S0-BZV-052

The Seven Deadly Sins

Studies in

Medieval and Reformation Traditions

History, Culture, Religion, Ideas

Founded by

Heiko A. Oberman†

Edited by

Andrew Colin Gow
Edmonton, Alberta

In cooperation with

THOMAS A. BRADY, JR., BERKELEY, CALIFORNIA

JOHANNES FRIED, FRANKFURT

BRAD GREGORY, UNIVERSITY OF NOTRE DAME, INDIANA

BERNDT HAMM, ERLANGEN

SUSAN C. KARANT-NUNN, TUCSON, ARIZONA

JÜRGEN MIETHKE, HEIDELBERG

M. E. H. NICOLETTE MOUT, LEIDEN

GUSTAV HENNINGSEN, COPENHAGEN

VOLUME CXXIII

The Seven Deadly Sins

From Communities to Individuals

Edited by

Richard Newhauser

Trinity University, San Antonio

BRILL

LEIDEN • BOSTON

2007

On the cover: Budapest, Kegyesrendi Központi Könyvtár MS. CX.2, fol. 249v (anno 1413): from Ulrich of Lilienfeld [?], *Conflictus "In Campo Mundi"*: The sin of Wrath. Photo: Richard Newhauser.

Brill has done its best to establish rights to use of the materials printed herein. Should any other party feel that its rights have been infringed we would be glad to take up contact with them.

This book is printed on acid-free paper.

A Cataloging-in-Publication record for this book is available from the Library of Congress.

BV
4626
.S482
2007

ISSN: 1573-4188
ISBN: 978-90-04-15785-9

© Copyright 2007 by Koninklijke Brill NV, Leiden, The Netherlands.
Koninklijke Brill NV incorporates the imprints Brill, Hotei Publishing,
IDC Publishers, Martinus Nijhoff Publishers and VSP.

All rights reserved. No part of this publication may be reproduced, translated, stored in a retrieval system, or transmitted in any form or by any means, electronic, mechanical, photocopying, recording or otherwise, without prior written permission from the publisher.

Authorization to photocopy items for internal or personal use is granted by Koninklijke Brill NV provided that the appropriate fees are paid directly to The Copyright Clearance Center, 222 Rosewood Drive, Suite 910, Danvers, MA 01923, USA.
Fees are subject to change.

PRINTED IN THE NETHERLANDS

CONTENTS

III. INDIVIDUALS

LIST OF ILLUSTRATIONS

Front Cover
Budapest, Kegyesrendi Központi Könyvtár MS. CX.2, fol. 249v (anno 1413): from Ulrich of Lilienfeld [?], *Conflictus "In Campo Mundi"*: The sin of Wrath. Photo: Richard Newhauser.

Hilaire Kallendorf, "Dressed to the Sevens, or Sin in Style: Fashion Statements by the Deadly Vices in Spanish Baroque *Autos Sacramentales*"
1. Avarice. From Cesare Ripa, *Iconologia, overo descrittione d'imagini delle virtù, vitij, affetti, passioni humane, corpi celesti, mondo e sue parti* (Padua, 1611), 35.
2. Gluttony. From Ripa, *Iconologia* (Padua, 1611), 209.
3. Wrath. From Ripa, *Iconologia* (Padua, 1611), 263.

Laura D. Gelfand, "Social Status and Sin: Reading Bosch's Prado *Seven Deadly Sins and Four Last Things* Painting"
1. Hieronymus Bosch, *Tabletop of the Seven Deadly Sins*, Madrid, Prado. Photo: Museo Nacional del Prado.
2. Jan van Eyck, *Arnolfini Wedding Portrait*, London, National Gallery. Photo: National Gallery, London.
3. Hieronymus Bosch, *Tabletop of the Seven Deadly Sins*: detail, *Imago Pietatis*. Photo: Museo Nacional del Prado.
4. Anonymous (single-leaf woodcut) from Munich, about 1490–1500: *The Four Christian Ages* (panel with the virtues and vices), woodcut, 35.4 × 19 cm. Basel, Kupferstichkabinett des Kunstmuseums Basel (Inv. X.1877). Photo: Kunstmuseum Basel.
5. Hieronymus Bosch, *Tabletop of the Seven Deadly Sins*, Madrid, Prado: Ira (detail). Photo: Museo Nacional del Prado.
6. Hieronymus Bosch, *Tabletop of the Seven Deadly Sins*, Madrid, Prado: Superbia (detail). Photo: Museo Nacional del Prado.
7. Hieronymus Bosch, *Tabletop of the Seven Deadly Sins*, Madrid, Prado: Luxuria (detail). Photo: Museo Nacional del Prado.
8. Hieronymus Bosch, *Tabletop of the Seven Deadly Sins*, Madrid, Prado: Accidia (detail). Photo: Museo Nacional del Prado.
9. Hieronymus Bosch, *Tabletop of the Seven Deadly Sins*, Madrid, Prado: Gula (detail). Photo: Museo Nacional del Prado.

ACKNOWLEDGMENTS

Permission is gratefully acknowledged here to the following institutions for the right to reproduce the illustrations in the volume: Museo Nacional del Prado, Madrid, for permission to reproduce Hieronymus Bosch, *Tabletop of the Seven Deadly Sins*; The National Gallery, London, for permission to reproduce Jan van Eyck, *Arnolfini Wedding Portrait*; the Kunstmuseum Basel, for permission to reproduce *The Four Christian Ages* (panel with the virtues and vices); and the Kegyesrendi Központi Könyvtár, Budapest, for permission to reproduce MS. CX.2, fol. 249v (anno 1413): Ulrich of Lilienfeld [?], *Conflictus "In Campo Mundi"*: the sin of Wrath.

The editor and contributors to this volume also take this opportunity to express our gratitude to the Master and Fellows of Darwin College, Cambridge University, and to Mr. Peter Brindle, Bursar of the college, for their willingness to put the resources of this institute for postgraduate study at the disposal of the summer seminar in 2004, something which contributed immeasurably to the success of this endeavor; to Ms. Abigayle Smyth, the administrative assistant for the seminar, for her unflagging support in countless tasks, without which the seminar would not have run as smoothly as it did; to the Program Committee of the 40th International Congress on Medieval Studies at Western Michigan University, Kalamazoo, MI, for permission to hold three sessions on "The Vices as Cultural Constructions" at the conference there in May, 2005, which gave many of the scholars represented in this volume an opportunity for the first time to present the findings of their research begun the year before to a wider academic audience; to the anonymous reader of the manuscript for the press for helpful observations about strengthening the volume; to Willis Salomon (Department of English, Trinity University) for reading and commenting on the Introduction; and to Professor Andrew Gow for his gracious support of this project. Above all, we wish to register our gratefulness to the National Endowment for the Humanities for its generosity in funding the Summer Seminar on "The Seven Deadly Sins as Cultural Constructions in the Middle Ages" in 2004. Great art is made possible through great patronage, as any study of the circumstances of the production of art in the past will amply demonstrate. In the same way, great scholarship flourishes in a nation when the enlightened institutions of government understand the leadership role of higher education in articulating, and evaluating, the values of the nation. No institution embodies its role as supporter of scholarship and teaching on all levels in the United States of America better than the National Endowment for the Humanities.

LIST OF CONTRIBUTORS

Dwight D. Allman, Department of Political Science, Baylor University, P.O. Box 97276, Waco, TX 76798–7276, USA; dwight_allman@baylor.edu

Bridget K. Balint, Department of Classical Studies, Ballantine 547, Indiana University, 1020 E. Kirkwood Ave., Bloomington, IN 47405–7103, USA; bkbalint@indiana.edu

V. S. Benfell III, Department of Humanities, Classics, and Comparative Literature, Brigham Young University, 3010 JKHB, Provo, UT 84602, USA; stanley_benfell@byu.edu

Dallas G. Denery II, Department of History, Bowdoin College, 9900 College Station, Brunswick, ME 04011–8499, USA; ddenery@bowdoin.edu

Laura D. Gelfand, Department of Art, FOLK 103, The University of Akron, Akron, OH 44325–7801, USA; lgelfan@uakron.edu

Susan E. Hill, Department of Philosophy & Religion, Baker Hall 150, University of Northern Iowa, Cedar Falls, IA 50614–0501, USA; susan.hill@uni.edu

Holly Johnson, Department of English, Mississippi State University, P.O. Box E, Mississippi State, MS 39762, USA; hj71@msstate.edu

Hilaire Kallendorf, Department of Modern and Classical Languages, ACAD 302D, Texas A&M University, College Station, TX 77843–4238, USA; h-kallendorf@tamu.edu

John Kitchen, Department of History and Classics, University of Alberta, 2–81 Tory Building, Edmonton, AB, T6G 2H4, Canada; john.kitchen@ualberta.ca

Rhonda L. McDaniel, Department of English, Middle Tennessee State University, PH 228C, Murfreesboro, TN 37132, USA; rlmcdani@mtsu.edu

Richard Newhauser, Medieval and Renaissance Studies Program, Department of English, Trinity University, One Trinity Place, San Antonio, TX 78212–7200, USA; rnewhaus@trinity.edu

Thomas Parisi, Department of Psychology, Saint Mary's College, Notre Dame, IN 46556, USA; tparisi@saintmarys.edu

Derrick G. Pitard, Department of English, Slippery Rock University, 1 Morrow Way, Slippery Rock, PA 16057, USA; derrick.pitard@sru.edu

INTRODUCTION:
CULTURAL CONSTRUCTION AND THE VICES

Richard Newhauser
Trinity University (San Antonio)

The present volume represents a selection of the research stimulated by my summer seminar on "The Seven Deadly Sins as Cultural Constructions in the Middle Ages," which was held at Darwin College, Cambridge University, July 12–August 13, 2004, and was supported by a generous grant from the National Endowment for the Humanities. For the five weeks during which they lived and worked together, the fifteen participants in the seminar intensively studied and debated both a conceptual history (*Begriffsgeschichte*) that views concepts not as pre-determined, set pieces for rote utilization, but as culturally constructed ideas partially shaped by the environments and functions in which they participate as well as by the individual choices of the thinkers in whose works they are inscribed. More specifically, the seminar dealt with the medieval development of the seven deadly sins as concrete examples of vitally-important ethical ideas which experienced new and constantly-changing definitions even as the vocabulary used to articulate them in a series of shifting communal, institutional, and individual surroundings remained remarkably stable. It is fitting to briefly introduce these areas here and to describe what will be added to previous scholarship on the vices by the essays in the present volume.

I. *Cultural Constructions*

All analysis of concepts from the past begins with the physical presence of conceptual transmission: a piece of parchment or paper (or today: the appearance of physical presence in the electronic flickering of a monitor) with text, image, and/or music; an illumination in glass, a monument of sculpture, or perhaps an entire building; actors addressing an audience, or a strip of celluloid or a DVD that preserves one or many versions of the acting ensemble's words and images. These documents or artifacts, and the range of genres of representation they

embody, both resonate with the concepts that inform them and participate in the creation and dissemination of these very concepts: there
is a continuum of contemporaneity that connects them with the past
and will remain palpable in the future. To understand how concepts
function as constructions, then, is to comprehend how they share, as
Reinhard Kosellek wrote some years ago, a "zone of convergence" of
the past and present.[1] Cultural communication from the past (word,
image, music) is always part of a tradition—by which it is neither wholly
determined nor which it can completely discard. Every concept is a set
of meanings negotiated within a cultural context as it changes through
time, and this diachronic factor is joined to a synchronic one in that a
concept is also given constantly new shape and new definition by the
cultural uses to which it is put by the members of a society who find
that concept a living, that is communicating, idea.

With great fruitfulness since at least the 1970s, and partially in opposition to the overwhelming dominance of positivist/empiricist science,[2] a
movement in the social sciences has developed a perspective that can be
of assistance to humanists in articulating the synchronic (and I would
add, though perhaps some of those in the social sciences would not,
also the diachronic) negotiations between concepts and culture that are
involved in *Begriffsgeschichte*. "Social constructionism"[3] conceives of the
objects of its study (patterns of behavior, emotions, knowledge about
the world) as something similar to the cultural construction of ideas,
namely as artifices of communal interaction:

> The terms in which the world is understood are social artifacts, products of
> historically situated interchanges among people. From the constructionist
> position the process of understanding is not automatically driven by the
> forces of nature, but is the result of an active, cooperative enterprise of
> persons in relationship. In this light, inquiry is invited into the historical
> and cultural bases of various forms of world construction.[4]

---

[1] Reinhart Koselleck, "Begriffsgeschichte und Sozialgeschichte," in *Soziologie und
Sozialgeschichte*, ed. P. Lutz, *Kölner Zeitschrift für Soziologie und Sozialpsychologie*, Sonderheft 16
(1972): 116–31; English trans. as "Begriffsgeschichte and Social History," in Reinhart
Koselleck, *Futures Past: On the Semantics of Historical Time*, trans. Keith Tribe (Cambridge,
MA, and London, 1985), 73–91, here 90.

[2] Kenneth J. Gergen, "Constructionism and Realism: How Are We to Go On?," in
Social Constructionism, Discourse and Realism, ed. Ian Parker (London, 1998), 147.

[3] For a collection of key documents in the developing articulation of this perspective
in the social sciences, see *Social Construction: A Reader*, ed. Mary Gergen and Kenneth
J. Gergen (London, 2003).

[4] Kenneth J. Gergen, "The Social Constructionist Movement in Modern Psychology,"
American Psychologist 40 (1985): 267.

Likewise, the emphasis on semantic analysis as an a priori route around what Rom Harré has termed the "ontological illusion" that something like the emotion of anger, for example, has an abstract reality that can be objectively researched translates into the philological foundation of much of the history of concepts that will be found in this volume. The contributors here consistently ask what meanings are indicated by the usage of any particular sin-designation as it was presented by an author or artist in the Middle Ages (and beyond) and what cultural function the artifact carrying that hamartiological term played as part of the cultural negotiations of the very meaning of the term. As Harré has written in dealing with emotions:

> Instead of asking the question, "What is anger?" we would do well to begin by asking, "How is the word 'anger,' and other expressions that cluster around it, actually used in this or that cultural milieu and type of episode?"[5]

Finally, the social constructionist perspective in emotionology, in particular, has emphasized the local moral evaluation of emotions as a key element in their production—the way in which those who use the vocabulary of emotions do so within socially restricted systems of duties and rights, obligations and conventions that serve as guidelines for the moral analysis of the terminology of emotions.[6]

It is here that the cultural constructionist view of the vices represented in the present volume is more expansive than its equivalent in the social sciences. Not only the local moral orders provided direction for the usage of the lexicon of behavior (or even more, of "abnormal" behavior), but the centralized and sanctioned vocabulary of morality reveals itself in the contributions to this collection of essays again and again to have been just as sensitive to local change. This is so, first of all, because the discourse on vices and virtues in the Middle Ages contained a decisive element of ambiguity that invited, even demanded, a differentiated resolution by moral analysis, as it does now, as well.[7] Second, even when one is dealing with what research

---

[5] Rom Harré, "An Outline of the Social Constructionist Viewpoint," in *The Social Construction of Emotions*, ed. Rom Harré (Oxford, 1982; reprint 1988), 4–5.

[6] Ibid., 8–9.

[7] Richard Newhauser, "Zur Zweideutigkeit in der Moraltheologie: Als Tugenden verkleidete Laster," in *Der Fehltritt: Vergehen und Versehen in der Vormoderne*, ed. Peter von Moos, (Köln, Weimar, Wien, 2001), 377–402; revised and expanded English version as "On Ambiguity in Moral Theology: When the Vices Masquerade as Virtues," trans. Andrea Németh-Newhauser, in Richard Newhauser, *Sin: Essays on the Moral*

can uncover as pejorative usages in the centralized lexicon of sinfulness, the particularity of the cultural contexts in which those semantic
items were found to be important demonstrates the actual flexibility of
this ecclesiastically-sanctioned vocabulary. Envy, for example, has been
taken by some social constructionists to be an anomaly in the common
list of the chief vices in the Middle Ages.[8] It is true that *Invidia* did
not enter the generally accepted scheme of seven deadly sins until the
work of Pope Gregory the Great (d. 604), but its Greek equivalent is
also found, though only once, in a work by Evagrius Ponticus (d. 399),
the first author to systematically examine the eight "evil thoughts" that
Gregory later transformed into seven sins.[9] Even more, envy can be
seen to be the same type of culturally constructed vice as the other six
normally surrounding it from Pope Gregory's work on, for it represents
an equivalent type of misdirected love, to speak with Augustine. Envy
fits perfectly in the list of seven deadly sins, as a cultural constructionist
analysis demonstrates, because it described a socially unaccepted desire.
As the contribution here by Bridget K. Balint reveals, in an academic
environment in the high Middle Ages, the pleasure of envy lay in its
ability to be used to describe one's rivals as harboring a sin, namely
the envy of oneself and one's own intellectual reputation.

Furthermore, the flexibility of a sanctioned moral vocabulary is also
demonstrated by the way in which particular genres of representation
variously weigh the discourse on vices and virtues: It is one thing, for
example, to find commercial activity being freed from the taint of the
sin of avarice in theoretical school tracts of the twelfth century, near
the beginning of the vast cultural changes to which the development
of a profit economy in medieval Europe contributed.[10] It is something
else again to find a century later that William Peraldus has included
a moral justification of commerce per se in the midst of treating
avarice in his very popular *Summa de vitiis*—intended as an aide for

---

Tradition in the Western Middle Ages, Variorum Collected Studies Series (Aldershot, 2007),
forthcoming.

[8] John Sabini and Maury Silver, *Moralities of Everyday Life* (Oxford, 1982), 14.

[9] Evagrius Ponticus included the term *phthonos* among the list of *logismoi* in *De vitiis
quae opposita sunt virtutibus*, 1, 4 (PG 79:1141, 1144).

[10] Richard Newhauser, "Justice and Liberality: Opposition to Avarice in the Twelfth
Century," in *Virtue and Ethics in the Twelfth Century*, ed. István P. Bejczy and Richard G.
Newhauser (Leiden, 2005), 295–316, here 311–12; Marcia L. Colish, "Another Look
at the School of Laon," *Archives d'histoire doctrinale et littéraire du moyen âge* 53 (1986):
7–22, here 20–21.

composing sermons to be preached, among other congregations, to the same urban populations which provided the manpower for this now valorized commercial activity.[11] In the practical contours of the genre of preaching aides, a sanctioned morality's amelioration of behavior that had formerly been considered central to the definition of the sin of avarice is a valuable indicator of a widespread alteration in how *avaritia* and related words were actually being used in a cultural milieu that was directly affected by both the moral vocabulary and commerce. Though the cultural constructionism of the contributions to this volume draws on the full variety of genres communicating moral valuations in a number of cultural milieus—from sermons to Dante's cosmological allegory, from clerical drama to Chaucer's *Canterbury Tales*, from works of monastic guidance to Bosch's meditative painting for the laity—, the editor and contributors are well aware of the differentiated value of moral expression in the wide variety of genres of representation treated in the volume and of the difficulties posed to a strict comparative method by the fullness of the evidence here.

II. *Previous Scholarship on the Vices*

The seven deadly sins (pride, envy, wrath, avarice, sloth, gluttony, lust—in their most frequent order, and the one adopted by Dante to organize Mount Purgatory [see the contribution here by V. S. Benfell III]) are still sometimes thought of as inflexible categories of medieval dogma or, when they are found in examples of contemporary popular culture (such as the feature-length film *Se7en*),[12] as signifiers for something of an arcane perversion, a vehicle for an evil which is both mysterious and ancient. Such a view, of course, does not address the longevity of the idea of these seven constructs as comprehending the basic categories of evil in medieval western culture. The very fact that even as this list of seven sins was being supplemented by psychological, utilitarian, and other models of behavioral analysis it could still be adopted from

---

[11] William Peraldus, *Summa de vitiis*, 4.2.4 ("De fraudibus negociatorum"), in Paris, Bibliothèque Mazarine MS. 794, fol. 52rb: "Qvarto loco inter species auaricie dicendum est de fraudibus negociatorum. Et notandum quod negociatio bona est in se et hominibus necessaria."

[12] *Se7en*, directed by David Fincher, written by Andrew Kevin Walker (New Line Cinema, 1995).

Catholic to Protestant use during the Reformation, and further adopted for secular utilization both before and after that point, makes the seven sins a worthy object of cultural inquiry as constructed ideas. Current research in the intellectual history of moral thought in the Middle Ages has demonstrated, moreover, how nuanced and differentiated the constructs actually were that came to be known as the seven deadly sins, how much their definition depended on a complex interaction with the cultural environments in which they were enumerated. The most recent research on this topic, in other words, has allowed these seven concepts to emerge from a narrowly theological inquiry and to be seen, individually and as a series, in the same light as other historically defined objects of study. In this way, current research does not define the categories of the sins merely as theological entities, but rather as differentiated articulations of what can be called discrete forms of an interrupted actualization of socially accepted forms of desire. Parallel to this definition, the virtues can be understood as ideals of the social-ization of desire.[13]

In the nineteenth and earlier twentieth century, and primarily in German scholarship, the sins were studied in three main contexts: First, they were seen as part of the history of Catholic dogma on matters of moral theology, something which appears clearly in the sub-title of the major work on the sins and dogma in this period, the monograph by Otto Zöckler.[14] Second, the origins of the sins became part of the historical study of monastic spirituality in Egypt, where established lists of *logismoi*, or "evil" thoughts (later altered and reformulated as the sins) first appeared. The focus here was on the debt this aspect of Egyptian monasticism owed to both Hellenism and Early Christian literature. Stefan Schiwietz's three-volume *Das morgenländische Mönchtum*, published between 1904 and 1938, is typical of endeavors in this second context, as is the monograph by Siegfried Wibbing.[15] Third, the iconography of vices and virtues formed the subject of a number of studies of medieval art, in particular in the tradition of Prudentius's *Psychomachia*, such as

---

[13] Richard Newhauser, "Virtues and Vices," in *Dictionary of the Middle Ages, Supplement 1*, ed. William Chester Jordan (New York, 2004), 628–33.

[14] Otto Zöckler, *Das Lehrstück von den sieben Hauptsünden: Beiträge zur Dogmen- und zur Sittengeschichte, in besonders der vorreformatorischen Zeit*, in O. Zöckler, *Biblische und kirchenhis-torische Studien*, 3 (Munich, 1893).

[15] Stefan Schiwietz, *Das morgenländische Mönchtum*, 3 vols. (Mainz, Mödling, 1904–1938); Siegfried Wibbing, *Die Tugend- und Lasterkataloge im Neuen Testament* (Berlin, 1959).

one can find in Adolf Katzenellenbogen's classic monograph.[16] The common factor in these studies is a tendency to examine their subject from structural and historical perspectives in which the content of the sins is imagined to be relatively stable.

Much of this earlier research was summarized and extended into the area of literary scholarship in 1952 in the monumental monograph by Morton Bloomfield,[17] which not only was the first major study of the sins in English, but also contributed a far more comprehensive view of the place of the sins in medieval culture and that was also sensitive to some of the major changes in the composition of the lists of sins in response to varying cultural factors. Bloomfield's work proved highly influential in the context of American universities, in particular, but it also served as the starting point for what is an ongoing interest among subsequent European medievalists in this aspect of medieval moral thought. The publication in 1967 of Siegfried Wenzel's study of sloth and his fundamental article in *Speculum* the next year detailing problems in the history of the sins not addressed by Bloomfield's work set the agenda for much historiographical work to come.[18] As a result, factors such as the place of the virtues in the comprehension of moral thought in the Middle Ages, the influence of Aristotle, and the genesis of rationales for the sins in Scholastic thought were the focus of some later work, such as the recent studies by Carla Casagrande and Silvana Vecchio.[19] At the same time, the study of individual sins has been, and continues to be, advanced in work by Lester Little, Alexander Murray, or

---

[16] Adolf Katzenellenbogen, *Allegories of the Virtues and Vices in Mediaeval Art from Early Christian Times to the Thirteenth Century*, trans. Alan J. P. Crick (London, 1939; reprint Toronto, 1989). For the use of Prudentius' text as a school book, see now Sinéad O'Sullivan, *Early Medieval Glosses on Prudentius' Psychomachia: The Weitz Tradition* (Leiden, Boston, 2004).

[17] Morton W. Bloomfield, *The Seven Deadly Sins: An Introduction to the History of a Religious Concept, with Special Reference to Medieval English Literature* ([East Lansing, MI,] 1952; reprint, 1967).

[18] Siegfried Wenzel, *The Sin of Sloth: Acedia in Medieval Thought and Literature* (Chapel Hill, NC, 1967); and "The Seven Deadly Sins: Some Problems of Research," *Speculum* 43 (1968): 1–22.

[19] Carla Casagrande and Silvana Vecchio, "La classificazione dei peccati tra settenario e decalogo (secoli XIII–XV)," *Documenti e studi sulla tradizione filosofica medievale* 5 (1994): 331–95; "Péché," in *Dictionnaire Raisonné de l'Occident Médiéval*, ed. Jacques Le Goff and Jean-Claude Schmitt (Paris, 1999), 877-91; and, most recently and comprehensively, *I sette vizi capitali: Storia dei peccati nel Medioevo*, Saggi, 832 (Turin, 2000).

more recently Richard Newhauser on avarice;[20] Mireille Vincent-Cassy on envy and gluttony;[21] and Pierre Payer or Ruth Karras on lust.[22]

Yet much scholarship of the last twenty years has also moved beyond an agenda in which the seven deadly sins are seen to function almost hegemonically in the environment of pastoral theology. John Bossy's well-known essay in 1988 articulated ways in which he felt the seven sins were seen by late-medieval culture to be inadequate, a topic which was in some regards anticipated by Bloomfield's work, but not fully realized there.[23] Likewise, analyses of other enumerations of morality in the Middle Ages, like Casagrande and Vecchio on the sins of the tongue,[24] or Newhauser on the nine accessory sins,[25] have called attention to the way in which cultural exigencies (such as the oral nature of preaching and confession) elicited a response that gives evidence of the flexibility of medieval moral thought. Likewise, one can see here, as well, the beginnings of a focus on new material on the sins largely unstudied in the past, such as texts on vices and virtues from medieval and early-modern Spain (see the essay here by Hillaire Kallendorf). But recent scholarship has also begun to address topics and use

---

[20] Lester K. Little, "Pride Goes before Avarice: Social Change and the Vices in Latin Christendom," *The American Historical Review* 76 (1971): 16–49; Alexander Murray, *Reason and Society in the Middle Ages* (Oxford, 1978), chapt. 3; Richard Newhauser, *The Early History of Greed: The Sin of Avarice in Early Medieval Thought and Literature* (Cambridge, Eng., 2000); "*Avaritia* and *Paupertas*: On the Place of the Early Franciscans in the History of Avarice," in *In the Garden of Evil: The Vices and Culture in the Middle Ages*, ed. Richard Newhauser (Toronto, 2005), 324–48; and "Justice and Liberality."

[21] Mireille Vincent-Cassy, "L'Envie en France au Moyen Age," *Annales E.S.C.* 35 (1980): 253–71; "La *gula* curiale ou les débordements des banquets au début du règne de Charles VI," in *La Sociabilité à table: Commensalité et convivialité à travers les âges*, ed. Martin Aurell, Olivier Dumoulin, and Françoise Thelamon ([Rouen], 1992), 91–102; and "Between Sin and Pleasure: Drunkenness in France in the Late Middle Ages," trans. Erika Pavelka, in *In the Garden of Evil*, ed. Newhauser, 393–430.

[22] Pierre Payer, *The Bridling of Desire: Views of Sex in the Later Middle Ages* (Toronto, 1993); Ruth Mazo Karras, "The Latin Vocabulary of Illicit Sex in English Ecclesiastical Court Records," *Journal of Medieval Latin* 2 (1992): 1–17; and "Two Models, Two Standards: Moral Teaching and Sexual Mores," in *Bodies and Disciplines: Intersections of Literature and History in Fifteenth-Century England*, ed. Barbara A. Hanawalt and David Wallace (Minneapolis, 1996), 123–38.

[23] John Bossy, "Moral Arithmetic: Seven Sins into Ten Commandments," in *Conscience and Casuistry in Early Modern Europe*, ed. Edmund Leites (Cambridge, Eng., Paris, 1988), 214–34.

[24] Carla Casagrande and Silvana Vecchio, *I peccati della lingua: Disciplina ed etica della parola nella cultura medievale* (Rome, 1987).

[25] Richard Newhauser, "From Treatise to Sermon: Johannes Herolt on the *novem peccata aliena*," in *De ore domini: Preacher and Word in the Middle Ages*, ed. T. L. Amos, Eugene A. Green, and Beverly Mayne Kienzle (Kalamazoo, MI, 1989), 185–209.

methodologies that open the question of the cultural use of the sins to a more diverse analysis and call into question some of the assumptions of earlier scholarship. Barbara Rosenwein et al. on anger, for example, is deeply invested in what was a current debate on the use and construction of the emotions in historical research;[26] Michael Theunissen has questioned the supposed historical break between the melancholy articulated in antique texts, sloth in the Middle Ages, and modernity's representation of depression.[27] Other approaches to the delineation of the moral categories of the sins have adopted methods of psychological research (Patrick Boyde, Edward Peters, and see Thomas Parisi's contribution to the present volume),[28] or the findings of anthropology (Richard Newhauser, and see the essay by John Kitchen in the present volume),[29] or a gender studies perspective (Ruth Karras, Richard Barton, and see Susan E. Hill's essay in the present volume) to yield new insight into the ways in which cultures fill the categories of moral analysis with an ever-changing content.[30]

III. *The Scholarship of the Present Volume*

The essays from the seminar that are selected and printed here confirm and extend these areas of scholarly analysis of the capital vices. In its widest context, the conceptual history of the seven deadly sins participates in the study of the political and social ethics of medieval communities. As Dwight D. Allman demonstrates, the construction of

[26] *Anger's Past: The Social Uses of an Emotion in the Middle Ages*, ed. Barbara Rosenwein (Ithaca and London, 1998).

[27] Michael Theunissen, *Vorentwürfe der Moderne: Antike Melancholie und die Acedia des Mittelalters* (Berlin and New York, 1996). See also Rainer Jehl, "*Acedia* and Burnout Syndrome: From an Occupational Vice of the Early Monks to a Psychological Concept in Secularized Professional Life," trans. Andrea Németh-Newhauser, in *In the Garden of Evil*, ed. Newhauser, 455–76.

[28] Patrick Boyde, *Human Vices and Human Worth in Dante's "Comedy"* (Cambridge, Eng., 2000); Edward Peters, "*Vir inconstans*: Moral Theology as Palaeopsychology," in *In the Garden of Evil*, ed. Newhauser, 59–73.

[29] Richard Newhauser, "Capital Vices as Medieval Anthropology," in *Laster im Mittelalter. Freiburger Kolloquium vom 20. bis 22. Februar 2006*, ed. Ch. Flüeler and M. Rohde (Fribourg, CH), forthcoming.

[30] Ruth Mazo Karras, "The Lechery that Dare Not Speak its Name: Sodomy and the Vices in Medieval England," in *In the Garden of Evil*, ed. Newhauser, 193–205; Richard E. Barton, "Gendering Anger: *Ira, Furor*, and Discourses of Power and Masculinity in the Eleventh and Twelfth Centuries," in ibid., 371–92.

a Christian kingship, a project to which Augustine of Hippo contributed in particular and that underscores the elevation of humility and
devaluation of pride, was a direct challenge to the classical tradition of
political philosophy and its practice in the Roman world of Augustine's
day. From Plato on, the major problem of political ethics in antiquity
had revolved around finding a way to reconcile the ruler's natural interest in his own good with the need for a politics of justice understood as
the common good of the ruled. For Augustine, however, the Christian
ruler exercises power in humility, which is to say he carries out his office
selflessly, not seeking temporal control, but only the reform of his own
immoral urges and the conversion of others to the worship of God:
right rule is the tempering of human depravity and service to God and
the Church. In the ninth century, Alcuin used Augustinian formulations
of the goals of kingship in developing a political theory of Christian
right rule; however, he also emphasized some of the civic orientation of
the ruler that Augustine had earlier diminished. Carolingian *renovatio*, in
fact, directed as it was to the Frankish aristocracy, adopted some of the
practical necessities of imperial rule that Augustine had characterized
as the moral opprobrium of *superbia*. In Alcuin's formulation, pride is
constructed as the sin of rebellion against legitimate political authority, such as that exercised by Charlemagne, not as the temptation of a
ruler to ignore the common good.

   Just as practical necessities play a role in the construction of a
social/political ethics in the Carolingian period, Bridget K. Balint demonstrates the way in which the cultural uses of envy among the Latin
poets of the high Middle Ages reflect new emphases on this sin. The
later eleventh and twelfth centuries witnessed a rise in the explanatory
power of envy to account for, and dismiss, one's critics. In Rome, *invidia*
had been conceived as a danger to both the envious person and the
object of his envy, but patristic and early-medieval writers emphasized
the harm done by the *invidus* to himself. Authors of the late eleventh
and twelfth centuries in northern France, however, such as Hildebert
of Lavardin, an anonymous female poet whose work is included in
London, BL MS. Add. 24199, Baudri of Bourgueil, and most famously
Peter Abelard, are among the first to turn to envy as an explanation
for their misfortunes or as a way of disarming criticism leveled against
them. The vocabulary of envy as a form of self-verification was fueled
by the revived interest in Ovid's amatory verse in the cathedral schools,
but it also confirms the growing independence of intellectuals (and
poets as intellectuals) in the high Middle Ages: envy is constructed

as an attack on one's intellectual prowess precisely when having an intellectual reputation takes on a palpable social and economic value. Our contemporary equation of gluttony with a harmful corpulence is certainly part of the reformulation in the twenty-first century of this sin as a matter of public health policy, but as Susan E. Hill's contribution reveals, it is also a decided narrowing of the semantic range of *gula* begun earliest as a reaction to the fashionableness of stout bodies in the seventeenth century. Medieval discourse on gluttony, on the other hand, draws attention to a particular understanding of social limits and a spiritual deficiency that threatens those limits, for the health of the individual mirrors that of the community throughout the Middle Ages. The concentric relationship between private bodies and the body politic is highlighted in the way in which the loss of the Edenic community was attributed to an act of gluttony (literally, eating the forbidden fruit) by many medieval authors, from John Cassian to the compiler of the fifteenth-century English catechetical treatise *Jacob's Well*. For Cassian, gluttony is an affront to the norms of communal harmony in the coenobium that depends on individual discipline, while in the work of Gregory the Great *gula* poses problems of discernment in knowing when eating fulfills the necessity of nature and when it is merely a matter of desire. Among lay authors of the later Middle Ages, such as *The Goodman of Paris*, gluttony remains a threat to the social order, but now because it leads to a loss of rationality or withdraws resources from the community for the misuse of one individual alone.

The institutional imperatives within the Church of formulating and teaching about the capital vices in the environment of the monastery, among the mendicant orders, pastorally from the pulpit, or dramatically in devotional performances exerted pressures of their own in the discourse on the vices. Five contributions here focus on the construction of the deadly sins in ecclesiastical environments, from the context of early-medieval and Anglo-Saxon monasticism to that of the Baroque church in Spain. Using Cassian's foundational texts on the vices, John Kitchen examines the implications of this writer's analysis of an aspect of lust, namely, nocturnal emissions, for an understanding of monastic ideology and the vexed question of Jesus's full human nature. Questions of sexuality reveal themselves to be discussions about core theological and social issues, and not just those comprehended in the term "purity" as an anthropological construct. Cassian's treatment of the secret of wet dreams has in common with Scriptural hermeneutics the fact that both demand a type of exegesis as a method of interpretation.

In fact, nocturnal emissions are problematic because they undermine monastic authority and point to a part of a monk's life that is hidden from his abbot as well as himself. When the same matter is applied to the question of Jesus's humanity, Christological limits are set, first of all, by Cassian's thinking on the concatenation of the sins. The establishment of how resisting one vice will preclude the next one also makes it imperative to read carefully the narrative sequence of Jesus's temptations in Scripture. In this way, the kinship of the vices works to guarantee orthodox Christology, for Jesus's defeat of the temptation of gluttony, as interpreted from Matthew 4:3, comprehends his resistance to all forms of the next vice, lust, before the question is even asked whether he experienced sexual longing. One witnesses here the widest anthropological implications for the list of sins that extend far beyond the merely practical functions to which they are sometimes considered to be limited. Rhonda L. McDaniel's contribution begins with the reception of Cassian's work on the vices by Aldhelm, abbot of Malmesbury and bishop of Sherborne in the late seventh and early eighth centuries. In the prose *De uirginitate*, addressed to nuns at Barking Abbey and elsewhere, Aldhelm analyzes the vices not just as a form of monastic discipline, but also as a way to quell the unrest among nuns who had been lifelong virgins against the spiritual and institutional authority that had begun to be exercised by women who had been married earlier, such as Cuthburg, former wife of the king of Northumbria and founder of Wimborne Abbey. Analogous to the later political ethics of the Carolingians, Aldhelm identifies the lifelong virgins' unwillingness to be ruled by abbesses who were formerly married as motivated by the sin of pride. In doing so, he borrows from both Cassian and Gregory the Great on the monstrous nature of the vices, but because of the long Benedictine tradition honoring the desert teachings on the capital vices, Cassian is a larger presence in such matters as the recommended cure for pride (the humility and poverty that comes with measuring one's monastic profession in terms of the heroic deeds of the saints), and in Aldhelm's poetic treatment of virginity in the "Carmen de uirginitate."

Questions of social control lie close to the surface of Aldhelm's thinking on the sin of pride, as they have, as well, in current scholars' consideration of strictures against lying that proliferated in the thirteenth century. As Dallas G. Denery II argues, however, there is more at stake in thinking about this sin of the tongue: inchoately formulated questions about the nature of language, for example, and the relationship between the inner and outer self. Although the lexicon for this discussion was supplied by Augustine of Hippo's consideration of lying, and most thirteenth-century authors supported his main definitions, they also discovered ways to adjust his conclusions to their own speculative needs. Augustine considered all lies categorically to be sins, regardless of their motivation or result, though this position taxed his ingenuity in finding ways to remove the stain of falsehood from Biblical examples of what were clearly lies told with divine approval. For mendicant theologians, however, Biblical liars were an inspiration for more refined analysis: Thomas Aquinas, for example, emphasized the distinction between words that are lies and deceptive deeds that are not; Alexander of Hales, and other Franciscan authors who followed him, allowed for deceptive acts that might be understood as prudent, instructive, or figurative; and Duns Scotus measured the possible justification of a lie solely on the intent of the one who tells it. For the mendicant orders, justifying mendicancy often required outer devotion even in the face of inner anxieties, so that the subtlety of their analysis of lying was as much intentionally self-directed as "objectively" analytical.

The pastoral and rhetorical appearance of clerical presentations of the sins for homiletic and dramatic purposes on clearly-defined occasions in the liturgical calendar is the focus of two essays. As Holly Johnson demonstrates, late-medieval preaching on Good Friday often created sets of correspondences between the seven deadly sins and Jesus's torments during the passion that accentuated the occurrence of sin, and the guilt of the sinner, as palpably corporeal experiences. On Good Friday, preachers often linked the sin-torment pairings to one of three things: the passion narrative, in which case each torment became a type of inversion, punishment, or remedy for a sin; instances of Jesus shedding his blood, where each occasion was understood as a cure for one of the sins; or specific wounds Jesus suffered during the passion, which were then considered admonitions against committing the corresponding sins. In this way, Jesus's tormented body and the related vices became a "meditative map" to understand the totality of the experience of sin and, as when Thomas Brinton employed the torment-sin pairings in a sermon preached in Rochester in 1375, they were also used to create a contemplative bridge between the sinner and the image of redemption. There is a good amount of flexibility in how the scheme of seven sins is used in Good Friday preaching, though the emphasis is always on the meditative connection between the congregation and the significance of Jesus's suffering during the passion. Through their rhetorical usefulness, the vices are transformed in Good Friday preaching to become not just indicators of immorality, but tools to foster devotion. Devotion is very much in the foreground of what Hillaire Kallendorf terms the "last great vestige of Scholasticism" in Spain, namely, the form of allegorical drama known as the Baroque *autos sacramentales*. These plays were written mainly by members of the clergy, above all by Pedro Calderón de la Barca (d. 1681), to be acted on Corpus Christi day, and had developed since the fifteenth century into open air productions on a system of mobile carts. The seven deadly sins appeared in the plays in elaborate dress, which at times used expected connections (Lust appears often as a woman), but can also be more complex (Gluttony and Sloth dress sometimes as wealthy peasants, not as low-class buffoons). Moral ambiguity in the plays replicates a social hierarchy in which upper-class vices could be recast as virtues and in which groups marginal to Spanish society could be satirized in the course of the *autos sacramentales*: Turks, Jews, Lutherans, etc., all are objects of scorn in the guise of the vices. The iconography for costumes was suggested by Biblical texts and emblem books, but the playwrights used clothing, and the act of changing costumes (in particular in the often dramatized parable of the wedding feast [Matthew 22:2–14]), to open larger issues of moral theology and social critique. The costumes of the vices were meant as a readable code through which the criticism of marginalized figures in Spanish society could be articulated, from a clerical perspective, and these groups characterized as moral evils.

Secular artists and authors participate in the construction of concepts of the sins by contributing both creatively and representatively to the artifacts of their expression. At the end of the Middle Ages, perhaps no one did this more decisively and successfully in the form of allegory than Dante. V. S. Benfell III demonstrates how Dante inherited a conception of the beatitudes in the Sermon on the Mount (Matthew 5:3–10) from a long tradition of Latin Biblical commentaries to which Augustine of Hippo contributed most importantly and, later, Thomas Aquinas, as well, in his attempt to reconcile Aristotelian concepts of virtue with the beatitudes. Dante constructed Mount Purgatory around the most common ordering of the seven deadly sins, but he also included the beatitudes structurally to mark the soul's overcoming of the vice of each terrace. Yet, his use of the beatitudes is not merely a traditional one, for he clearly alters the way in which the defeat of sloth, avarice, and gluttony is signaled on terraces 4–6. Overcoming sloth is related to the blessing of those who mourn because this beatitude introduces the next stage in the narrative of purgation in which Dante moves on to correct the desire for things that may be considered goods, but not the highest good. The defeat of avarice and gluttony is marked by references to the blessing of those who thirst and hunger for justice because both of these sins, and their remedies, are conceived in highly (though not exclusively) Aristotelian terms. The importance of avarice for the *Purgatorio* can be found in Dante's conception of this sin as an ecclesiastical and political transgression, and the transition from vice to beatitude as a path marked by the need for earthly justice to counter greed as preparation for receiving grace. Avarice is also the focus of Derrick G. Pitard's contribution on Chaucer's "Summoner's Tale," in which the satire of the fraternal orders applies both to their false commodification and their linguistic hollowness: instead of engaging in the economy of salvation by offering penance to sinners, they seek to use the empty form of confession for monetary advantage, but their pretensions are revealed by the startling expression of Thomas' vernacularity when he farts in Friar John's hand instead of giving him money. Though Chaucer mocked the academic discourse in which anti-fraternalism was first articulated, he drew much from the type of critique of the friars' apostolic pretensions found in the work of William of St. Amour. William's accusation that mendicancy in all its manifestations was a source of sin forms part of the charge against Friar John and his ilk in the "Summoner's Tale." Beyond this, the competition between the friars and the secular clergy for resources from the lay community, the corruption of confession by the friars, their false appropriation of the learned language of Biblical interpretation and Scholastic debate—all of this is amplified by Chaucer's vernacular perspective. Friar John cannot even understand the full extent of Thomas' flatulent insult because (and here Chaucer's satire adds a new layer to its inherited anti-fraternalism) his greedy desire for acquisition drives him to try to appropriate the fart as an academic exercise.

The connection between the vices and social class is, as Laura D. Gelfand argues, an integral part of Hieronymus Bosch's painting, *The Seven Deadly Sins and the Four Last Things* (ca. 1490), often wrongly described as a "tabletop." This remarkable presentation of visual stimuli was designed to produce an effect of contrition in the viewer (perhaps a member of Bosch's own religious confraternity) and to provide the viewer's imagination with a set of contemplative images. The unblinking divine eye at the center of the painting transforms the representations of social status seen in the vices ranged in a circle around it by providing them with an admonitory focal point to encourage the viewer's self-examination of his/her conscience about each sin and how one sin leads to the next. The painting shows that the sins were constructed to articulate differences in social classes in Bosch's environment: lust and pride typify the aristocracy; envy undermines the moral status of both this class and the merchants, who are further characterized by their avarice and sloth; while the peasantry is exemplified by the bestiality and irrationality of gluttony and wrath. Bosch used clothing, iconographic markers, the genre settings of the vices, and narratives implied by gestures to bring together markers of class and immorality. The presence of money bags in almost all sin-portraits demonstrates the ubiquity of avarice, above all, in Bosch's thinking about the vices, and in the secular social environment for which he produced his painting.

At the end of the volume, Thomas Parisi returns to the "zone of convergence" found to connect the past and present in all *Begriffsgeschichte*. He reads Dante's existential cosmology, based as it is on sin, expiation, and the possibility of achieving a beatific state, as a map of Freud's project, but one in which Freud, like Virgil, cannot lead the way completely out of a sin-bound world. The first nexus of both thinkers is the importance of love: Dante's account of the sins as types of disordered love in the *Purgatorio* mirrors Freud's account of psychological development, Dante's desire to overcome misery to achieve felicity resounds in Freud's desire to transform neurosis into common unhappiness. But beyond love, three anthropological correspondences delineate the connection between Freud and Dante: citizenship, which demands a providentially-guided justice in Dante, becomes in Freud more of a functional necessity in the process of maturation; character and fate, where Dante and Freud converge in seeing that the search for pleasure inherent to human beings has programmed into them difficulties that will arise regularly, all of which can be understood to spring from pride (Dante) or its Freudian equivalent, narcissism; and language and desire, where, at least partially, the inability to use language is understood by Dante to result from the loss of reason that comes along with the moral depravity at the bottom of the *Inferno*, as in Freud a "linguistic-motivational rupture" becomes characteristic of aphasia. Reading Freud and Dante together foregrounds their anthropologies and makes it clear to what degree moral investigation and biological psychology have much to contribute to each other.

In fact, this fruitful sharing of ideas across the humanities and the social sciences reproduces the *raison d'être* of the 2004 seminar on the vices and the guiding methodology in our long and animated discussions that summer examining the seven deadly sins as cultural constructions.

COMMUNITIES

SIN AND THE CONSTRUCTION OF
CAROLINGIAN KINGSHIP

Dwight D. Allman
Baylor University

Abstract: This paper focuses on political and civic dimensions of the Carolingian *renovatio*, particularly on attempts to work out a conception of Christian kingship and a public moral/spiritual order (in systematic engagements with the capital vices) to sustain the construction of a Christian empire. Drawing especially on the work of Alcuin of York, I explore how Carolingian thinkers confronting the issues of governing an expanding territory beset by pagan resistance and hostility appropriate and employ patristic-era political thought, most importantly from Augustine of Hippo. I consider the ways in which Carolingian treatments of sin build on systematizations by Gregory the Great and others, and the ways in which adaptations of theoretical and theological constructs inherited from Christian thinkers—constructs that often represent responses to hegemonic Greco-Roman traditions concerned with right rule, the best life, and the just polity—reveal a negotiation of pressing political realities that earlier Christian thinkers did not face.

As early architects of Christendom, the Carolingians took their building materials from diverse sources, but especially from storehouses of social-theological reflection erected by an earlier generation of Christians confronting the late-antique clash of cultures between a politically ascendant community of believers in Jesus as the resurrected Messiah and the contracting imperial world of an aristocratic, pagan Rome. Among the most important of these storehouses was Augustine's mammoth apologetic of the Christian faith against its pagan detractors, *De civitate Dei contra paganos*—a favorite work of Charlemagne, and in fact the only one named by Einhard, his official biographer.[1]

Augustine's tome, almost fifteen years in the making (413–427), documents tectonic movements in the metaphysical firmament of the

---

[1] See Einhard, *Vita Caroli Magni*, 24, in Éginhard, *Vie de Charlemagne*, ed. and trans. Louis Halphen (Paris, 1923), 70–72.

Latin world that marked the close of pagan antiquity and the rise of medieval Europe. Perhaps no passage more ably records these developments than the brief preface Augustine composed for the first book of *De civitate Dei*. Here, the Bishop of Hippo trumpets "the excellence of humility" [*virtus humilitatis*] to a neo-pagan elite for which the term *humilitas* had traditional associations with those in Roman society whose abject station set them conspicuously apart from, even beneath the notice of, cultured men devoted to virtue.[2] Augustine employs *humilitas* only once in his preface, but in such a way as to place the classical world of Virgil's *Aeneid* in comparative relation to the moral universe of Christian scripture.[3] He begins by noting the particular difficulty he confronts in attempting to bring "the proud" (by whom he means especially those whose distinction in the "arts" of ruling Virgil describes at *Aeneid*, 6.853),[4] to recognize how great *virtus humilitatis* is. He thereby implies that those who trace their self-understanding to the *Aeneid* do not perceive *humilitas* to be a form of excellence. He suggests, in fact, that for pagan Romans the word names something close to its opposite, since "the inflated arrogance of a proud spirit" leads them to assume for themselves a role ("To spare those humbled by conquest [*subiectis*] and to subdue the proud")[5] which Holy Scripture assigns to God, who alone properly "resists the proud but bestows grace upon the humble [*humilibus*]."[6] The juxtaposition makes Virgil's *subiectus* into a kind of pagan gloss on *humilis*, highlighting the contesting valuations at the crux

---

[2] As a political term, the valences of *humilitas* are governed, in the first instance, by the notion of power and position in society. The condition described by *humilitas* is fundamentally that of the powerless who, as a consequence, have no standing in society. See, for example, Cicero, *Tusculan Disputations*, 5.103; *Pro Quinctio*, 95. But the word can therefore also signify a depraved and contemptible status, one that is beneath the notice of cultivated people and refined taste; see Pliny, *Naturalis Historia*, 14.7.

[3] On Augustine's construction of *De civitate Dei* around a juxtaposing of Virgil's formative work of Roman nationalism with the Bible, see Peter Brown, *Augustine of Hippo: A Biography*, new ed. (London, 2000), 306: "After twenty years of studying the Bible, Augustine was convinced that the Christians also had a literature of inexhaustible richness. 'Your' Vergil is now deliberately juxtaposed, at every turn, with 'Our' Scriptures."

[4] "...remember, Roman, these will be your arts: to teach the ways of peace to those you conquer, to spare defeated peoples, tame the proud." Translation taken from *The Aeneid of Virgil*, trans. Allen Mandelbaum (New York, 1981), 160–61.

[5] Augustine of Hippo, *De civitate Dei libri XXII*, 1.praef., ed. B. Dombart and A. Kalb, 5th ed. (Stuttgart, 1981; reprint München, 1993), 1:4: "Parcere subiectis et debellare superbos" (my translation).

[6] *De civ.*, 1.praef. (1:3): "[Deus] superbis resistit, humilibus autem dat gratiam" (my translation). Augustine is here quoting James 4:6. Cf. also 1 Pet 5:5.

of the rivalry between these two moralities. As Augustine represents it, Roman assertion of the arts of rule amounts simply to overweening pride, a capital vice for Christians, while humility, the foundation of Christian virtue, denotes a condition to which the pagan conception of virtue does not apply. In short, Augustine rests citizenship in the Heavenly City upon a quality of soul connected by Roman aristocrats to a social-political standing identified with an utter lack of capacity for human or civic excellence.

The elevation of *humilitas* underlies Augustine's case for a distinctly Christian form of kingship, a key innovation in his articulation of a political theory rooted in Christian theology. It is by God's grace that true rulers acquire their defining capacities, the most important of which are the uniquely Christian virtues of faith, hope, and love, but it is only to those conditioned by *humilitas* that God affords grace. My examination of early medieval political thought rests on the contention that Augustine's teaching on the right rule of the Christian king, and therefore on the unique possibilities for a just society when Christians preside, challenges the compounded wisdom of the classical tradition of political philosophy descending from Socratic idealism. The public-spirited current of that tradition expressed itself as a persistent concern with the practical task of cultivating governors who might properly be artisans of just rule. It sought, moreover, to foster an elite culture capable of nurturing such a politics by attaching the love of honor to a Socratic engagement with the question of the best and most just life, and to sustain this configuration through the institution of friendship.[7]

It is within the practical works of Aristotle that we encounter the mature expression of this ambition. At the beginning of his *Nicomachean*

---

[7] This summary of the public-spirited ends of Socratic political philosophy deserves a full elaboration and defense in its own right, which cannot be undertaken here. A proper treatment of this thesis constitutes, in fact, a principal aim of my book-length study of *The Citizen and The Soul*, now in progress. For accounts of the Socratic practice of philosophy as centrally concerned to promote moral and civic improvement in the interest of fostering the ability to lead as just a life as possible, see Peter Euben, *Corrupting Socrates: Political Education, Democratic Culture, and Political Theory* (Princeton, 1997); Alexander Nehamas, "A Fate for Socrates' Reason: Foucault on the Care of the Self," in *The Art of Living: Socratic Reflections from Plato to Foucault* (Berkeley, 1998), 157–88; Dana Villa, *Socratic Citizenship* (Princeton, 2001). For accounts that emphasize, at the same time, the radical and subversive character of the philosophic life that Socrates recommends and the essential tensions, therefore, between philosophizing and the public life of the polis, see Pierre Hadot, "The Figure of Socrates," in *Philosophy as a Way of Life* (London, 1995), 147–78; Paul A. Rahe, *Republics Ancient & Modern*, vol. 1 (Chapel Hill, NC, 1994); Leo Strauss, *The City and Man* (Chicago, 1964).

Ethics, Aristotle sets the focus of his treatise on those devoted to honor through a life of public-political activity only to explain how honor fails as a description of the highest good, since it is sought not for its own sake but as a means of affirming the excellence of the honored.[8] A dialectical unfolding of Aristotle's teaching in the *Ethics* is thereafter dictated by the civic ambition to cultivate genuine statesmen among those prompted, in the first instance, by the yearning for honor. Aristotle attempts, in other words, to direct his audience to the pursuit of those qualities of character and intellect upon which right rule depends by linking a dominant passion for honor to an ascending catalogue of virtues and by refining a taste for popular acclaim into a concern with the esteem and approval of those most accomplished in virtue.[9]

With this essay I seek, first, to examine briefly the conversation about the problem of just rule that emerged originally among Greek philosophers before turning to an exploration of Augustine's rival case for a solution to that problem once Christianity achieved political currency. Having traced the outlines of a quarrel between Augustine and the ancient philosophers on the problem of just rule, I consider finally Carolingian negotiations of theory and practice in the attempt to institute a proper Christian politics. The Carolingians, of course, also had to wrestle with pressing realities confronted in the exercise of actual political power in an expanding and newly defined kingdom frequently beset by pagan resistance and hostility, a set of circumstances that Augustine never had to address.

I seek, in particular, to explore political and civic dimensions of the Carolingian *renovatio*, for it represents in part the working out of a conception of Christian kingship and a public moral/spiritual order to sustain the construction of a Christian empire. The public culture that the Carolingian reformers sought to put in place was essentially a theological and religious structure. A central pillar of this structure was the catalogue of "principle vices" that the *Moralia in Job* by Gregory the Great (ca. 540–604) first translated from the exclusive realm of

---

[8] See *Nicomachean Ethics*, 1095b.22–30; also, 1124a.20–29.

[9] Commentators on Aristotle's political works that see these writings as structured, at least in part, by a practical concern with the education of statesmen or those who might rule include Mary Nichols, *Citizens and Statesmen: A Study of Aristotle's Politics* (Lanham, MD, 1992); Lorraine Smith Pangle, *Aristotle and the Philosophy of Friendship* (Cambridge, Eng., 2002); Thomas W. Smith, *Revaluing Ethics: Aristotle's Dialectical Pedagogy* (Albany, NY, 2001); Aristide Tessitore, *Reading Aristotle's Ethics: Virtue, Rhetoric, and Political Philosophy* (Albany, NY, 1996).

monastic spirituality and discipline to the work-a-day world of the laity. This development alone marks a pronounced shift from an ancient world in which public life coalesced around attention to the virtues, not the vices. I am here particularly concerned to investigate Carolingian formulations of Christian kingship and the interplay of conceptions of vice and virtue in those formulations. The study of Carolingian kingship provides a strategic window on the emerging practice of Christian rule. And in its applications, deviations, and/or modifications of the moral and political thought of the patristic era, we find an excellent vantage point from which to begin to adjudicate, both philosophically and historically, one of the formative, if often neglected, quarrels in the tradition of western social thought. The now well-rutted convention of tracing the rise of modern political theory to *la querelle des anciens et des modernes* obscures the extent to which modern political thought represents a mediation and outgrowth of the contest staged by Christian thinkers such as Augustine with the progenitors of Greco-Roman traditions of theory and practice.

I. *Classical Political Philosophy and 'Rule in the Strict Sense'*

The opening book of Plato's *Republic* culminates in an exchange between Socrates and an ambitious young teacher of rhetoric named Thrasymachus, who responds to Socrates' query about the nature of justice by provocatively announcing that justice is "nothing other than the advantage of the stronger."[10] Justice, in other words, describes the ability of those who possess power to compel those subject to that power to serve their designs; in effect, the word denotes a kind of rhetoric by which the powerful dress up the imposition of their power. Identifying justice with obedience to their commands, rulers facilitate the pursuit of their own advantage. As such, justice benefits not those who practice it (the law-abiding), but those who define it (the lawmakers). Politics is reduced to a contest in which the victors win the opportunity to define their own interest as the just. But if justice is not profitable for those who practice it, the very goodness of justice is brought into question.

---

[10] Thrasymachus makes this declaration at *Republic*, 338c. Stephanus page references to the *Republic* will be contained in the text hereafter. All translations are my own and based on *Platonis opera*, vol. 4, ed. J. Burnet (Oxford, 1982).

The exchange with Thrasymachus marks a point in the dialogue at which Socrates' role in the conversation shifts from simply directing an inquiry into what justice is to also defending justice as something good.[11] At the same time, the Socratic practice of political philosophy emerges as involving considerably more than the mere application of philosophical analysis to the phenomenon of politics. Plato's grand dialogue on justice suggests that it likewise entailed a public-spirited kind of philosophizing.

Socrates ultimately reduces Thrasymachus to silence by leading the conversation towards an examination of ruling, and by co-opting a key professional assumption of those like Thrasymachus who offered their wisdom on politics for sale: ruling is an art (*technē*) and, as such, can be taught (cf. 340c–41a). As a result, the examination of this sophistic formulation of justice comes to turn on an understanding of *technē* that teachers of rhetoric, and all others who profess to know how to instruct and to prepare their young charges for a successful career in politics, necessarily embrace.[12] Socrates is thus able to bring Thrasymachus to admit that it is in the nature of a *technē* to concern itself with the good of those to whom it is applied (as, for example, does medicine). Consequently, ruling "in the strict sense"[13] must concern the welfare and happiness of the ruled, not of the ruler (341d–42d).

The ambivalent conclusion of this line of reasoning is the famous philosopher-king thesis: only if and when philosophers rule, Socrates insists, will justice prevail and the ills that now characterize political life find resolution (473d–e). For both moral and epistemological reasons philosophers are uniquely qualified to rule. They alone are prepared to wield power in accordance with an art concerned strictly with servicing the welfare of those subject to such power. In almost the same breath, however, Socrates makes clear that this formula for eliminating injustice and setting the human condition aright looks to be an utterly paradoxical (if not quixotic) one.[14] As rulers, philosophers would have to trade in a life of contemplation for a life of action, thereby ceasing to practice philosophy. Only if the happiness of the ruler could somehow be

---

[11] On this point, see Devin Stauffer, *Plato's Introduction to the Question of Justice* (Albany, NY, 2001), 57–58.

[12] On this point, see *The Republic of Plato*, trans. Allan Bloom, 2nd ed. (New York, 1991), 330.

[13] The Greek text reads *kata ton akribē logon* at 340e. See also 341b.

[14] Socrates concludes his introduction of the idea that philosophers must rule at 473e by noting *hōs polu para doksan* ("how very paradoxical") it appears. See also 592a–b.

made identical with service to the good of the ruled, would the ruler's interest in his own good be productively aligned with the terms of just governance. But prospects of any such achievement appear especially problematic when the matter of just rule is considered in relation to another question to which the *Republic* gives thematic attention—the question of the *happiness* of the guardian-rulers.[15] Conceived as strict observance of the art of ruling, the just life proves to be less than its own reward, since the art of caring for the welfare (body and soul) of the ruled does not encompass the happiness of the ruler. In fact, ruling in this sense necessarily competes with and detracts from the care of oneself.[16] Socrates therefore observes that the right-thinking individual will readily choose to be well-ruled, to be the object and beneficiary of the genuine ruler's art, rather than to take on the chore of ruling (see 347a–48a).

The untidy conclusion with which Plato's *Republic* appears to leave us, namely, that the problem of the just ruler is not amenable to a complete solution, only perhaps to a pragmatic one (albeit one guided by the insight which philosophy provides into the nature of the problem), appears to have fostered an ongoing reflection, extending from Aristotle to Cicero, that aimed at a practical resolution of the problem of just rule. The crux of that practical problem consisted in finding a way to reconcile the ruler's natural interest in his own good to the imperatives of a just politics conceived in terms of the common good of the ruled.[17]

II. *Augustine's Case for Christian Kingship*

Book 5 of *De civitate Dei* marks the conclusion of the first part of Augustine's lengthy defense of Christianity, now ensconced as the

---

[15] This theme is introduced explicitly at 419a, after which it begins to drive Socrates' treatment of the guardian-class, particularly with respect to the erotic nature of the philosopher-rulers. See *Republic*, trans. Bloom, 413; Jacob Howland, *The Republic: The Odyssey of Philosophy* (New York, 1993), 38–42.

[16] On the tensions between caring for the city and caring for oneself, see *Republic*, trans. Bloom, 331–34, 372–79.

[17] For more on the background of justice as the moral response to the common good, see Richard Newhauser, "Justice and Liberality: Opposition to Avarice in the Twelfth Century," in *Virtue and Ethics in the Twelfth Century*, ed. István P. Bejczy and Richard G. Newhauser (Leiden, 2005), 295–316, here 295–97.

official religion of Rome, against its pagan critics. In the final chapters of Book 5, he contends for the superiority of the Christian emperors Constantine and Theodosius to their non-Christian forerunners and adversaries. Through the first five books, Augustine has argued against the view that recent calamities—in particular, the sack of Rome by Alaric and his Visigoths in 410, a symbol for many of the city's declining fortunes—could be reasonably attributed to Rome's abandonment of its worship of the pagan gods. This argument culminates in a defense of the political efficacy of the rulers responsible for elevating Christianity to its official status and presiding role within the empire. In this way, Augustine disputes the charge circulating among neo-pagan aristocrats that the embrace of Christianity initiated by Constantine marked the onset of Rome's descent from political preeminence.[18]

In chapter 24, Augustine identifies the locus of their *happiness* as the basis of what he represents as the superior governance of these Christian rulers, for the happiness of the Christian rests not in the "consolations of this wretched life," but in anticipation of "eternal felicity." The Christian ruler does not look for his fulfillment in the exercise or exploitation of worldly power, or even in the unhindered realization of his mortal will. He is moved neither by the flattery "of those who accord [him] sublime honors," nor by the prospect of "empty glory" (*DCD*, 5.24, 232).[19] His peculiar state of soul is perhaps best summed up in the fact that, though politically supreme, he cherishes most his status as disciple and servant of the true God. Accordingly, Augustine emphasizes that Theodosius never ceased "to assist the Church in her labours against the ungodly by means of the most just and merciful laws," and that he "rejoiced more in being a member of the Church than in being the ruler of the world" (*DCD*, 5.26, 235).

As a Christian, he rests his life on the promise of eventual salvation and can therefore be simply "happy in hope" (*DCD*, 5.24, 232).

---

[18] On the contentious question of Christianity's relation to the decline of the Roman empire, see Arnaldo Momigliano, "Christianity and the Decline of the Roman Empire," in *Paganism and Christianity in the Fourth Century*, ed. A. Momigliano (Oxford, 1963), 1–16. On the neo-pagan challenge to Christianity's political efficacy, see Brown, *Augustine of Hippo*, 302ff.

[19] English quotations from *De civitate Dei* (DCD) will be cited in the body of the essay simply by book, chapter, and page numbers, as they appear in *The City of God Against the Pagans*, ed. and trans. R. W. Dyson (Cambridge, Eng., 1998). For a discussion of the first five books (part 1) as a response to the contention that the gods should be worshipped "for felicity on earth," see Brown, *Augustine of Hippo*, 302–03.

According to Augustine, it is Christianity's illumination of *what permanently is* as opposed to *what presently appears* that enables the Christian king to devote himself so single-mindedly to the task of just rule. That perspective entails not only viewing temporal conditions in the light of eternal verities, but also embracing the idea that history unfolds in strict accord with providential design. The faithful ruler, therefore, strives simply to execute the designs of providence through his office. In this way, Augustine recounts how only after he had consulted and received assurances from John, "a hermit established in Egypt" who was "gifted with the spirit of prophecy," did Theodosius determine that he should wage war against "the tyrant Maximus," who seized control of the eastern empire by slaying Gratian and usurping his younger brother Valentinian (*DCD*, 5.26, 233–34). By the same token, such a ruler must be prepared to lay down his sword, submitting even to the unjust rule of another, if providence so designs.[20] Moreover, the beliefs that define the self-understanding of the Christian ruler necessarily direct him toward the right worship of God, a mode of devotion that begins with the Christian experience of *humilitas*. Unlike pagan piety, this form of devotion eventuates in a comprehensive ordering of desire and will in obeisance to divine authority and the temporal pursuit of justice. At the same time, it disparages worldly honors and the love of glory. In right worship, the faithful Christian finds an object for his passions commensurate with his deepest longings. Right worship, thus, enables the disciple of Christ to bring an end to the strife among the different parts of himself that otherwise defines his mortal being.[21] By the same token, it inoculates the Christian ruler against the many temptations that attach to positions of power. What principally distinguishes the

---

[20] On this point, see Rowan Williams' rich discussion of "the paradox that the only reliable political leader, the only ruler who can be guaranteed to safeguard authentically *political* values (order, equity, and the nurture of souls in these things) is the man who is, at the end of the day, indifferent to their survival in the relative shapes of the existing order, because he knows them to be safeguarded at the level of God's eternal and immutable providence, vindicated in the eternal *civitas dei*." See "Politics and the Soul: A Rereading of the *City of God*," *Milltown Studies* 19, 20 (1987): 67.

[21] The strife that constitutes the mortal self, and that can only be resolved by coming to worship the true God, is a central theme of Augustine's *Confessions*. See Book 10, in particular. On the peace that all things seek and that results from a right ordering "of equal and unequal things in such a way as to give to each its proper place," including of the body to the soul and the human to the divine, see *DCD*, 19, especially chapter 13, 938–40.

Christian ruler from his pagan counterparts is, in short, the moral and
intellectual constitution of his soul.

The spiritual formation fostered by right worship leads the Christian
ruler to pursue his happiness through the selfless conduct of his
office, which he prizes not as a means of achieving political status or
wielding temporal power, but of controlling and reforming "wicked
desires." At the same time, he seeks to make his office and influence
into instruments for winning converts to, in order to promote further
the worship of, the true God (*DCD*, 5.24, 232). Augustine insists that
right rule ultimately requires the participation of *both* rulers *and* their
subjects or fellow citizens in the right worship of God (cf. *DCD*, 19.13
and 17, 938–40, 945–47). His teaching therefore promotes a politics
whose defining purpose is to extend right worship—and, therein, the
prospects for a Christian *rule in the strict sense*—throughout the empire.
Because he attaches greater importance to his "being a member of the
Church" than to his standing as "ruler of the world," the Christian
emperor conceives of his office as a service to God and the Church
(*DCD*, 5.26, 235). With his account of Theodosius, Augustine is at
pains to detail the political utility of the Christian emperor's spiritually
upright reign. Broadly stated, this is the conclusion to which Augustine
leads his readers through the first five books of his *apologia* contra the
neo-pagan critics of Christianity who blamed the upstart religion for
Rome's political tribulations. As a historical matter, Augustine's theory
of just government, anchored in the right-worshipping rule of an
evangelizing ruler, may well have pointed the way, at least implicitly, to
an imperial Christianity. But, if so, one is obliged to observe that the
Christian politics defended in *De civitate Dei* represent a more nuanced
teaching than is manifest by its historical influence.

The extended argument of that work identifies household management and domestic relations as vitally implicated in civic health and
concord. With an explanation calibrated for an audience schooled in
ancient philosophy's pervasive concern with harmony and due proportion,[22] Augustine treats the household in its relation to the city as a part
to its whole, concluding that, inasmuch as "every part has reference
to the integrity of the whole of which it is a part," the spiritual state

---

[22] As Brown, *Augustine of Hippo*, 304, makes clear, Augustine's work "was no transi-
tory pamphlet for a simple audience: it was a book which men of leisure, learned men,
must be prepared to read again and again to appreciate."

of the household fundamentally shapes that of the city: "the ordered concord of domestic rule and obedience has reference to the ordered concord of civic rule and obedience" (*DCD*, 19.16, 945). The domestic realm thus becomes a kind of "laboratory of the spirit," nurturing each member with an appropriately "pastoral care" within a family structure that reflects a divinely instituted *ordo* of hierarchy and rule.[23] Similarly, Augustine intimates that the social practices and virtues that make civic harmony conceivable are best cultivated within a context structured by the self-transformation and eternal understanding that Christianity uniquely makes available.[24] Civic life is always a social life, and the pilgrim-citizen, who participates already in the heavenly peace that sets the City of God apart from all worldly associations, is necessarily the most social of animals. As Rowan Williams has put it, "the *pax* of the individual soul and the *pax* of the universe are parts of a single continuum."[25]

The qualities that recommend an individual to social life here and now thus reflect the universal order whose final realization is the Heavenly City that the Christian pilgrim seeks. In a similar vein, Theodosius illustrates for Augustine the Christian life of civic engagement as pastoral care, within which the usual boundaries demarcating the distinct realms of family, city, and nation take on the provisional status of fleeting realities whose claims must always be viewed in light of eternal participation in the City of God. Because the pilgrim-citizen and/or pilgrim-ruler so exemplifies the civic, social and moral qualities that a well-ordered polity requires, Augustine's defense of Christianity against the charge that it is the source of disorder and corruption serves at the same time as a recommendation of Christianity to the role of moral educator for Rome. However, a central tenet of that education concerns the fallen condition of humankind, a state of fundamental antagonisms: the body is at war against the soul, as is every man against his neighbor, and every nation against every other nation and against itself. It is to this predicament that Augustine traces what he terms *libido*

---

[23] See Williams, 64.

[24] In *Epistle 91* Augustine describes himself as "a citizen of a country which is above, in holy love," but whose plain, essentially domestic virtues are nevertheless recognized by "those very books…from which you imbibed the sentiment of a loyal subject" as the qualities that characterize a polity "in full flower." Quoted in Jean Bethke Elshtain, *Augustine and the Limits of Politics* (Notre Dame, IN, 1995), 41.

[25] Williams, 63.

dominandi,[26] the "lust for mastery" with its endless struggle for power and domination that circumscribes human relations and political affairs, and that severely limits the prospects for temporal justice. Accordingly, the pilgrim-citizen must fix his love of justice on that heavenly site where the faithful will be transformed and redeemed from their fallen state. While the pre-Christian tradition of political philosophy emphasizes human excellence as a solution for politics, Augustine inaugurates a tradition of Christian political thought that makes an understanding of man's depravity the basis of right rule. This orientation necessarily implies a radically different construction of practical wisdom or prudence from that promoted by classical political philosophy. As Williams emphasizes, Augustine's model statesman comes to light as the embodiment of a paradox: "the only ruler who can be guaranteed to safeguard authentically *political* values (order, equity, and the nurture of souls in these things) is the man who is, at the end of the day, indifferent to their survival in the relative shapes of the existing order, because he knows them to be safeguarded at the level of God's eternal and immutable providence, vindicated in the eternal *civitas Dei*."[27] The Augustinian solution to the problem of right rule grounds itself in otherworldly commitments that entail an acknowledgement of the parsimonious limits assigned to politics. Right rule, therefore, must be ever prepared to sacrifice its temporal kingdom if only that will preserve its alliance with the City of God.

The idea that right rule is an extension of right worship also represents, of course, the premise underlying the contention of conservative critics that Rome had lost its way since it abandoned its traditional gods for Christianity. Augustine therefore labors to illustrate and to document the moral corruption that worship of the pagan gods engendered. He takes up the challenge posed by neo-pagan opponents of Christianity in the broadest possible way with an examination of Rome's failure to realize its own ideals even at the peak of its achievement. And to make his case against the public culture of pagan Rome, he turns to the indigenous critique of Roman political life, to the moral-political evaluations of Rome's political history and public life pronounced by

---

[26] See, for example, Augustine's discussion "Of the impiety of the war which the Romans waged against the Albans, and of the victories gained through their lust for mastery" (*DCD*, 3.14, 109–13).

[27] Williams, 67.

its own poets, historians, and public officials.[28] Augustine emphasizes, in turn, a framework of social-political assumptions that he shares with—or, more accurately, takes from—the pagan world he would displace. Like Cicero (cf. *DCD*, 2.21, 76–80), he ultimately traces good governance to the well-ordered soul, a contention that points back to Socrates' defense of his life as a philosopher-citizen in Athens. As noted above, the political priority of caring for the soul likewise stands at the center of the inquiry into the problem of justice that constitutes Plato's *Republic*, and it undergirds Aristotle's *epistemē politikē* as documented by both his *Politics* and *Ethics*. In Cicero, this central teaching of classical political thought finds not only its most important Roman voice, but also perhaps its ultimate instantiation in the form of a leading man of action whose activity grounds itself in an abiding reverence for philosophy and in an ongoing relationship to philosophizing. Augustine's political defense of Christianity thus continues a tradition of conversation about just rule initiated by classical political philosophy, but constitutes at the same time the inauguration of an important quarrel with that tradition, particularly with its pragmatic negotiation of the problems posed by rule in the strict sense. To be sure, he makes common cause with classical political philosophy in its critique of pagan popular religion. However, in his portrait of Theodosius—arguably the original *mirror* of a Christian prince—Augustine contends for the superiority of Christianity in resolving the matter that classical political philosophy had located among the defining problems of politics.

III. *Augustinian Kingship and the Carolingian Construction of Empire*

Alcuin of York (ca. 730–804) was arguably the most important of the luminaries engaged in the Carolingian *renovatio*.[29] Brought from England

---

[28] Cf. Brown, *Augustine of Hippo*, 301ff., where he explores how Augustine dispels the mythology put forth by contemporary neo-pagan aristocrats who revere the ancient ways and believe restoration of these ways to represent the only solution to the crisis of political decline that Rome now faces.

[29] However, a leading authority on Alcuin, Donald A. Bullough, whose recently published biography *Alcuin: Achievement and Reputation* (Leiden, 2004) represents the most exhaustive study to date, forcefully challenges the "received notions" of Alcuin as heading up Charlemagne's court school, where he supposedly figured as the dominant figure in the Carolingian *renovatio*. See Bullough, 336–46.

by Charlemagne to his court school at Aachen,[30] Alcuin became a key figure in the Carolingian *translatio studii*—the "transference" or transmission of Christian learning that had come to be concentrated in the British Isles back to continental Europe. During the years of his service to Charlemagne, Alcuin took on the task of tutor, advisor, and emissary of the great king. And the court school at Aachen functioned, rather like schools of government today, as a conduit through which storehouses of monastic and clerical learning became available for social/political purposes. Among the intellectual tasks that Alcuin appears to have taken upon himself was that of formulating a conception of Christian kingship. However, Alcuin broke no new conceptual ground in thinking through the matter of the Christian ruler. As Luitpold Wallach convincingly argued over forty years ago, Alcuin's construction of Charlemagne as the model Christian ruler plainly bears the theoretical fingerprints of Augustine.[31] Alcuin's teaching on kingship holds particular interest for what it can teach us about the unfolding practice of a Christian politics fundamentally shaped by Augustine, since it was Augustine's model of kingship that supplied the paradigm of right rule for medieval political theory.

Alcuin attaches to Charlemagne Augustine's designation of the Christian emperor as *felix imperator*, the temporal ruler whose happiness is vouchsafed by his membership in the eternal city of God. Like Augustine, moreover, Alcuin holds that the Christian ruler is spiritually formed through right worship of God, which leads him to identify his pursuit of happiness with the ends of just rule and the selfless conduct of his office. For Augustine, then, the Christian ruler properly conceives of serving his subjects in terms of the pastoral ethic of those who in commanding function as "the servants of those whom they seem to command" (*DCD*, 19.14, 942), for which Christ's redeeming sacrifice of himself for the sake of his followers stands as the model.[32] Such a ruler likewise seeks to make his political office and authority into an instrument for winning converts to, and for promoting the worship of, the true God. Accordingly, Alcuin sometimes describes Charlemagne

---

[30] Bullough contends that Alcuin arrived at Aachen only in 786 (not 781/82), making highly improbable the received account of his founding role in the court school (cf. Bullough, 346). But Bullough nevertheless concludes that "if Alcuin's part is hardly the familiar 'headship of a palace school,' it is not less significant in its outcome" (372).
[31] See Luitpold Wallach, *Alcuin and Charlemagne: Studies in Carolingian History and Literature* (Ithaca, NY, 1959), 48–72.
[32] Cf. Luke 22:25–27.

as a *praedicator* (preacher) who spreads the word of God to his subjects, having been ordained by God *populo praeesse et prodesse* (to guide and to help the people).[33] In a correspondence with Charlemagne from 799, Alcuin includes a list of duties pertaining to the ruler that clearly has its origin in Augustine's enumeration of the qualities that define the *felix imperator*.[34] And in a letter from 801, less than a year after Charlemagne had been crowned emperor in Rome, Alcuin even compares the felicitous state of a people *qui sapiente et pio regitur principe* (who are ruled by a wise and pious prince) to the Platonic ideal of a regime in which philosophers, or *amatores sapientiae* (lovers of wisdom), govern.[35]

On at least one occasion,[36] however, Alcuin applies the term *pontifex* to Charlemagne, conveying in a word his conviction that Christian kingship, strictly conceived, joined temporal authority over the material world of dominions, property, and persons to a spiritual responsibility for the souls of the governed. Alcuin thereby emphasizes, in Wallach's words, "the exalted position" to which he assigns Charlemagne, while underscoring his belief that, because he was a true king, it was "impossible to corrupt him."[37] One might be led by this to conclude that the Carolingian formulation of kingship as a union of consummate temporal power with the highest spiritual authority models itself on Old Testament exemplars. Indeed, among the appellations applied to Charlemagne, "the new David" was a favorite.[38] But in choosing to address Charlemagne as a *pontifex*, Alcuin also appears to be consciously recovering and rehabilitating a title that the Christian rulers who first took over the pagan office of Roman emperor—among them, Gratian

---

[33] Cf. Alcuin, *Epistolae*, 178 and 257, as cited in Wallach, 16.

[34] Compare Alcuin, *Epistolae*, 177.17–34, ed. Ernst Dümmler, in *Epistolae Karolini aevi* 2, MGH Epistolae 4 (Berlin, 1895; reprint, 1994), 292–93, with *DCD*, 5.24, 231–32.

[35] *Epist.*, 229.2–4, ed. Dümmler, 372. Wallach, 26, observes how Alcuin carefully alters the expression used by Boethius, his source for what he knows of the Platonic *kalipolis*. Where Boethius speaks of "blessed republics" (*beatae res publicae*) perceptible only to the mind's eye, Alcuin invokes the flesh-and-blood *felices imperatores* that Augustine believes Christianity makes possible.

[36] See Alcuin, *Adversus Elipandum Toletanum libri*, 1.16, PL 101:251D.

[37] Wallach, 13.

[38] In his discussion of Carolingian politics, Henry Mayr-Harting argues that Old Testament commentaries by important English scholars preceding Alcuin—in particular, the Venerable Bede—served to educate succeeding generations about the Old Testament office of kingship. See Mayr-Harting's examination of "Christianity and the Political Order" in "The West: the Age of Conversion, 700–1050," chapter 3 of *The Oxford Illustrated History of Christianity*, ed. John McManners (Oxford, 1996), 101–10. See also Bullough, 409–10.

and Theodosius—had purposely abandoned. Here, we catch perhaps first sight of a subtle negotiation with key aspects of the Augustinian ideal of kingship, as Alcuin attempts to imbue Augustine's *paterfamilias*[39] with something of the imposing grandeur and immutable authority that attached to the Roman *pontifex maximus*. What comes into view looks like a certain concession to the civic orientation and ambition of pagan religion that Augustine consistently derides. Confronting the limits of human justice, Carolingian Christians seem to have found that prudence called for the building of civic bridges across the theological chasm separating the city of God from the city of man.

In a letter from August, 799, Alcuin exhorted Charlemagne with words that shed an even sharper light on his attempts to negotiate the realities of imperial rule within the framework of Augustinian political theory:

> Spare your Christian people and defend the churches of Christ that the blessing of the King on high may make you strong against the pagans. We read that when one of the old poets sang about the praise of the Roman emperors, and what sort [of rulers] they should have been, he said, if I recall correctly: "Spare those humbled by conquest and subdue the proud," which verse blessed Augustine, in his book *On the City of God*, explained with much praise.[40]

The verse, which Alcuin would have Charlemagne take to heart here, is the very one that Augustine cites from the *Aeneid* (6.853) to introduce the fundamental contest of beliefs leading to his great apology for the Christian faith. As Wallach notes, it contains Virgil's formulation of "the high mission of the Roman."[41] But, as we have seen, Augustine uses it to illustrate the central theme of his work—the essential conflict between the earthly city in its self-aggrandizing quest to subdue its world and the heavenly city, where citizenship is extended by divine grace

---

[39] At *DCD*, 19.16, 944, Augustine contends that "those who are truly 'fathers of their families' are as much concerned for the welfare of all in their households, in respect of the worship and service of God, as if they were all their children." See also Williams, 64–65, for a sustained examination of the pastoral dimensions of Augustine's Christian ruler.

[40] Alcuin, *Epist.*, 178, ed. Dümmler, 294: "Parce populo tuo christiano, et ecclesias Christi defende, ut benedictio superni Regis te fortem efficiat super paganos. Legitur quendam veterum dixisse poetarum, cum de laude imperatorum Romani regni, si rite recordor, cecinisset, quales esse debuissent, dicens: 'Parcere subiectis et debellare superbos,' quem versiculum beatus Augustinus in libro de civitate Dei multa laude exposuit." My translation.

[41] Wallach, 21.

only to those who submit themselves to a merciful God. In the context of Augustine's preface, the verse serves to define the condition that Augustine later describes as "a perverted imitation of God" (*DCD*, 19.12, 936). Roman *superbia* (pride), which nourishes the desire "to impose its own dominion upon its equals, in place of God's rule" (*DCD*, 19.12, 936), stands in essential opposition to Christian *humilitas*, the precondition of true virtue and just rule (cf. *DCD*, 19.25–27, 961–64).

Alcuin's recommendation of this verse to Charlemagne, by comparison, appears to betray a fully self-conscious (N.B., "if I recall correctly") reassessment of Augustine's condemnation of the spirited pride that Virgil would arouse for the imperial mission of imposing a Roman order upon the world. Alcuin quietly transforms Augustine into a proponent of imperial Christianity, rehabilitating in the process the pagan culture of imperial Rome for the edification of a Christian ruler. To this end, he expressly reverses Augustine's condemnation of Roman self-assertion and moral presumption, recommending to Charlemagne the very posture that Augustine identified with "the swollen fancy of the proud-spirited" (*DCD*, 1.preface, 3) from which arises "that lust for mastery which, among the other vices of the human race, belongs in its purest form to the whole Roman people" (*DCD*, 1.30, 45). In contrast to Augustine's portrait of Theodosius as the humble, self-effacing servant (cf. *DCD*, 5.26, 233–35), Alcuin paints the Holy Roman Emperor with elevated hues suited to an imaging of divine authority.

To explore yet further the question of Alcuin's practical negotiations of moral and theological constructs inherited from earlier Christian thinkers, it proves instructive to look closely at Alcuin's treatment of the vices, particularly the vice of *superbia*, in his *De virtutibus et vitiis liber* (Book on the Virtues and the Vices). From a passage in chapter 27 we read:

> There are eight principal vices—or [eight vices] marking the beginning of all the vices—out of which, as if from roots, they produce all the vices of diverse evils from a corrupt mind or a degraded body. We have decided to say a few words about them, namely which branches of vicious germination might be seen to grow out of which roots, in order that each individual, by pulling up the roots, might know how he can more easily destroy the branches. The first vice is a spiritual one, pride, of which it is said: "The beginning of all sin is pride" (Sir 10:15), which is the queen of all evils, by which angels have fallen from heaven, [and] which arises out of contempt for the commandments of God. It arises, moreover, when the mind is elevated from good works and esteems itself better than others, while, in fact, it is worse than others in the very thing

in which it deems itself better. Pride arises, likewise, through rebellion from authority, when men have contempt for obeying their superiors. Now, from pride all disobedience is born, and all presumption, and all obstinacy, quarrels, heresies, insolence...all of which evils the true humility of the servant of God will easily be able to conquer.[42]

Alcuin modifies the otherwise Cassianic order of the vices employed in his text by moving *superbia* to the top of the list,[43] seemingly because Scripture (i.e., Sir 10:15) teaches that it is the *initium omnis peccati* (the beginning of all sin) and, by implication, *regina omnium malorum* (the queen of all evils). But he thus places what he designates a "spiritual vice," or *vitium spirituale*, at the head of an ordering that proceeds from the sins of the flesh to those of the spirit, violating the tidy logic of Cassian's original list that ranks the sins in accordance with the theological priority of the soul over the body. Alcuin also reverses the order of *tristitia* and *acedia*, while he denotes lust not as *luxuria* but as *fornicatio*. However, it is Alcuin's repositioning and application of pride that raises, once again, the possibility of a different, more broadly civic than theological, ambition lying behind his appropriation of the moral constructs inherited from a fledgling Christian tradition. The status of pride as the "root" or "origin" of all sin establishes it as the most socially significant vice. It is, of course, the moral failing most commonly identified with political authority—the vice of kings and the king

---

[42] Alcuin, *De virtutibus et vitiis liber ad Widonem comitem*, 27, PL 101:632D–38A: "Octo sunt vitia principalia vel originalia omnium vitiorum, ex quibus quasi radicibus omnia corruptae mentis vel incasti corporis diversarum vitia pullulant iniquitatum. De quibus pauca dicere ratum duximus, vel ex quibus radicibus qui rami vitiosae germinationis crescere videantur; ut sciat unusquisque radicibus exstirpatis, facilius ramos praecidere posse. Primum vitium est spirituale, superbia, de qua dicitur: Initium omnis peccati superbia (Eccl. X, 15), quae regina est omnium malorum, per quam angeli ceciderunt de coelo, quae fit ex contemptu mandatorum Dei. Fit etiam, quando attollitur mens de bonis operibus, et se meliorem aestimat aliis, dum in eo ipse pejor aliis est, quo se meliorem putat. Fit etiam per contumaciam superbia, quando despiciunt homines senioribus obedire suis. Ex ipsa vero nascitur omnis inobedientia, et omnis praesumptio, et omnis pertinacia, contentiones, haereses, arrogantia,...quae omnia mala vera humilitas famuli Dei perfacile vincere poterit." My translation.

[43] On the Cassianic order of the vices (*gula, luxuria, avaritia, ira, tristitia, acedia, vana gloria, superbia*), see Carole Straw, "Gregory, Cassian, and the Cardinal Vices," in *In the Garden of Evil: The Vices and Culture in the Middle Ages*, ed. Richard Newhauser (Toronto, 2005), 35–58; Richard Newhauser, *The Treatise on Vices and Virtues in Latin and the Vernacular* (Turnhout, 1993), 181–88; Morton Bloomfield, *The Seven Deadly Sins: An Introduction to the History of a Religious Concept, with Special Reference to Medieval English Literature* ([East Lansing, MI:] 1952; reprint, 1967), 69ff.

of vices.[44] And yet, what Alcuin stresses here is not the connection of pride to elite pretensions, or even to the abuse of political power, but its role in fomenting rebellion from lawful and/or legitimate authority: "Pride arises, likewise, through rebellion from authority, when men have contempt for obeying their superiors." There is, in fact, no hint of pride being a particular temptation for rulers. It comes to light only as a failing of the well-ruled. Scrupulously avoiding any identification with power and authority, Alcuin points to the rebellion against God by fallen angels as the classic instance of the vice.[45] It is plainly not the "superiors," least of all Charlemagne, to whom this treatment of pride is immediately addressed.

Alcuin's treatment of pride departs not only from Cassian's ordering of the vices, but also from the account provided by Gregory. For Cassian, the path of vice ascends from sins of the flesh (*gula, luxuria*), to longings for conquest and control (*avaritia*) that provoke, in turn, anger (*ira*) at resistance, followed by states of sadness and deflation (*tristitia, acedia*), as anger turns inward, to finally the distending sins of vainglory and pride (*vana gloria, superbia*).[46] Gregory, on the other hand, separates out *superbia*, the root of all sin, and constructs a trajectory that moves from the spiritual (*vana gloria, ira, invidia, tristitia*) to the bodily vices (*avaritia, gula, luxuria*), a course of self-diminution antithetical to that plotted by Cassian.[47] Wallach (who must be credited with the yeoman's work of tracking down the sources informing Alcuin's account of the virtues and the vices) greatly misrepresents the matter in suggesting that his description of *superbia* is simply "copied from Gregory."[48] Although he starts with *superbia*, as the root-sin, Alcuin largely adheres to the Cassianic pattern that proceeds from carnal appetites to failings based

---

[44] In the iconographic tradition, pride is often represented (especially in the High Middle Ages) as a lion, the king of the vices. Another popular representation is that of a royal figure (frequently a queen) enthroned. Bloomfield notes that both Gregory the Great and Isidore of Seville, whose respective treatments of the vices stand as two of the most influential, portray *superbia* as "the queen of the seven sins." Bloomfield, 77; see also, pp. 145, 183, 199, 377n278.

[45] On "Lucifer as the prototype of pride," see Bloomfield, 109 and 382n16.

[46] For Cassian's account of the unfolding course of the vices, see John Cassian, *The Conferences*, trans. Boniface Ramsey (New York, 1997), 177–210.

[47] For Gregory's listing of the vices, see *Moralia in Iob*, 31.45.87–88, ed. M. Adriaen, CCSL 143B (Turnhout, 1985), 1610–11.

[48] Wallach, 245.

on higher capacities of the soul.[49] Moreover, the identification of pride with the problem of men having contempt for legitimate authority is a distinctly social-political assessment of this vice that corresponds to Alcuin's peculiar situation as advisor to, and sometime emissary for, an emperor staging an unprecedented attempt to mold his society into a Christian kingdom.

In sum, the outlines of a revealing pattern begin to come into focus: in his correspondence with Charlemagne, Alcuin is regularly at pains to synthesize elements of pagan Rome's political culture into the Christian emperor's self-understanding in ways that seem to underscore the deficits of a tradition which places its main emphasis on avoiding the vices, and which, to the extent that it promotes virtues, privileges qualities of soul that do not specifically aim at the achievement of excellence in political affairs. By the same token, Alcuin's treatment of the vices seems generally to observe an implicit boundary dividing the ruled from their rulers. Alcuin returns to classical constructions of kingship in attempting to give new emphasis to qualities and capacities that the effective administration of an expanding empire would most likely demand, while largely directing his teaching on the vices to the task of shaping the body of those subject to kingly power. If these observations are correct, they point perhaps to an important line of further investigation in the study of the virtues and the vices in the Middle Ages. They suggest, in other words, that beginning with the Carolingian project of founding a Christian kingdom here and now, the practical exigencies of governance prompted a new interest in what Augustine termed the "splendid vices" of pagan antiquity and a complex interweaving of the virtues forged by the ancient world's esteem for political life into the theological frame of the Christian soul.

---

[49] Bloomfield, 80, by contrast, correctly notes that Alcuin "follows the Cassianic list, often using Cassian's own words." At the same time, he documents that Alcuin was the first Latin author "to utilize Gregory of Nyssa's relating of sin and the human soul" in order to apply it to the cardinal sins. Alcuin thus traces "gluttony, lechery, and avarice" to the concupiscent part of the soul, "sadness and accidie" to the irascible part, and "pride and vainglory" to the rational part (cf. 80–81).

ENVY IN THE INTELLECTUAL DISCOURSE OF THE HIGH MIDDLE AGES

Bridget K. Balint
Indiana University

Abstract: In theological controversies and poetic rivalries of the early Middle Ages, it was common to accuse one's critics of, e.g., malevolence and incompetence, and to answer such accusations by rhetorical demonstrations of wit and good will. In the later eleventh century, however, the discourse of rivalry began to focus on the "envy" of the writer's "detractors," and the tone of intellectual exchange became in general much more aggressive. Reasons for the new prominence of envy include: 1) widespread reading of Ovid's amatory poetry, which provided a lexicon of envy; and 2) competition among rival masters that fueled increasingly ostentatious self-promotion. By the time the seven-fold schema of the sins came into its widest circulation, *invidia* had come to be more frequently associated with its manifestation as carping criticism (*detractio, médisance*) than with the internal state of mind of the envious person per se.

The twelfth-century scholar and theologian Peter Abelard is one of the better-known personalities of the high Middle Ages, but one of the least sympathetic. His primary complaint in his autobiographical *History of My Calamities*, that he is persecuted by lesser men envious of his talent and success, sounds hollow even to readers encountering Abelard for the first time. While Abelard's proto-scientific application of reason to theological, philosophical, and even historical problems inspires admiration, the high-handed manner in which he assumes the superiority of his own arguments is unattractive. Even his contemporaries remarked upon it: he "thought even the saints inferior" wrote one.[1] In addition to publishing savage criticisms of his teachers and peers,[2] Abelard habitually

---

[1] Fulk of Deuil in a letter addressed to Abelard, quoted by M. T. Clanchy, *Abelard: A Medieval Life* (Oxford, 1997; reprint, 1999), 327.

[2] E.g., his comments about Anselm of Laon, one of the great teachers of the late eleventh century, include remarks such as "he had a remarkable command of words but their meaning was worthless and devoid of all sense." *The Letters of Abelard and Heloise*, trans. B. Radice (New York, 1974), 62.

asserted his own brilliance, making statements about his work in the
following vein:

> the treatise [*On the Unity and Trinity of God*] . . . began to please everyone, as
> it seemed to answer all questions on the subject. It was generally agreed
> that the questions were peculiarly difficult and the importance of the
> problem was matched by the subtlety of my solution.[3]

One begins to sympathize with Abelard's persecutors, and to suspect
that the "envy" suffered by Abelard was simply well-deserved antipathy
under another name.

Abelard, however, was not the only twelfth-century writer who imagined himself as the object of the "hatred of another's good fortune."[4]
Indeed, *invidia* turns out to be a persistent presence in texts from the late
eleventh and early twelfth centuries. So many writers, most of whom
were far less provoking in their behavior than Abelard was, accused
their critics of envy that it became a commonplace of contemporary
intellectual discourse. This paper will sketch some of the implications
of envy among the learned in the eleventh and twelfth centuries, and
investigate its appearance as the most feared sin and the one most often
disclaimed by writers of Latin from ca. 1050 until ca. 1200.

I. *The Roots of Envy*

Any well-read person in the High Middle Ages would have had two
primary frames of reference for the term *invidia*: the Greco-Roman, and
the Biblical-Patristic. The writings of the Roman philosopher Seneca the
Younger, read widely in the Middle Ages, conveyed the Stoic teaching
that envy was a powerful and harmful passion.[5] It is not surprising that

---

[3] *The Letters of Abelard and Heloise*, 78.

[4] Augustine defines envy as "odium felicitatis alienae" in several of his works, including *De Genesi ad litteram*, 11.14, ed. J. Zycha, trans. P. Agaësse and A. Solignac (Paris,
1972), 258; and *Enarrationes in Psalmos*, 104, ed. E. Dekkers and J. Fraipont, CCSL 40
(Turnhout, 1956), 1545.

[5] As is the case when discussing "emotional" or psychological experience in any
ancient society, it is difficult to reconstruct precisely what feelings and actions a Roman
labeled with the term *invidia*. Robert Kaster has constructed a detailed and convincing taxonomy of the "scripts" that the Latin term can refer to. The range is quite
broad, not least because the single Latin term is used for "emotional" experiences that
Aristotle, for instance, distinguished with two separate terms, *nemesis* and *phthonos*. See
Robert Kaster, "*Invidia* and the end of *Georgics* 1," *Phoenix* 56 (2002): 275–295; idem,
"Invidia, Νέμεσις, Φθόνος, and the Roman Emotional Economy," in *Envy, Spite and*

Seneca, who had intimate dealings with the intrigue-ridden Neronian court, writes about both active and passive envy—the experience of the envier as well as the suffering of the envied—as if they were hardly to be escaped by anyone living. In his *Consolation to Marcia* on the death of her son, he calls the deceased young man fortunate because he has now escaped the suffering caused by envy of another's happiness.[6] Considering the other side of the question, Seneca elsewhere advises a wise man to avoid inciting envy by keeping his advantages and his good fortune to himself.[7] The average Roman would have found this advice sensible: belief in the "Evil Eye," a concrete manifestation of envy, was widespread in Rome as it was in other Mediterranean cultures.[8] The word *invidere*, "to envy," literally means "to look at someone with hostile intent," and it sheds etymological light on the close relationship between the abstract vice "envy" and the much-feared phenomenon of the Evil Eye. It was thought that a person with the Evil Eye could bring harm upon the prosperous simply by directing a malevolent gaze at them. Indeed, many apotropaic tokens survive whose purpose was clearly to distract and discourage a potentially injurious gaze.[9] One method of discouraging the Evil Eye was to remind potential enviers of the suffering that would await them, the gnawing, choking feeling of "eating one's heart out."[10] Apotropaic depictions of Envy thus often show a figure throttling himself with both hands, a vivid externalization

---

Jealousy: The Rivalrous Emotions in Ancient Greece, ed. David Konstan and N. Keith Rutter (Edinburgh, 2003), 253–76. The polyvalence of the term may be partly responsible for its popularity in the High Middle Ages.

[6] Seneca, *Dialogorum libri*, 6.19.6, ed. L. D. Reynolds (Oxford, 1977), 154: "...non invidiae felicitatis alienae tangitur." Cf. *Dial.*, 11.9.4, p. 276 for a similar sentiment.

[7] *Ad Lucilium Epistulae Morales* 105.3, ed. L. D. Reynolds (Oxford, 1965), 2:443–4: "Invidiam effugies si non te ingesseris oculis, si bona tua non iactaveris, si scieris in sinu gaudere."

[8] See, e.g., K. M. C. Dunbabin and M. W. Dickie, "Invida rumpantur pectora. The Iconography of Phthonos/Invidia in Graeco-Roman Art," *Jahrbuch für Antike und Christentum* 26 (1983): 7–37; T. Rakoczy, *Böser Blick, Macht des Auges und Neid der Götter: eine Untersuchung zur Kraft des Blickes in der griechischen Literatur* (Tübingen, 1996). For the iconography of envy in the Middle Ages, see now F. N. M. Diekstra, "The Art of Denunciation: Medieval Moralists on Envy and Detraction," in *In the Garden of Evil: The Vices and Culture in the Middle Ages*, ed. Richard Newhauser (Toronto, 2005), 431–54.

[9] E.g., floor mosaics and wall-paintings in the houses of the prosperous, as well as protective amulets worn upon the person.

[10] The Latin word *livor*, "bruise" or "rust" (in fruit), comes to be used as a synonym for *invidia*, perhaps because the injurious discoloration or taint was seen as analogous to the experience of the envier. The metrically convenient phrase *livor edax*, "gnawing envy," first appears in Ovid and quickly becomes proverbial.

of the envier's distress.[11] The Romans conceived of envy, then, as a vice that adversely affects two people, both the envier and the person envied; and this conception was common to the society as a whole, philosophers and illiterate farmers alike.

The Bible and its early commentators provided the High Middle Ages with an additional perspective on envy that differed in some respects from the Roman view. Although patristic interpretations often echo Roman ideas about envy, and envy is often named, without further explanation, as the motive for anger and violent actions, nevertheless, when the Fathers write in detail about the term and its meaning, they seem less concerned about the damage the envier might do than about the spiritual health of the envious person.

Gregory the Great (d. 604), for example, discusses envy at length in several passages of the *Moralia in Job*, as the word *invidia* appears numerous times in the Biblical text. Of particular interest is his comment on a phrase from Job 5:2, *et parvulum occidit invidia*, "and envy slayeth the little one," where Gregory explains that, contrary to what the passage might initially imply—that the envious person has the power to cause real harm—experiencing envy is an indication of inferiority, and the "little one" in the passage is, in fact, the envier himself.[12] The *Moralia* and other early discussions of envy maintain this focus on the spiritual damage that the envier inflicts upon himself. They often depict his suffering as graphically as the Romans had, with the helpful support of a phrase from Proverbs 14:30, *putredo ossium invidia*, "envy is a rottenness of the bones."[13] This is not to say that the Fathers deny envy's potential for harming others: indeed, Irenaeus, Cyprian, and others attribute the fall of Lucifer as well as his subsequent machinations against mankind to his envy of humanity for being created in God's image, or of the salvation won for them by Christ.[14] "By the envy of the devil, death came into the world" (Wis 2:4) is often cited in this

---

[11] Dunbabin and Dickie, "Invida," 8–9 and *passim*.

[12] Gregory the Great, *Moralia in Iob*, 5.46.84, ed. M. Adriaen, CCSL 143 (Turnhout, 1979), 281.

[13] Gregory the Great, *Mor.*, 5.46.85–86, CCSL 143:281, quoted at length by many other authors including, e.g., the ninth-century archbishop Hincmar of Reims, *De cavendis vitiis et virtutibus exercendis*, 1.6, ed. D. Nachtmann (Munich, 1998), 151.

[14] Cyprian, *De zelo et livore*, 4, ed. M. Simonetti, CCSL 3A (Turnhout, 1976), 76–77; see N. Adkin, "Pride or Envy? Some Notes on the Reason the Fathers Give for the Devil's Fall," *Augustiniana* 34 (1984); J. Petruccione, "The Persecutor's Envy and the Martyr's Death in Peristephanon 13 and 7," *Sacris Erudiri* 32 (1991): 69–70.

context. Additionally, a great deal of Biblical discord is ascribed to anger or hatred that has its roots in envy: Cain, Esau, the brothers of Joseph, and Saul are envious before they are murderous.[15] Medieval commentators also find that the dangerous enviers of the Old Testament anticipate typologically Jesus handed over to Pilate by envious Jews, as the gospels of Matthew (27:18) and Mark (15:10) say of Pilate that "he knew that the chief priests had delivered him up out of envy." Patristic writers insist, however, that even the most threatening envy, that of the devil, is ultimately futile. The arch-envier has lost the ultimate good, the salvation bestowed upon humanity, and can never again possess it, nor take it from mankind. In consequence, the Fathers effectively embrace envy as a part of salvation history, and the envier, excluded from a serene existence just as Lucifer was excluded from heaven, is less to be feared than pitied, as Cyprian makes clear when he addresses the envious, perhaps with a classical vision of the self-throttling Envy in mind: "Wherever you are, your adversary is with you, your enemy is always in your own breast."[16] Envy jeopardizes the envier's own salvation, whereas any harm done to the envied person is temporary rather than eternal.

Perhaps for this reason, very few late antique and early medieval writers complain about being envied themselves, nor do they make any efforts to avert the envy of their peers.[17] When *invidia* does occur in their writings, whether historical, homiletic, epistolary, or lyric, and when the term itself is not the focus of the discussion (as it was in examinations of the capital vices), it is usually used to explain an individual's hatred, seizure, or destruction of another's worldly goods, i.e., wealth, property, power, or status. Gregory of Tours (d. 594), for example, ascribes envy to many such evildoers; he assumes that his readers understand envy as a vice directed at the material advantages enjoyed by others, as in the following: "[Count] Eulalius took a girl by force from the convent at Lyons and married her. But his concubines, who some say were motivated by envy, deprived her of her senses by

---

[15] Cyprian, *De zelo*, 5, ed. Simonetti, 77.
[16] Cyprian, *De zelo*, 9, ed. Simonetti, 80.
[17] Jerome is the notable exception: he sees himself besieged by the envious, much to the frustration of his friends and correspondents, including Augustine, who declares that he'll call an end to their debate about scriptural interpretation if Jerome cannot continue it "free from the suspicion of envy." See Letter LXXIII.9 in Augustine, *Epistulae LVI–C*, ed. K. Daur, CCSL 31A (Turnhout, 2005), 50.

witchcraft."[18] Early medieval tales of disputes about possessions and status are replete with envy in this way, but it is not a term that occurs often in conflicts among intellectuals, whether in controversies over points of religious doctrine or in instances of poetic rivalry. Abelard's complaints about envious detractors who caused him misfortune on account of his greatness would have made little sense to an earlier scholar. Even Godescalc of Orbais (ca. 800–868/9), the most Abelardian figure of the early Middle Ages in terms of the doctrinal controversies he stirred up and the ecclesiastical condemnations he suffered, apparently did not imagine that envy was to blame for the way his writings were received. Although Godescalc paraphrases Job 5:2 at one point in his short treatise *On Predestination*, remarking dryly, as he resumes the work that had been interrupted by institutional interference, that he has "not wished to be killed by anger like the fool or by envy like the little ones," it is a statement of strength rather than a claim on the sympathy of the reader: as Job's friend reminds him in the Biblical passage, only the childish worry about envy. *Invidia* makes no further appearance in any of Godescalc's extant works.[19]

Envy is also absent, for the most part, from less weighty intellectual rivalries in the early Middle Ages. The poetic productions of the scholars whom Charlemagne gathered at his court, for instance, abound in explicit attempts to win royal favor that use abject flattery on the one hand and satirically exaggerated criticism of a perceived poetic rival on the other. In the competitive atmosphere at court, the expression of envy at a rival's success might be expected, but it does not in fact appear. The Carolingian scholar-poets Peter of Pisa and Paul the Deacon, for instance, exchange verses in which each strives to ridicule the other's learning. At one point, Peter satirically exaggerates Paul's much-vaunted knowledge of Greek. Abelard, in Paul's position, would have responded by pointing out Peter's own utter ignorance of that language, and ascribing the criticism to envy. In his versified reply, however, Paul merely points out his awareness that he is a target of satire;[20] and after several verses deprecating his own knowledge, he

---

[18] Gregory of Tours, *Libri Historiarum X*, 10.8, ed. B. Krusch, 2nd ed. (Hanover, 1951), 490.

[19] *De Praedestinatione*, in *Œuvres théologiques et grammaticales de Godescalc d'Orbais*, ed. C. Lambot (Louvain, 1945), 342. The editor of the *De Praedestinatione* remarks *à propos* of this passage, "Il s'y montre décidé à déjouer les plans de ses adversaires."

[20] Paul writes: "All this, I see, is bandied about to make a fool of me, / all this is thrown with irony in my teeth. / Alas, derided by praise, I am the butt of ridicule!" The

appends a translation of a Greek poem as an undeniable token of his prowess. It is a graceful and witty exchange, even if the wit is rather barbed, and envy is entirely absent. For these and other early medieval writers, envy is neither a motivation for criticism nor an excuse for the poet's own failures or misfortunes, even though patronage and material gain may have been at stake.

II. *The Expanded Rhetorical Role of Envy*

In the eleventh century, however, envy gains a new textual prominence, most notably in works that were written by clerics and others associated with the cathedral schools in northwestern France. The definition of envy expands to include almost any kind of unfavorable criticism, as writers become acutely sensitive to any critical eye cast upon their works or those of their friends.[21] A striking early example occurs in Hildebert of Lavardin's epitaph for Berengar of Tours, probably written not long after Berengar's death in 1088. Berengar was a scholar and cleric who argued against the notion of transubstantiation, and so ended up on the losing side of the Eucharistic controversy that played out in the middle decades of the eleventh century. In 1079, Berengar was finally condemned and silenced; he died in 1088.[22] Hildebert, who was probably Berengar's student, wrote a verse epitaph for him in which the only reference to this famous and long-drawn-out controversy is framed in terms of envy: "Envy mourns him whom she had earlier carped at; nor did she carp and hate as much as she now praises and loves."[23] Rather than admit his teacher had erred or that he had been bested in argument,

---

poems are printed in *Poetry of the Carolingian Renaissance*, ed. and trans. Peter Godman (Norman, OK, 1985), 82–89.

[21] Envy, originally a sin of the covetous eye, thus expands to include *detractio*, slander. Gregory had included slander among the army of vices that accompany envy in *Moralia*, 31.45.87, ed. Adriaen, 1610, but envy and slander now begin to become inseparable. See Mireille Vincent-Cassy on the meaning of "envie" in Old French, which by the thirteenth century is synonymous with slander: "L'Envie en France au Moyen Age," *Annales: E.S.C.* 35 (1980): 253–71, here 258.

[22] For a full account of the controversy, see Charles M. Radding and Francis Newton, *Theology, Rhetoric, and Politics in the Eucharistic Controversy, 1078–1079: Alberic of Monte Cassino against Berengar of Tours* (New York, 2003).

[23] *Carmen 18*, 45–46, in *Carmina minora*, ed. A. B. Scott (Munich, 2001), 9: "livor eum deflet quem carpserat antea, nec tam/carpsit et odit eum, quam modo laudat, amat."

Hildebert attempts to save face by invoking envy, instantly placing all attackers of Berengar in the wrong. Instead of naming Berengar's opponents, among whom were the well-respected Lanfranc of Bec and Alberic of Monte Cassino, the poet portrays Berengar as an innocent beset by a vice personified. Of course, one would not expect a full exposition of Berengar's arguments in his epitaph, but encapsulating the controversy in the moralizing term "envy" is a rhetorical move that frames Berengar's situation in an entirely new way. Because envy is immoral, and the actions it inspires are sinful, Hildebert's poem draws a moral equivalence between criticism of Berengar's arguments about the Eucharist and the murderous action of Count Eulalius's concubines, "impelled by envy." Framing the outcome of an academic, theological dispute in these terms, as saintly innocence vs. aggressive sinfulness, is a way of forestalling any further argument. It is a shortcut to the desired conclusion, that Berengar was the victim of an unjust attack. Naturally, Hildebert sympathized with the plight of his teacher, but it is curious—and typical of the rhetorical role envy plays from the late eleventh century through the thirteenth—that the poet should appeal to the reader's emotions by emphasizing Berengar's position as innocent victim, instead of representing and defending Berengar's ideas.

Another alleged victim of intellectual envy makes a rather more convincing case that she has been wronged. In a poem found in an anthology of eleventh- and twelfth-century Latin verse (London, BL MS. Add. 24199, whose anthology section was copied in the late twelfth century), a woman expresses bitter resentment at the fact that her learning and writing have been criticized as unseemly. Discovering envy at work, she indignantly exposes it:

> O what new cunning: but known to us—envy seeks its place under the guise of correctness. It is not for holy women to compose verses, nor for us to ask who Aristotle might be.... Your mind desired to condemn what it could not do, to disparage good things, if they were worthy of praise.[24]

The poet's observation that "envy seeks its place under the guise of correctness" provides us with an important key to understanding the

---

[24] "O nova calliditas—sed nobis cognita: quaerit / Sub specie recti livor habere locum. / Non est sanctarum mulierum fingere versus, / Quaerere nec nostrum quis sit Aristotile.... / Detrectare bonis se quae laudanda fuerunt, / Quoque nequit vestra mens cupit argueres." In Constant Mews, *The Lost Love Letters of Heloise and Abelard: Perceptions of Dialogue in Twelfth-Century France* (New York, 1999), 164–66.

use of the term *invidia* in the eleventh and twelfth centuries. Her bitter words reveal a deep conflict about the nature of knowledge, which had been developing since the early days of the eleventh-century revival of learning. Until that time, all species of learning had been accommodated more or less comfortably in the monastic and cathedral schools. The late eleventh and early twelfth centuries, however, witnessed a sudden expansion in the range of subjects available for study—Aristotle, for one; Roman amatory poetry, for another—that seemed to have, at best, a tenuous relevance to religious life. Add to this a new emphasis on adversarial performance as a badge of learning, the various movements towards ecclesiastical reforms both within monasteries and without, and a renewed pressure for all clerics to cultivate monastic virtues, and conflict within the once homogeneous intellectual community was inevitable.[25] Increasingly divergent ideas about what constituted "correctness" in religion and education resulted in disputes like the one that the intellectual woman was apparently involved in, whose acrimony was at least partly due to the fact that the antagonists were both members of the learned religious population, as, indeed, were Berengar and his critics.

Nor did "envy in the guise of correctness" limit its targets to women. In the generation before Abelard, we find envy an extraordinarily prominent motif in the poetry of the abbot Baudri of Bourgueil (later Archbishop of Dol in Brittany). In the poetic preface to his collection of verse, he gives some advice to his little book, as he sends it out on its way: go only to friendly readers, he advises, "so that no snare or gnawing envy will injure you."[26] Envy is definitely the most threatening force in Baudri's world: he refers to it even more than Abelard does, at least thirty-five times in the poems. Remarkably, every one of his references to envy imagines it as a menace directed not at wealth, power, or influence, but at literary prowess. Unlike Abelard, Baudri is

---

[25] On the prominence of dialectical disputation beginning in the mid-eleventh century, see Peter von Moos, "Literatur- und bildungsgeschichtliche Aspekte der Dialogform im lateinischen Mittelalter: Der *Dialogus Ratii* des Eberhard von Ypern zwischen theologischer *disputatio* und Scholaren-Komödie," in *Tradition und Wertung: Festschrift für Franz Brunhölzl zum 65. Geburtstag*, ed. G. Bernt, F. Rädle, and G. Silagi (Sigmarigen, 1989), 165–210, here 167. Gregorian reformers set great store by the extension of monastic discipline within and beyond monastic communities. See, e.g., Karl F. Morrison, "The Gregorian Reform," in *Christian Spirituality: Origins to the Twelfth Century*, ed. Bernard McGinn and John Meyendorff, 177–93, here 188–89.

[26] *Baudri de Bourgueil: Poèmes*, 1.126, ed. and trans. Jean-Yves Tilliette (Paris, 1998–2002), 1:4: "ne tibi fascinus aut livor edax noceat."

quite eager to avert any *invidia* that might be directed at him; further, he is anxious to be judged innocent of envy himself. The rhetorical strategies he employs to forestall envy can give us a fuller picture of just what he conceived it to be.

Baudri sees a great risk that envy will arise in any relationship between himself and another writer. In poems addressed to others, he often makes remarks that are best construed as apotropaic, in which he invokes envy in order to prevent it, as in a poem to Marbod that proposes an exchange of poetry, to be conducted "so that the muse may speak, with envy expelled and kept far away."[27] In addition to such requests for mutual freedom from envy, Baudri softens almost any criticism or advice he delivers with a disavowal of *invidia*. For example, after reminding a brilliant young man that his talent is God's gift rather than his own possession and so should not be an occasion for pride, he points out that, "I myself do not envy you, nor am I speaking with evil intent."[28] This certainly shows excessive anxiety about the expression of justifiable and valuable criticism. It also implies a distressing readiness on the part of intellectuals to raise the charge of envy and its accompanying ill-will when faced with any criticism at all.

In spite of his constant prayers against and disavowals of envy, Baudri claims in numerous passages that he has been its victim. That he should be so sensitive to criticism is curious. After all, as abbot of an affluent monastery and subsequently an archbishop, Baudri had likely heard many of the sort of disparaging remarks that are regularly leveled against administrators, but he does not complain about any such: only his poetry seems to have suffered from invidious attacks. Much like Abelard, Baudri casts himself as an innocent target: "I have a playful muse, but a chaste life; still, envy ensnares me, although I am innocent."[29] "They tear innocent me apart with teeth of abuse, / and envy clamors for the death penalty against me."[30] Baudri also admits that the darts of envy have injured him so much that they are having their desired effect, that is, the limiting or silencing of his poetry: "The fury of envy is such a cruel stepmother to correctness / that I often lose

---

[27] Poem 86.13, in Baudri, *Poèmes*, 1:82: "ut procul abiecto livore camena loquatur."
[28] Poem 113.29, in Baudri, *Poèmes*, 1:120: "ipse nec invideo nec iniqui garrio more."
[29] Poem 193.107–08, in Baudri, *Poèmes*, 1:116: "musa iocosa michi, sed vita pudica iocoso, / et tamen innocuum fascinat invidiam."
[30] Poem 194.45–46, in Baudri, *Poèmes*, 1:118: "Insontem lacerant me dentibus obloquiorem, / Meque reum mortis clamitat invidia."

my enthusiasm for study."[31] Here, once again, we see the same "envy in the guise of correctness" that the woman poet had come to deplore. In Baudri's case, it is not difficult to imagine what manner of arrows were aimed at him: he writes jesting and occasionally flirtatious poems, some addressed to well-known noble and/or religious women. As with the woman poet, Baudri responds to criticism that was not directed at his command of Latin poetic idiom, but at the moral conduct of his life as demonstrated by his poetry. In spite of Baudri's repeated protests that his life and his poetic fictions remained quite separate, he apparently failed to convince every reform-minded reader that this was indeed the case. Unable to prevent the misreading of his poems, Baudri resorts to some moralizing of his own, attributing all criticism to *invidia*.

The divergent opinions expressed in this period about the role of literary learning in religious life make it clear that morality and literacy were closely interrelated; but how did "envy" come to be the term used to describe what writers perceived as misdirected moral criticism, and why is it so prevalent in Latin texts from this period? Part of the explanation can be found in the classical poetic tradition that was revived to spectacular effect in the eleventh-century cathedral schools. In Roman poets, we find an envy that differs greatly from the envy of philosophers, exegetes, or homilists, and one that sounds rather more like Baudri's and Abelard's: envy aims to injure the famous and the clever in particular, and a writer can do nothing except try to disarm it by naming it publicly. Virgil, Horace, and Martial, among others, develop the theme. The works of the first-century poet Ovid, however, are the source for a disproportionately large percentage of eleventh- and twelfth-century references to envy.[32] One of the most important passages is from the middle of Ovid's *Remedia amoris*, the *Cures for Love*, a book of instructions for disentangling oneself from undesirable relationships, written as a tongue-in-cheek sequel to his scandalous *Ars amatoria / Art of Love*, a book of poetic advice for the conduct of illicit affairs. In the middle of the *Remedia* Ovid inserts a lengthy defense of his poetry against his critics, who are motivated, he says, by envy. The

---

[31] Poem 194.51–52 in Baudri *Poèmes*, 1:118: "Ut furor invidiae probitati est seva noverca, / quocirca tepeo sepius a studio."

[32] The expanded influence of Ovid upon literary writing beginning in the mid-eleventh century is well-documented. See, e.g., Franco Munari, *Ovid im Mittelalter* (Zürich, 1960), 9–11; Jean-Yves Tilliette, "Savants et poètes du moyen âge face à Ovide: les débuts de l'*aetas Ovidiana* (v. 1050–v. 1200)," in *Ovidius redivivus: von Ovid zu Dante*, ed. Michelangelo Picone and Bernhard Zimmermann (Stuttgart, 1994), 63–104.

passage provides a lexicon and an attitude for later Latin writers who felt themselves under attack for whatever reason:

> Some people have recently been carping at my books, / complaining that my Muse is shameless. / But as long as I am pleasing the public, as long as I am sung in the whole world, / let anyone who wishes assail my work. / Envy slandered the talents of great Homer, / but whatever fame you have, Zoilus, you have from him. / Impious tongues chewed apart your poems, too, / you who led the defeated Trojan gods to Rome [i.e., Virgil]. / Envy seeks the heights; the winds whip the mountaintops, / the thunderbolt from Jove's right hand seeks the heights /.... Burst, gnawing envy! We have a great name already, / and it will be greater, as long as we keep going the same way we began.[33]

This is precisely what Hildebert, the woman poet, and Baudri mean when they say "envy": the carping, petty criticism of art or wit that the critic himself is not talented enough to produce. It is not difficult to understand why the passage would be so appealing to these later writers. Ovid combines the traditional Roman image of "gnawing" Envy with characteristics of particular relevance to a poet. For him, envy is nearly synonymous with *detractio*, slander, and it is a powerful destructive force, like gales and thunderbolts. To be its victim is, however, a mark of excellence: if envy seeks the heights, the envied poet has a place on the peak of Parnassus. Abelard quotes this line aptly, since Ovid's own experience could be a source of consolation for the embattled intellectual. Although the poet was exiled by Augustus on account of a famously unspecified *carmen et error*, a poem and a faux pas, his fame did not suffer any lasting damage from the emperor's condemnation. To conquer envy, Ovid implies, one should meet it with defiance rather than humility, for the fame of the truly enviable writer will indeed be immortal. Note also that this source text, quoted and alluded to by so many, is taken from a Roman poem that many of its medieval readers found objectionable. Conrad of Hirsau, for one, says, "Even if Ovid should be tolerated in certain of his minor works.... who in his right mind would tolerate his croaking about love?"[34] A writer who took up the Ovidian stance on envy, then, was not merely answering criticism:

---

[33] Ovid, *Remedia Amoris*, 361–370, 389–90, ed. A. Ramirez de Verger (Munich, 2003), 283–84.

[34] "Etsi auctor Ovidius idem in quibusdam opusculis suis...tolerandus esset, quis eum de amore croccitantem...si sanum sapiat, toleret?" Conrad of Hirsau, *Dialogus super auctores*, ed. R. B. C. Huygens (Leiden, 1970), 114.

by doing so he or she publicly proclaimed allegiance to the idea that some texts are worth reading even if they might explicitly contravene the ideals of monastic discipline.

It is, thus, not difficult to understand why certain writers of verse invoke their fellow-poet Ovid; but that a professional philosopher like Abelard should adopt the attitude of a Roman love poet might seem incongruous. In certain intellectual circles, however, poetry had a privileged role. The noted teacher Bernard of Chartres, for one, asserted that the foundations of philosophy could be found in Classical poets,[35] and many scholars of the period, notwithstanding the objections of pedagogues like Conrad of Hirsau, were trained to read poetry as a rich source of veiled truths before they graduated to the more advanced philosophical and theological texts written in prose. Classical poets were viewed as having special access to knowledge about the way the world, and indeed the universe, works.[36] Having read that an admirable Roman poet had responded to criticism by accusing his critics of envy, many twelfth-century intellectuals—not only poets—would find it reasonable to adopt this stance themselves.

Yet the availability of the Ovidian model was not the only factor contributing to the expanded role of envy in intellectual discourse. Baudri's poems mark an incipient awareness of intellectual prowess as something worthy, in the same sense that wealth, honors, and ecclesiastical preferment were worthy and thus enviable if attained by another. Among Baudri's peers, recognition as a poet was as much sought after as material advancement. The growing coterie of wealthy patrons may have had something to do with this, but only a small percentage of Baudri's extant poems are written to his (generally female) patrons, while poems that mention envy are generally addressed to his (mostly clerical) peers. In the case of *magistri* in the newly-flourishing urban schools who, like Abelard, earned their living based upon how many

---

[35] John of Salisbury quotes Bernard as follows: "Excute Virgilium, aut Lucanum, et ibi cuiuscumque philosophiae professor sis, eiusdem inuenies condituram." *Metalogicon* 1.24, ed. J. B. Hall, CCCM 98 (Turnhout, 1991), 52.

[36] This is certainly the case in the Chartrean educational tradition, which was one of the dominant modes of education in the twelfth century, but certainly not the only one: the Cistercians and Victorines, for instance, rejected Roman poetry as a foundation for wisdom. See Winthrop Wetherbee, *Platonism and Poetry in the Twelfth Century: The Literary Influence of the School of Chartres* (Princeton, 1972), 5. A fine brief overview of twelfth-century uses of Roman poetry can be found in Jean Jolivet, "Poésie et philosophie au XIIème siècle," *Perspectives médiévales* 17 (1991) 51–70.

paying students they could attract, intellectual reputation did in fact have economic value, so detractors, whether motivated by envy or not, were certainly to be feared.[37]

Nourished by Ovid, divergent views of acceptable learning, and the increasing worth of an intellectual reputation, envy soon becomes a literary commonplace.[38] Although Abelard himself makes no attempt to avert the envy of others, many writers make great efforts to do so, and they set about their task in various ways. Very often, authors place remarks meant to disarm the envious in their prologues, to ensure that the reader approaches in a benevolent frame of mind, or in epilogues, to quiet anticipated criticism when the work has been read. Strategies for turning envy aside include disavowal, as so often in Baudri; pleas,[39] resignation,[40] or defiance.[41]

Anti-invidious remarks became so regular that, by the later twelfth century, writers felt free to play upon their reader's expectations regarding envy. The *magister* Matthew of Vendôme begins his *Ars versificatoria* with an apparently sincere plea to his readers: "Let the spirit of envy retreat, let the enemy not gnaw at my little textbook."[42] But he then adopts an Ovidian attitude of defiance by stating that he offers in this work "food for envy, torment for enmity, nourishment for slander." He proceeds to address some rather harsh invective at a colleague whom he accuses of, naturally, *invidia*: "Let Rufinus, that disgrace to mankind, the dregs of humanity, set a guard on his mouth to stop him, puffed up with envy as he is, from making rash criticisms without thinking them

---

[37] Bruno Roy and Hugues Shooner, "Querelles de maîtres au XIIᵉ siècle: Arnoul d'Orléans et son milieu," *Sandalion* 8–9 (1985–1986): 315–41.

[38] Cf. the remark made by Roy and Shooner, "Les procédés adoptés par chacun pour se mettre en valeur sont si énormes...qu'on en vient à se demander si au XIIe siècle le motif de l'invidia n'était pas un simple motif littéraire...," "Querelles," 333n69. A complete list of authors who decry envious readers would exceed the available space, but it would include Vitalis of Blois, Geoffrey of Monmouth, and Alexander Neckham, as well as countless twelfth-century poets, many anonymous.

[39] Eberhard appends to his *Laborintus* a plea for suggestions to improve the work, but only if readers "let envious slander sleep." *Laborintus*, ed. E. Faral, in *Les Arts poétiques du XIIᵉ et XIIIᵉ siècle* (Paris, 1924), 377.

[40] John of Salisbury steels himself to bear the darts of envious detractors at the beginning of his *Metalogicon*, ed. Hall, 9.

[41] Many poets, including the Roman Martial and the twelfth-century bishop Marbod, develop Ovid's confident exclamation "burst, gnawing envy!," wishing their critics would burst *with* envy: Martial, *Epigrammata*, 9.97, ed. D. R. Shackleton Bailey (Stuttgart, 1990), 311; Marbod of Rennes, "Contra invidiam," ed. A. Beaugendre, in *Venerabilis Hildeberti...Opera tam edita quam inedita...*(Paris, 1708), 1619.

[42] *Ars versificatoria*, prologus, in *Opera*, ed. F. Munari (Rome, 1977–88), 3:39.

through…instead let him go play with his concubine, that red-headed Thais…"[43] To round off this outrageous set of insults, he twists the now-clichéd disavowal of *invidia* into a metrically elegant but entirely scurrilous epigram about Rufinus's love life, avowing that he, Matthew, is not envious of such good fortune (having Thais as a mistress), even though he had to pay for what Rufinus gets for free.[44] The commonplace of benevolent disavowal of envy in the face of someone else's "good fortune" becomes, in Matthew's hands, a foul insult of his rival's promiscuous girlfriend—and an indication that intellectual envy, once feared, is now merely a cliché.

Abelard's earnest self-presentation as the victim of envious slanderers, then, is in large part a nod to a literary convention of the early and middle twelfth century—a convention that reflected the simultaneously increasing status and insecurity of the ecclesiastic intellectual. As the twelfth century waned, however, the factors which brought envy to prominence in Latin literature also receded: poetic momentum shifted to the vernacular languages, while the establishment of universities brought some measure of security to professional teachers, standardized, to a certain extent, the appropriate material for study, and regularized the makeup of the student population. Envy became less prominent in discussions of the status of intellectuals, perhaps because that status was becoming more clearly defined. In the late twelfth and thirteenth centuries, envy returns to its material roots, as it begins to play a large part in courtly vernacular literature, where excellence in nobility, wealth, and love are its objects, notably in the *Lais* of Marie de France and the Arthurian tales of Chrétien de Troyes.[45] With the thirteenth-century promulgation of the Seven Deadly Sins, Envy personified takes on recognizable traits and becomes an enforcer of social norms in both literature and art. For those writing in Latin, however, the once-powerful envy of their peers has been masked by the screen of literary commonplace, and is no longer as threatening as it once had been.

---

[43] *Ars vers.*, ed. Munari, 3:40.

[44] *Ars vers.*, ed. Munari, 3:41. In Aubrey Galyon's translation: "Truly, I am not envious: If she has borne me up, a scholar, for pay, let the red she-goat bear Rufus as her buck." *The Art of Versification* (Ames, 1980), 25.

[45] See Sarah Spence, "Double Vision: Love and Envy in the *Lais*," in *In Quest of Marie de France, a Twelfth-Century Poet*, ed. Chantal Maréchal (Lewiston, 1992), 262–79.

"THE OOZE OF GLUTTONY":
ATTITUDES TOWARDS FOOD, EATING, AND EXCESS IN THE MIDDLE AGES

Susan E. Hill
The University of Northern Iowa

Abstract: An historical approach to the meanings of the fat body cannot ignore gluttony, since the glutton is often characterized as the excessive eater, inevitably corpulent. This contemporary western view of the vice of gluttony is challenged by the puzzling notion found throughout the Middle Ages that Adam and Eve, with their first bites of forbidden fruit, commit the sin of gluttony. How can ingesting so little food be gluttonous? Working with Mary Douglas's notion that the way a culture thinks about food reflects and reveals the structures of its "whole experience of life" ("Culture and Food," 78), I argue that medieval conceptions of gluttony present a world in which the state of one's soul is directly connected to the maintenance of one's proper physical boundaries and balance, a condition which extends to, and helps to maintain, the social body.

"It's no sin to be fat, but it might as well be."[1] Jeremy Igger's comment a decade ago highlights the precarious cultural location of the fat body. As Anne Scott Beller writes, "obesity has been identified as a 'disease' with a stipulated cure (dieting) and an acknowledged etiology (gluttony)."[2] And, although we now rarely use the use the specific word "gluttony" to describe how fat bodies are created, this is because we have defined gluttony simply as overeating, often use that term instead, and assume—perhaps rightly so—that gluttony or overeating necessarily leads to corpulence. Moreover, while being fat is not officially a sin, it is true that in the contemporary West, there is a tendency to attribute moral failings to the fat body. Natalie Allon suggests that, "fat people are viewed as 'bad' or 'immoral'"; they suffer from "societal opposition

---

[1] Jeremy Iggers, "Innocence Lost: Our Complicated Relationship with Food," *The Utne Reader* 60 (November/December 1993): 54–60, here 54.

[2] Anne Scott Beller, *Fat and Thin: A Natural History of Obesity* (New York, 1977), 5.

to gluttony."[3] In the contemporary western mind, fat people are "out of control," or "out of bounds," and their inability to be in command of themselves is literally displayed on their fat bodies.[4]

This implicit connection between gluttony and corpulence—and our concomitant disdain for fatness—is, however, a relatively recent cultural phenomenon. Ken Albala traces "the modern anxiety over obesity" to the seventeenth century, "when fat was fashionable."[5] New ideas about body chemistry and physiology at that time led medical professionals to begin to question whether being fat was unhealthy, thereby creating "a nascent fear of fat."[6] As time went on, the bond between gluttony and corpulence solidified, underscoring our current assumption that the glutton is, necessarily, corpulent.

Prior to the seventeenth century, however, such a strong connection between gluttony and corpulence is lacking.[7] Medieval medical and health treatises, such as Hildegard of Bingen's *Cause et cure*, written in the twelfth century, assume that the four bodily fluids—blood, phlegm, black bile and yellow bile—along with the four primal elements—heat, cold, wetness, and dryness—determine an individual's constitution. Different temperaments and body types result from the domination of one of the four humors in each person's body. In Hildegard's text, for instance, it is important for thin people to bathe often, while those with "fat flesh will harm themselves with water baths because they are warm and moist within."[8] Hildegard harbors no particular disdain for any type of body, for bodies simply are what they are, though everyone must strive to maintain his or her humoral balance.

Despite the lack of connection between gluttony and corpulence in medieval medical discourse, the Middle Ages is a time when moral discourse about gluttony—one of the seven deadly sins—flourished.

---

[3] Natalie Allon, "The Stigma of Overweight in Everyday Life," in *Psychological Aspects of Obesity*, ed. Benjamin B. Wolman (New York, 1982), 130–174, here 131, 135.

[4] See *Bodies Out of Bounds: Fatness and Transgression*, ed. Jana Evans Braziel and Kathleen LeBesco (Berkeley, 2001), for nuanced analysis of contemporary ideas of fatness.

[5] Ken Albala, "Weight Loss in the Age of Reason," in *Cultures of the Abdomen*, ed. Christopher Forth and Ana Carden-Coyne (New York, 2005), 169–183, here 169.

[6] Albala, 169–171.

[7] Albala also notes that fatness was not linked to gluttony in the Middle Ages, although he argues that theologically, gluttony was primarily about a lack of charity towards others. I argue here that gluttony has a much broader range of social meanings in the Middle Ages than Albala suggests.

[8] Hildegard of Bingen, *On Natural Philosophy and Medicine, Selections from "Cause et Cure"*, trans. and ed. by Margaret Berger (Cambridge, Eng., 1999), 96.

Gluttony's status as a capital vice suggests an earlier origin for our contemporary moral disdain for fatness: our contempt for the fat body may be connected to ancient and pervasive formulations about gluttonous excess. Yet, an exploration of the idea of gluttony in the Middle Ages further complicates our contemporary equation of gluttony with overeating by revealing a significant disconnection between being a glutton and being fat. Instead, discussions about gluttony in the Middle Ages highlight a distinctly medieval understanding of social limits and the excesses that threaten them, thereby creating a moral discourse about food practices that, I surmise, will later lend moral weight to the equation of gluttony with fatness.[9] Indeed, unlike today, when corpulence seems to reveal a simple lack of personal willpower and moral fortitude, many medieval writers viewed gluttony as a marker for a particular form of spiritual deficiency. The idea of gluttony in the Middle Ages—whether it is considered to be the first sin, or whether it is discussed in the monastery or the town—depends on the assumption that an individual's bodily behavior makes a significant contribution to the spiritual health, not only of the individual, but of the community, as well.[10] An understanding of ideas about gluttony in the Middle Ages can, thus, not only provide insight into how the medieval world viewed the relationship between the individual and society, it can provide a historical context for recognizing how we perceive the societal effects of gluttony today.

The distinct character of gluttony in the Middle Ages can be seen in medieval interpretations of Genesis. Although the sin of Adam and Eve is most often discussed in the context of sexuality or gender hierarchy during this time,[11] some writers suggested that the first sin is that of gluttony. That one bite of the apple could suffice to render the first humans guilty of gluttony certainly defies our contemporary understanding of gluttony as overeating, and points to the idea that gluttonous behavior includes more than overindulgence. In John Cassian's *Conferences*, for

---

[9] This article is part of a larger project on the moral history of corpulence and gluttony in the West. Here, I seek to articulate the nature of the moral discourse about gluttony in the Middle Ages as a precursor to our contemporary understanding of fatness as morally suspect. Exactly where and how those connections are made is the focus of my broader project.

[10] Of course, this connection also works the other way: one's spiritual health can influence one's bodily behavior, and thereby influence the body politic.

[11] *Eve and Adam: Jewish, Christian and Muslim Readings on Genesis and Gender*, ed. Kristen E. Kvam, Linda S. Schearing, and Valarie H. Ziegler (Bloomington, 1999), 169.

example, composed in the early fifth century for monastic communities, Adam is used to exemplify the notion that gluttony is both a natural and an unnatural vice, that is, it can arise solely from "the instigation and itching of the flesh" but requires "external matter in order to be consummated."[12] Adam "would not have been able to be deceived by gluttony had he not had something to eat and immediately and lawlessly misused it," though it is clear that "it was by gluttony that he took the food from the forbidden tree."[13] For Cassian, gluttony in the Garden of Eden was characterized by a misuse of food that resulted in human "ruin and death."[14]

In the thirteenth century, as Thomas Aquinas considers whether gluttony is a "serious" sin, he suggests that a sin's punishment can tell us how much weight we are to give it. Quoting John Chrysostom, Aquinas writes, "By the belly's incontinence was Adam expelled from Paradise."[15] Since the first act of gluttony resulted in Adam and Eve's expulsion from the Garden of Eden, Aquinas argues that gluttony is, indeed, a most serious sin. Following Cassian, Aquinas concludes that the gluttonous act of Adam and Eve was less about the apple itself, and more about "the abuse of divine things" that becomes "the occasion of other sins."[16]

Gluttony's status as the first human sin is not confined to the work of monastic or academic theologians. This idea can also be found in *Jacob's Well*, a series of sermons written in the early fifteenth century by a parish priest for use by other preachers and teachers, as well as for "lay people preparing for confession."[17] Although *Jacob's Well* is closely related to a number of other pastoral manuals written in the Middle Ages,[18] its "elaborate and carefully constructed"[19] allegory, which rep-

---

[12] John Cassian, *The Conferences*, trans. Boniface Ramsey (New York, 1997), 183.

[13] Cassian, *Conferences*, trans. Ramsey, 183, 185.

[14] Cassian, *Conferences*, trans. Ramsey, 186.

[15] Thomas Aquinas, *Summa theologiae*, 2a 2æ, 148.3, Blackfriars ed. (London and New York, 1964–81), 43:123. See also William Ian Miller, "Gluttony," in *Wicked Pleasures: Meditations on the Seven Deadly Sins*, ed. Robert C. Solomon (Lanham, 1999), 19–49, here 22.

[16] Aquinas, *Summa theol.*, 2a 2æ, 148.3, Blackfriars ed., 43:125.

[17] Leo Carruthers, "'Know Thyself': Criticism, Reform and the Audience of *Jacob's Well*," in *Medieval Sermons and Society: Cloister, City, University*, ed. Jacqueline Hamesse, et al. (Louvain-la-Neuve, 1998), 219–40, here 219.

[18] Leo Carruthers, "'And what schall be the ende': an Edition of the Final Chapter of *Jacob's Well*," *Medium Ævum* 61:2 (1992): 289–97, here 289.

[19] Carruthers, "And what," 289.

resents the sinful human body as a pit of "oozy water and mire"[20] on a quest for purification through penance, provides a unique example of the use of the body as a symbol for the relationship between the individual and society. In this text, the "ooze of gluttony...destroys both body and soul, and a man's good" (*JW*, 141). The devil "seeks the throat of man by gluttony, as the wolf seeks the sheep" just as he "took Adam and Eve, when they ate the apple" (*JW*, 141). As with Cassian and Aquinas, *Jacob's Well* articulates the notion that gluttony results in the inappropriate use of food that leads to a rift between humans and God.

These medieval interpretations of Genesis suggest an orientation to the sin of gluttony that is primarily about the misuse and abuse of food, and sometimes, drink.[21] Eating too much, which is how we currently think of gluttony, may be one of the ways in which humans can abuse food, but it is neither the only nor the primary characteristic of gluttony in the Middle Ages. Moreover, fatness, as a sign of the gluttonous person, is rarely considered to be a significant marker of gluttony. Indeed, that Adam and Eve can be gluttons underscores the notion that being fat is not the glutton's sin; rather, the importance of the sin of gluttony is that the misuse of food can have a significant negative impact, not only on an individual's spiritual journey, but also on the creation and maintenance of a community.

Take, for instance, John Cassian's *Institutes*, one of the first texts to treat systematically a list of eight vices (which later developed into the seven deadly sins). Writing for his fellow monks about "the causes and remedies of the principal vices" for "the improvement of our behavior and the attainment of the perfect life," Cassian's interest in the vices is to investigate their hidden natures, expose their causes, and propose remedies for them.[22] The challenge of the vices is that "until they have been revealed they are unknown to everyone, even though we are all hurt by them and they are found in everyone" (*Inst.*, 117). It

---

[20] *Jacob's Well, An English Treatise on the Cleansing of Man's Conscience*, ed. Arthur Brandeis, EETS os 115 (London, 1900), vi, hereafter cited parenthetically as *JW*; all translations are mine, with gratitude to Holly Johnson for her generous assistance.

[21] For an excellent account of drinking as a part of gluttony in the Middle Ages, see Mireille Vincent-Cassy, "Between Sin and Pleasure: Drunkenness in France in the Late Middle Ages," trans. Erika Pavelka, in *In the Garden of Evil: The Vices and Culture in the Middle Ages*, ed. Richard Newhauser (Toronto, 2005), 393–430.

[22] John Cassian, *The Institutes*, trans. Boniface Ramsey (New York, 2000), 13, 117, hereafter cited parenthetically as *Inst.*

is the insidiousness and pervasiveness of the vices that makes them dangerous; revealing them will allow the monks "to be led to a place of refreshment and perfection" (*Inst.*, 118).

What is fascinating about this text is that Cassian clearly recognizes that, although each monk has different challenges in his struggle to be obedient to God, the community, as a whole, must develop a consistent approach to food. Each monk has his own skills and talents: one may be better at controlling his desire for food, one may be a better scholar or worker. Thus,

> a uniform rule concerning the manner of fasting cannot easily be kept because not all bodies have the same strength, nor is it, like the other virtues, achieved by firmness of mind alone.... There are different times, manners, and qualities with respect to eating that are in accordance with the varied conditions, ages, and sexes of bodies, but there is one rule of discipline for everyone with regard to an abstinent and virtuous mind. (*Inst.*, 119)

The goal of abstinence for the monk is achieved by "the setting of times and the quality of food" but is also dependent upon the judgment of each monk's conscience (*Inst.*, 121):

> For each individual must calculate for himself the degree of frugality that his bodily struggle and combat require. The canonical rule for fasting is useful indeed and by all means to be observed, but unless this is followed by temperate eating habits it will be unable to attain to the goal of integrity. (*Inst.*, 121)

The successful monastic community must, then, be able to create this delicate balance between each individual's talents and challenges, while maintaining consistent rules for the community.

Cassian's articulation of three forms of gluttony reflects his sense of the individual's relation to the community. The first kind of gluttony is "that which urges the anticipation of the canonical hour for eating" or eating before the proper time (*Inst.*, 131). One might wonder why snacking or eating a bit early amounts to gluttonous downfall. Yet, in the context of the monastic community, eating at the wrong time necessitates breaking established communal rules, which are based on "the most ancient tradition of the fathers" (*Inst.*, 132). Moreover, eating out of the proper time defiles the community: "Whatever is eaten that does not fall under regular practice and common usage is polluted by the disease of vanity, boastfulness, and ostentation" (*Inst.*, 132).

The second kind of gluttony is "that which rejoices only in filling the belly to repletion with any food whatsoever" (*Inst.*, 131). This form of gluttony is closest to the contemporary idea that the glutton is a habitual overeater, though for Cassian being corpulent is never the glutton's challenge. Rather, "voracious satiety" is problematic because food affects the mind in the same way as drink:

> ... [T]he mind that is suffocated and weighed down by food cannot be guided by the governance of discretion. It is not an excess of wine alone that ordinarily inebriates the mind. Too much food of any kind makes it stagger and sway and robs it of every possibility of integrity and purity. (*Inst.*, 120)

The problem with overeating is not that it will make one fat, but rather that eating too much makes one incapable of clear thinking, and hence, of proper monastic discipline. Eating too much violates the monastic requirement of restraint and obedience, for "even while desiring it, we should approach with restraint the food that we are obliged to eat in order to sustain our life" (*Inst.*, 121). Thus, theoretically, at least, the fat—or "hale and hearty" (*Inst.*, 121)—monk may have few issues with gluttony, while the thin monk may have a greater task at food discipline if he is inclined to an excessive desire for food. Indeed, gluttony pollutes precisely because it defies the proper course of one's spiritual life: "Only thus is our life's course to be laid out, so that there is no longer any time wherein we may feel that we are being diverted from spiritual pursuits beyond that which compels us to descend to the necessary care of the body, on account of its fragility" (*Inst.*, 125).

Cassian's third kind of gluttony is "that which is delighted with more refined and delicate foods" (*Inst.*, 132). Monastery food must be "easy to prepare" and "cheap to purchase," and a monk must content himself with inexpensive food whose function it is to take care of the body's needs (*Inst.*, 131, 132). Cassian's idea of delicate and refined foods is beans, vegetables and fruit, which suggests just how dull his monastic diet truly was. His point, though, is that the desire for food not readily available in the monastery reveals a lack of virtue, discretion and obedience to monastic ideals (*Inst.*, 132).

Thus, for Cassian gluttony has more to do with one's recognition of the proper place of food in one's life and in the community as a whole than it does with the body's heft. Although Cassian recognizes that some monks will be challenged by gluttony more than others, and that whether and how one gains discipline with regard to food is up to each individual, he nonetheless maintains that gluttony, like all of the vices, is a communal burden, precisely because the challenge of food is the challenge of spiritual discipline.

As concern with the vices leaves the monastery, Cassian's three types of gluttony remain fairly constant, though they are often reinterpreted for the lay context or supplemented with others. For Pope Gregory (590–604), whose ideas about the seven deadly sins became influential throughout the Middle Ages, gluttony tempts us in five ways: to eat too early, to eat foods that are too dainty or expensive, to eat food that requires too much preparation, to eat too much, or to eat too greedily.[23] Gregory's analysis of the seven deadly sins depends on Cassian's earlier vision: both authors focus on the development of discretion and self-control to overcome the vices.[24] Unlike Cassian, however, who encourages monks to develop their faculties of discretion so that they can recognize that different kinds of bodies require different kinds of food discipline, Gregory focuses more generally on the temptations of pleasure, and the difficulties humans have in discerning the difference between need and desire. While gluttony certainly means eating "beyond the measure of necessity" (*Morals*, 30.61, 406), the significant challenge of gluttony is that "pleasure so veils itself under necessity, that a perfect man can scarce discern it" (*Morals*, 30.62, 407). Although we are able to recognize the difference between bodily hunger and a raw desire for food, it is much trickier to detect when pleasure "connects itself with that very eating which is necessary" (*Morals*, 30.62, 407). For Gregory, then, one of the difficulties with the idea of gluttony is that it is hard for an ordinary person to figure out when one is submitting to the necessities of nature by eating, and when one is submitting to one's own desire. And, although Cassian expresses a similar concern, Gregory's focus on this issue suggests that, within the larger society outside the monastery, this challenge is even more difficult.

This tension between desire and necessity increases even further when Gregory speaks of the cure for gluttony, for the suppression of one's desires for food can lead to greater bodily demands for it. Although Cassian argues that one should approach the temptations of food with "restraint," Gregory argues that even the practice of self-control can pose challenges:

---

[23] Gregory the Great, *Morals on the Book of Job*, 30.60, trans. J. Bliss (Oxford, 1844–50), 4:405, hereafter cited parenthetically as *Morals*.
[24] An insightful analysis of the relationship between Cassian and Gregory can be found in Carole Straw's "Gregory, Cassian, and the Cardinal Vices" in *In the Garden of Evil*, ed. Newhauser, 35–58.

> But often, whilst we incautiously condescend to necessity, we are enslaved
> to desires. And sometimes, while we endeavour [*sic*] to oppose our desires
> too immoderately, we increase the miseries of necessity. For it is necessary
> for a man so to maintain the citadel of continence, as to destroy, not the
> flesh, but the vices of the flesh. For frequently, when the flesh is restrained
> more than is just, it is weakened even for the exercise of good works, so
> as to be unequal to prayer also or preaching, whilst it hastens to put out
> entirely the incentives of vices within itself. (*Morals*, 30.63, 407)

In other words, it is necessary for a person to develop self-discipline
when it comes to food, though too much self-discipline will also leave
one incapable of doing those acts necessary to express one's faith. For
Gregory, achieving the tricky balance between giving the body enough
and not too much, something for which each individual must continually
strive, is the only possible way to live well with this tension:

> And, thus, whilst we allow our vices, when checked, to struggle against
> us, and yet prohibit their engaging with us on equal terms, it comes to
> pass that neither our vices prevail against our virtue, nor does our virtue
> again settle down to rest with entire extinction of our vices. In which way
> alone our pride is utterly extinguished, because though it may serve for
> victory, yet a continual fight is reserved for us, to keep down the pride
> of our thoughts. (*Morals*, 30.63, 408)

To be able to battle successfully and regularly against a temptation that
is always present is Gregory's best solution for overcoming the vices.
Indeed, Gregory's concern with the psychological effects of the vices
overshadows completely their physical effects: whether a person is fat
is of no interest to him. Gregory is only concerned with whether a
person can successfully maintain the psychological and spiritual balance
between the desire for and necessity of food.

Gregory's understanding of the meaning and purpose of the vices
sets the stage for lay commentaries after the sixth century, though
many of these texts do not achieve his theological and psychological sophistication. *The Goodman of Paris*, "the most exhaustive treatise
on household management which has come down to us from the
Middle Ages,"[25] is a book of instructions written near the end of the
fourteenth century by a much older Frenchman for his 15-year-old

---

[25] *The Goodman of Paris: A Treatise on Moral and Domestic Economy by a Citizen of
Paris*, trans. Eileen Power (Avon, England, 1992), 5, hereafter cited parenthetically as
Goodman.

wife. As Christine Rose points out, such conduct books were written to ensure that women (and men) would assume their proper place in the social system.[26] The author's discussion of gluttony and the other deadly sins is found in his explanation of how a good wife avoids sin and manages the inner life of her soul.[27] Both *The Goodman of Paris* and the fifteenth-century penitential text, *Jacob's Well*, use Gregory's schema of the five temptations of gluttony and continue to focus on the communal effects of gluttony. At the same time, however, although food remains of major concern in these works, gluttony's communal effects also frequently expand to encompass such ideas as excessive drinking and harmful speech, highlighting the consequences of gluttony in the context of ordinary life.

The association of gluttony with drinking and hurtful speech, for example, can be found in nascent form in Cassian and Gregory, but are more thoroughly developed in works written primarily for lay communities. So, for instance, drinking too much is gluttonous, for the "tavern is the Devil's church, where his disciples go to serve him" (*Goodman*, 58). Indeed, overindulgence in drink leads to the final form of gluttony, harmful speech, for when people go to the tavern, "they go upright and well spoken, wise and sensible and well advised, and when they return they cannot hold themselves upright, nor speak; they are all fools and madmen and they return swearing, beating and giving the lie to each other" (*Goodman*, 58). The problem with drinking too much is that the Devil teaches human beings "gluttony, lechery, forswearing, slandering, backbiting, to scorn, to chide, to despise, to renounce God, to steal, to rob, to fight, to slay, and many other such sins" (*JW*, 148). Each of the lessons taught by the Devil when one has drunk too much is a specific harm to human relationships that affects the community in negative ways. Despite the fact that the definition of gluttony has grown over time from its beginnings in monastic discipline, it still has little to do with bodily corpulence, underscoring the idea that the consequences of gluttony—in all of its manifestations—have a profound impact on the spiritual health and well-being of the individual and the community.

In both *The Goodman of Paris* and *Jacob's Well* we find Cassian's initial forms of food gluttony, reformulated for the lay community. Eating

---

[26] Christine M. Rose, "What Every Goodwoman Wants: The Parameters of Desire in *Le Menagier De Paris / The Goodman of Paris*," *Studia Anglica Posnaniensia* 38 (2002): 393–410, here 395.

[27] Rose, 399.

at the wrong time, for instance, is often connected with breaking fast
before going to church:

> The first branch [of gluttony] is when a person eateth before he ought:
> to wit too early in the morning, or before saying hours and going to
> church and hearing the word of God and His commandments; for every
> creature ought to have the good sense and discretion not to eat before the
> hour of tierce, save by reason of illness, or weakness or some necessity
> constraining thereto. (*Goodman*, 38)

Not bound by monastic rules, the lay person is nonetheless encouraged
to maintain a sense of the proper time for eating and its connection to
ecclesiastical rules. The writer of *Jacob's Well* specifically highlights how
eating at the improper time can lead an individual to a host of other
sins, as well as undermine the orderly structure of the community:

> The first branch of gluttony is to eat or drink at the wrong time, too soon
> or too late. It is a foul ooze to a man of age and of will that will not abide
> by the time of eating; for that is of lust, from which may come many sins.
> Such use makes a man to say, "I cannot fast, nor do penance, nor go to
> church, nor sleep in my bed, for I have a bad head." He says such, for
> his evil use has made him so. To fast until evening to get worldly goods
> grieves him not; to fast until noon for the blessings of heaven and for
> God's love, that you cannot do. You eat and drink too late, until midnight,
> in sumptuous suppers, in riot and vanity, and you lie long in bed in the
> morning. You ignore the time that God has ordained, for you make day
> of night, and night of day, and so you spend the time of both in vanity,
> at chess, at the tables, at dice, in displeasing your God, in hindering your
> body and soul. Yet this gluttony is not wicked enough, for to this gluttony
> and riot you draw others from their goodness. (*JW*, 142)

Gluttony not only leads to lust, which leads to many more sins, it
keeps one from church. Taking God for granted, the glutton focuses
on worldly things, paying attention to fasting only when its rewards are
immediate and tangible. The true problem with eating at the wrong
time, however, is that it leads to a willful repudiation of creation's order,
as the glutton exchanges God's carefully formed days and nights for
the chaos of wild gaming, which inevitably also leads others astray. In
Jacob's Well, eating at the proper time reflects the proper order of the
world as a whole; eating at the improper time leads to excesses that
have serious and damaging social consequences.

Eating too much is also condemned in these texts, though not because
it makes one fat or, as Cassian suggests, muddles the mind. Rather,
eating too much aligns one with Satan, and transforms a human being
into an animal:

> The sin of too much eating and drinking pleaseth the Devil. It is written in the Gospels that God gave the Devil power to enter into the belly of the swine, by reason of their gluttony, and the Devil entered into them and drove them into the sea and they were drowned; even so enters he into the body of gluttons, who lead a dishonest life, and pushes them into the sea of hell [....] For, as the Scripture saith: once upon the day to eat and drink it is angelic, and to eat twice a day is human, and thrice or four times or more often is the life of a beast and not of a human being. (*Goodman*, 57–58)

Overeating turns humans into dishonest animals, destined for hell. In eating too much a human performs the idolatrous act of making one's stomach divine: "You who live by your flesh, you slay your soul, for you make your belly your God. If you live for jollity, and love vanity, and riotousness, and the company of folly, you can keep no measure" (*JW*, 143). Self-control clearly has moral value, for it is what keeps humans human, and turns them away from their animalistic impulses.

Eating foods that are too expensive is also a form of gluttony in these works, but again, for very different reasons than in the monastery. Eating costly food suggests selfishness, and a lack of interest in helping the poor. "The fourth branch of the ooze of gluttony is to eat too dainty foods, for you spend more for a meal than forty men might live by. Such sin in many ways, that is, in great outrage of expenses, in using food in too great pleasure, in vainglory, not only in gluttony but out of pomp, to make many different dishes" (*JW*, 144). To seek out "delicious viands" means that one can "do good to fewer others and cannot withhold himself so that he may help a poor man, or two, or more" (*Goodman*, 59). The value of helping others in community outweighs the selfish pleasure that one may experience with food.

It is in the final two forms of gluttony not found in Cassian that we find some variation. In *The Goodman of Paris*, the author writes that the third branch of gluttony "is when a person eats and drinks so much in a day that ill befalls him, and he is drunk and sick and must take to his bed" (*Goodman*, 58). The fifth branch "is when a person eats so greedily of a dish that he doth not chew it and swallows it whole and before he ought" (*Goodman*, 59). Thus, this text ignores the notion of eating food that requires too much preparation, and subdivides eating too much into two distinct categories: one about eating too much and not needing to, and another about eating so much one becomes sick. In *Jacob's Well*, the third branch of gluttony "is when you eat too quickly, like a hound" (*JW*, 144). The fifth branch is "curiosity, to seek what foods you like the most" (*JW*, 144). These two follow Gregory's schema.

These last two forms of gluttony come the closest to the contemporary concern about food and health. In *The Goodman of Paris*, there is an acknowledgement that eating too much can, indeed, make one ill. In *Jacob's Well*, illness from too much food stems from one's curiosity about, and desire for, many different kinds of food.

> Innocent says[28] . . . measure and temperance is so despised, and excess and superfluity is so desired in diverse food and drink and in diverse causes, that delight knows no manners and greediness exceeds measure; through this the stomach is troubled, sick and aggrieved, the wit is dulled and impaired, the understanding is oppressed. From this comes not health, but sickness and death. Therefore, he says, the sentence of the wise man, be not too desirous and too greedy in your eating, do not fall on each delicacy out of measure, for in many foods and diverse drinks is great sickness, and many because of gluttony have perished and died. (*JW*, 145)

This commentary echoes Cassian's idea that overeating leaves one as inebriated as excessive alcohol, and foreshadows the numerous medical warnings for obesity today. Yet, even in this context, it is not the state of obesity caused by gluttony that causes death. Rather, it is the eater's attitude towards food that matters. In *Jacob's Well*, for instance, various food practices are associated with venial and deadly sins. To enjoy one's food too much is a venial sin; to break a fast commanded by the church is a deadly sin (*JW*, 145).

Thus, medieval attitudes towards food, eating, and excess focus primarily on the role of food in an individual's struggle to create balance between desire and necessity, which in turn helps to create and maintain a balanced, healthy community. The sin of gluttony is not merely the sin of overeating: although overeating can reflect a host of other communal transgressions, like denying food to the poor, or succumbing to the animalistic parts of the self that seem to deny our very humanity, it is certainly not the only—or even the most damaging—gluttonous act. Indeed, the most injurious acts of gluttony are those which violate the carefully fashioned boundaries of Christian society, especially those which deflect a person's attention from God. Being fat in the Middle Ages is not, as it is today, an obvious mark of gluttonous excess.

One of the most vivid contemporary descriptions of the glutton can be found in Henry Fairlie's 1978 book, *The Seven Deadly Sins Today*:

---

[28] As Brandeis suggests in the introduction to *Jacob's Well*, there are many references in the text that are misquoted or are stated in "strangely mutilated form" (*JW*, x). This is one of them.

Watch a gluttonous man at his food. His napkin is tucked in his collar and spread across his paunch, announcing the seriousness of the business in which he is engaged. His bulging face and popping eyes are fixed on his plate. Only occasionally does he look up at his companions with a glazed look. His mouth has only one function, as an orifice into which to push his food. Now and then he may grunt at what someone has said. Otherwise, he stuffs. He is like a hog at its swill. He may ignore his companions; but they cannot ignore him. Even if they can avert their eyes from the spectacle—the swamp in his mouth, where the tide ebbs and flows, the seepage from its corners—they are unable to block their ears to the noise. He sucks each spoonful through his teeth as if it were the Sargasso Sea. He does not chew his meat but champs and chomps, crunches and craunches. He crams, gorges, wolfs, and bolts. He might as well be alone.[29]

Fairlie's description of the glutton reconfirms all of our contemporary associations with the glutton: he's fat and disgusting, eating his way through mountains of food; our available vocabulary is not sufficient to describe his eating. For Fairlie, the problem with the glutton is that his interest in food takes him away from community, and leaves him condemned to solitude.[30] It is in this contemporary assumption about gluttony's effect on community that we can see the greatest conceptual difference between the Middle Ages and current conceptions of food practices. Whereas we may worry that gluttonous behavior cuts us off from our communities, in the Middle Ages the glutton's sin is his destructive intervention into a community whose boundaries are marked by a desire for spiritual strength and communal well-being.

---

[29] Henry Fairlie, *The Seven Deadly Sins Today* (Washington, 1978), 155.
[30] Fairlie, 155.

THE INSTITUTION OF THE CHURCH

CASSIAN, NOCTURNAL EMISSIONS, AND THE SEXUALITY OF JESUS

John Kitchen
University of Alberta

Abstract: How Christian communities regarded nocturnal emissions reveals not simply the prominence of purity issues in early medieval culture, but also the fissures of the belief system itself. Focusing primarily on Cassian's discussion of the issue, this inquiry first considers Scripture's function in conditioning the discourse on nocturnal emissions. By examining how the discovery of the Bible's hidden meanings relates to a monastic self-scrutiny that renders transparent the secrets of monastic sexuality, my paper argues that Cassian's problematization of wet dreams actually frames the monk's body as a text, with purity of mind and flesh emerging as the precondition of the *hermeneutica spes*. The discussion then turns to the related question of exegesis and the concatenation of the sins. On this point, my study highlights how Cassian utilizes his sin-scheme as an exegetical tool safeguarding orthodox Christology on the question of Jesus's sexuality—and whether the Savior himself experienced "nightly sullying."

In the opening pages of *Fragmentation and Redemption*, Carolyn Bynum registers—and challenges—the retreat of medievalists from the current (argumentative) "fun." Of course, not all "departed from the fray," but as to the reason why a majority apparently did she offers no explicit explanation. Even so, her description of medievalists forfeiting debates on new approaches is telling:

> ...aside from a few mavericks among intellectual historians, Americans who study medieval history have folded their tents and slunk away. Absent from contemporary debates, they seem unaware of trends and novelties.... Today there is a war between the practitioners of new historical methods and the guardians of the old order. Some of the rhetoric is unattractive, to be sure.... But by and large the war is a rather cheerful, noisy one, in which the casualties...are few. Some of the debate is stimulating and productive. But medievalists play no role. It seems a shame to miss the fun.[1]

---

[1] Caroline Walker Bynum, *Fragmentation and Redemption: Essays on Gender and the Human Body* (New York, 1992), 21–22.

When considering her research in light of the opposing camps, she claims not to have "aligned" herself "with any current dispensation," while also noting that her work has often been regarded as "typical of the new history," that her analysis of medieval texts "has resonances with...postmodern feminism, deconstruction or poststructural anthropology." Chief among the reasons why her scholarship tends to be regarded as an example of the "new cultural poetics" is its focus. "Fun" for Bynum entails the treatment of emblematic subjects: "sexuality, gender, the body and [not surprising for a medievalist] death."

The first three might be expected to figure prominently in an essay on seminal emissions. As with the reception of Bynum's scholarship, just writing on such a topic might signal an author's allegiance. However, I propose something different, perhaps paradoxical. Nocturnal emissions present a phenomenon in which a war between mavericks and old guards is unwinnable. As we shall see, the discourse on wet dreams has a centripetal quality, a way of drawing the actual physical experience of seminal discharge into debates on the religion's core teachings, as if the disclosure of night emissions is pulling the thought of monastic practitioners toward Christianity's center. One may set out to study the phenomenon as an explicit example of how male sexuality, gender and the body figure prominently, only to find that the actual texts undercut such categories, that sources detailing responses to this particular bodily discharge stubbornly compel one to confront the massive weight of a religious tradition still in the making by the time Cassian wrote about such episodes in the fifth century.[2] In other words, the problem of nocturnal emissions opens up beyond itself, eliciting such wide-ranging discourse that the issue hardly may be classified as merely sexual—too much is at stake, much more than the indulgence in a trendy preoccupation with the private lives of past people.

Consider, for instance, the remarkable variation in early Christian attitudes toward nocturnal emissions as detected by Brakke.[3] Once we

---

[2] For the biographical details and modern studies, see Columba Stewart, *Cassian the Monk* (New York, 1999).

[3] See David Brakke, "The Problematization of Nocturnal Emissions in Early Christian Syria, Egypt, and Gaul," *Journal of Early Christian Studies* 3,4 (1995): 419–60. As Brakke summarizes (419), "the question of whether men who have had a nocturnal emission should commune or not provided a rare occasion for early Christians authors to use the male—rather than female—body to reflect on the purity of the individual Christian and the identity of the church." This paper is deeply indebted to Brakke's insightful discussion. For developments extending beyond the period Brakke addresses,

try to take full account of the implications arising from his meticulous observations, we immediately notice that broad, crucial questions emerge, questions at the core of a particular religious world-view, specifically: Christianity's relationship with Judaism, the tension between clerics and ascetics, the body-soul nexus, intentionality, the harsh reality of a fallen world, and most perplexing of all, the question of Jesus's full humanity, a subject whose difficulty undergoes dramatic accentuation when Christian thinkers confront the issue of whether their savior ever experienced "nightly sullying." To state the obvious, wet-dreaming is the stuff of theology. Christian discourse on the matter exposes cracks in a fragile belief system.

A thorough-going attempt to explicate that discourse will require an interpretive move between the current lines of contention in humanistic scholarship, a move mandating far more methodological and theoretical reflection than I have space for here. While some basic literature in anthropology and cultural studies marks my inquiry, the main focus is the sources themselves, particularly how these sources treating an explicitly sexual issue bring to light one of those fault lines marking Christianity's theological and social landscape. For reasons that will become apparent, I shall approach the subject of nocturnal emissions in Cassian's writing by turning first to the religion's core material, its Scripture, which conditions the treatment of the issue at a more subtle and far deeper level than modern authorities have hitherto recognized, even as they cite the obvious passages from Leviticus (7:20–21; 15:16–17) and Deuteronomy (23:10–12) on the question of "pollution."[4] To be sure, Cassian's use of such texts eliciting reflections on "purity" is crucial. But I shall underscore the significance of Biblical verses containing no explicit reference to certain bodily fluids as "unclean."

Coming next under our analysis is the role of an interpretive apparatus Cassian uses in his treatment of the problem, an apparatus logically tight but also the "mouthpiece" of a contested Christology.[5] Building

---

see Dyan Elliott, "Pollution, Illusion, and Masculine Disarray: Nocturnal Emissions and the Sexuality of the Clergy," in *Constructing Medieval Sexuality*, ed. Karma Lochrie, Peggy McCraken, and James A. Schultz (Minneapolis, 1997), 1–23.

[4] Elizabeth A. Clark, *Reading Renunciation: Asceticism and Scripture in Early Christianity* (Princeton, 1999), 138, 223–24; Brakke, "Problematization," 442, 447.

[5] Here I borrow from the work of Jean Danielou, *From Shadows to Reality: Studies in the Biblical Typology of the Fathers*, trans. Wulstan Hibberd (London, 1960), 44. As we shall see later, with respect to its role in supporting orthodox theological positions, the "concatenation" of the sins serves the same purpose as typological exegesis: "Typology...is

on the intriguing observations offered by Demyttenaere, I shall try to
formulate an argument that brings into focus more fully how Cassian's
system of concatenating the sins itself functions as a hermeneutical tool
safeguarding orthodox Christianity.[6] Such a function would suggest the
distinctive workings of a theologically (and ideologically) far-reaching
sin-scheme—precisely the kind of function that one of the pioneering
and foremost thinkers on the *principalia vitia* seems to have regarded as
only marginal to the purpose of the "the seven deadly sins" in medieval
literature.[7]

I. *The Body and Scripture: Secret Texts*

Students of both the desert writings and medieval vernacular literature
have explored the notion of the body as text.[8] The representation of the
monastic body in Cassian's discussion of nocturnal emissions warrants
a similar attention. But we may be more precise about the nature of
this carnal text when we see its relation to the Scriptural text.

As the current war between trend-setters and traditionalists confirms,
texts elicit distinctive kinds of interpretation depending on the interpretive tools critics apply. The aim of these interpretive strategies is to
reveal what texts conceal. As we shall see, the monastic body's involun-

---

the mouthpiece of theology: the dogma of Christ as the new Adam, and of Mary's
mediation rests on the typological significance of the Genesis account. To dispute this
typology would be to go against the whole of ecclesiastical tradition."

[6] Albert Demyttenaere, "The Cleric, Women and the Stain," in *Frauen in Spätantike
und Frühmittelalter. Lebensbedingungen, Lebensnormen, Lebensformen: Beiträge zu einer internationalen Tagung am Fachbereich Geschichtswissenschaften der Freien Universität Berlin, 18. bis 21.
Februar 1987*, ed. Werner Affeldt and Ursula Vorwerk (Sigmaringen, 1990), 141–65.
On Cassian's concatenation of the sins, see also Carole Straw, "Gregory, Cassian, and
the Cardinal Vices," in *In the Garden of Evil: The Vices and Culture in the Middle Ages*, ed.
Richard Newhauser (Toronto, 2005), 35–58, here 37 and 40.

[7] Siegfried Wenzel, "The Seven Deadly Sins: Some Problems of Research," *Speculum*
43 (1968): 12–13: "What significance did the Seven Deadly Sins really have in medieval
culture? Were they among those key notions which opened up revealed truths, gave
new insights into the meaning of life or the nature of man.... One soon realizes that
the scheme served primarily a very *practical purpose*, that it did not so much furnish
theoretical insight into human behavior as provide a guide for a life directed toward
moral perfection."

[8] Douglas Burton-Cristie, *The Word in the Desert* (New York, 1993), 30: "The holy
person became a new text and a new object of interpretation." See also E. Jane
Burns, *Bodytalk: When Women Speak in Old French Literature* (Philadelphia, 1993); and *The
Book and the Body*, ed. Dolores Warwick Frese and Katherine O'Brien O'Keeffe (Notre
Dame, 1997).

tary discharge and the *sacrae litterae* evoke a similar response: exegesis. Techniques of interpretation, whether applied to Scripture or nocturnal emissions, uncover hidden inner-workings of the respective texts. To put the matter succinctly, in a way that develops the insight offered in another context by De Certeau, "the precondition for hermeneutics," whether a hermeneutics of Scripture or the flesh, is "the secret."[9] In short, Cassian's analysis of the problem compels us to view the wet-dreamer's body as a text with a secret to disclose.

Consider first the description of Abba Theodore. While nothing in it refers to nocturnal emissions, the way the depiction links interpretation to revealed secrets of the self will prove useful for underscoring a key feature in Cassian's presentation. In a scene articulating the reason why the Bible poses interpretive challenges, we see an elder's "lived hermeneutics" blurring boundaries between sacred text and monastic flesh.[10] Understanding only "a few words of Greek," Theodore openly lacks formal Biblical training. He remains not simply indifferent to patristic *auctoritates*; he eschews the written tradition of exegesis, claiming that monks have no need to read commentaries. Instead, to decipher Biblical mysteries, a holy man must search for the secret passions vitiating his life. Interpretive acumen entails moral perfection. Here, the technique of self-examination assumes the role of exegetical tool, for the detection of vice, of secret flaws, lifts the veil of the self and the Bible. Exposing a heart once clouded by bodily sin renders transparent a Biblical corpus. An accurate and authoritative hermeneutics presupposes ascetic self-disclosure:

> When some brothers...were asking him about certain interpretations of Scripture, he said to them: "A monk who desires to attain to a knowledge of Scripture should never toil over the works of commentators. Instead, he should direct the full effort of his mind and the attentiveness of his heart toward the cleansing of his fleshly vices. As soon as these have been driven out and the veil of the passions has been lifted, the eyes of his heart will naturally contemplate the mysteries of Scripture, since it was not in order to be unknown and obscure that they were delivered to us by the grace of the Holy Spirit; rather, they were made obscure by our vices, when the veil of our sinfulness clouds over the eyes of the heart. Once these latter have been restored to their natural healthfulness, the

---

[9] Michel de Certeau, *The Mystic Fable, Volume One: The Sixteenth and Seventeenth Centuries*, trans. Michael B. Smith (Chicago, 1995), 99.

[10] Burton-Christie, *Word*, 23; for the standard scholarship on Cassian's use of Scripture, ibid., 29.

very reading of Holy Scripture—even by itself—will be more than sufficient for the contemplation of true knowledge...."[11]

The story of Theodore's method suggests that corporeal vices vitiate
with a three-fold opacity: they conceal themselves, the meaning of Scripture and, by implication, man's redemption. Their hidden nature also
corresponds with how the Bible conditions the approach to eradicating
sins. Biblical quotation actually lays down the method for detecting flaws
rooted in the monk's deepest self. Again, Cassian's description highlights
the secret workings of sin, secret workings linked to key Biblical texts
appropriated by the elder and applied to a monk's body. Judging by
the verses and the interpretive attention they draw, investigating and
exposing vice is a violent affair. A text from Isaiah indicates that an
elder's interrogation shatters the passions, portrayed as tyrannical rulers
with internal fortresses holding monks hostage. The elder's discovery
and destruction of the passions' strongholds liberates the junior monk.
It is a moment when the self is exorcised of secret sins after submitting
to an abbatial scrutiny authorized by Scripture:

> Although the causes of these passions are recognized by everyone as soon
> as they have been exposed by the teachings of the elders, until they have
> been revealed they are unknown to everyone, even though we are all hurt
> by them.... But we are confident that we can explain them somewhat if,
> through your prayers, the word of the Lord is also addressed to us which
> was uttered through Isaiah: "...I will smash bronze gates and I will break
> iron bolts. And I will open to you hidden treasures and concealed secrets"
> [Is 45:2–3]. Then the word of God will precede us and first humble the
> powerful of our earth—that is these same harmful passions that we wish to
> subdue and that claim dominion for themselves and a most cruel tyranny
> in our mortal body—and it will make them submit to our investigation and
> our exposure. And breaking open the gates of ignorance and smashing

---

[11] Cassian, *De institutis coenobiorum*, 5.33–34, ed. Michael Petschenig, CSEL 17 (Vienna,
1886), 107: "...quibusdam fratribus...ab eodem quosdam scripturarum sensus inqui-
rentibus ait, monachum scripturarum notitiam pertingere cupientem nequaquam debere
labores suos erga commentatorum libros inpendere, sed potius omnem mentis industriam
et intentionem cordis erga emundationem uitiorum carnalium detinere, quibus expulsis
confestim cordis oculi sublato uelamine passionum sacramenta scripturarum naturaliter
contemplarentur, siquidem nobis non, ut essent incognita uel obscura, spiritus sancti
gratia promulgata sint, sed nostro uitio uelamine peccatorum cordis oculos obnubente
reddantur obscura: quibus rursum naturali redditis sanitati ipsa scripturarum sanctarum
lectio ad contemplationem uerae scientiae abunde etaim sola sufficiat...." All translations of Cassian are by Boniface Ramsey: John Cassian, *The Institutes* (New York, 2000);
John Cassian, *The Conferences* (New York, 1997).

the bolts of the vices that shut us from our true knowledge, it will lead us to our concealed secrets and, according to the Apostle, it will, once we have been enlightened, reveal to us "the hidden things of darkness and make manifest the counsels of hearts" [1 Cor 4:4].[12]

Darkness, concealment, basically sin as secret—that is what also marks the discourse of nocturnal emissions. Indeed, as soon as the issue arises, at the end of a *conlatio*, we find it dramatically suspended, with the elder gently postponing (*"differatur"*) a full disclosure of his knowledge.[13] More important, and related to the connection between the hidden, sinful self discovered and exegetical power thereby attained, is the fact that the *Conferences'* interlocutor, Germanus, immediately associates the topic of involuntary seminal emissions with "a most obscure inquiry...unknown to many" (*"obscurissimam questionem...multis...incognitam"*). In addition, we again find Scripture linked to the physicality of monks, a specific verse signifying and foreshadowing the discussion on the mysterious bodily condition of wet dreams. Significantly, the authority on the subject, Theonas, first responds to Germanus's request to learn more about the problem by situating it within the context of internal circumcision:

> ...you are inquiring carefully and not about external purity and outward circumcision but about that which is hidden, knowing that the fullness of perfection does not consist in this visible abstinence of the flesh, which can be possessed either out of necessity or out of hypocrisy even by the faithless, but in the willed and invisible purity of heart, which the blessed

---

[12] *De inst.*, 5.2, CSEL 17:82: "Quarum passionum causae quemadmodum, cum patefactae fuerint traditionibus seniorum, ab omnibus protinus agnoscuntur, ita priusquam reuelentur, cum ab ipsis uniuersi uastemur...ab omnibus ignorantur. uerum eas ita nos aliquatenus explicare posse confidimus, si intercessionibus uestris ad nos quoque ille qui per Esaiam prolatus est sermo domini dirigatur:...portas aereas conteram, et uectes ferreos confringam. et aperiam tibi thesauros absconditos, et arcana secretorum, ut nos quoque uerbum dei praecedens primum terrae nostrae potentes humiliet, id est has easdem quas expungare cupimus noxias passiones dominationem sibi ac tyrannidem saeuissiman in nostro mortali corpore uindicantes, easque faciat indagini nostrae atque expositioni subcumbere, et ita ignorationis portas effringens ac uitiorum uectes excludentium nos a uera scientia conterens ad secretorum nostrorum arcana perducat ac secundum apostolum inluminatis nobis reuelet ea quae sunt abscondita tenebrarum et manifestet consilia cordium...."

[13] *Conlationes patrum*, 21.36, ed. Michael Petschenig, CSEL 13 (Vienna, 1886), 613: "...tamen quia satisfieri desiderio uestro ad plenum non potest (breue enim quod superest spatium noctis ad indagandam hanc abstrusissimam non sufficit quaestionem), congruum reor ut interim differatur." As the next conference indicates, the discussion is actually postponed for seven days.

apostle preaches thus: "He is not a Jew who is flesh, but he is a Jew who is so inwardly, and circumcision is of the heart, in spirit and not in letter, the praise of which is not from men but from God [Rom 2:28–29], who alone searches out the secrets of hearts."[14]

Keeping the above passages in mind, we see the reason why wet dreams are problematic: They undermine monastic authority and the monk's life, a life that is supposed to be utterly transparent. As Brakke shows, frequent nocturnal emissions point to a hidden part of a person, a part unknown not only to the elders but possibly even to the monk himself.[15] Illustrating the point is the case of a monk repeatedly awakening damp before taking communion.[16] The elders proceed by ruling out possible causes, almost all of which point to a failing on the monk's part, but a failing that the monk himself may miss were it not for the probing and systematic procedure of abbatial questioning. Again, we are witnessing the monk as text and the interrogators as interpreters skilled in the hermeneutics of the flesh, exegetes of body and mind asking the source decisive questions that yield answers, thus creating a narrative generated by the wet dreamer's secret. We are, in other words, at a moment in which "the hidden begins to take on the aspect of plot."[17] After excluding as causes of the discharge impure thoughts and an excess of bodily fluid due to the gluttonous intake of food and drink, the elders identify demonic malevolence as the culprit, thereby exonerating the "sullied" monk. With his innocence demonstrated, communion is encouraged. He experiences the problem never again.

Now we may add two points to Brakke's findings (though the first is really a matter of emphasizing what he discovered and considering it in light of implications not falling within the scope of his impressive survey). First, we should stress the reason why, with Cassian, "wet dreams are subjected to a level of analysis deeper and literally more

---

[14] *Conl.*, 21.35–36, CSEL 13:612–13: "...nec enim de exteriore castimonia et circumcisione manifesta, sed de illa quae in occulto est diligenter inquiritis, scientes in hac uisibili carnis continentia perfectionis plenitudinem non inesse, quae haberi uel per necessitatem uel per hypocrisin etiam ab infidelibus potest, sed in illa cordis uoluntaria et inuisibili puritate, quam beatus apostolus ita praedicat: non enim qui in manifesto, Iudaeus, neque quae in manifesto in carne, est circumcisio, sed qui in occulto, Iudaeus, et circumcisio cordis spiritu non littera, cuius laus non ex hominibus sed ex deo est, qui solus scilicet cordium secreta rimatur."

[15] Brakke, "Problematization," 448–58.

[16] *Conl.*, 22.6, CSEL 13:621–23.

[17] De Certeau, *Mystic Fable*, 97.

'microscopic' than anything we have...encountered."[18] That is because Cassian configures wet dreams in terms of a secret. Their hidden nature, their deeply layered causes, makes them subversive. They present obscure narratives resistant to closure; as such, they also call for a thorough-going, systematic, and penetrating analysis. The technique of interpretation thus matches the kind of text to be interpreted. Hence, we find in Cassian's treatment all that the secret text gives rise to: eroticism, narrative expansion (exegesis), forensic-like interrogation—indeed, all the elements that De Certeau associates with the way the secret marks the discourse of early modern "mystics." More important, with respect to elders and sullied monks, this secret "...designates a play between actors. It circumscribes the terrain of strategic relations between the one trying to discover the secret and the one keeping it.... [It] organizes a social network."[19] Therefore, to be as precise as possible, let us note that the issue here is not so much "the problematization of nocturnal emissions" as it is "the problematics of secrecy."

By now, the second point to add is obvious. We can readily grant what was asserted at the essay's beginning: Biblical texts having nothing to do with "impure" bodily fluids bear on the matter of wet dreams. The Scriptural references appearing in the context of a discussion on bodily vices underscore secrecy as the issue at stake. That observation is meant not to diminish the importance of those passages that do deal with purity issues in Cassian's writings; it is intended to suggest that Biblical texts of an entirely different sort condition his discussion. Indeed, if we recall the kind of citations initiating the dialogue, we are able to see the full implications coming at the end of his narrative on the troubled monk. Here, we find not only an example of an investigative procedure aimed at uncovering the unknown cause of a wet dream; we also have an instance in which the elders' interrogation fulfils Scripture, for with the unfolding of that story comes the actualization of the Isaian passage—gates have been smashed, concealed secrets opened up.

So far, then, the interconnectedness of Scripture, interpretation, and the body's mysterious workings emerges as the key to understanding Cassianic discourse on wet dreams. In what remains, I propose to continue to pursue the connection between the three, but this time as they figure in a different context from the one just examined.

---

[18] Braake, "Problematization," 446.
[19] De Certeau, *Mystic Fable*, 97.

II. *The Implied Question: Did Jesus Have Wet Dreams?*

Nagy suggests that the end of Achilles "may have been unsuitable for the *kléos* of the Iliadic tradition... *because the audience itself was involved in his death.*" The death of Patroklos, "his surrogate," is substituted because the passing of Achilles, foreshadowed by "his other self," is "too painful... to be treated directly."[20] As in the *Illiad*, substitution and indirect speech also figure in Cassian's presentation of an unspeakable matter, one with the potential to detract from the "glory" (*kléos*) of his God. His treatment of Christ's nature simultaneously warrants and silences discussion on the possibility of the savior's experiencing wet dreams. What closes this theological aporia is the Cassianic sin-scheme deployed with typological exegesis, rhetorical surrogates that imply a question and its answer.

As I have suggested, the discourse on night emissions moves to Christianity's core. Now at stake is the question of the relationship between Christ's humanity and divinity. Demyttenaere brings the Christological matter to our attention with great breadth, situating Cassian's record of the desert fathers' position within the perspective of ecclesiastical attitudes toward women, menstruation, and purity regulations in early medieval religion. He offers a rich synthesis of wide-ranging texts and their anthropological relevance, a thought-provoking reflection to which the present discussion is greatly indebted. However, because he is treating "the stain" in relation to broader questions, he (understandably) confines his discussion on Cassian to "a few words." Furthermore, in offering such a clear and perceptive summary of the source, he may give the impression that the question of Christ's wet dreams arises directly, as if Cassian forthrightly asked: "Was the God-man Jesus bothered by nightly sullying?"[21]

In taking up Demyttenaere's discussion, I propose to pay close attention to the actual steps in Cassian's argument and to delineate the methods Cassian uses in formulating his position. In addition, I emphasize the subtlety in the way the issue itself quietly emerges. Rather than treating the matter explicitly, Cassian approaches it indirectly, adducing signifiers that enable him to preclude the possibility of

---

[20] Gregory Nagy, *The Best of the Achaeans* (Baltimore, 1981), 113; and the "Forward" to this volume, with James M. Redfield, x.

[21] Demyttenaere, "Cleric," 155–56.

Jesus's experiencing an "impure flow" at the very moment the question begins to loom. That question then arises only by implication, as if the inquiry itself verges on the taboo. To put the matter in another way, one consistent with the previous observations, here Cassian's rhetorical strategy itself suggests a secret, a hidden thought that must be acknowledged and confronted but in such a way that imposes limits to what is, Christologically speaking, possible. His approach brings a rapid and logically tight closure not just to a theological issue, but to the imagination, to what monks can legitimately envisage about their flesh and blood God. As we shall soon see from a passage quoted at length, the methods Cassian employs circumscribe the boundaries of Christological curiosity.

Concatenating the sins is the first means by which limits are imposed. Cassian's method entails a complex set of relationships brought to bear on the relevant Biblical texts, relationships rooted in narratological time and the vices' affinity. In his recounting of the devil's tempting of Jesus, the question of narrative sequence assumes prominence as he fits the various temptations into specific categories of vice. Given the interconnectedness of certain sins, the order of the temptations becomes paramount, for successfully resisting one vice implies the defeat of another most closely related to it. In other words, the vices' "kinship" (*cognatio*) functions as a principle of Biblical interpretation used to safeguard orthodox Christology. The implications are far-reaching: Cassian can approach the categorization of certain sins represented in the Biblical passage as a fluid construct, as a semiotic system in which one vice of Jesus's temptation signifies and implies another; and because concatenation creates fluid hamartiological categories, Christ can be regarded as fully man even if he never had a wet dream, for his defeat of gluttony entails a victory over lust; and a victory over lust, in turn and again by implication, cancels out the possibility of dreaded emissions.

The key passage is Matthew 4:3.[22] Satan says to a fasting Jesus: "If you are the Son of God, tell these stones to become loaves of bread." As already suggested, the decisive component in Cassian's consideration of whether his savior succumbed is the interconnected sin scheme. Because lust springs from gluttony, Matthew's recounting of Jesus's

---

[22] On the importance of this passage's interpretation in the history of hamartiology, see Richard Newhauser, *The Early History of Greed: The Sin of Avarice in Early Medieval Thought and Literature* (Cambridge, Eng., 2000), 55–57.

temptation to transform stones into bread warrants Cassian's conclusion that his incarnated God vanquished lust. In defeating gluttony—and Cassian's understanding of that sin would render even the satiety from eating bread while fasting a form of gluttony—Jesus therefore defeated lust.[23]

The second means by which limits are imposed consists of Biblical typology. Christ as the second Adam restores what the first Adam lost through sin. As with the first, the second Adam has "real flesh," but the second Adam does not have "real sin." We may infer from the rhetoric that real sin includes wet dreams, though absent are the vivid references to "the stain of vile fluid" (*sordidi liquoris contagium*) or "an impure flow in sleep" (*inmundo fluxu dormiens*) that often appear in frank conversations between elders and junior monks. Instead, the incarnated Christ remains free from the "carnal desire" arising involuntarily but naturally in man. The typological mode of thought and rhetoric marking the very place where Cassian implies the question of Christ's wet dreams serves a purpose common to this interpretive strategy: It establishes both similarity and difference in the type represented, creating the tension as well as the harmony Christian commentators find between Old and New Testament figures and events.[24] Thus, a later Biblical figure, while sharing traits with a forerunner, surpasses the earlier type (as with Christ's restoring Adam's lost paradise). In the present case, not just

---

[23] *Conl.*, 5.6, CSEL 13:124–25: "In illis enim passionibus etiam ipse temptari debuit incorruptam imaginem dei ac similitudinem possidens, in quibus et Adam temptatus est, cum adhuc in illa inuiolata dei imagine perduraret, hoc est gastrimargia, cenodoxia, superbia, non in quibus post praeuaricationem mandati imagine dei ac similitudine uiolata suo iam uitio deuolutus inuoluitur. gastrimargia namque est qua interdicti ligni praesumit edulium, cenodoxia qua dicitur: aperientur oculi uestri, superbia, qua dicitur: eritis sicut dii, scientes bonum et malum. In his ergo tribus uitiis etiam dominum saluatorem legimus fuisse temptatum, gastrimargia, cum dicitur ei a diablo: dic ut lapides isti panes fiant, cenodoxia: si filius dei es, mitte te deorsum, superbia, cum ostendens illi omnia regna mundi et eorum gloriam dicit: haec tibi omnia dabo, si cadens adoraueris me...." On the "kinship" and "concatenation" of certain vices (gluttony, lust, wrath, sadness and *acedia*), Cassian states: "Haec igitur octo uitia licet diuersos ortus ac dissimiles efficientias habeant, sex tamen priora, id est gastrimargia, fornicatio, filargyria, ira, tristitia, acedia quadam inter se cognatione et ut ita dixerim concatenatione conexa sunt, ita ut prioris exuberantia sequenti efficiatur exordium. nam de abundantia gastrimargiae fornicationem, de fornicatione filargyriam, de filargyria iram, de ira tristitiam, de tristitia acediam necesse est pullulare" (*Conl.*, 5.10, CSEL 13:129–30). See Wenzel, "Seven Deadly Sins," 4; Morton Bloomfield, *The Seven Deadly Sins: An Introduction to the History of a Religious Concept, with Special Reference to Medieval English Literature* ([East Lansing, MI], 1952; reprint, 1967), 70.

[24] On Christian uses of typology, see, in general, Daniélou, *From Shadows to Reality*.

the difference but the symmetry Cassian creates between the two also assumes a crucial role: As the second Adam, Christ can be tempted only by as many sins as the first Adam—but not by more. Typological interpretation, combined with concatenation, effectively sets a limit to the number of temptations experienced by Jesus. Concatenation and typology thus regulate Christology:

> Therefore both the one and the other [Christ] are called Adam, the former having been the first to go to ruin and death and the latter having been the first to go to resurrection and life.... It behooved him [Christ], then, to suffer temptations, but it was not necessary that they be excessive. For one who had conquered gluttony could not be tempted by fornication, which proceeds from the former's repletion and from its root. Even the first Adam would not have been struck by this if he had not been deceived by the enticements of the devil and contracted the passion [gluttony] which generates it. For this reason the Son of God is not said to have come without qualification, in sinful flesh but rather "in the likeness of sinful flesh" [Rom 8:3]. Although he had real flesh, which is to say that he ate and drank and slept and was also really fastened by nails, he did not have real sin contracted through wrongdoing but only what seemed to be such. For he did not experience the burning pricks of carnal desire that even arise when we do not want them, due to nature's action, but he experienced a certain similarity through participating in our nature. The devil tempted him, then, only with the vices by which he had also deceived that first man, conjecturing that, as a man, he could be mocked in other ways too if he saw that he was seduced by the things with which he had overthrown the first man. But he was unable to inflict him with a second disease [lust], sprouting from the root of the principal vice that served as a source, since he was defeated in the first battle....[25]

---

[25] *Conl.*, 5.6, CSEL 13:125–26: "...ideoque et ille Adam dicitur et iste Adam, ille primus ad ruinam et mortem, hic primus ad resurrectionem et uitam...huius ergo ut suscipere eum temptationes oprtuit, ita excedere necessarium non fuit. nec enim qui gastrimargiam uicerat poterat fornicatione temptari, quae ex illius abundantia ac radice procedit, qua ne ille quidem primus Adam fuisset elisus, nisi ante generatricem eius passionem deceptus inlecebris diaboli recepisset. et ob hoc filius dei non absolute in carne peccati uenisse dicitur, sed in simultudine carnis peccati, quia, cum esset in eo uera caro, manducans scilicet et bibens et dormiens, clauorum quoque confixionem in ueritate suscipiens peccatum eius quod praeuaricatione contraxit uerum non habuit sed imaginarium. Non enim ignitos aculeos concupiscientiae carnalis expertus est, qui etiam nolentibus nobis natura iam administrante consurgunt, sed huius quandam similitudinem naturam participando suscepit. Nam cum omnia quae officii nostri sunt in ueritate conpleret et uniuersas infirmitates gestaret humanas, consequenter huic quoque passioni putatus est subiacere, ut per has infirmitates etiam condicionem huius quoque uitii atque peccati uideretur in sua carne portare. denique in his eum tantummodo uitiis diabolus temptat, in quibus et illum primum deceperat, coniciens hunc quoque uelut hominem similiter in ceteris inludendum, si eum in illis quibus priorem

If the premises are accepted, a number of possible conclusions are eliminated. The very terms of the discussion preclude a free-wheeling *disputatio*. Interpretive methods set binding parameters. Christ can have been tempted only by as many sins as Adam; and in overcoming the temptation of one vice (*gula*), which also tempted Adam, Jesus the antitype overcomes that vice's closest kin (*fornicatio*). Therefore, the "God-man" did not experience nightly sullying, though Cassian never puts it so explicitly. Indeed, he never has to say it at all. His exegetical moves render direct utterance of the looming question superfluous— signification and implication silently bear the question and the answer. His method arrests the very idea of a sullied Christ before it becomes dialogue.[26]

III. *Asceticism as Ideology*

Cassian's utilization of a concatenated sin scheme creates a kind of surrogate signifier—that is *gula* both bears and subsumes *fornicatio*. Closure to the Christological problem raised here could not be accomplished without a notion of the sins' kinship, for Cassian's Biblical interpretation would collapse, and with it the Scriptural justification for the Christology he advocates. The combination of hamartiology and typology validates the assertion of Christ's full humanity while it also precludes the savior's experience of wet dreams.

In addition, concatenation endorses an ideology, namely asceticism. The question of asceticism as ideology also arises in Harpham's challenging work. The book treats asceticism not simply as a product of early Christianity, but also as a feature "common to all culture."[27] His broad and provocative discussion conceptualizes asceticism as "a hyperarticulated" and ambivalent form of resistance: "the durability of asceticism lies in its capacity to structure oppositions [e.g., between flesh and spirit], without collapsing them, to raise issues without settling them."[28] Certainly, his observations on asceticism as a "cultural

---

deiecerat sensisset elisum. uerum ei secundum iam morbum, qui de radice principalis uitii pullularet, primo certamine confutatus inferre non potuit."

[26] The point coincides with the impression Cassian has left on his modern interpreters: "What is most striking in Cassian's work are his silences"; see Stewart, *Cassian*, 3.

[27] Geoffrey Galt Harpham, *The Ascetic Imperative in Culture and Criticism* (Chicago, 1987), xi.

[28] Ibid., xii.

imperative" keeping moral tensions tight constitute an intriguing thesis impressive for its critical scope and dense analysis yet difficult to encapsulate here, not simply because its subtlety resists easy summary, but also because its references to "ideology" in the context of asceticism require more precise explication—"ideology" remains undefined throughout the study. A definition, though, is needed, as indicated by the vast and divergent scholarly literatures treating the term and by the prominence Harpham's inquiry itself gives to it: The long foundational section of the book is called "The Ideology of Asceticism."[29] Of course, we may infer from the way he associates the word with key historical and theological developments that the ideological components of asceticism include, though are not limited to, "self-denial, belief in God, and the tireless effort to starve out or punish the animal elements of the human condition."[30] In light of those features, then, we may say that concatenation endorses the ideology of asceticism, for the "kinship" between the sins, as we have seen, enables Cassian to validate an ascetic Jesus, to present an eremetical God-man conquering temptation with a pure body, heart, and mind. In other words, concatenation serves the ideology of asceticism by precluding the attribution of "animal elements," such as defiling emissions, to the savior's humanity.

But we may be more precise. In particular, I have in mind the criteria for using the term as set out by contemporary thinkers on ideology, criteria taken up by Biblical scholars who have applied theories on ideology to Scripture and other early Christian sources. In pursuing their insights here, it is important to recall one Biblical critic's comment: " 'ideology' has an extremely wide and confusing set of possible definitions."[31] As a sound guide for using the diverse studies treating the

---

[29] Ibid., 3–88. In commenting on Harpham's study, I regret not being able to address at length the work's numerous and invaluable insights. The mild criticism I offer above is in no way intended to diminish the far-reaching significance of his treatment. Furthermore, Harpham's opening reflection offers a compelling statement against critics who may find "a proper procedural rigor" lacking in his analysis: "...without a relaxation of certain kinds of academic rigors, I would not have been able to exercise certain speculative freedoms—freedoms which, as anyone who works in this way understands, carry with them other duties, other rigors" (xiii).

[30] Ibid., xiv. It is also important to note how Harpham goes on to qualify this view: "...asceticism does not oppose the body in any simple way. For by characterizing an entire life as an 'imitation of Christ' or as 'a pattern for believers,' asceticism both denigrates and dignifies the body, casting it at once as a transgressive force always on the side of 'the world' and as the scene or stage for discipline, self-denial, ascesis."

[31] John Kloppenborg, "Ideological Texture in the Parable of the Tenants," in *Fabrics of Discourse: Essays in Honor of Vernon K. Robbins*, ed. David Gowler, L. Gregory

term, Kloppenborg's work is invaluable for the way it offers a synthesis of the theoretical literature on the subject, in his attempt to identify the "ideological textures" of a Biblical passage.

I take the "descriptive or anthropological definition," rather than the "pejorative" and "positive senses" of ideology, as the most fruitful place for applying "ideological criticism" to Cassian's writings. Ideology, then, may be defined as "an integrated system of beliefs, assumptions and values, not necessarily true or false, that reflect the needs and interests of a group or class at a particular time in history."[32] In light of that definition, we may succinctly express what is ideological about Cassian's discussion on seminal emissions and Christology. In that discussion, concatenation and typology are not merely interpretive tools; they convey, in a rigorous and systematic fashion, the needs and interests of a specific group, by "encoding" the beliefs, assumptions and values of orthodox ascetics.

In addition, and as Kloppenborg stresses when pursuing the implications of the above definition, "ideology is not merely a set of beliefs…but beliefs that serve the power interests of those who hold and promote them."[33] That qualification opens up the range of ideological content in the sources we have been examining. For instance, the account of an elder's interrogation aimed at determining the hidden cause of a wet dream also has an "ideological texture." The story shows how the secret "organizes a social network," to be sure, but embedded in that portrayal of a social network is also the privileged (and perhaps contested) status of elders who exercise their power as authorized interpreters not just of a junior monk's body and mind, but also of the Scriptures used to legitimize and condition the investigation.[34] At both levels, Cassian's

---

Bloomquist, and Duane Watson (Harrisburg, 2003), 65, where the author cites the standard theoretical literature on the subject of ideology.

[32] The definition is taken from David Brion Davis, *The Problem of Slavery in the Age of Revolution, 1770–1823* (Ithaca, 1975), 14; see also: Vernon Robbins, *The Tapestry of Early Christian Discourses: Rhetoric, Society, and Ideology* (London, 1996), 96; John Elliott, *A Home for the Homeless: A Sociological Exegesis of 1 Peter, Its Situation and Strategy* (Minneapolis, 1990), 268; and Kloppenborg, "Ideological Texture," 66–67. I rely extensively on Kloppenborg's essay in my consideration of asceticism and ideology.

[33] Kloppenborg, "Ideological Texture," 67.

[34] Cassian's portrayal of elders probing the inner states of monks reveals the continuity between the practices of late antique ascetics and later confessors scrutinizing the thoughts of penitents. See Richard Newhauser, "Zur Zweideutigkeit in der Moraltheologie. Als Tugenden verkleidete Laster," in *Der Fehltritt. Vergehen und Versehen in der Vormoderne*, ed. Peter von Moos (Köln, Weimar, Wien, 2001), 377–402, with reference to Cassian's influence at 387. Since inner states are fraught with ambiguity, especially with respect to intention, and since sins may remain unknown even to the sinner, the

CASSIAN, NOCTURNAL EMISSIONS, AND THE SEXUALITY OF JESUS   89

literary productions encode the power interests of senior ascetics, and with respect to concatenation those power interests extend beyond the monastic milieu, as concatenation also encodes orthodoxy, the prescribed set of beliefs on Christological matters.

The specific ways such ideological encoding operates may also be identified. The Cassianic texts presented here "coerce" a particular reading of Scripture through the deployment of rhetorical strategies that also serve and reflect the interests of Cassian's monastic practitioners. As Biblical scholars assert, "ideological coercion takes place in several ways: first, by stripping events of their particularity and referring the resulting abstractions to some generalized schema; second, by the supplying of cross-references or analogies; and third, by framing."[35] Each one of those methods is at work in the sources we have examined.

---

need for decipherers of thoughts becomes justified. As we sense from Newhauser's observations (378–79), the justification for examining others' inner states also legitimizes the power of moral theologians in the lives of medieval believers: "Dabei ist die Frage der Intentionalität unabdingbar, denn erstens bringt sie die Kontrolle über die Art und Weise zur Sprache, in der dem mittelalterlichen Gläubigen innere Zustände zugerechnet wurden, die auch unabsichtlich beliebig fehlerhaft sein könnten. Sie zeigt zweitens, dass es dem Interesse der Moraltheologen förderlich gewesen ist, diese inneren Zustände als so labil zu charakterisieren, dass debei ihre eigene Rolle als Fürsprecher und Interpreten gerechtfertigt wurde." Michel Foucault offers similar observations when treating Cassian, confession, and elders: "About the Beginning of the Hermeneutics of the Self: Two Lectures at Dartmouth," ed. Mark Blasius *Political Theory* 21,2 (1993): 216–19: "...the first point about the self-examination in the monastic life is that the self-examination in this kind of Christian exercise is much more concerned with thoughts than with actions.... The monk has to examine the nearly imperceptible movements of the thoughts.... How is it possible to perform this necessary hermeneutics of our own thoughts? The answer given by Cassian and his inspirators [sic] is both obvious and surprising. The answer given by Cassian is, well, you interpret your thoughts by confessing not of course your acts, not confessing your faults, but in confessing continuously the movement you can notice in your thought. Why is this confession able to assume this hermeneutical role? One reason comes to mind: in exposing the movements of his heart, the disciple permits his *seigneur* to know those movements and, thanks to his greater experience, to his greater wisdom, the *seigneur*...can better understand what's happening. His seniority permits him to distinguish between truth and illusion in the soul of the person he directs." Foucault also discusses Cassian and confession in "The Battle for Chastity," in *Western Sexuality: Practice and Precept in Past and Present Times*, ed. Philippe Ariès and André Béjin, trans. Anthony Forster (Oxford, 1985), 14–25; see also, in general, Foucault, *The History of Sexuality*, 1: *An Introduction*, trans. Robert Hurly (New York, 1990), with a critique of Foucault's treatment of medieval confession offered by Karma Lochrie, *Covert Operations: The Medieval Uses of Secrecy* (Philadelphia, 1999), 12–42. For the implications of Foucault's thought on asceticism, see Elizabeth A. Clark, "Foucault, the Fathers, and Sex," *Journal of the American Academy of Religion* 56 (1988): 619–41; and, especially, her recent book *Reading Renunciation*, which astutely treats the strategies of ascetic exegesis.

[35] Kloppenborg, "Ideological Texture," 75, citing David Penchansky, "Up for Grabs: A Tentative Proposal for Doing Ideological Criticism," *Semeia* 59 (1992): 35–41.

Indeed, the concatenation of sins is itself a "generalized schema" to which the Biblical narrative recounting Jesus's temptations is referred and by which the pericope is "stripped of its particularity." In addition, both typology and concatenation furnish Cassian with "cross-references" and "analogies": Genesis, "the Old Adam," and "the kinship" of certain sins, for instance. Finally, these references frame the question of Christ's humanity and divinity.

The framing is especially important for showing us the way concatenation helps to construct a reading of the Biblical account. Cassian's use of concatenation to interpret the temptations of Jesus coincides with a salient feature of "ideological coercion." Such coercion "occur[s] ... by creating a narrative syntax that implies causal relationships between discrete elements."[36] With one sin able to "spring" (*pullulare*) from another, the causal connection inherent in the notion of concatenation creates a relationship between the otherwise "discrete elements" of the Biblical narrative recounting the temptations. Fasting now becomes crucial in determining the question of Jesus's sexuality, even though no such connection exists between the two in the Scriptural passage under consideration. The "abstraction" of a concatenated sin-scheme clearly frames Cassian's interpretation of Jesus's temptations. The notion that fasting curtails wet dreams thus leads to a particular reading of the Biblical source, a reading that is congenial with an entire tradition of ascetic exegesis;[37] congenial, too, with the concerns of elders clearly perplexed at the way wet dreams undermine abbatial authority; and, most important, congenial with defenders of a Christology in which the savior, though human, does not exhibit the "animal elements of the human condition." The strategies at work here all aim at coercing a reading of the Biblical narrative that buttresses asceticism, the authority of elders, and Christian orthodoxy. That, indeed, is ideology at its core.

---

[36] Kloppenborg, "Ideological Texture," 77.

[37] Besides highlighting the importance of Evagrius in the development of interpretation of Matt 4:1–11, Newhauser's analysis (*Early History of Greed*, 55–56) also reveals how Evagrius, who deeply influenced Cassian, ties together exegesis, the causal connections between sins, and the ascetic mentality: "Before the anchorite could move on to higher stages of monastic discipline, Evagrius taught, he had to be successful in particular in expelling the same evils Jesus had had to contend with, for once he was wounded by one of these three [gluttony, avarice or vainglory], he would quickly fall into the hands of the battalions which followed them."

IV. *Conclusions*

The salient point to emerge from such observations again relates to the insights offered by thinkers considering the meaning and role of ideology in Western culture. As we may already sense from the material examined so far, "ideology functions...especially in the context of conflict."[38] It is in just such a context that theologians of late antiquity formulate their positions on Christ's human and divine natures. Clearly, such a context also conditions Cassian's discussion on nocturnal emissions.[39] Significantly, concatenation stamps the two longest Christological sections of the *Conferences*, both of which treat "Christ's relationship to sin and raise the issue of his temptations."[40] To draw the obvious conclusion, Cassian uses concatenation to deflect the most daunting problem in late antique Christianity, the mystery of Christ's full humanity and divinity.

Concatenation thus offers a way to address that mystery, and to contain it, during an era marked by Christological controversies. Cassian's Christ is one among many, and we need not confine ourselves to the theological literature to appreciate the point. In a challenging study of the period's iconography, Thomas Mathews surveys the visual depictions of Jesus in light of the era's Christological debates. He uncovers a "chameleon," everything from a magical gynecologist to the hermaphroditic Jesus of Ravenna's Arian baptistery.[41] Like these images, Cassian's discussion of wet dreams, his use of concatenation and his construction of an ascetic Jesus reveal not so much a stable belief system as they do a struggle to grasp who this God is. Significantly, the salient feature Matthews uncovers is Christ's mysteriousness. Again we are in the realm of the secret:

> We who live in a post-Christian world think we have arrived at a certain
> objectivity about Christ.... The new converts of the fourth and fifth
> century did not find it so easy. To them he was still utterly mysterious,
> undefinable, changeable, polymorphous. In the disparate images they have
> left behind they record their struggle to get a grasp on him; the images

---

[38] Kloppenborg, "Ideological Texture," 67.

[39] On the Christological and theological polemics engaging Cassian, see Stewart, *Cassian*, 4–5, 10–11, 16, 21–24, 28, 77–78.

[40] *Conferences*, trans. Ramsey, 178.

[41] Thomas Matthews, *The Clash of the Gods: A Reinterpretation of Early Christian Art*, revised and expanded ed. (Princeton, 1999), 54–141.

were their way of thinking out loud on the problem of Christ. Indeed, the images are the thinking process itself.[42]

When we situate Cassian's discourse on wet dreams within the era's theological polemics and iconography, we are compelled to recognize that his sin scheme is of the greatest significance, serving more than a mere "practical purpose," for here the theological stakes are high. Clearly, hamartiology is crucial to the religion's episteme.

I also add that it would be churlish not to qualify my response to Wenzel's position. In downplaying what the chief sins accomplished with respect to their insights into "the meaning of life or the nature of man," he obviously has in mind scholastic and pastoral authors, who inherited schemes after Cassian that had undergone transformations and intense refinement as practical guides in monastic and clerical circles. Even so, based on the analysis offered here, I think it worth resisting the tendency to view the sins in merely practical terms; for from the analysis also arises the question of whether later authors, particularly exegetes, used hamartiology in a similar way, which is all the more likely if Cassian's influence marked medieval Christianity.

Yet rather than take Wenzel's position as a point of contention, I prefer to view it as an invitation to address the problem his observation frames. After all, hamartiology's most crucial role discussed here is in Christology. How does Christology defended by hamartiology give "theoretical insight into human behavior"?

Consider concatenation as a symbol of monastic culture, with its function in Cassian's Christology akin to that special device worn by the Chagga and colorfully portrayed by Becker. Notice that what he says of the anthropological literature on "primitives" resonates with the Judaeo-Christian tradition, especially regarding menstruation. Notice, too, that the cultural symbols employed pertain to secrecy—"disguises" and "mysterious processes":

> To say that someone is "anal" means that someone is trying extra-hard to protect himself against the accidents of life and danger of death, trying to use the symbols of culture as a sure means of triumph over natural mystery.... When we comb the anthropological literature we find that...primitives have often shown the most unashamed anality of all. They have been more innocent about what their real problem is, and they have not well disguised their disguise, so to speak, over the fallibilities

---

[42] Ibid., 141.

of the human condition. We read that men of the Chagga tribe wear an anal plug all their lives, pretending to have sealed up the anus and not to need to defecate. An obvious triumph over mere physicalness. Or take the widespread practice of segregating women in special huts during menstruation.... [I]t is obvious that man seeks to control the mysterious processes of nature as they manifest themselves within his own body. The body cannot be allowed to have ascendancy over him.[43]

In light of Becker's insight, we may say that concatenation represents the cultural "disguise" stopping Christ's slippage into a vitiated human nature, vitiated along the lines mentioned by Gregory the Great when he refers to the moral status of hunger or the monthly courses of women.[44] In other words, concatenation is a culturally constructed way of asserting Jesus's triumph over a mysterious bodily process that reeks of fallen humanity. It does give us insight into human behavior: it suggests that Cassian's monastic culture will ingeniously create and apply artifices to make space—however small—between an incarnated but full-fledged divinity and a human body that (*sponte sua*) defecates, menstruates, and ejaculates.

In introducing *Purity and Danger*, Douglas claims that "the more we know about primitive religions the more clearly it appears that in their symbolic structures there is scope for meditation on the great mysteries of religion and philosophy."[45] Cassian's discourse on wet dreams confirms her observation, it lays open the "profound themes" she hints at when speaking about purity issues as "an entry to comparative religions." Like Becker and Matthews, Douglas also presents cultural symbols as devices for comprehending "mysteries." That is precisely what the Cassianic literature indicates—"the problem of wet dreams" induces a

---

[43] Ernest Becker, *The Denial of Death* (New York, 1973), 32; compare Mary Douglas, *Purity and Danger: An Analysis of Concepts of Pollution and Taboo* (London, 2000), 201; see, in general, Otto Raum, *Chaga Childhood* (New York, 1940).

[44] As Demyttenaere, "Cleric," 157–58, notes (citing Bede, *Historia Ecclesiastica*, 1.27): "This human condition, marked by original sin, serves as an argument for the ambiguous papal advice concerning the communion of women during menstruation. He [Pope Gregory the Great] elaborates: 'it is a feature of righteous people to acknowledge a fault even where there is no personal fault, because a blameless action may often spring from fault. For instance, eating when we are hungry is no fault, but being hungry originates in Adam's sin; similarly, the monthly courses of women are not a fault, because nature causes them. However, as nature itself is vitiated to such a degree that it even appears to be defiled against its will, the vitiation springs from sin, and in this vitiation human nature may recognize itself as it has been made by Divine Judgement. And man, who has sinned willingly, may bear the burden of guilt unwillingly.'"

[45] Douglas, *Purity*, 6–7.

struggle to understand, through the symbolic structure of Christianity's interpretive methods, what resists knowing. And characterizing such a struggle in an ascetic culture confronting the mystery of its incarnated and transcendent God is the need to protect a delicate longing, the often frustrated though nonetheless earnest desire to harmonize—and to keep (somewhat) apart—what is holy and what is human.

PRIDE GOES BEFORE A FALL: ALDHELM'S PRACTICAL APPLICATION OF GREGORIAN AND CASSIANIC CONCEPTIONS OF *SUPERBIA* AND THE EIGHT PRINCIPAL VICES

Rhonda L. McDaniel
Middle Tennessee State University

Abstract: The Anglo-Latin author, Aldhelm, occupies an important place in the history of the reception and transmission of the Cassianic and Gregorian schemes of the principal vices. He knew the pertinent works of both earlier authors and in the prose version of his *De uirginitate*, Aldhelm apparently attempted to combine or reconcile the two. In the later, metrical version of *De uirginitate*, however, he abandoned any attempt to merge the two schemes and chose to portray the Cassianic organization of the vices with no further mention of Gregory's contribution to the idea. Understanding Aldhelm's choice requires a careful consideration of his own background, ideas, and conception of the audience for whom he wrote the *De uirginitate*. Such an understanding will help explain why Cassian's order of the principal vices endured in Anglo-Saxon England into the eleventh century despite the greater influence and authority of the writings of Gregory the Great.

The eight principal vices (out of which grew later conceptions of the seven deadly sins) were first recorded by Evagrius in his writings on the practice of solitary asceticism that had developed during the fourth century CE in the regions of Egypt and Syria. Evagrius referred to the vices as λογισμοί (thoughts), mental tendencies that would lead to sin if not overcome and that had to be rooted out by ascetic discipline.[1] This psychology of sin was introduced to the Christian lands of western Europe in writing by John Cassian in his *Conferences* and *Institutes*, which he produced in the early fifth century after emigrating from the east and settling in Gaul, where he established two monastic communities, one for men and one for women, in Marseilles. The reception of ascetic practice in Gaul before the early 400s CE had not

---

[1] Evagrius Ponticus, *Praktikos*, 6–14, in *Évagre le Pontique: Traité pratique ou le moine*, ed. and trans. Antoine Guillaumont and Claire Guillaumont, SC 170–71 (Paris, 1971), 2:506. For the English translation, see Evagrius Ponticus, *The Praktikos*, trans. John Eudes Bamberger (Kalamazoo, MI, 1981), 16–26.

been encouraging, but the tide of opinion was turning when Cassian arrived in Marseilles:

> Augustine in Africa, Martin in Gaul, Paulinas of Nola and Ambrose in Italy, Priscillian in Spain, had by their prowess and reputation sanctified asceticism in the eyes of a section of the population. But the movement had not fully captured the loyalty of the leaders of society as a whole. Not only the unsympathetic pagans but sporadic Christian opinion denounced the monks as irresponsible and bizarre wretches.[2]

In a time when Benedict of Nursia had yet to write his famous *Rule* and monastic observance was by no means uniform nor even particularly well-defined in western European lands, Cassian's works met the need for a fundamental theology of asceticism in the Latin west and the need for firsthand instruction from one who knew the customs of the fathers of Syria and Egypt. Through the *Institutes* and *Conferences*, Cassian contributed to the growing conception of what ascetic practice might look like beyond the boundaries of Syria and Egypt, especially cenobitic asceticism, or the observance of ascetic life in community with others instead of as a solitary hermit.

Despite receiving criticism from Cassiodorus and Prosper of Aquitaine for the semi-Pelagian views expressed especially in *Conference* 13, Cassian's writings on cenobitic monastic practice were recommended by Cassiodorus (with a caveat regarding Cassian's teaching on grace and free will) and later in the *Rule* of Benedict of Nursia.[3] The pall of Cassian's apparent semi-Pelagian stance in opposition to the teachings of Augustine of Hippo on the matter of grace, however, was enough to:

> make Augustinians suspicious and to begin requests for modified editions of the *Conferences*.... Nevertheless both semi-Pelagian and Augustinian writers of the fifth and sixth centuries had read [Cassian]; and the demand for epitomes and expurgation proves that in spite of these disadvantages his ascetical theology was meeting a long-felt need.[4]

The numerous extant manuscripts of Cassian's writings on ascetic practice testify to the continued popularity of these works throughout the Middle Ages.[5] It comes as no surprise, then, to find that manuscripts of Cassian's works followed the monks, Roman and Irish, who

---

[2] Owen Chadwick, *John Cassian: A Study in Primitive Monasticism* (Cambridge, Eng., 1950), 43.
[3] Ibid., 171.
[4] Ibid., 170–71.
[5] Ibid., 162.

evangelized the pagan Anglo-Saxon tribes that had overwhelmed the Celts and established themselves in Britain after the collapse of Roman governance in the early 400s.

The new Anglo-Saxon converts lost no time in establishing monastic communities and schools for the study of holy writings. The rapid proliferation of monastic establishments reflected the rapidity with which the new religion gained converts among the royal houses of the Anglo-Saxons and with which the value of literacy and religious education for both men and women rose as a consequence. One important center for instruction was established at Canterbury, where the first missionaries from Rome had built a community. Within seventy-five years of its founding, Canterbury had become one of the premier places of instruction in western Europe. Under the able direction of Archbishop Theodore and the teacher, Hadrian, the school at Canterbury produced many learned men, according to Bede.[6] The writings of the earliest English Christian authors indicate that they were familiar with Cassian's works. As Stephen Lake's study of Cassian's influence up to 817 CE shows, "[t]he evidence . . . demonstrates a definite presence of copies of Cassian's writings in sub-Roman Britain and in Anglo-Saxon England, and probably in Ireland. The most concentrated study of his writings is found at Canterbury, where his *De institutis* was employed as a schoolroom text . . ."[7] Certainly both the *Institutes* and *Conferences* were known to the earliest Anglo-Saxon "man of letters," who had studied under Hadrian at Canterbury: Aldhelm, abbot of Malmesbury (c. 673– c. 705) and bishop of Sherborne in Dorset (c. 705–c. 709).[8]

Aldhelm's writings provide a clear witness to his prodigious learning, earning him a reputation as "the most widely learned man produced in Anglo-Saxon England during its first four centuries of Latin Christendom."[9] Aldhelm's impressive reading list included both classical Latin authors and the writings of the major (and many minor) figures

---

[6] Bede, *Historia ecclesiastica gentis Anglorum*, 4.2, ed. and trans. B. Colgrave and R. A. B. Mynors (Oxford, 1969), 332–35.

[7] Stephen Lake, "The Influence of John Cassian on Early Continental and Insular Monasticism to c. AD 817," Ph.D. diss., Cambridge Univ., 1996, 217. I am grateful to Andy Orchard for calling my attention to Lake's dissertation.

[8] Aldhelm, *The Poetic Works*, trans. Michael Lapidge and James L. Rosier (Cambridge, Eng., 1985), 1; and Aldhelm, *The Prose Works*, trans. Michael Lapidge and Michael Herren (Cambridge, Eng., 1979), 153–54.

[9] Lapidge and Herren, "Introduction," in *Prose Works*, 1. See also Jane Barbara Stevenson, "Theodore and the *Laterculus Malalianus*," in *Archbishop Theodore*, ed. Michael Lapidge (Cambridge, Eng., 1995), 207; and M. R. James, *Two Ancient English Scholars: St Aldhelm and William of Malmesbury*, (Glasgow, 1931), 8–11.

of early western Christianity. M. L. W. Laistner observes that among the texts with which Aldhelm was acquainted were "some writings of Augustine and much of Jerome; the *Collationes* of Cassian; Gregory the Great and Isidore . . . and a considerable body of hagiographical literature," to mention just a few.[10] Aldhelm's own writings in turn quickly became school texts in England and in the Anglo-Saxon missions on the Continent and his verbose Latin style was studied and imitated by students up through the eleventh century.[11] The texts of his best-known work, the *opus geminatum* (twinned work), *De uirginitate*, survive in numerous manuscripts of both its prose and its metrical versions, attesting to their importance and popularity.[12] Though these works were apparently studied in the schools principally for their Latin style rather than their content, Aldhelm himself, in the "Prosa de uirginitate" especially, seems concerned to address a particular problem in the developing monasteries in his area of influence.

In the preface to his "Prosa de uirginitate," Aldhelm writes that several nuns appealed to him to compose for them a work in praise of virginity. Few scholars would argue anymore that Aldhelm merely exercised a common literary *topos* when he made these comments and dedicated the prose work to Hildelith and several other nuns by name.[13] Hildelith's identity has been accepted as that of the abbess of the double monastery of Barking Abbey during the later years of the seventh century when Aldhelm probably composed the work. The other women named by Aldhelm have customarily been thought to be other nuns under Hildelith at Barking, but Scott Gwara has recently challenged this view and argued that at least some of the other named dedicatees were abbesses of other double monasteries in Aldhelm's sphere of influence. If Gwara is correct, then Aldhelm's immediate audience for the "Prosa de uirginitate" may have been the communities of two or more double monasteries rather than just the community at Barking. The matter of audience takes on greater significance when Aldhelm

---

[10] M. L. W. Laistner, *Thought and Letters in Western Europe, AD 500 to 900*, rev. ed. (Ithaca, NY, 1957), 155.

[11] Scott Gwara, "Introduction," in Aldhelm, *Prosa de uirginitate cum glosa Latina atque Anglosaxonica*, ed. Scott Gwara, CCSL 124A (Turnholt, 2001), 70.

[12] Ibid.

[13] Stephanie Hollis, *Anglo-Saxon Women and the Church: Sharing a Common Fate* (Rochester, NY, 1992), 76. Hollis also speculates that Hildelith, the abbess of Barking, may have been formerly married (ibid., 80).

gives his reason for including comments on the vices in a work meant as a treatise in praise of virginity:

> But what compelled me to debate and discuss concerning the disgraceful roots of the eight sins ... was that certain people, elevated on the lofty pinnacle of virginity and raised up on the peaks of a chaste way of life ... believe that they have incomparably surpassed the renown of the others.[14]

Aldhelm apparently read between the lines of the letters these women had sent to him, thinking about them "with a certain natural curiosity about hidden things," and received the impression of virgins "pulling rank" in a spiritual sense over those women who had formerly been married before taking up a monastic life.[15] Uppermost in Aldhelm's mind, perhaps, was Cuthburg, the former wife of Aldfrith, king of Northumbria and sister of Ine, king of Wessex where Aldhelm's monastery was located. Sometime during Aldhelm's tenure as abbot of Malmesbury, Cuthburg founded Wimborne Abbey, which is specifically associated in a charter (albeit a spurious one) with Aldhelm by name.[16] This former queen has been associated with the Cuthburg named among the dedicatees of the "Prosa de uirginitate" by William of Malmesbury and scholars of Aldhelm's writings ever since.[17] While it is impossible to determine with certainty, the founding of Wimborne Abbey may have sparked the tension between virgins and the formerly married that Aldhelm describes here, since Wimborne was ruled by an

---

[14] Aldhelm, *Prose Works*, trans. Lapidge and Herren, 70; *Prosa de uirginitate*, 13, CCSL 124A:159–61: "Sed nos de flagitiosis.VIII. uitiorum radicibus, unde reliquorum perniciosa facinorum frutecta uelut spissa uirgultorum uimina lentis frondibus succrescunt, ea potissimum causa disceptare et disputare coegit, quod nonnulli edito uirginitatis fastigio sublimati et pudicae conuersationis arcibus exaltati secundum castitatis gradum acsi contemptibilem sibique longe disparem arbitrantes ceterorum praeconia se incomparabiliter transcendere confidunt illud quodammodo obliterantes et postergum ponentes: *omnis, qui se exaltat, humiliabitur, et qui se humiliat, exaltabitur.*" In the interests of space, I have omitted the translation of some of Aldhelm's clauses that merely rephrase or add color to the point he is making.

[15] Aldhelm, *Prose Works*, trans. Lapidge and Herren, 59; *Prosa de uirginitate*, 2, CCSL 124A:31: "naturali quadam ... latentium rerum curiositate." The passage has been discussed in Richard Newhauser, "Towards a History of Human Curiosity: A Prolegomenon to its Medieval Phase," *Deutsche Vierteljahrsschrift* 56 (1982): 568–69.

[16] William of Malmesbury, *The Deeds of the Bishops of England (Gesta Pontificum Anglorum)*, trans. David Preest (Rochester, NY, 2002), 258; idem, *Gesta pontificum Anglorum libri quinque*, 5.225, ed. N. E. S. A. Hamilton (London, 1870), 379.

[17] See Gwara, "Introduction," 48–50.

abbess who had entered monastic life after being married and divorced. While it was not uncommon for royal widows to enter the monastic life and found their own monasteries, the circumstances of Cuthburg's entry into the chaste life, divorce from a living husband, complicated the issue. Aldhelm's prose work upholds the degrees of chastity established by earlier Church fathers in terms of the honor and reward due to each degree: the highest grade is lifelong virginity; the second grade, chaste widowhood; and the third grade, marriage. But Aldhelm expands the second grade to include those who had divorced from their spouses in order to enter a monastic life. Aldhelm also observes that the second grade of chaste former spouses can surpass even the virgins in virtuous life:

> And yet—unfortunately—it usually occurs . . . that the station of the inferior life, advancing on all fronts little by little, takes the place of the superior grade as it languished tepidly; and . . . he who was counted last through the negligence of his past life, henceforth, kindled by the flame of divine love, is in first place, reminding (us) of the maxim in the Gospels, "Many sins are forgiven her because she hath loved much [literally: one who is forgiven much, loves much]." And he who had been merely a follower in pious resolve, rejecting the pleasures of the world with contempt like the scourings of filth and repressing the enticements of carnal delight, and having undertaken manfully the novitiate of a chaste way of life . . . becomes the leader through the diligence of his labor.[18]

This passage in Latin uses the masculine form of the relative pronoun *qui*, translated by Lapidge and Herren as "he who," because it refers to the antecedent *gradus*, which is a masculine noun. In fact, however, the *inferioris uitae gradus*, "the station of the inferior life" as it is rendered by Lapidge and Herren, can refer equally to either female or male members of that station. Thus, while the translators have correctly rendered the grammatical gender of the antecedent noun by translating "he who" for *qui*, Aldhelm's Latin can refer to either a woman or a man in the second grade of chastity, and the sense of the passage might be more

---

[18] Aldhelm, *Prose Works*, trans. Lapidge and Herren, 66–67; *Prosa de uirginitate*, 10, CCSL 124A:111–15: "Et tamen plerumque, pro dolor, immutatis ordinibus versa vice contingere solet, ut inferioris uitae gradus usquequaque paulatim proficiens superiorem tepide torpentem praeoccupet et . . . qui existimabatur praeteritae conuersationis negligentia posterior, deinceps diuinae caritatis flamma succensus existat anterior euangelicae reminiscens sententiae: *cui multum dimittitur, multum diligit*, et qui contempta mundi blandimenta uelut quisquiliarum peripsema respuens ac carnalis luxus lenocinia refutans in sancto proposito successor extiterat, sumpto uiriliter castae conuersationis tirocinio . . . cum sudoris industria efficiatur antecessor."

accurately rendered into modern English as "one who," or even "she who." The idea that Aldhelm was thinking of a female member of the second grade is strengthened by his allusion to Luke 7:47, which refers to a woman. His use of *uiriliter* (manfully) to describe the way a member of the second grade can undertake a novitiate into the monastic life need not limit the unspecified subject of this passage to a male monastic. This Latin term was used for both men and women in patristic and hagiographical writings to indicate those of both sexes whose minds were steadfast and constant in their commitment to chastity and the ascetical pursuit of perfection in Christ.[19] It is possible, then, that these words refer to Cuthburg and others like her, especially given Aldhelm's comments about someone from the second grade becoming a leader, since Cuthburg established her own monastery at Wimborne.

In fact, Aldhelm goes on to inveigh against "those of either sex who, inflated with the puffed up arrogance of pride, exult in the integrity of the flesh alone. . . . [They] are so much the less eager to devote themselves to moans of lamentation . . . inasmuch as they trust themselves to be deformed by no blemishes and stains, and fouled by no blackness of secular slag."[20] He bemoans the fact that the virgins were shipwrecking their lives of holiness because of their pride while the formerly married were surpassing them in holiness even though members of this second group had lost their bodily integrity. Of the lifelong virgins, however, he notes that "because they judge themselves to be chastely celibate and to be thoroughly free from all the dregs of filth, inflated with (over-) confidence in their virginity, they arrogantly swell up and in no way do they turn away the most cruel monster Pride, devourer of the other virtues, with the nose-ring of humility."[21]

---

[19] For a discussion of patristic use of *uir* and *uiriliter* in reference to women, see the section on Jerome in Chapter Two, "The Sins of the Fathers," in my dissertation, "Male and Female He Created Them: Ælfric's *Lives of Saints* and Patristic Theories of Gender," Ph.D. diss., Western Michigan Univ., 2003, 26–39.

[20] Aldhelm, *Prose Works*, trans. Lapidge and Herren, 67; *Prosa de uirginitate*, 10, CCSL 124A:115–19: "illis dumtaxat in utroque sexu . . . qui tumido elationis supercilio inflati de sola carnis integritate gloriantur, . . . tanto minus lamentorum fletibus incumbere gestiunt . . . quanto se nullis naeuorum maculis deformatos, nullo saecularis scoriae atramento foedatos fuisse confidunt."

[21] Aldhelm, *Prose Works*, trans. Lapidge and Herren, 67; *Prosa de uirginitate*, 10, CCSL 124A:121: "quod se caelibes castos et ab omni spurcitiae sentina funditus immunes arbitrentur, fiducia uirginitatis inflati arroganter intumescunt et nequaquam crudelissimam superbiae balenam, ceterarum virtutum deuoratricem, humilitatis cercilo declinant."

In his description of the trouble between the virgins and the formerly married, Aldhelm diagnoses the fundamental problem as arising from Pride, and this diagnosis provides a specific context for his comments on the principal vices.

This context seems to be the driving force for Aldhelm's reference to the Gregorian and Cassianic schemes of the vices. Commenting on the "Prosa de uirginitate," Morton Bloomfield notes that Aldhelm's depiction of the vices "shows the influence of Gregory and his concept that of Prudentius," and then adds in an endnote, "Cassianic influence can also be seen in his treatment of the Sins."[22] Indeed, Aldhelm presents the vices as an aggressive army and comments that "in the conflict of the eight principal vices, although Pride is placed last, yet like a fierce queen she is known to usurp for herself the authority of tyrannical power and the sway of government more so than the others,"[23] drawing upon Gregory's language in describing Pride and its relationship to the other vices in this passage from the *Moralia in Iob*:

> For of the tempting evils that fight against us in an invisible contest on behalf of Pride, who reigns over them, some go first in the manner of warlords, and others follow in the manner of troops.... For when Pride, herself queen of the vices, has fully possessed a conquered heart, she hands it over quickly to the seven principal vices, as if to some of her warlords, to destroy it.[24]

Looking at the *Institutes*, however, we find that Cassian uses this same kind of language and he probably influenced Gregory's depiction: "But when [Pride] seizes the unhappy mind and captures the citadel of the virtues set on high, like a most savage tyrant it lays waste and overturns the whole city from its foundations. It levels the once lofty

---

[22] Morton W. Bloomfield, *The Seven Deadly Sins: An Introduction to the History of a Religious Concept, with Special Reference to Medieval English Literature* ([East Lansing, MI], 1952; reprint, 1967), 78 and 361 n. 85.

[23] Aldhelm, *Prose Works*, trans. Lapidge and Herren, 67; *Prosa de uirginitate*, 11, CCSL 124A:121–23: "in conflictu octo principalium uitiorum, licet ultima ponatur, tamen quasi atrox regina tyrannicae potestatis imperium et dominandi monarchiam prae ceteris sibi usurpare denoscitur."

[24] Gregory the Great, *Moralia in Iob*, 31.45.87, ed. Marc Adriaen, CCSL 143B (Turnholt, 1985), 1611: "Temptantia quippe uitia, quae inuisibili contra nos proelio regnanti super se superbiae militant, alia more ducum praeeunt, alia more exercitus subsequuntur.... Ipsa namque uitiorum regina superbia cum deuictum plene cor ceperit, mox illud septem principalibus uitiis, quasi quibusdam suis ducibus deuastandum tradit." My translation, but cf. Gregory the Great, *Morals on the Book of Job*, trans. J. Bliss (Oxford, 1844–50), 3:489.

bulwarks of holiness to the ground of vice."[25] All three authors use the metaphor of pride as a conqueror and destroyer of the citadel of the virtuous soul. Aldhelm clearly uses Gregory's conception of Pride as a queen who exercises authority and rules over the other vices (a metaphor not found in Cassian's discussion of pride in the *Conferences*, although he uses the idea of pride as a tyrant in the *Institutes*). Yet, Aldhelm also specifically mentions pride's place in Cassian's order of the vices practically using Cassian's own words from the *Institutes*.[26] By blending the Gregorian and Cassianic descriptions of the effects of pride, Aldhelm uses the authority of the two earlier authors to validate the comments he makes in addressing issues of pride in his audience. Any reader of Aldhelm's work who looked up the passages on the vices in Gregory's *Moralia* or Cassian's *Institutes* and *Conferences* would find the same language Aldhelm used, and thus could find reinforcement and support for Aldhelm's characterization of pride.

Aldhelm seems to have adopted Gregory's language regarding the bestial nature of the vices and their armies when he urges his audience to:

> fight with muscular energy against the horrendous monster of Pride and at the same time against those seven wild beasts of the virulent vices, who with rabid molars and venomous bicuspids strive to mangle violently whoever is unarmed and despoiled of the breastplate of virginity and stripped of the shield of modesty.[27]

Aldhelm's language here shows his close familiarity with Gregory's comments from Book 31 of the *Moralia*, in which Gregory writes:

> The leaders, however, are well described as encouraging, the armies as howling...while they drag [the mind] to every madness, confuse it

---

[25] John Cassian, *The Institutes*, trans. Boniface Ramsey (New York, 2000), 256; *De institutis coenobiorum*, 12.3.2, ed. Jean-Claude Guy, SC 109 (Paris, 1965), 452–54: "Haec uero cum infelicem possederit mentem, ut quidam saeuissimus tyrannus sublimissima capta arce uirtutum uniuersam funditus ciuitatem diruit atque subuertit, excelsa quondam sanctitatis moenia uitiorum solo coaequans...." For the influence of Cassian on Gregory the Great's concept of the vices, see Carole Straw, "Gregory, Cassian, and the Cardinal Vices," in *In the Garden of Evil: The Vices and Culture in the Middle Ages*, ed. Richard Newhauser (Toronto, 2005), 35–58.

[26] Cassian, *De inst.*, 12.1, SC 109:450.

[27] Aldhelm, *Prose Works*, trans. Lapidge and Herren, 68; *Prosa de uirginitate*, 11, CCSL 124A:129: "contra horrendam superbiae bestiam simulque contra has uirulentorum septenas uitiorum biluas [sic], quai rabidis molaribus et uenenosis genuinis inermes quosque ac uirginitatis lorica spoliatos pudicitiaeque parma exutos atrociter discerpere nituntur, lacertosis uiribus dimicandum est."

with a sort of bestial shouting. . . . The howling army clearly follows [the exhortation by each one of the warlords among the vices] because the unhappy soul, once captured by the principal vices, while being over-thrown into madness by sins that have multiplied, is now destroyed with wild savageness.[28]

While Gregory maintains the allegorical context of his comments on a verse from Job by referring to the hordes of lesser vices as howling beasts, Cassian specifically calls pride a beast: "Therefore the athlete of Christ . . . must also and in every respect strive to destroy this most sav-age beast [of pride], since it devours all the virtues."[29] As he addresses the problem at hand, Aldhelm takes the middle ground, calling all of the concepts involved beasts: both the monstrous leader, pride, and the other seven vices commanded by pride.

There is no ambiguity in Aldhelm's position: Pride will rob the virgins in his audience of the hundred-fold reward for their total devotion to Christ in body and soul. Bodily integrity alone will not gain for them the holiness they seek, but they must root out this usurping queen of vices with humility or else they will have maintained their bodily virgin-ity in vain. But how is one supposed to discipline oneself to humility? Cassian's answer to this question provides the framework for Aldhelm's "Prosa de uirginitate" as a whole and provides the controlling idea that brings together the work's praise of virginity, examples from the lives of the saints, and instruction on the eight principal vices.

In book twelve of the *Institutes*, "The Spirit of Pride," Cassian instructs his readers on preconditions necessary for humility to flourish and the characteristics of humility towards one's brethren in the monastic com-munity. He asserts that, "Humility . . . can never be acquired without poverty."[30] Throughout the examples of both female and male saints' lives in the prose and metrical versions of the *De uirginitate*, Aldhelm uses

---

[28] Gregory the Great, *Moralia in Iob*, 31.45.90, CCSL 143B:1611: "Bene autem duces exhortari dicti sunt, exercitus ululare, . . . dum hanc ad omnem insaniam pertrahunt, quasi bestiali clamore confundunt. . . . Quam uidelicet exercitus ululans sequitur, quia infelix anima semel a principalibus uitiis capta, dum multiplicatis iniquitatibus in insaniam uertitur, ferali iam immanitate uastatur." My translation; cf. Gregory, *Morals*, trans. Bliss, 3:491.

[29] Cassian, *Institutes*, trans. Ramsey, 272–73; *De inst.*, 12.32, SC 109:498: "Quapropter athleta Christi, qui spiritalem agonem legitime certans a Domino desiderat coronari, hanc quoque ferocissimam bestiam ut deuoratricem cunctarum uirtutum omnimodis festinet extinguere."

[30] Cassian, *Institutes*, trans. Ramsey, 272; *De inst.*, 12.31, SC 109:496: "Humilitas uero nullatenus poterit absque nuditate conquiri."

hagiography to equate worldly wealth with marriage, and he encourages his audience(s) to shun both in pursuit of humility and purity for the sake of Christ.[31] He also castigates monastics of both sexes who dress opulently, a practice that Aldhelm associates with arrogance and vanity.[32] He clearly considered such attire to be evidence of pride and contrary to the cultivation of humility.

This issue of opulent clothing makes specific the general message of Aldhelm's rehearsal of the saints' lives, associating wealth and rich clothing with the worldly vanity that his readers should have rejected when they took up the humility of the monastic life. Aldhelm applies the point bluntly, thus bringing the association of humility with poverty into sharp focus and using that connection as part of his cure for the pride he senses in his audience. The controlling idea for Aldhelm's broad-ranging cure in the "Prosa de uirginitate" is apparently based on Cassian's main instruction on the cure of pride in the *Institutes*, which comes at the very end of Book 12 where he writes that one can overcome pride only by:

> keep[ing] ever in mind the sufferings of our Lord and of all the holy ones, consider[ing] that we are being tried with lighter pains because we are that much further removed from their deserts and their way of life, and realiz[ing] as well that in a short while we shall depart from this world and soon, having put a quick end to this life, be their companions. The contemplation of this is deadly not only to pride but to all the vices in general.[33]

This focus on contemplating the lives of holy ones as a cure for pride blended well with the emphasis on humility that formed a mainstay of patristic treatises on virginity. It also explains why Aldhelm made the saints' lives such a large part of his own work, though he did not limit his examples to the ascetics from Egypt and Syria. Having identified pride as a problem among the members of his audience, he applied

---

[31] See the section on Aldhelm from Chapter Three, "The Sins of the Sons," of my dissertation, "Male and Female He Created Them," 92–114.

[32] Aldhelm, *Prose Works*, trans. Lapidge and Herren, 124–26; *Prosa de uirginitate*, 55–56, CCSL 124A:715–25.

[33] Cassian, *Institutes*, trans. Ramsey, 273; *De inst.*, 12.33.1–2, SC 109:500: "si mente iugiter recolamus uel Domini nostri uel sanctorum omnium passiones, considerantes tanto leuioribus nos iniuriis adtemptari, quanto longius a meritis eorum et conuersatione distamus, pariter etiam cogitantes in breui nos de hoc saeculo migraturos eorumque nos celeri uitae huius fine mox futuros esse consortes. Peremptoria namque est haec contemplatio non solum superbiae, uerum etiam generaliter omnium uitiorum."

Cassian's recommended cure by making brief hagiographical accounts the centerpiece of both the prose and metrical versions of *De uirginitate*. The diverse nature of his audience explains why Aldhelm's catalog of saints includes both virgins and a widow, males and females, saints in spiritual marriages and saints whose sanctity and notable deeds came after the experience of carnal relations.

Aldhelm may have succeeded with the "Prosa de uirginitate" in rooting out the tension of pride between the virgins and the formerly married women in his audience, for when he later produced his metrical "Carmen de uirginitate," he not only declined to render his former rebuke into hexameters, but he also omitted all mention of Gregory's *Moralia*, giving instead a lively description of the eight vices as found in Cassian's fifth *Conference* with Abba Serapion. Although Aldhelm draws on the metaphor of a battle with the vices in his prose treatise, his treatment in the metrical version is much more graphic, calling to mind Prudentius's *Psychomachia*.[34] As Gernot Wieland observes, however, the connection to Prudentius is tenuous. Among other differences, Wieland notes that, "[o]nly one pair of vices and virtues have the same names in both Aldhelm and Prudentius, namely Ira and Patientia, and this . . . does not say too much about Prudentius' influence."[35] Nevertheless, Aldhelm's treatment of the conflict between the vices and their opposing virtues presents Cassian's descriptions of the sins that spring from each vice along with images reminiscent of Prudentius' work. Aldhelm depicts Pride as a ferocious warrior amassing an army:

> which brandishes weapons of sin at the warriors of Christ. With pompous deceit she aims to gather a band of followers, and strides ahead always accompanied by vile Disdain; and while in deceit she moves her feet through the sins of the world, her crested head shakes under dark clouds. . . . From that root is born a black and leafy bush . . . at first there is contempt of (one's) elders who teach (the) precepts, while pride of mind swells in a conceited breast; then the menace of envious hatred arises, which with swelling arrogance is wont to despise those who are equals and . . . to reign proud. For such death-bringing power thrives through envy. . . . Thence the mutterings of proud voices are born, as well as the

---

[34] Alternatively, Peter Godman sees Aldhelm's treatment of the eight principal vices in the metrical *De uirginitate* as a "poetic excursus" essentially unrelated to the rest of the metrical work or the prose version, in "The Anglo-Latin *Opus Geminatum*: From Aldhelm to Alcuin," *Medium Ævum* 50,2 (1981): 215–29, at 221.

[35] Gernot Wieland, "Aldhelm's *De Octo Vitiis Principalibus* and Prudentius' *Psychomachia*," *Medium Aevum* 55,1 (1986): 85–92, at 87–88.

sin of the heart which refuses to obey commands, and also the savage slander of the tongue which lacerates men.[36]

With one exception, all of Aldhelm's "leaves" produced from the root of pride appeared earlier and in the same order in Cassian's fifth *Conference*, where he noted that pride produces "contempt, envy, disobedience, blasphemy, murmuring, and slander."[37] The one exception is blasphemy. Aldhelm did not forget this sin, but rather illustrated the idea with the story of Lucifer, who proudly blasphemed by boasting that in his own strength he could be equal to God.[38] Aldhelm abandoned any attempt to try to blend in the Gregorian scheme of the sins that follow the vices, for Gregory's description of the characteristics of the vices varies too greatly from Cassian's. In Gregory's scheme, pride is the root of the seven vices of vainglory, envy, anger, *tristitia*, avarice, gluttony, and *luxuria* (rather than Cassian's *fornicatio*). While one might argue from Cassian that all of the vices originate in pride, Cassian himself still emphasizes the point that there are eight vices, not seven, and pride itself is one of the eight.[39] In addition, of the seven vices other than pride listed by both Gregory and Cassian, only three—avarice, anger,

---

[36] Aldhelm, *Poetic Works*, trans. Lapidge and Rosier, 162–63; "Carmen de uirginitate," 2703–07, 2710–18, 2727–29, in *Aldhelmi opera*, ed. Rudolf Ehwald (Munich, 1919; reprint, 1984), 463–64:

Militibus Christi torquentem pila piacli;
Quae glomerare studet ventos fraude maniplos
Et graditur semper fastu comitata maligno,
Dumque pedes pergit per mundi crimina fallax,
Sed cristata caput quassat sub nubibus atris;
. . . . . .
Nascitur atra frutex ex ista radice frondens
Et nemus umbrosum diro de semine surgit:
Primo contemptus procerum praecepta docentum,
Dum mentis typhus ventoso pectore turget;
Necnon invidiae pestis progignitur inde,
Quae solet aequales tumido contemnere fastu
Atque satellitibus spretis regnare superba.
Namque per invidiam letalia sceptra vigebant,
Dum praedo pellax et tetrae mortis amator
. . . . . .
Inde superbarum nasacuntur murmura vocum
Et crimen cordis dicto parere negantis
Ac lacerans homines trux detractatio linguae.

[37] John Cassian, *The Conferences*, trans. Boniface Ramsey, (New York, 1997), 198; *Collationes patrum*, 5.16, ed. E. Pichery, SC 42 (Paris, 1955), 209.

[38] Aldhelm, *Poetic Works*, trans. Lapidge and Rosier, 163; "Carmen de uirginitate," 2730–51, ed. Ehwald, 464.

[39] Cassian, *Institutes*, trans. Ramsey, 255; *De inst.*, 12.1, SC 109:450.

and vainglory—share the same characteristics. Gregory's vice of gluttony combines the characteristics of Cassian's vices of gluttony and
fornication, while Gregory's description of *tristitia* combines Cassian's
descriptors for *tristitia* and some of the descriptors for *acedia*. The other
traits of Cassian's *acedia* are then attributed by Gregory to *luxuria*, thus
eliminating *acedia* altogether. Gregory then makes envy one of the seven
vices, whereas Cassian lists envy as a sin that follows from pride. The
chart below shows how the two lists compare with each other:

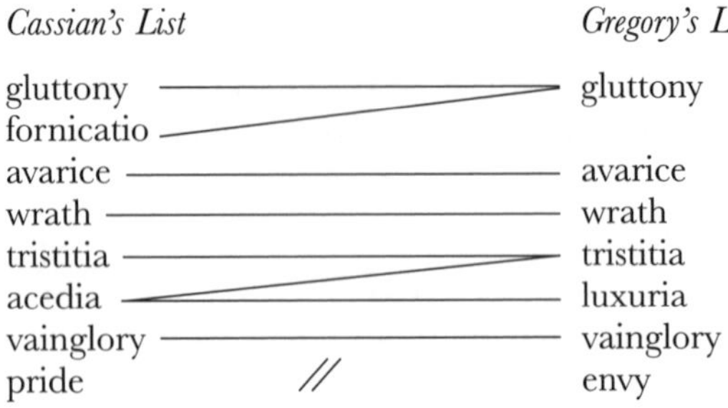

Cassian's List   *Gregory's List*

gluttony —————————— gluttony
fornicatio ——
avarice ———————————— avarice
wrath ——————————— wrath
tristitia ——————————— tristitia
acedia ———————————— luxuria
vainglory ———————————— vainglory
pride   //   envy

Figure 1: Relationships between characteristics of the vices in Cassian's
scheme and the vices in Gregory's.

As Aldhelm creates his elaborate description of the vices in the "Carmen
de uirginitate," he must chose which set of descriptions he will follow,
since Gregory clearly differed from Cassian both in the vices that made
up his list and the characteristic sins that grew out of each principal
vice. His choice is clear, for Aldhelm's scheme and his approach to
opposing and overcoming the vices is thoroughly Cassianic rather than
Gregorian. Aldhelm does not comment on his reasons for choosing
Cassian's scheme rather than Gregory's, but the simplest explanation
may be that he expected his readers to be more familiar with Cassian's
works because they were recommended reading according to the *Benedictine Rule*. Aldhelm appears to expect some if not all of his intended
audience to be familiar with Benedict's *Rule* when he writes in the
"Carmen de uirginitate" regarding Benedict that, "He was the first
to set forth the struggle of our life, the way in which the monasteries
might hold to a desired rule, and the way in which a holy man might
hasten . . . to the lofty heights of the heavens."[40] In light of such a com-

---

[40] Aldhelm, *Poetic Works*, trans. Lapidge and Rosier, 122; "Carmen de uirginitate,"
870–73, ed. Ehwald, 390:

ment, Aldhelm may have assumed that his audience, whether in one monastery or several, would be more likely to have access to and be familiar with the scheme of the principal vices presented in Cassian's writings since these works were recommended for regular reading as an encouragement to those in monastic life. Gregory's *Moralia*, on the other hand, might not have been readily available to many in his audience (especially if they were spread out across many monasteries) given the length of the work and the expense that would have been necessary for producing or obtaining a copy.[41]

The prose and metrical versions of *De uirginitate* thus illustrate for us the way in which one early Anglo-Saxon abbot applied Cassian's precepts concerning the eight principal vices, especially Cassian's teachings on pride, in order to correct a problem that he discerned in the letters and communications of several women dedicated to the communal life of monasticism and then to encourage these women (and perhaps a more general audience) in the pursuit of lives of virtue. Aldhelm did not try to browbeat his audience into an outward obedience that left the root of pride untouched. Rather, he attempted, as Cassian had advised, to encourage his audience to strive for the holiness and virtue of God and of the holy ones who had gone before them, to urge them to recognize the shoot of pride that was springing up among them and to assert themselves to overcome that vice with the virtue of humility. In doing so, Aldhelm provides us with an early example of how the eight principal vices were applied to address problems in an organized monastic community.

Primo qui statuit, nostrae certamine vitae
Qualiter optatam teneant coenubia normam
Quoque modo properat directo tramite sanctus
Ad supera scandens caelorum culmina cultor.

[41] Helmut Gneuss indicates that there is no complete text of the *Moralia* in the extant manuscripts from Anglo-Saxon England dating to the seventh or early eighth centuries. We have two fragments of the text and some glosses in three Northumbrian manuscripts, as well as one manuscript dated to the second quarter of the eighth century, possibly from Southern Mercia, that contains books 32–35 of the *Moralia*: Würzburg, Universitätsbibliothek MS. M.p.th.f.149a. Helmut Gneuss, *Handlist of Anglo-Saxon Manuscripts: A List of Manuscripts and Manuscript Fragments Written or Owned in England up to 1100*, (Tempe, 2001), 129, 132–33, and 146.

BIBLICAL LIARS AND
THIRTEENTH-CENTURY THEOLOGIANS

Dallas G. Denery II
Bowdoin College

Abstract: In *On Lying*, Augustine argued that every lie (regardless of the circumstance) is a sin. Writers of popular medieval religious handbooks explicitly accepted Augustine's pronouncements, as did scholastic theologians beginning with Peter Lombard in the twelfth century and continuing through Gabriel Biel in the fifteenth century. While recent work on medieval and early modern "sins of the tongue" treats this tradition in the clerical and scholastic discourse of lying as a form of social control, there is something else at stake in the subtle tensions and muted controversies that rest just beneath the surface of this seemingly inert debate. Can we lie with our actions or only with our words? What is the difference between a liar and a hypocrite? In the final analysis, these are questions about the nature of language, the relation between our inner and outer selves and about our duty to the world around us.

According to William Peraldus, the thirteenth-century Dominican pastoral writer, there are any number of reasons why a person ought to detest lies. Towards the very end of his extremely popular treatise, *Summa de vitiis* (written in conjunction with the popular, if not as widely-transmitted, *Summa de virtutibus*), in a section given over to an analysis of the "sins of the tongue," Peraldus lists at least twelve reasons. Among other things, he notes that lies are diabolical. It was the devil himself who spoke the first lie when he assured Eve that she would not die if she ate the apple and we, in turn, become sons of the devil when we follow this fatal example. Lies are like a poison, a deadly venom, and to this day snakes are poisonous precisely because it was in the form of a serpent that the devil deceived Eve. But the poison of lies is worse than any snakebite. They do not kill the body, but the soul itself. And, so it goes, liars are counterfeiters and thieves exchanging the valuable coin of truth for worthless fakes, they are traitors who do great harm not only to themselves, but to the church and to society at large.[1]

---

[1] William Peraldus, *Summae virtutum ac vitiorum* (Antwerp, 1571), 2:266v–67v.

Peraldus' opening salvo against the sin of lying consists of a barrage of images designed to reveal the deadly, if often unrecognized, reality of this common vice. And while many of the arguments and images he employs to lead his readers (and listeners) to a detestation of this sin were really little more than the typical stock and trade that pastoral writers had offered up for centuries to the laity, there is something in the sheer volume, the excess and overflow of examples and Biblical quotations, that gives a hint of Peraldus' originality and helps to explain the *Summa de vitiis'* enduring popularity.[2] For all that, having concluded his list of reasons to detest lies with his twelfth one ("He who falls into this sin deeply wounds himself"), Peraldus then proceeds to do something less original, though no less interesting. "Next I will describe the various categories of lies of which there are many," he writes, and what follows is a more or less straightforward recitation of what any informed reader would have immediately recognized to be the standard division of this sin into eight species and three general types.[3] Peraldus claims to take this list from Augustine and perhaps he did. He could have taken it from practically anyone who had written on the topic of lies and deception from at least as early as the twelfth century when Peter Lombard included it as the centerpiece of his analysis of lying, which itself was part of his more general analysis of the ten commandments in the third book of his *Sentences*.[4] After Peter, no aspiring theologian, from the Franciscan Alexander of Hales in the early thirteenth-century through the Dominican Gabriel Biel in the fifteenth century failed to rehearse and endorse Augustine's division of this sin, not to mention his more general conclusion that we should never lie, that every lie (no matter what the circumstance) is a sin. Augustine's authority held sway over pastoral writers as well. Peraldus

---

[2] Edwin D. Craun, *Lies, Slander, and Obscenity in Medieval English Literature: Pastoral Rhetoric and the Deviant Speaker* (Cambridge, Eng., 1997), 14–16, discusses Peraldus' originality in elevating "the sins of the tongue" to the level of a capital sin. On Peraldus' influence and popularity, see Antoine Dondaine, "Guillaume Peyraut: Vie et oeuvres," *Archivum Fratrum Predicatorum* 18 (1948): 162–236; Richard Newhauser, *The Treatise on Vices and Virtues in Latin and the Vernacular* (Turnhout, 1993), 127–30; and Siegfried Wenzel, "The Continuing Life of William Peraldus's 'Summa vitiorum,'" in *Ad litteram: Authoritative Texts and Their Medieval Readers*, ed. Mark D. Jordan and Kent Emery, Jr. (Notre Dame, IN and London, 1992), 135–63. For the most complete analysis of the sudden thirteenth-century flurry of interest in the "sins of the tongue" see Carla Casagrande and Silvana Vecchio, *Les péchés de la langue: discipline et éthique de la parole dans la culture médiévale*, trans. Philippe Baillet (Paris, 1991).

[3] Peraldus, *Summae virtutum ac vitiorum*, 2:267v.

[4] Peter Lombard, *Sententiae in IV libris distinctae*, 3.38.1–2 (Grottaferrata, 1981), 2:213–15.

is only one in a long list of writers, including Angelus of Clavasi, both the real and the pseudo-Vincent of Beauvais, and John Bromyard, to include Augustine's opinions as definitive. Given all this, it is not that surprising that when, in the early seventeenth century, the Englishman John Downame took up the cause in his aptly named essay, *A Treatise Against Lying*, confirmed anti-papist though he was, he happily relied again and again on Augustine's enduring treatise, *Against Lies*, as well as on Thomas Aquinas' very Augustinian take on the matter.[5]

If lying has a history, it is a history that at first glance seems to have slowed to a crawl under the weight of Augustine's authority. Scholastic debates and pastoral accounts of lying all too often seem like little more than rote rehearsals of unquestionable facts. While recent work on medieval and early modern "sins of the tongue" treats this particular strain of Augustinian-influenced pastoral and scholastic discourse as a form of social control, as a clerical attempt to extend its moral and disciplinary authority over the day-to-day life of the laity, there seems to be something else at stake in the subtle tensions and muted controversies that rest just beneath the surface of this only apparently inert debate.[6] Indeed, the very appearance of inertia in this case is important, suggesting that the need to repeat, to reaffirm, and to retrench in support of certain elements of these inherited ideas was of central importance to at least one significant line of medieval and early modern religious and intellectual thought. The very questions these writers raised when considering the sin of lying already suggest as much. Why must every lie be a sin? Can we lie with our actions or only with our words? Can a lie ever be justified? In the final analysis, these are questions about the very nature and function of language, about the relation between our inner and outer selves and about our duty to God, to ourselves, and to those around us. Augustine may well have framed the terms in which most thirteenth-century religious writers thought and argued about these questions, but within that framework they explored and staked out a variety of positions, and in so doing altered Augustine's ideas even as they reaffirmed his most fundamental definitions.[7]

---

[5] John Downame, *A Treatise Against Lying* (London 1636), 15, sets the tone for the rest of the work when he begins his second chapter, "*Wherein it is shewed what a Lye is*" with Augustine's definition of a lie: "Saint *Augustine* briefely defineth it thus; A Lye is a false signification with a will to deceive."

[6] Craun, *Lies, Slander and Obscenity*, 25 and Casagrande and Vecchio, *Les péchés de la langue*, 29.

[7] In a recent essay, Marcia Colish, "Rethinking Lying in the Twelfth Century," in *Virtue and Ethics in the Twelfth Century*, ed. István P. Bejczy and Richard G. Newhauser

According to Augustine every lie is a sin. Whether you tell a lie to save someone's life or to steal his property, it makes no difference. Some liars incur more guilt because of the lies they tell, some less, but no liar is guiltless. Following Augustine, nearly every writer served up an eight-fold division of the species of lies based on their culpability. The worst were malicious lies, lies designed to harm someone. The very worst of these were lies against God and the faith. Next came lies that harmed someone and helped no one, followed closely by lies that harmed one person while helping someone else. A fourth species consisted in lies told simply for the love of lying (and this type, Augustine adds, "is a pure lie"). There are even lies that are told simply to please others. Rounding out the list were a variety of beneficial lies, lies that harm no one and were told to help someone in need. These could be lies that helped a person protect his possessions or his physical well-being. Finally, there was the beneficial lie told to protect another's virtue, such as lies told to prevent a man from being raped.[8]

What bound together these various divisions, at least in Augustine's mind, was that in each case the liar had a will to deceive someone, be it for harmful or charitable reasons. A person lies, Augustine writes, "who has one thing in his mind but expresses something else with words or any other sort of indication." In other words, the liar's intention fundamentally (though not exclusively) determines the quality of his act.[9] The objective truth or falsity of the statement matters less than the speaker's intention. "A lie," Augustine will argue, and this is the defini-

---

(Leiden, 2005), 155–73, demonstrates that the twelfth century must not be viewed as "an unadulterated *aetas Augustiniana*" when it comes to attitudes about lying. Augustine's opinions were influential, but not all determining. For an outline of this debate among the Church Fathers, see Boniface Ramsey, "Two Traditions on Lying and Deception in the Ancient Church," *The Thomist* 49 (1985): 504–33. Thirteenth-century theologians knew that other Church fathers, like Ambrose, had suggested that some lies were acceptable. Regardless, they tended to condemn these non-Augustinian positions and instead explored the parameters of acceptable speech within Augustinian limits. For one notable exception which falls outside the scope of this paper, see Albert the Great's *Super Ethica*, Book IV, lecture XIV, in *Opera omnia*, vol. 14, ed. W. Kübel (Münster, 1968), 288, where, borrowing from an anonymous Greek commentary on Aristotle's *Ethics*, Albert introduces a distinction between civil and theological virtue into the analysis of mendacity: "Sed virtus civilis ordinatur ad boum finitum, quia ad consistentiam civilitatis, et ideo potest commodum vel damnum in altera parte praeponderare, ut scilicet utendum sit quandoque civiliter mendacio, ut evitetur aliquid per quod magis civilitas periclitetur."

[8] Augustine, *De mendacio*, 14.25, ed. Josephus Zycha, CSEL 41 (Vienna, 1900), 444–46.

[9] Augustine, *De mendacio*, 3.3, CSEL 41:414–16, and especially 4.4, CSEL 41:417.

tion that John Downame still repeated as definitive in the seventeenth century, "is a false signification made with a will to deceive."[10] To prove his point, Augustine works through a variety of complex scenarios in which the liar knowingly states a factual untruth or states the truth (while thinking it is false), in which the liar states a falsehood precisely because he suspects the listener will not believe him, or in which the liar speaks the truth because he knows the listener will not believe him. At the end of these circuitous analyses, whose moral valences are subtle and difficult to work through at best, Augustine for all intents and purposes throws up his hands and simply concludes that it is safest to always speak the truth: "For there is no need to be afraid of any of those definitions when the mind has a good conscience as it utters what it either knows, or opines, or believes to be true, and has no wish to make anything believed but what it utters."[11] Should unjust killers knock on the door, he holds up the model of the Bishop Firmus who underwent torture, proudly proclaiming to agents of the pagan Roman emperor that he could neither lie about nor betray the whereabouts of the man they sought. For Augustine, the results of Firmus' actions, however hard for the rest of us to emulate, proved their own value. Having withstood torture, he was brought before the emperor who so admired his conduct that, without any difficulty, Firmus obtained the fugitive's pardon.[12]

There was something deeper and much more fundamental organizing Augustine's thought about lying, something that went well beyond good results at the end of a long, painful day. The very structure of language, the very being of words, required that they be used truthfully to represent our innermost thoughts. What is of central importance here, what would be of central importance to many medieval theologians and pastoral writers, is the idea that the mental word precedes and has precedence over the spoken word. Verbal signs signify mental concepts, they exist for the sake of correctly expressing our inner states and ideas to others.[13] "There is no reason for us to signify something,"

---

[10] Augustine, *Contra mendacium*, 12.26, ed. Josephus Zycha, CSEL 41 (Vienna, 1900), 507: "Mendacium est quippe falsa significatio cum voluntate fallendi."

[11] Augustine, *De mendacio*, 4.4, CSEL 41:419: "Nulla enim definitionum illarum timenda est, cum bene sibi conscius est animus hoc se enuntiare quod uerum esse aut nouit aut opinatur aut credit, neque uelle aliquid nisi quod enuntiat persuadere." He reaches the same conclusion after a similar analysis of scenarios at 13.22, CSEL 41:441–42.

[12] Augustine, *De mendacio*, 13.23, CSEL 41:442.

[13] Augustine, *De trinitate libri xv*, 15.10–11, ed. W. J. Mountain and Fr. Glorie, CCSL

Augustine writes in *On Christian Doctrine*, "that is, to give a sign, except to express and transmit to another's mind what is in the mind of the person who gives the sign."[14] While Augustine derived the philosophical basis for this conception of language from the Stoics, much of his theory of signs and language is tied up in a Christology of the word, in which the word becomes flesh, in which the word saves, and in which the Bible is the expression of Christian truth. Within this context any lie constitutes not merely a misuse of language, but a rejection of the saving power of the word, a rejection of truth and, even, of God.[15]

Augustine faced one great stumbling block to all this. There are passages in the Bible in which it seems that lies are told and told well, that is, told without guilt and without sin. There are, for example, the Hebrew midwives who, when Pharaoh asked why they had not killed every male child as soon as it was born, replied, "Because the Hebrew women are not like the Egyptian women; for they are vigorous and give birth before the midwife comes for them." Jacob, following his mother's advice, pretends to be his brother Esau and obtains his blind father Isaac's benediction. In this case Jacob goes so far as to wear goat skin so that should his father touch him, he will feel like his (apparently very) hairy brother. Abraham at one point announces that his wife Sara is his sister. There are even problematic moments in the Gospels. For example, following his resurrection, Jesus pretends to walk further than he really intends.[16] Augustine worries repeatedly over the possible consequences of lowering his absolute standard and admitting the acceptability of certain sorts of lies. "He who says that there are some just lies," Augustine writes in *Against Lies*, "must be regarded as saying

---

50A (Turnhout, 1968), 483–90. See also Paul Vincent Spade, "The Semantics of Terms," in *The Cambridge History of Later Medieval Philosophy*, ed. Norman Kretzman et al. (Cambridge, Eng., 1982), 188–90. For Augustine's Stoic inheritance, see Marcia Colish, "The Stoic Theory of Verbal Signification and the Problem of Lies and False Statements from Antiquity to St. Anselm," in *Archéologie du signe*, ed. Lucie Brind'Amour and Eugene Vance (Toronto, 1982), 17–43.

[14] Augustine, *De doctrina christiana*, 2.2.3, ed. and trans. R. P. H. Green (Oxford, 1995), 56–59. See also R. A. Markus, "St. Augustine on Signs," *Phronesis* 2 (1960): 70–76.

[15] Marcia Colish, "The Stoic Theory of Verbal Signification," 30–31. Colish is quite good in this article at pointing out the circumstances that inflect Augustine's various treatments of lying. On Augustine's sign theory and incarnation specifically, see Mark Jordan, "Words and Word: Incarnation and Signification in Augustine's *De doctrina Christiana*," *Augustinian Studies* 11 (1980): 177–96.

[16] The story about the midwives appears at Exod 1:19, Jacob's claim to be Esau at Gen 27:1–40, Abraham's assertion that Sarah is his sister at Gen 20:2, and Jesus' long walk at Luke 24:28.

nothing else than that there are some just sins and, consequently, that some things which are unjust are just."[17] Not only does such a standard result in unacceptable logical and moral paradoxes, it also introduces a slew of practical problems. If some lies are acceptable, then how would we ever know when to believe a person's statements and when not to? More importantly, how could we be sure that any given passage from the Bible itself had been asserted as truth? On what basis could adjudication be made to determine whether on this occasion, these words, in this statement, were being offered sincerely or duplicitously, as models of holy behavior to emulate or sacrilege to condemn?[18]

Faced with these challenges, Augustine deploys his prohibition against lying as the basis for something like a nascent literary theory and hermeneutic for the Bible. Since God cannot lie and every lie is a sin, there can be no justifiable lies in the Bible. In all these cases of apparent Biblical deception, Augustine will therefore find it necessary to argue that either the alleged lie is no lie at all or that, if it clearly is a lie, that the lie itself is not approved, not held up as a model for behavior. In the case of the midwives, for example, God rewarded them not for lying, but for saving the lives of the Hebrew babies. Augustine suggests that even their ignorance, their acculturation into the ways of the Egyptians, not to mention the impossibility before the dispensation of Christ of their having clearly known the ethical imperative of truth-telling, all served as mitigating factors in God's eyes.[19]

By contrast with this clear case of Biblical lying, Augustine adopts a variety of different strategies to remove the taint of falsehood from other alleged cases of Scriptural untruthfulness. Considering Abraham, Augustine distinguishes concealing the truth from lying. Abraham speaks the truth because he and Sara share the same father (although not the same mother); he simply "conceals something of the truth." Extending this line of thought, Augustine writes, "It is not a lie when truth is passed over in silence, but when falsehood is brought forth in speech."[20]

---

[17] Augustine, *Contra mendacium*, 15.31, CSEL 41:511: "Nihil autem judicandus est dicere, qui dicit aliqua justa esse mendacia, nisi aliqua justa esse peccata, ac per hoc aliqua justa esse, quae injusta sunt."

[18] Augustine, *De mendacio*, 8.11, CSEL 41:429–30, and *Contra mendacium*, 18.37, CSEL 41:520–22.

[19] Augustine, *Contra mendacium*, 15.32–33, CSEL 41:512–14.

[20] Augustine, *Contra mendacium*, 10.23, CSEL 41:499: "Aliquid ergo veri tacuit, non falsi aliquid dixit.... Non est ergo mendacium, cum silendo absconditur verum, sed cum loquendo promitur falsum."

Augustine's analysis of silence is anything but thorough, and certainly not clear. Later in the same work, he considers whether, if asked, we ought to tell a gravely ill man that his son is dead, information that we know will precipitate the man's own death. Do we lie and tell him that we don't know or that his son is alive? Do we tell him the truth or do we remain silent? A similar example occurs in *On Lying*. Imagine we are asked if someone we know is hiding in a certain place, in our house (and Augustine assumes in this example that we do, in fact, know). How do we respond? With silence, with a lie, or with some variety of truthful statement? In both these cases, Augustine rejects silence not because it is tantamount to lying, but because *in this case* it is not a particularly efficacious speech act. If we fail to answer his question, the dying man will know exactly what has happened, will know that his son has died.[21] Likewise, our poor fugitive's pursuers will interpret our silence as a tacit acknowledgment that he is hiding in our house. In fact, in this last case Augustine rejects even a non-mendacious response like "I will not answer your question," for precisely the same reasons. They will interpret our refusal as proof that he is in the house. Better in this case proudly to announce, "I know where he is and I will never disclose it," not because it is the only truthful response, but simply because it is the truthful response that has the best chance of securing the fugitive's safety.[22]

Jacob's apparent lie presents a much tougher case, but one that Augustine resolves by stressing, again, the dangers of assuming there are acceptable lies in the Bible. The very possibility of reading parts of Scripture allegorically, as mysteries or figures, depends upon this prohibition. "If we call it a lie," writes Augustine, "then all parables and figures for signifying anything which are not to be taken literally, but in which one thing must be understood for another, will be called lies."[23] In other words, the presence of an apparent lie or deceptive act

---

[21] Augustine analyzes the case of the sick man and his dead son at *Contra mendacium*, 18.36, CSEL 41:519–20.

[22] Augustine, *De mendacio*, 13.24, CSEL 41:443–44, makes it clear that he contrasts both the silent and the stated refusal to answer with any sort of mendacious response: "Ita per nostram uel taciturnitatem uel talia uerba homo proditur, ut intret qui quaerit, si potestatem habent inuenit eum: qui tamen ab eius inuentione mendacio nostro posset auerti." Contrast this reading with Marcia Colish, "St. Augustine's Rhetoric of Silence Revisited," *Augustinian Studies*, 9 (1978): 16–18, who rightly stresses the importance of specific circumstances in determining the meaning of silence, but wrongly reads Augustine as asserting that silence constitutes a lie in these instances.

[23] Augustine, *Contra mendacium*, 10.24, CSEL 41:499: "Quae si mendacia dixerimus,

in the Bible, one that is neither condemned, nor shown not to be a lie at all (as in Abraham's case), provides something like the justification, even the need, to engage in a figurative reinterpretation of the act that will render it truthful. As Augustine puts it in *On Lying*, the prophets of the Old Testament "did and said all that is related about them in a prophetic manner."[24] While it would certainly seem as if Jacob lied to his father when he announced, "I am Esau thy firstborn" and deceived him when he extended his goatskin-covered hand, Augustine will claim that Jacob had no intention of deceiving Isaac. Here it is a matter of relocating Jacob's words and deeds within a broader context, not as a response to his father's question, a question posed at a specific time and at a specific place, but rather in terms of what Jacob intended to signify, the transference of the elder brother's primacy and inheritance to the younger, of the future transference of God's covenant from the Jews to the Christians.[25] Augustine attempts to reel in the potential for interpretive excess when he contends that what is presented as a mystery in one place in Scripture must be presented clearly and openly in another—the Bible as a whole forms the proper context for interpreting such speech acts.[26] And yet, this strategy reveals a deeper problem that Augustine seems to recognize but ignores. How do such prophetic cases from the Bible relate to ordinary, non-Biblical, non-prophetic acts of communication in which, given the proximate causes and contexts, not to mention the reasonable expectations of the other participants, such statements and actions could plausibly be thought to be mendacious?

These interpretive tensions, underplayed and passed over as they were in Augustine's own writings, provided thirteenth-century scholastic and pastoral authors the room to proclaim their allegiance to Augustine while quietly reshaping his actual position. Just as important to this process was the very nature of scholastic academic practice, dependant as it was on authorities, while simultaneously governed by the method of the *quaestio*, in which the topic under consideration was broken down and analyzed as a series of discrete questions or problem points. In response to each

---

omnes etiam parabolae ac figurae significandarum quarumque rerum, quae non ad proprietatem accipiendae sunt, sed in eis aliud ex alio est intelligendum, dicentur esse mendacia...."

[24] Augustine, *De mendacio*, 5.7, CSEL 41:421: "Unde credendum est illos homines, qui propheticis temporibus digni auctoritate fuisse commemorantur, omnia, quae scripta sunt de illis, prophetice gessisse atque dixisse."

[25] Augustine, *Contra mendacium*, 10.24, CSEL 41:501–2.

[26] Augustine, *Contra mendacium*, 10.24, CSEL 41:500–1.

question, the author would present a series of authorities in support
of, as well as against, the question. He would then navigate through
these varied positions as he sought to give his own response, a response
ever more nuanced than those of his predecessors.[27] If Augustine could,
after lengthy and convoluted analysis, simply adopt the principle that it
is safest not to lie at all rather than to risk relying on flawed reasoning,
scholastic writers had no such option. Augustine, of course, was writing in response to specific questions, arising out of specific real world
contexts and specific, not to mention, useful responses were expected.
Scholastic writers were no less concerned with the world around them
and, for all their abstract reasoning and technical terminology, scholastic
theology must always be understood as a reflection of and a response
to its contemporary social, cultural, and religious world. Nevertheless,
the immediate context that shaped scholastic discourse was the medieval
university itself and in that setting, detail was everything. Analysis, not
synthesis, was the order of the day and there was more than enough
slippage in Augustine's own thought to create the possibility for original
analysis, while still claiming allegiance to Augustine's central ideas.[28]

Not surprisingly, those very same Biblical examples of apparent deception that had exercised Augustine's attention provided a starting point
for many scholastic elaborations on Augustine's ideas. Sometimes these
elaborations were implicit, perhaps even unintended. When, in the late
1260s, the Dominican theologian Thomas Aquinas asks whether every
lie is a sin, his immediate response is yes, and yes for very Augustinian
reasons having to do with the nature and function of language itself.
"Words by their very nature," he writes, "being signs of thought, it is
contrary to their nature and out of order for anyone to convey in words
something other than what he thinks."[29] He then considers those classic
cases of apparent Biblical deception, the Hebrew midwives, Abraham
and Sarah, Jacob and Isaac, citing and agreeing with Augustine's answer

---

[27] On the method of the *quaestio*, see Marie Dominique Chenu, *Toward Understanding Saint Thomas*, trans. and corrected by A. M. Landry and D. Hughes (Chicago, 1964), 79–96.

[28] Edward Grant, *The Foundations of Modern Science in the Middle Ages* (Cambridge, Eng., 1996), 127–31, makes this same point about the scholastic reception of Aristotle. The contrast between "analysis" and "synthesis" is his.

[29] Thomas Aquinas, *Summa theologiae*, 2a 2ae, quaest. 110, art. 3, response, in *Opera omnia iussu impensaque Leonis XIII P. M. edita* (Rome, 1897), 9:425: "Mendacium autem est malum ex genere. Est enim actus cadens super indebitam materiam: cum enim voces sint signa naturaliter intellectum, innaturale est et indebitam quod aliquis voce significet id quod non habet in mente."

in each case. In the case of Abraham, Thomas notes the difference between "hiding the truth" and telling a lie, suggesting that Abraham did the former, not the latter. A little later in the same set of responses, however, Thomas pushes this line of thought a bit further when he notes that while "it is unlawful for anyone to lie in order to rescue another, no matter what the peril, one may, however, prudently mask the truth, as Augustine explains."[30] Now, it is not at all clear that this is what Augustine explained, or at least had intended his readers to think had been explained. Perhaps Abraham's claim that Sarah was his sister required this sort of justification in order to render it truthful, but when Augustine turned to the sorts of examples he expected his readers to follow (and which Thomas' use of the word "peril" here would imply he had in mind—when a well-told lie or dissimulation might save a hidden fugitive from unjust pursuers), Augustine's actual advice, as we saw, was anything but one of coy dissimulation or silence. In Thomas' hands, however, that is precisely the valence that Augustine's advice has assumed.

This weakening of Augustine's standards, however muted in Thomas' writings, becomes more evident in a line of thought that developed among certain Franciscan writers. Considering Jacob's claim to be his brother, Alexander of Hales, writing in the 1230s, considers a problem that Augustine himself had noticed, only to more or less pass over it, when he notes that it might well be objected that Jacob really had intended to persuade his father that he was Esau. Alexander meets the objection, for all intents and purposes, by accepting it. "It ought to be said," he writes, "that given the circumstances [*occasionaliter*], Jacob may have intended this, but principally he intended to claim for himself his due benediction; his statement was therefore simply true. . . ."[31] In other

---

[30] Thomas Aquinas, *Summa theol.*, 2a 2ae, quaest. 110, art. 3, ad 4, in *Opera omnia*, 9:425: "Et ideo non est licitum mendacium dicere ad hoc quod aliquis alium a quocumque periculo liberet. Licet tamen veritatem occultare prudenter sub aliqua dissimulatione: ut Augustinus dicit, *contra Mendacium.*" Pedro Zagorin, *Ways of Lying: Dissimulation, Persecution and Conformity in Early Modern Europe* (Cambridge, MA, 1990), 28–31, makes a similar observation about Thomas, but interprets it within a larger history culminating in debates about mental reservation and Catholic-Protestant persecution.
[31] Alexander of Hales, *Summa theologica*, Pars II, inquisitio III, tractatus II, sect. I, quaestio II, titulus VIII, caput VI (Quaracchi, 1924–79), 4:582A–B: "Quod ergo obicit quod 'intendebat persuadere quod esset Esau personaliter', dicendum quod, etsi intendebat facere aliquid, quo facto Isaac crederet ipsum esse Esau, occasionaliter intendebat hoc; nam principaliter intendebat benedictionem sibi debitam vendicare; verbum vero simpliciter verum erat, quia allegorice et transumptive erat enuntiatum."

words, Alexander invokes something like a hierarchy of intentions. Jacob primarily intended his words and actions to signify at the allegorical or figurative level. In order to accomplish this allegorical signification, however, it was necessary, given the specific circumstances in which he found himself, for Jacob to speak and act in ways which would deceive his father, or any other normal interlocutor for that matter. Whereas Augustine considered only the speaker's (i.e., Jacob's) intention as crucial for determining the exclusive contexts within which to determine the truth or falsity of his statements, Alexander recognizes that the actual communicative context in which Jacob spoke has its own standards against which Jacob's intentions must be understood and measured. According to these standards, his words and deeds cannot but be understood as somewhat deceptive.

Alexander's willingness to complicate Jacob's speech act, to recognize the multiple interpretive contexts it inhabited and intentions it contained, combined with his very Augustinian stance against lying, no doubt played a part in his distinction between words and deeds. Repeating and affirming Augustine's definition that a lie is a false statement made with the intention of deceiving someone, Alexander adds that this definition does not strictly apply to deeds. Unlike words, actions were not instituted for the sole purpose of communication, for revealing to others what is in our minds, and as a result there is some leeway in how we can use actions to communicate.[32] A version of this distinction was already present in Augustine and Thomas picked up on it when he analyzed the relation between words and deeds. "As Augustine says," writes Thomas, "among all signs words occupy first place. In the saying, then, that lying is a false meaning in words, by 'words' every sort of

---

The jury is still out on the complete authenticity of this treatise and the extent to which it contains redactions and interpolations from Alexander's students, especially Jean de la Rochelle. On the treatise's authorship and its continuing importance as a marker of mid thirteenth-century Franciscan theology, see Casagrande and Vecchio, *Les péchés de la langue*, 143–44. For convenience, I will refer only to Alexander as the author.

[32] Alexander of Hales, *Summa theol.*, Inq. III, tractatus III, sect. II, quaes. II, caput I (3:402): "Ad primo autem obiectum dicendum est quod mendacium non proprie dicitur in factis, licet sit ibi simulatio. Verbum enim proprie ordinatur ad significandum, mendacium autem dicitur a dictione mentis; quia ergo mens dicit per verbum, ideo recte dicitur mendacium 'falsa vocis significatio.'" Alexander expands on this later, *Summa theol.*, Pars II, inquisitio III (4:581B): "In opere potest simulari facto quod non est; ergo et sermone potest simulari quod non est—dicendum quod non sequitur. Et ratio est, quia factum non est institutum ad significationem mentis conceptum, sermo autem ad hoc institutus est ut sit nuntius mentis et interpres."

sign is meant. Hence, were one to intend to convey something false by nodding, one would not be innocent of lying."[33] Despite this apparent strengthening of the relation between words and actions, Thomas later adds, again following Augustine, that "to pretend is not always to lie."[34] Alexander would not have disagreed with any of this, but his analysis of the problem is more subtle than Thomas'.

Alexander contends that there are three categories of praiseworthy simulations, that is, types of actions in which a person, without incurring guilt, without lying, can pretend to be someone he is not or pretend to do something he does not intend to do. Citing the usual array of Biblical examples, he defines these as prudent, instructive, and signifying or figurative deceptions. Jehu, for example, engaged in prudent deception when he pretended to be a member of the cult of Baal so that he could kill their priests.[35] Jesus, by contrast, engaged in instructive deception when he pretended not to stop walking when he and his disciples had reached the village that was their destination. He was teaching them about the importance of deeds of mercy and hospitality. Finally, when he donned goatskin and stated, "I am Esau your firstborn," Jacob did not lie so much as engage in a figurative deception. In each case, the action is laudable because of the overarching intention and goal, to instruct or to signify a spiritual truth.[36] Regardless, the immediate action with its potentially deceptive aspects remains. Alexander says little more about this, but at least in the case of Jacob, it seems as if the higher figurative ends justify the potentially unworthy means, especially when

---

[33] Thomas Aquinas, *Summa theol.*, 2a 2ae, quaest. 110, art. 1, ad 2, in *Opera omnia*, 9:422: "...sicut Augustinus dicit...voces praecipuum locum tenent inter alia signa. Et ideo cum dicitur quod mendacium est *falsa vocis significatio*, nomine *vocis* intelligitur omne signum. Unde ille qui aliquod falsum nutibus significare intenderet, non esset a mendacio immunis."

[34] Thomas Aquinas, *Summa theol.*, 2a 2ae, quaest. 111, art. 1, ad 1, in *Opera omnia*, 9:429: "Ad primum ergo dicendum sicut Augustinus dicit, in libro de *Quaest. Evang.*, *non omne quod fingimus mendacium est.*"

[35] This interpretation would prove controversial; both Thomas Aquinas and John Duns Scotus would reject it.

[36] Summarizing this lengthy section, Alexander of Hales, *Summa theol.*, Pars II, inquisitio III, tractatus II, sect. I, quaest. I (4:581A–B), writes: "Dicendum ergo generaliter quod mendacium de se dicit vituperabile et contrarium veritati, et ideo non potest recte fieri, sive sit in voluntate, sicut primo modo, sive in facto, sicut secundo modo, sive in dicto, sicet tertio modo. Solvendum ergo per interemptionem, cum dicit quod mendacium potest esse licitum in operibus simulatis. Non est enim mendacium simulatio cautelae vel doctrinae vel figurae in facto, sed illa quae est duplicitatis et fallaciae."

those means consist in actions which, unlike words, were not solely instituted for the sake of truthful communication.

While he rejects hypocritical actions outright as lies, Alexander recognizes that certain potentially laudable actions carry with them degrees of deception that verge upon, but perhaps do not constitute lies. What separates these actions from hypocritical actions is the individual's overall intention. Of course, intention was central to Augustine's own conception of what it meant to lie, but then again, so was the nature of language itself as a vehicle for truthful communication. As Augustine, as Thomas, as many other scholastic writers would echo, a lie is necessarily sinful because, no matter what the justification, a lie is a misuse of language. Unlike fornication and killing, which can be done blamelessly and without sin given the right circumstances (for purposes of procreation between married adults on the one hand, and as a proper administration of justice by duly vested individuals on the other), no circumstances can alleviate or entirely wash away the stain of sin that comes with even the most benevolent of lies.[37] Alexander's recognition that the communicative context matters in determining whether a statement is or is not a lie placed even greater emphasis on the morally determinative role of intention. In certain situations, it is the speaker's intentions and not, say, the expectations of his interlocutor given the circumstances in which they find themselves that determine the interpretive contexts within which the speaker's statement and actions should be taken as truthful.[38]

Another Franciscan, Duns Scotus, writing in the early 1300s, would push this line of thought further in his own *Sentence* commentary. Again accepting the Augustinian standard that all lies are sinful, Scotus considers and rejects Thomas' argument that lies are necessarily sinful because they misuse language. Appealing to God's absolute power, Scotus argues that if God so chose, he could revoke the commandment, "Thou shalt

---

[37] Thomas Aquinas, *Summa theol.*, 2a 2ae, quaest. 110, article 3, response, in *Opera omnia*, 9:157–59. Although at question 110, article 4, response, Thomas notes that circumstances can alleviate or exacerbate the sin connected with any lie, he is very clear in asserting in question 110, article 3, ad 4, that no good intention can justify the telling of a lie. In this he follows Augustine, *Contra mendacium*, 7.18, CSEL 41:489–91.

[38] Compare Martin W. F. Stone, "In the Shadow of Augustine: The Scholastic Debate on Lying from Robert Grosseteste to Gabriel Biel," in *Herbst des Mittelalters? Fragen zur Bewertung des 14. und 15. Jahrhunderts*, ed. J. A. Aertsen and M. Pickavé (Berlin, 2004), 287–89, who presents Alexander as less innovative and less interested in exploring the tensions in Augustine's thought.

not kill," in which case we could blamelessly kill others. Scotus considers the example of Abraham and Isaac. God ordered Abraham to kill Isaac, and had Abraham followed through on this command (as he intended) his action would have been meritorious. If this is acceptable in the case of murder, Scotus reasons, then it is certainly the case with lying, especially since giving someone a wrong opinion hardly seems as bad as murder.[39] It is not the misuse of language that guarantees that lying is sin. Rather, Scotus contends the culpability of lying rests entirely on the bad intention. It is the bad intention alone that constitutes the necessary and sufficient circumstances and contexts to render any given speech act culpable or laudable.[40]

The consequences of this subtle interpretive shift, this now exclusive emphasis upon the will and upon intention, show up in Scotus' handling of those now well trod Biblical examples. Considering the case of the Hebrew midwives, Scotus first offers as "probable" an interpretation that extends at least as far back as Augustine's *Contra mendacium* and had been more or less repeated verbatim ever since. The midwives did in fact lie and because that sin precluded an eternal reward, God granted them a temporal reward for their charity. Significantly, Scotus then proceeds to what he believes to be an even more probable interpretation. "One could say," he writes, "that theirs was a polite or white lie, because it was useful in saving the Jewish children and harmed no one. God would have rewarded their good motives and would still not have

---

[39] John Duns Scotus, *In librum tertium sententiarum*, dist. 38, quaest. 1, in *Opera Omnia*, vol. 25, ed. Luke Waddington (Paris, 1894), 866: "[M]inus enim malum est auferre proximo opinionem veram, vel occasionaliter generare in eo opinionem falsam, quam auferre sibi vitam corporalem, imo non est quasi comparatio." For a facing-page translation of the entire question, see *Duns Scotus on the Will and Morality*, trans. Allan B. Wolter (Washington, D.C., 1986), 480–501. Richard Cross, "Duns Scotus on Goodness, Justice, and What God Can Do," *Journal of Theological Studies*, 48 (1997): 67n61, corrects several defects in Wolter's Latin text. Despite Scotus' own arguments here, Stone, "In the Shadow of Augustine," 302, notes that among most subsequent theologians, "Scotus was never construed to hold the view that that lying is wrong as long as God wills it to be so." For a concise summary of Scotus' conception of the relation between voluntarism and ethics, see Richard Cross, *Duns Scotus* (Oxford, 1999), 89–95. Scotus, Cross suggests, 192n79, probably holds that while lying is not intrinsically evil, it can never be in accord with the intrinsic nature of things. "After all," Cross writes, "God can dispense from the obligation not to lie; and we presumably would want to claim that under such circumstances lying is not morally bad." For an overview of thirteenth-century ethical debates about voluntarism see Bonnie Kent, *Virtues of the Will: The Transformation of Ethics in the Late Thirteenth Century* (Washington, D.C., 1995).

[40] Scotus, *In librum tertium sententiarum*, dist. 38, quaest. 1, ed. Waddington, 866.

denied them eternal life for their sin, which was only venial."[41] In other words, Scotus' emphasis on the will and intention enables or compels him to enter into the very sort of moral calculating that Augustine had been so keen to avoid. With the case of the midwives in mind, Scotus immediately asks whether "because of a powerful motive of charity" one should commit a venial sin, tell a venial lie. Although he chooses to postpone a full examination of the problem, Scotus' own position is clear, "Since such an evil is of itself not eternal but temporal," he concludes, "it does not seem one ought to omit something which of itself is the cause in some way of an eternal good."[42] Perhaps every lie is a sin—indeed, Scotus is clear, as clear as Thomas, Alexander, and Augustine were before him, that every lie is a sin—but this does not prevent us from sometimes recognizing the need and even the merit in telling them.

The thirteenth-century reception of Augustine's prohibition against lying was anything but a passive rehearsal of forever repeated truisms. Certainly, there was a great deal of repetition, a constant reaffirming of truisms and principles, but this appearance of stability, even stagna- tion, masks what, in the final analysis, is a vibrant debate. Indeed, it is precisely this contrast between the need to maintain a prohibition against lying and the constantly shifting set of reasons offered in sup- port of those precepts that makes the discourse of lying so valuable a measure of the tensions and changes at work in thirteenth-century intellectual and religious life. The immediate context for these changes (not to mention the façade of stability that at first renders them invis- ible) is the medieval university itself, with its simultaneous reliance on authorities and analysis. University theologians subjected Augustine's

---

[41] Ibid., ed. Waddington, 956: "Vel probabilius dici potest, quod mendacium illud fuit officiosum, quia utile ad salutem parvulorum Judaeorum, et nulli nocivum; et Deum remunerasse eas pro bono motu, et tamen non abnegasse eis vitam aeternam pro illo peccato quod erat in eis veniale."

[42] Ibid.: "De obstetricibus autem teneri potest ad propositum, quod non peccabant nisi venialiter, quia mendacium earum erat penitus officiosum; et motus pietatis, si fuis- sent ibi alia requisita ad meritum, fuisset meritorious vitae aeternae, et etiam alicujus boni temporalis, quia Deus pro tempore illo remuneravit cultures suos bono temporali." Compare this reading of Scotus' position with Silvana Vecchio, "Mensonge, Simula- tion, Dissimulation," in *Vestigia, Imagines, Verba: Semiotics and Logic in Medieval Theological Texts (XIIth–XIVth century)*, ed. Constantine Marmo (Turnhout, 1997), 126, who stress- es Scotus' "condamnation absolue du mensonge verbal," and Stone, "In the Shadow of Augustine," 303–04, who notes Scotus' condemnation of the midwives' lie, but ignores the mitigating role of intention and charity in Scotus' overall assessment of their actions.

arguments and examples to a degree of scrutiny they could not entirely withstand and, in doing so, necessarily came upon gaps and slippages in his thought. Why theologians almost inevitably used these gaps as excuses to expand the limits of acceptable speech requires a different set of contexts and explanations. No doubt one is the extremity of Augustine's prohibition, an extremity which attracts and troubles even modern ethicists.[43]

More immediately relevant to the concerns and interests of thirteenth-century theologians were the mendicant religious orders with their explicit obligation to live the life of witness in both word and deed. It was an obligation that brought problems concerning truth and falsity, appearance and reality, and simulation and deception, to the foreground.[44] In his thirteenth-century guide for Franciscan novices, David of Augsburg gives voice to these concerns when he suggests that there will be times when even the best of novices must present a false front. "If you should lack interior devotion," he writes in the *De institutione novitiorum*, "at least humbly maintain discipline and a grave exterior demeanor out of reverence for God and as an example to others."[45] No scholastic theologian would have objected to this advice, would have judged such behavior to be deceitful, but it is worth noting that scholastic discussions of lying almost inevitably conclude with discussions of hypocrisy that almost inevitably focus on those who present themselves as holy while lascivious or at least lukewarm emotions stir within them. What is the difference between laudable deception and vile hypocrisy?[46]

These are concerns that move us to the very heart of mendicant life—to the public preacher with his duty not merely to edify and instruct his audience, but to move and excite it with the desire to confess. In this respect, the thirteenth-century Dominican Humbert of Romans' *On the Formation of Preachers* is unique only because of its sustained

---

[43] Sisella Bok, *Lying: Moral Choice in Public and Private Life* (New York, 1978), 32–46.

[44] I address the impact of this obligation in *Seeing and Being Seen in the Later Medieval World* (Cambridge, Eng., 2005), 22–30.

[45] David of Augsburg, *De institutione novitiorum*, in Bonaventure of Balneoregio, *Opera omnia*, ed. A. C. Peltier (Paris, 1868), 12:294: "Si autem non habes devotionem interius, saltem conserva disciplinam et morum gravitatem humiliter exterius, propter reverentiam Dei et aliorum exemplum."

[46] For a semantic history of hypocrisy up until the 12th century see Frederic Amory, "Whited Sepulchres: The Semantic History of Hypocrisy to the High Middle Ages," *Recherches de Théologie ancienne et médiévale* 53 (1986): 5–39.

examination of the preacher's need to cultivate his public persona. Humbert makes it clear that the preacher must adapt his words and appearance to an ever changing set of circumstances and audiences, while simultaneously maintaining a careful watch on his intentions. The preacher must make sure that the dramatic and rhetorical effects he deploys are never intended for self-glorification, but only for the good his listeners.[47] Franciscan and Dominican *exempla* and training manuals attest to how difficult it was to perform this balancing act. While it is entirely possible that the pastoral literature devoted to the sins of the tongue was part of a vast church-sponsored effort at social discipline, scholastic debates about lying seem to be just as crucially focused on the mendicants themselves—careful explorations through traditional Biblical models of the range of prudent, instructive, and figurative deceptions. Behind the subtleties of scholastic debates about lying, behind their quiet examination and extension of permissible speech and actions, lay an entire world of religious life, duty, and worry.

---

[47] Humbert of Romans, *De eruditione praedicatorum*, in *De vita regulari*, ed. Joachim Joseph Berthier, vol. 2 (Rome, 1889), 373–484. On Humbert's treatise and mendicant tensions between public performance and inner intention, see Denery, *Seeing and Being Seen*, 19–38, and Claire Waters, *Angels and Earthly Creatures; Preaching, Performance and Gender in the Later Middle Ages* (Philadelphia, 2004), 31–56.

"THE HARD BED OF THE CROSS": GOOD FRIDAY PREACHING AND THE SEVEN DEADLY SINS

Holly Johnson
Mississippi State University

Abstract: The use of the seven deadly sins in late-medieval Good Friday sermons reflects a changing conception of sin from external act to internal disposition. In many sermons, the seven deadly sins are used largely rhetorically, rather than doctrinally: where theological points are made, they are made idiosyncratically; there is no fixed formulation to which preachers resorted, nor are the sins integral to the sermons. As redemption of sin is the focus of Good Friday, this idiosyncrasy suggests a diminished interest in the seven deadly sins as a matter of theology while preachers continued to rely on them as rhetorical conveniences. The larger goal in the invocation of these sins is affective, an attempt to make personal and immediate Christ's suffering and death. Preachers were less interested in enumerating forbidden behaviors than in encouraging a more positive rejection of sin born out of a close identification with Christ in his suffering.

I. *Introduction*

That each sin crucifies Christ anew was a medieval commonplace, central to the meaning of Good Friday. During the Good Friday liturgy, Christ's Passion and death were not just liturgically reenacted, but were believed to be recurring: Christ was again, each Good Friday, redeeming the sins of the world, bearing them on the cross, including those sins of the contemporary congregation. This commonplace was made vivid by rituals such as the Veneration of the Cross, during which the congregation approached the cross on its knees while it heard the chanting of the *Improperia*, a series of reproaches placed in Christ's mouth that contrast what Christ had done for the Jews in the Old Testament with the treatment they inflicted on him during the Passion. The liturgical placement of the *Improperia* made the contemporary audience complicit in inflicting this suffering on Christ; a contemporary sinner was thus no different from the first-century Jews. To make the audience feel its complicity—that their sins continue to crucify Christ— and thus respond to Christ's suffering as an ongoing event, preachers of late-medieval Good Friday sermons found ways to connect as closely as possible the events reenacted on Good Friday with the daily sins of their audience. In Good Friday sermons Christ's Passion is presented as the consequence of sin, an antidote to sin, and the antithesis of sin; the emphasis in most sermons, however, is not on sin itself, but on an experience of and the appropriate response to the Passion—not on what not to do, but on how to feel.

The seven deadly sins, a convenient and popular way to categorize sin, offered preachers one tradition on which they could rely to make Christ's suffering immediately present to their congregation. The most common appearance the sins make in late-medieval Good Friday sermons is in a series of juxtapositions in which each deadly sin is paired with one of Christ's torments. Such juxtapositions in Good Friday sermons function both mnemonically to underscore the relationship between the Passion and sin and rhetorically to solicit feelings of guilt, gratitude, and compassion.[1] They thus helped to forge the connection between Christ's Passion and the contemporary sinner. Because this is a seemingly simple set of juxtapositions, the combination of sins and torments was recognizable as a set to medieval audiences, and part of the response preachers could anticipate comes by way of this recognition. The juxtapositions thus constitute a topos of Good Friday preaching, but, as with other medieval topoi, this does not suggest that they were the result of a preacher's lack of ingenuity when composing sermons. Not only are there many variations of this topos, but within a single example there are variations in the ways sins are paired with torments. The pairings arise from a variety of ways of conceiving both the seven deadly sins and Christ's redemptive suffering and death. Preachers could assume audiences knew the basic shape of this topos, but they manipulated the details to achieve their own ends. The topos thus reveals what these ends may have been, and because it results from an amalgamation of traditions, both aesthetic and doctrinal, it reveals the way the medieval imagination reworks and recombines material to create new sets of associations and images. By connecting the sins to

---

[1] The juxtaposition also appears, for instance, in *Le Manuel des Péchés*, the thirteenth-century Old French treatise on the vices and virtues, which includes a variation of this topos when it discusses Christ's Passion in a section on the articles of the Creed. *Roberd of Brunne's Handlyng Synne (Written A.D. 1303); with the French treatise on which it is founded, Le Manuel des Pechiez by William of Wadington . . .*, ed. F. J. Furnivall (London, 1862), 418.

Christ's physical suffering, the topos also reveals something about the late-medieval conception of sin as something tangible, intrinsically connected to one's own body. All this makes the topos a rhetorically rich tool for preaching about sin and redemption and for drawing audiences into the liturgical reality of Good Friday, into an immediate experience of Christ's suffering and death.

II. *Variations and Connections*

The pairing of the seven deadly sins with Christ's torments appears in several variations, examples of which can be grouped in three broad, but overlapping, categories depending on how the torments are conceived: as events of the Passion narrative, as instances when Christ actively shed his blood, or as specific wounds he received on Good Friday. In examples from the first category, Christ's torments are often treated in general terms, each of them encompassing a broad aspect of the Passion, and these generalized torments become the inversions of the sins that caused them. For example, Christ was utterly humbled to defeat pride, naked and impoverished to defeat avarice. In examples of the first type, Christ's torments are also sometimes treated as specific events within the Passion story, and these specific events are not always absolute inversions of the sins they are paired with, but are still their logical counterparts—such as when he was given gall and vinegar as a counterpart to gluttony, or when he prayed for his enemies as a counterpart to envy. Most examples in the first category include both generalized torments and specific torments, whichever suits the sin with which they are paired. Examples in the second category present the torments as the blood Christ shed at different times, blood which cleanses each of the seven deadly sins. One sermon calls these his seven baths, and the baths include such events as the sweating of blood in the garden of Gethsemane and the scourging.[2] Another variation of this second

---

[2] London, Lambeth Palace MS. 352, fol. 224v. This is a lengthy macaronic (Latin and Middle English) Good Friday sermon, extant in a late-14th or 15th-century manuscript. For a description of the manuscript, see Montague Rhodes James and Claude Jenkins, *A Descriptive Catalogue of the Manuscripts in the Library of Lambeth Palace* (Cambridge, Eng., 1930–32) and Siegfried Wenzel, *Macaronic Sermons: Bilingualism and Preaching in Late-Medieval England* (Ann Arbor, MI, 1994), 33–34. This sermon has been ed. and trans. H. Johnson, "Preaching the Passion: Good Friday Sermons in Late-Medieval England," Ph.D. diss., Univ. of North Carolina, 2001, 57–177.

type appears in Middle English lyrics, in which a sinner prays to Jesus to be delivered of the seven deadly sins.[3] These prayers proceed in the chronological order of the blood sheddings, not in one of the traditional orders of the sins, beginning with Christ's circumcision juxtaposed to lust and ending with the wound in Christ's side juxtaposed to envy. Such prayers were probably used as aids to devotion, not as parts of sermons. In the third category, each of Christ's individual wounds is connected to one of the seven deadly sins, usually set forth in the following pairings: the crown of thorns and pride, the wound in the right or left hand and anger, the wound in the side and envy, the wound in the feet and sloth, the wound in the other hand (whichever one is not connected to anger) and avarice, being made to taste vinegar and gall and gluttony, and the scourging and lust.[4] This version is often presented in Middle English lyrics, in each stanza of which Christ beseeches the viewer to behold a certain wound and reflect on the sin associated with that wound. Although the seven deadly sins are a well-established, widely-known, and standard formulation, there is no standard formulation for what constitutes Christ's seven torments.

Nor is there a consistent logic underlying why certain torments are juxtaposed to certain sins, even within a single example. We can see how whimsical these associations are just by looking at one of Bonaventure's uses of the topos from the first of his two Good Friday sermons in the Quaracchi edition (vol. 9 of his *Opera omnia*).[5] In one section of this

---

[3] Examples of such verse prayers can be found in *Religious Lyrics of the XIVth Century*, ed. Carleton Brown (Oxford, 1924), no. 123, and *Religious Lyrics of the XVth Century*, ed. Carleton Brown (Oxford, 1939), no. 62.

[4] I know of one example of this variation used in a Good Friday sermon (Cambridge, Jesus College MS. 13, fols. 86v–87r), but there are two examples in John of Grimestone's Preaching handbook within his section on the Passion, one of which translates a Latin verse. See *A Descriptive Index of the English Lyrics in John of Grimestone's Preaching Book*, ed. Edward Wilson (Oxford, 1973), nos. 199 and 218. For a discussion of the relationship between John of Grimestone's handbook and preaching, see Siegfried Wenzel, *Preachers, Poets and the Early English Lyric* (Princeton, NJ, 1986), chaps. 4–5. For preaching in England, see G. R. Owst, *Preaching in Medieval England: An Introduction to Sermon Manuscripts of the Period c. 1350–1450* (Cambridge, Eng., 1926); idem, *Literature and Pulpit in Medieval England*. 2nd rev. ed. (New York, 1961); and H. Leith Spencer, *English Preaching in the Late Middle Ages* (Oxford, 1993). For a discussion of Good Friday sermons, see Nicole Bériou, "Latin and Vernacular. Some Remarks about Sermons Delivered on Good Friday during the Thirteenth Century," in *Die deutsche Predigt im Mittelalter*, ed. Volker Mertens and Hans-Jochen Schiewer (Tübingen, 1992), 268–84; Wenzel, *Preachers, Poets*, 146–63; and H. Johnson, "Preaching the Passion."

[5] Volume 9 of the Quaracchi edition includes two sermons intended for Good Friday, in both of which this topos occurs. Apparently, Bonaventure found it rhetorically useful.

sermon, Bonaventure names each of the seven deadly sins, beginning with pride and ending with lust, admonishing his audience, if they are tempted to commit a certain sin, to look on or consider Christ's antithetical torment, for this contemplation will conquer the devil. Bonaventure curiously jumps from addressing the audience to addressing the devil and back to addressing his audience, as if caught up in his own contemplation:

> Thus, by considering the Passion of Christ, the devil tempting through pride is conquered by all people. I see Christ humbled on the Cross, made the reproach of men; I should not desire honors. Go your way, Lucifer, tempter of enviousness; consider Christ praying for his enemies. When he tempts you with sloth, see Christ transfixed by nails and say, "I also will hang on the cross of penance." [...] If [the devil] tempts you with avarice, consider Christ naked on the cross; his mother alone is said to have covered him there. If [he tempts you] with gluttony, think about the bitterness of his drink; if with lust, consider the hard bed of the cross.[6]

Although anger does not appear, Bonaventure otherwise lists the seven deadly sins in their traditional order, connecting each to one way that Christ suffered, and the connections all seem to make the same point: Christ's specific torment offers the one tempted by a certain sin something that, when visualized, will naturally overcome the temptation. But that "something" varies from pair to pair. Some of the pairs work as polar opposites, and these opposites suggest an array of related meanings. When Bonaventure sets Christ's humiliation against pride, Christ embodies the antithesis or inversion of this sin; he is not only humiliated as opposed to being honored, but he becomes an emblem of humility, as if the abstraction "humility" assumed concrete form. This visual emblem also suggests Christ's interior disposition: because he submits willingly to treatment at which a proud man would balk, he presumably does not desire what a proud man desires. The inversion has both symbolic and psychological resonance. Likewise, when Christ's nakedness is set against avarice, he becomes a portrait of poverty, and this physical

---

[6] *Opera omnia iussu et auctoritate*, ed. Patres Collegii a S. Bonaventura (Ad Claras Aquas [Quaracchi], 1882–1902), 9:261, col. 2: "Unde considerando passionem Christi vincitur ab omnibus diabolus (tentans) de *superbia*. Video Christum in cruce humiliatum, *factum opprobrium hominum* [Ps 21:7]; non appetam honores. Vade viam tuam, Lucifer, tentator de *malignitate*; considera Christum orantem pro inimicis suis; quando tentat te de *accidia*, vide Christum clavis confixum et dicas: ego etiam pendebo in cruce poenitentiae [...]. Si tentat te de *avaritia*, considera Christum in cruce nudum; sola Mater sua dicitur eum texisse ibi. Si de *gula*, cogita amaritudinem potus; si de luxuria, considera durum lectum crucis."

nakedness represents Christ's inner disposition: because he wears
nothing, he presumably desires nothing, in contrast to those who desire
many things and cover themselves with expensive clothing. These two
torments, Christ's humiliation and his nakedness, are not specific events
but broad aspects of the Passion, and they convey both physical and
psychological suffering. Christ suffers physically, but this suffering makes
concrete his interior state, just as the sinner is tempted physically but the
temptation is something interior, coming as it does from the devil.

At the same time that these two torments represent polar opposites
of the sins with which they are paired, they simultaneously embody the
remedial virtues for these sins, becoming a visual image, an icon, of that
virtue. Humility was considered the remedy of pride in a wide variety
of pastoral literature,[7] and voluntary poverty the remedy for avarice.[8]
Similarly, Christ's motionlessness on the cross (though forced) is used
as an example of his steadfastness in purpose and thus the remedial
virtue for sloth: whereas the slothful desire to shirk their religious
responsibilities and are restless, Christ stayed true to his purpose and
remained—literally—motionless. It might have seemed more logical
to connect sloth to Christ being made to stay awake for three days, a
medieval commonplace, but the topos relies more on images and Christ
as hieratic icon than it does on events; when events are evoked, these
events overlap each other as if they were all happening simultaneously.
Creating a narrative is apparently not the objective of this topos. These
three images create symbolic pictures of the virtues that remedy pride,
avarice, and sloth, but they do not present active examples of how one
should behave. Only in one of Bonaventure's juxtapositions does Christ
perform the remedial virtue in an active way. When Christ prays for
his enemies, he offers an example of charity, the remedial virtue for
envy. Here he not only embodies the virtue; he enacts it. He had not
actively chosen to be humiliated or stripped of his clothing or nailed to
the cross; he was a passive victim of these torments, inflicted on him for
sinners. While he exemplifies the remedial virtues of humility, poverty,
and steadfastness, he does so incidentally. Only when he prays for his
enemies does he actively exemplify the remedial virtue. Presenting an
exemplum of the virtues is thus not the primary function of the topos,

---

[7] See, for example, *Summa Virtutum de Remediis Anime*, ed. and trans. Siegfried Wenzel
(Athens, GA, 1984), chapt. 2.

[8] See, for example, *Fasciculus morum: A Fourteenth-Century Preacher's Handbook*, ed. and
trans. Siegfried Wenzel (University Park and London, 1989), Part IV, section xii.

but all four of these pairings evoke the sins' remedial virtues, making a logical doctrinal connection between sin and torment.

When Bonaventure connects gluttony to Christ being given gall and vinegar, the relationship differs markedly from the above pairings. Being forced to taste something repugnant does not exactly embody the remedial virtue for gluttony; Christ is not forced to taste gall and vinegar as an example of abstinence or temperance. Nor is it an emblematic antithesis of gluttony; starvation would serve that purpose. Rather, Christ must taste something repugnant because gluttons indulge in food and drink pleasing to the taste. Here, Christ suffers an appropriate punishment for the sin, thus redeeming the sinner by taking the punishment on himself and literally bearing it. As the sinners do in Dante's *Inferno*, Christ suffers the sin's *contrapasso*, and he does so on behalf of those who committed the sin and *as if* that is the reason he suffered in this specific way. Many of the torments discussed above can also be seen as their sins' *contrapassos*. Christ is humiliated and stripped because people are proud and wear expensive clothing; he is nailed to the cross and made to stand motionless because people are restless. But the connection between gluttony and being given gall and vinegar is narrower and seems to embody only the sin's *contrapasso*, not its antithesis or its remedial virtue. Furthermore, it works primarily on the level of the senses. It forges an experience of the torment and a memory of that experience via the sense of taste. Another example of this sort of sense experience is when Bonaventure tells those tempted to lust to consider the "hard bed of the cross." The connection here is again visceral: one presumably engages in acts of lust while lying on a soft bed; Christ suffered in all his body by being stretched on a hard cross. If one feels lustful, one need only remember Christ's body racked in pain. Bonaventure need not belabor the point; the metaphor speaks for itself. But it is less of a theological point than a rhetorical one: Christ was not stretched on a cross as an example of chastity and the cross as a bed can be intended only in a grimly ironic way.[9] The connections thus sometimes rely on the tradition of seeing the virtues as remedies

---

[9] Interestingly, *Le Manuel des Péchés* connects the sin of sloth to Christ's "hard bed of the cross." A Middle English translation of this treatise reads: "Whanne his fete were nailed to þe cross, in so muche he hath chasted slow men þat ligeth longe in here bedde. Þey wol noþynge do for Ihesus Criste; þey wol lepe by folie, but to cherche þey wol nat renne. Ihesus Criste in þe cros hadde a ful hard bed. 3e schulde serue hym with gode wille þat bow3te 3ow so dere." See *Of Shrifte and Penance: The ME Prose Translation of Le Manuel des Péchés*, ed. Klaus Bitterling (Heidelberg, 1998), 37.

for the seven deadly sins and sometimes, often at the same time, on
the doctrine of the redemption, making concrete the belief that Christ
bore the sins of the world by presenting him as literally bearing a sin's
contrapasso. And sometimes the connections are primarily visceral and
metaphorical. Bonaventure seems more interested in making apt and
suggestive correspondences than he is in making his connections share
the same underlying logic.

Bonaventure presents a static image that encompasses many aspects of
the Passion, and this image is connected to one of the seven deadly sins,
usually simply summed up by their traditional names: *superbia, avaritia,
accidia*, etc. Something different, but related, happens in the variation of
the topos that connects the seven deadly sins to specific wounds instead
of to generalized torments. Examples in this category give the torments
narrow specificity while also presenting the sins in an active form. For
example, in one Middle English lyric, Christ is imagined as saying,
"Through my right hand the nail was driven / Think on that if you will
live / And worship God with alms deeds / that at your death heaven
may be your reward."[10] There is no theological basis for associating the
wound in the right hand (or sometimes the left) with avarice, though the
connection of avarice with hand movements (in counting money, etc.) is
traditional.[11] His utter nakedness and poverty work better as antitheses
of the sin than does an individual wound. But the wounded open hand
acts well as a synecdoche for Christ's generosity and as a easy mnemonic
that sums up the sin by connecting it with one part of the body, the
part literally connected with taking and giving. The sin of avarice is not
named at all in the Middle English text; it is only implied by the call to
give alms by which one will receive one's true reward in heaven, a verse
that alludes to Christ's words in the Gospels about putting one's treasure
where one's heart is (Matthew 6:19–21; Luke 12:33–35). By giving alms,
one shows the same generosity Christ shows by holding open his hands.
Giving alms is made to stand in for any number of ways one might be
generous, just as Christ's wounded open hand stands in for the many
ways he showed generosity.

---

[10] *Cambridge Middle English Lyrics*, ed. Henry A. Person (Seattle, 1953), 10: "Thrugh
my right hand þe nayle was driffe / Thynke þer on if þou wilt liffe / And worshipe
god with almysdede / þat at þi deyng heuen may be þi mede."
[11] See Richard Newhauser, *The Early History of Greed: The Sin of Avarice in Early
Medieval Thought and Literature* (Cambridge, Eng., 2000), 82, 136.

Such connections between the sin and a part of Christ's body ultimately derive from the iconographic tradition that attaches each sin to the part of the body with which one commonly commits that sin.[12] Sloth, for example, is iconographically connected to the foot and is thus, in this variation of the topos, connected to the wounds in Christ's feet, as opposed to the more encompassing image of Christ being unable to move on the cross. For example, in a stanza from a Middle English lyric, Christ berates the slothful by saying, "Rise up, slothful man, out of your bed, / Behold my feet, how they are bled, / How they are nailed onto the tree, / Thank me for this; it was for you."[13] Here the sin of sloth is summed up (again, not named) in the image of a sinner sleeping late. Christ being pierced through his feet has nothing whatever to do with that kind of laziness; the only connection seems to be by way of the iconographic tradition. And this lyric reduces the sin of sloth to its common denominator—staying too long in bed. But this reduction of sloth to sleeping late and Christ's pierced feet as a remedy for sloth become shorthand—and memorable—ways to convey larger concepts. Sleeping late stands in for any number of ways one fails to do one's duty, and while lazing around, one need only think of Christ's pained feet to remember one's failure. While the lyric clearly arises from the iconographic tradition of associating sloth with the foot, the image presented here can also recall the image created in many examples of the first type, in which Christ's motionlessness is paired with sloth. While the lyrics rely on simple rhymes and homely images, this simplicity still evokes a rich array of meanings.

The absence of a uniform or consistent relationship between the seven deadly sins and the torments is evidence that preachers did not use this topos to offer insight into the sins or to explicate the Passion. In other words, the torments are not used to teach the audience something new about sin and the sins are likewise not used to teach the audience

[12] Walter Hilton's *The Scale of Perfection* offers an interesting example of this iconography, creating an "image of sin" by connecting each sin with one part of the body. Hilton begins with pride connected to the head and ends with sloth connected to the feet, and he dramatizes each sin by an action committed with that body part. For example, Hilton says that the arms are wrath "in as mickle as a man wreaketh him of his wrath by his arms." *The Scale of Perfection*, ed. E. Underhill (London, 1923), 205.
[13] Cambridge, Jesus College MS. 13, fol. 86v: "Rys vp, slaw man, owt of thy byd, / Behold my feeth how yt arn bled, / Qwow yt be nayled on to the tre, / Thank me ther of yt was for the."

something new about Christ's redemptive suffering and death. Nor
are the seven deadly sins a means for remembering various aspects of
Christ's suffering. This is made apparent by the use of the wounds in
examples from the third category. There is no significance in the overall
Passion narrative to separating the wounds in the right and left hands
as two distinct torments, except perhaps to make the point that Christ
was nailed, and not just tied, to the cross. But separating them is not
necessary as an aid in remembering that Christ had one nail in one hand
and another nail in the other. Christ's five wounds, including the two in
his hands, were by that point well established medieval devotions. This
topos is not mnemonic in the usual sense of providing a structure either
for remembering the seven deadly sins or for remembering the Passion.
Instead, what is remembered is the entire experience—perhaps, for
example, the physical pain the congregant felt in his or her own hands
when connecting them to Christ's pierced hands and the concurrent
feelings of compassion and guilt.

III. *Function and Effect*

All variations of this topos have one thing in common when used
by preachers: they are all primarily rhetorical. They seek to create a
memorable experience, very like the experience created by the medieval
art of meditation, by which Christians imaginatively enter into the life
of Christ and see themselves as actively participating in this life. The
meditation was intended to foster in the meditators greater compassion
for Christ and a desire to imitate in their lives what they see in Christ's.[14]
Evidence for this meditative experience comes partly by way of the
juxtapositions themselves, which are sometimes theological, sometimes
metaphorical, sometimes purely mnemonic, but never rigidly systematic.
By juxtaposing each of Christ's torments with one of the seven deadly
sins, preachers make of Christ's body a meditative map, the parts of
Christ's body or the generalized torments becoming foci for meditation.

---

[14] The two texts central to this tradition are the *Meditationes vite Christi*, traditionally
attributed to Bonaventure but now believed to have been written by John of Caulibus,
and Ludolph of Saxony's *Vita Jesu Christi*. For a new edition of the former, see *Iohannis
de Caulibus Meditaciones vite Christi: olim S. Bonaventuro attributae*, ed. M. Stallings-Taney,
CCCM 153 (Turnhout, 1997), and for the latter, see Ludolph of Saxony, *Vita Jesu
Christi*, ed. L. M. Rigollot (Paris, 1870).

The form of the Middle English verses reveals this meditative emphasis implicitly. In each stanza Christ himself speaks to an individual viewer and he speaks in the immediate moment; the viewer is imagined as even at that moment performing the sin. If the viewer is slothful, he is at that moment lying in bed, and Christ's feet are at that moment being pierced with nails and are bleeding while Christ beholds the lazy sinner. The lyrics become a speaking *imago pietatis*, the image of Christ as the Man of Sorrows, who looks out at the viewer from the timeless now and points to his wounds, which are still—and eternally—bleeding. A connection is thus not only forged between sin and wound but also between sinner and Christ, who simultaneously behold one another and are linked by the actions they perform with the same parts of their bodies. By connecting wounded hands with avarice, and therefore with giving and taking, or with anger, and therefore with striking or embracing, or wounded feet with rising and moving, the Middle English verses foster a close identity with the suffering Christ by way of what congregants have in common with him. Such foci not only elicit an affective response to Christ's suffering, but act as mnemonic hooks. When linked to the individual's own hands and feet, Christ's suffering becomes at once more painful and therefore more memorable.

Such a meditative response is made explicit by the fourteenth-century English monk-bishop Thomas Brinton who uses the topos in two of his Good Friday sermons.[15] In one of these sermons preached in 1375 in the Rochester cathedral, he prefaces the topos by directing his audience's attention to the crucifixion hanging in the church and asserting that, if each sinner contemplates the crucifixion, he can wash himself from spiritual stains.[16] Brinton then presents the topos by not only naming each sin and connecting it to its antithetical torment, but also by creating pictures of the sins either by adding a telling detail or by using lively verbs that themselves summon up the sins, like "swelling with pride" or "delighting in gluttony." At the same time he creates lively pictures of Christ suffering:

---

[15] W. A. Pantin calls Brinton an "outstanding monk-bishop," well known "above all as a preacher [...] thanks especially to the collection of 103 sermons, preached between 1373 and 1383, that has survived." *The English Church in the Fourteenth Century* (Cambridge, Eng., 1955), 182–83. These sermons have been edited by M. Devlin, in *The Sermons of Thomas Brinton, Bishop of Rochester (1373–1389)* (London, 1954).

[16] Brinton, *Sermons*, ed. Devlin, 2:253: "Hoc enim speculum in medio ecclesie est appensum vt peccator quilibet illud videns faciem anime possit tergere et lauare."

For if we swell with pride, let us consider Christ humbled and despised; indeed, he humbled himself until death, death moreover on a cross. If we are moved to anger and envy, not loving our neighbor or also our enemy, let us consider Christ praying for his crucifiers. If we delight in gluttony and pleasures, let us consider Christ who drank gall and vinegar. If we are charmed by feasts and clothing, let us consider Christ hanging naked on the bare cross.[17]

At this point in the topos, Brinton develops a vivid image of Christ hanging from the cross—how Christ was constrained to the cross, how he could not lift one foot over the other, had nowhere to lay his head, could not lay down or sit—an image often connected to sloth, but sloth is not mentioned.[18] Instead, Brinton turns to despair, saying, "If we despair of our multitude of sins, we should see Christ extending his arms to embrace us and prepared even to shed his blood if need be."[19] Brinton may have sloth in mind when developing this last juxtaposition, as despair was connected to sloth.[20] Christ's arms extended on the cross as if in an embrace is also a devotional commonplace associated with Bernard of Clairvaux and probably made popular by Jacobus de Voragine's *Legenda aurea*.[21] Christ's arms are of course literally stretched out because he is being crucified, but this image becomes a visual symbol of his love revealed by his willingness to be crucified. Thus, after piling up images of sins, Brinton shifts the attention to a devotional image perhaps to make clear that, ultimately, meditating on the crucifixion should inspire gratitude and greater affection, not merely guilt and the avoidance of sin. The topos itself becomes a lesson in meditation: Brinton not

---

[17] Ibid.: "Nam si superbia turgestamus, respiciamus in cruce Christum humilem and despectum, immo se humiliatum vsque ad mortem, mortem autem crucis. Si ad iram et inuidiam moueamur non diligentes proximum vel eciam inimicum, respiciamus Christum pro crucifixoribus exorantem. Si gula et deliciis delectemur, respiciamus Christum felle et aceto potatum. Si in lectisterniis et vestibus fuerimus delicati, respiciamus Christum nudum super nudosam crucem pendentem."

[18] Ibid.: "... que crux ita stricta erat quod non potuit vnam pedem iuxta alterum ponere sed oportuit vnum super alterum perforari, ita stricta quod non habuit vbi caput reclinaret, ita exilis quod non potuit iacere vel sedere sed tantum pendere."

[19] Ibid.: "Si pre multitudine peccatorum desperemus, respiciamus Christum brachia extendentem nos ad amplectandum et se paratum pro nobis sanguinem suum ad fundendum eciam si opus sit."

[20] See Siegfried Wenzel, *The Sin of Sloth: Acedia in Medieval Thought and Literature* (Chapel Hill, NC, 1967), 82, 87–88.

[21] See Jacobus de Voragine, *The Golden Legend: Readings of the Saints*, trans. W. G. Ryan, (Princeton, 1993), 2:210. For the *Legenda*'s influence in popularizing devotional writings, see Thomas Bestul, *Texts of the Passion: Latin Devotional Literature and Medieval Society* (Philadelphia, 1996), 32.

only asserts that such a meditation is effective in cleansing one of one's sins, but, by creating images of Christ sufferings and connecting these sufferings to images of sin, he enacts the meditation himself.

In a Good Friday sermon preached to the Benedictine priory of Rochester, Brinton uses the topos in such a way that again reveals this meditative concern, but he makes the topos specific to a congregation of monks. He juxtaposes Christ's torments with the seven deadly sins by means of a series of rhetorical questions, all of which follow the same form: How can you feel this sinful inclination when you see Christ suffering in this way? These rhetorical questions establish how one should respond when contemplating Christ's torments, and they confirm that it is this response that remedies sin, not the torments themselves. Brinton begins with pride and asks, "Who is so proud or presumptuous, who, if he contemplated the king of kings vehemently despised and humiliated by death on the cross, would not become humble at once?"[22] He not only connects the sin of pride and Christ's humility; he also presents a striking portrait of that humility by calling Christ the king of kings, thus the very one who ought to receive the honor the proud man desires and who does not deserve the humiliating treatment he receives. Brinton moves through each of the sins and ends, curiously, not with the usual final sin in the concatenation of sins, lust, but with sloth, perhaps because sloth is a sin particularly tempting to the monks who make up his audience; and, indeed, he makes the portrait of the sin apply specifically to monastic practices:

> Who is so impatient and irreligious, for whom the yoke of religion appears intolerable, the commands of his superior irrational, keeping vigil and staying quiet in the cloister painful and unpleasant, that he would not find all those things sweet if he were to contemplate Christ resting on the tree of the cross, so constricted that he could not put one foot next to the other, so restricted that he had nowhere to lay his head, so destitute and pained that he could not sit or lie down but only hang?[23]

---

[22] Brinton, *Sermons*, ed. Devlin, 2:309: "Quis enim tam superbus et presumptuosus, qui si contempletur regem regum proterue despectum et ad mortem crucis humiliatum quin statim fiat humilis?"

[23] Brinton, *Sermons*, ed. Devlin, 2:309–10: "Quis tam impaciens et irreligiosus, cui si iugum religionis appareat intolerabile, preceptum superioris irracionabile, multum vigilare et in claustro quiescere penale et non delectabile, quin ista omnia erunt satis dulcia si attendat Christum in crucis arbore quiescentem, tam stricta quod non potuit vnum pedem iuxta alium ponere, tam curta quod non habuit vbi caput posset reclinare, tam exili et penali quod non potuit sedere vel iacere sed tantum pendere?"

The implication behind all of Brinton's rhetorical questions is that it would be unnatural for anyone not to throw off the particular sin in response to the related form of Christ's suffering, but Brinton makes this especially vivid for the surly monk: if such a monk, inclined to shirk his religious duties out of boredom and restlessness, contemplated Christ hanging motionless and constricted on the cross, that monk would naturally throw off his sloth; any monk who does not respond this way is an ungrateful fool. It is not so much that Christ's torment remedies the sin or even takes away the sin by his literally bearing it on the cross; it is that the one who reflects on this torment will, out of compassion and gratitude, *want* to give up the sin. Devotional feelings play a larger role in encouraging good behavior than doctrinal exposition. And, at the same time as Brinton calls on the audience to imagine these torments, he creates the images themselves, placing them in the audience's imagination. The juxtapositions are again used as training in meditation.

If the associations between Christ's torments and the seven deadly sins have any effect on encouraging virtue, it is not because of the theological teaching about redemption or sin or because of the complexities of meaning created by specific juxtapositions. Certainly, a medieval audience would not be expected to tease out all the nuances of meaning. Rather, the topos creates a meditative experience—an experience of Christ's suffering and of the appropriate response to that suffering—and what is memorable is that experience. Many of the juxtapositions forge a visceral connection between Christ and sinner. Thus, not only do preachers present graphic visual images of Christ suffering, images that the congregant is asked to "behold" or "consider" or "contemplate," but preachers also implicitly ask the congregant to *feel* that suffering. They do so by using metaphor ("the hard bed of the cross"), by suggesting connections between what the congregant naturally shares with Christ (limbs, sense of taste, simple actions), and by presenting Christ's suffering as happening in the present moment and the sins as those performed—or felt—in that same moment. The sinner is not only entreated to behold the suffering body of Christ, but it is clear that he is simultaneously being beheld by Christ. The topos thus forges a close identity between sinner and Christ by way of the body and by way of ordinary activities—rising, sitting, tasting, and lying in bed.

IV. *Conclusion*

The use of this topos in Good Friday sermons tells us at least three things about the late-medieval concept of the seven deadly sins. First, it tells us that the seven deadly sins were still considered a handy way to categorize sin, a way to organize a general sense of sinfulness into manageable chunks, but that, while they are convenient tools, they are not dogmatically rigid. If a preacher wants to vary one sin, as Brinton does by substituting despair where one expects sloth, he seems to have felt no qualms about doing so. Second, the use of the topos tells us that the various strands of the seven deadly sins tradition—theological, pastoral, iconographic—could be blended to create something rhetorically rich and multi-layered. For instance, preachers draw readily (although perhaps not consciously) from the tradition of seeing the sins in relationship to the remedial virtues or of seeing them in relationship to parts of the body, and they combine such traditions with Christ's suffering. They also amalgamate various theological conceptions of Christ's Passion, presenting Christ's torments as active remedies for sin, as necessary consequences of sin, and as a substitution for the punishment that sinners justly deserve: Christ suffers for the sins and redeems them; he becomes both their victim and their antidote. And third, the topos tells us something about the late-medieval conception of sin as having a visceral or tangible reality, intrinsically connected to one's physical body, which reflects one's interior disposition, just as Christ's physical suffering reflects his interior disposition. And the tangible nature of sin makes possible a sinner's identity with Christ, who literally bore his or her sins on the cross.

Preachers of Good Friday sermons do not seem inclined to belabor the nature of sin or to enumerate sinful behavior.[24] Such enumeration may have been appropriate for treatises on the sins or preaching about sin, but it is not a concern on Good Friday, when experiencing the events of

---

[24] The one exception I know of is one of John Wyclif's Good Friday sermons in which he juxtaposes the seven deadly sins with Christ's seven Last Words from the cross. Wyclif, unlike many preachers, spends more time detailing the cause and effect of each sin than he does explicating Christ's Last Words. But, like the other preachers, he makes sin concrete by connecting each sin to one stage in the decomposition of a dead body, beginning by connecting a dead body's stiffness with pride and ending by connecting a dead body's stench with lust. See *Sermones*, ed. Iohann Loserth (London, 1890), 4:330–37.

the Passion takes precedence over knowing what not to do. Most of the preaching thus focuses on the cost of the redemption, rather than on the sins being redeemed. The goal seems to be to inspire humble gratitude and reverence, to fashion the right disposition—a desire to be good born out of a close identity with Christ in his suffering. This desire should and may well lead to good behavior, but mainly as a by-product. For late-medieval preachers, the seven deadly sins are rhetorical conveniences, suggesting perhaps their usefulness for fostering devotion even when they were no longer of great interest to academic theologians.

DRESSED TO THE SEVENS, OR SIN IN STYLE: FASHION STATEMENTS BY THE DEADLY VICES IN SPANISH BAROQUE *AUTOS SACRAMENTALES*

Hilaire Kallendorf
Texas A&M University

Abstract: Stage directions conserved with the manuscripts of seventeenth-century Spanish liturgical dramas offer fascinating insights into the clothing that was scripted to be worn by actors and actresses playing the parts of the Seven Deadly Sins onstage. *Autos sacramentales* were public spectacles performed in and around religious festivals. The costumes worn by the Vices both illustrate and problematize certain racial and social tensions and stereotypes operating within Spanish society of this time period. The theme of dressing, specifically discussed by the playwrights in the context of the Vices, also raises questions about identity, essence, mutability, performativity, and the Pauline injunction to "clothe oneself" with righteousness.

I. *Introduction*

In recent years the academy has paid increasing attention to fashion, perhaps in part because of the impact of the *Annales* historians.[1] Theorists such as Roland Barthes, Henri Lefebvre, Jean Baudrillard, Gilles Lipovetsky, and Michel Maffesoli have all weighed in with various theories or systems of fashion.[2] An almost universal conclusion reached by these theorists is that there is no such thing as "semiotically innocent" fashion.[3] Instead, clothes function as a sort of "symbolic intersubjective casing"[4] which is forever in need of interpretation, as dress can be at the same time both material and metaphor.[5] The discussion becomes

---

[1] Michael Sheringham, "Fashion, Theory, and the Everyday: Barthes, Baudrillard, Lipovetsky, Maffesoli," *Dalhousie French Studies* 53 (2000): 144.
[2] See Sheringham; and Roland Barthes, *The Fashion System*, trans. Matthew Ward and Richard Howard (New York, 1983).
[3] Dani Cavallaro and Alexandra Warwick, *Fashioning the Frame: Boundaries, Dress and Body* (Oxford and New York, 1998), 3.
[4] Ibid., 4.
[5] Linda B. Arthur, "Dress and the Social Control of the Body," in *Religion, Dress, and the Body*, ed. Linda B. Arthur (Oxford and New York, 1999), 6.

even more complicated in reference to the specific clothing of theatrical costume, for "[c]lothes as theatrical properties were simultaneously economic capital, material memory-systems, and transgressors of every social boundary."[6] In the early modern period in particular, clothes on the stage were "material mnemonics."[7] The challenge for the dramatist is to "prevent the clothing from obstructing the message."[8] But what happens when the clothing *is* the message, such as when the costume of a character onstage makes the figure recognizable as one of the Seven Deadly Sins?

It should be remembered that "[w]ithin medieval society the body was prioritised as the dwelling-place of the soul, inner character was displayed through outward signs and clothing could not avoid implication in such a problematic moral arena."[9] Cavallaro and Warwick echo this assessment of the function of clothing during the Middle Ages:

> Dress, then, could be described as a deep surface, a system of signs that fundamentally relies on superficial modes of signification for the purposes of expressing the underlying beliefs of a given culture and the character of the subjects fostered therein. This function of dress can easily be traced back to the Middle Ages.[10]

During the early modern period, however, the function of dress was not so transparent—except perhaps within the confines of that last great vestige of Scholasticism, the dramatic art form known as the Spanish Baroque *auto sacramental*.

II. *Description of the Genre*

The *autos sacramentales* could best be described as "devotional drama"[11] composed as part of the popular celebration of the feast of Corpus

---

[6] Peter Stallybrass, "Properties in Clothes: The Materials of the Renaissance Theatre," in *Staged Properties in Early Modern English Drama*, ed. Jonathan Gil Harris and Natasha Korda (Cambridge, Eng., 2002), 195.

[7] Ann Rosalind Jones and Peter Stallybrass, *Renaissance Clothing and the Materials of Memory* (Cambridge, Eng., 2000), 11.

[8] Marilyn R. DeLong and Patricia A. Hemmis, "Historic Costume and Image in Emblem Analysis," in *The Telling Image: Explorations in the Emblem*, ed. Ayers L. Bagley, Edward M. Griffin, and Austin J. McLean (New York, 1995), 120.

[9] C. Breward, *The Culture of Fashion* (Manchester, 1995), 34.

[10] Cavallaro and Warwick, 135.

[11] Alexander A. Parker, *The Allegorical Drama of Calderón: An Introduction to the* Autos Sacramentales (Oxford, 1968), 65.

Christi, which included a grand procession.[12] The authors were generally priests: Lope de Vega, Tirso de Molina, Mira de Amescua, and José de Valdivielso are prominent examples. Although they were written by a variety of different authors, the *autos sacramentales* as a genre came to be virtually synonymous with the name of a single playwright, Pedro Calderón de la Barca, because he received an exclusive contract from the crown to write all the *autos* for Madrid from 1649–1681.[13] Thus, it is indisputable that he wrote far more *autos*, and pieces of much higher quality, than anyone else.

The *autos* had actually begun in the fifteenth century as liturgical dramas performed by priests inside the church.[14] Over the centuries, however, the art form evolved, moving out to the courtyard and then taking to the streets. Each year either two or four new *autos* were performed: there were four per year from 1592 to 1646, and two per year

---

[12] Todd Arthur Price, "The Stage in the Streets: Calderón de la Barca's *autos sacramentales* in the Urban Landscape of Madrid," Ph.D. diss., Univ. of Virginia, 2004, 13–14, describes the procession and how it evolved: "In 1317, Pope John XXII added an octave and a procession to the celebration of Corpus Christi, laying the groundwork for what would become in the seventeenth century the most elaborate and splendid annual procession in Spain. The procession quickly became a mix of the sacred and the profane, and as early as 1392 secular elements, such as a dragon leading the procession, became central to the festivities. Although some criticized the secular elements of Corpus Christi, such as the dragon, the parade of giants, and the dances, others offered the justification that David himself danced before the ark of the covenant. Initially each city in Europe celebrated Corpus Christi in its own manner, but in 1551 the Council of Trent tried to impose some unity and order on the festivities. . . . In Madrid, the procession began with a parade of giants, dwarfs wearing oversized masks, dancers, an elaborate dragon, floats, and groups of children. The giants, which were common to many religious celebrations in Spain, represented the four corners of the earth, signifying both that all the nations of the world paid homage to Christ and the glories of imperial Spain. The dances were popular in nature, often employing peasants from the villages surrounding Madrid. While other religious festivals incorporated dragons, the Corpus Christi dragon, known as the *tarasca*, was far more elaborate than those that appeared at other celebrations. The arms of the *tarasca* were operated by children, who were so adroit that, according to the account of a French traveler, they could snatch the hats off spectators. On the back of the *tarasca* rode a woman, who displayed the latest fashions for the upcoming year. The giants and the *tarasca* would eventually be banned from the Corpus Christi celebrations in 1772 by the Bourbon monarchy. In 1780, all popular elements were prohibited." This process of development differs from that of the Corpus Christi plays in England, which began not as liturgical drama but instead unfolded on an independent but parallel track with them. See Lawrence M. Clopper, *Drama, Play, and Game: English Festive Culture in the Medieval and Early Modern Period* (Chicago and London, 2001).

[13] Ibid., 11.

[14] Alfonso Reyes, "Los autos sacramentales en España y América," *Boletín de la Academia Argentina de Letras* 5 (1937): 351.

until the *autos* were prohibited in 1765. The city officials selected and financed the writing and production of the *autos*. Theatrical companies were paid exceedingly well for these productions, making the feast of Corpus Christi the single most lucrative event of the year for both actors and producers. The most important factor economically was the monopoly they received for commercial productions in the *corrales* from Easter until the feast of Corpus Christi in June.[15]

The *autos sacramentales* were performed in the open air upon a system of mobile carts:

> Originally, the *auto* was performed with two carts, each known as a *medio carro*, and a stage mounted on wheels, called either a *carrillo* or *medio carrillo*. The combination of two *medios carros* and a *carrillo* formed a *carro*. For important performances, such as those before the king, a stationary stage would replace the *carrillo*. The carts, which contained both an upper and lower staging area, were decorated with elaborate scenery and contained the latest innovations in scenic effects.[16]

The mobility of these platforms contributed to the versatility of the genre. Originally performed inside the church, the *autos* with their *carros* were soon removed to the courtyard immediately outside the church. Often the *autos* would be performed in this sacred context for their first run, but then be repeated throughout the city in various plazas to which the *carros* could be moved. Frequently the first few performances after the one at the church would be reserved for the king or prominent government officials (the *autos* would literally be performed in the plazas outside their palaces, so all they had to do was look out the window to watch). Sometimes there were squabbles over which officials would receive personal stagings of the *autos* and in what order, as it was considered a great honor to be recognized publicly in this way. Finally, around 1647 the *autos* began to be performed after the festival in the public theaters known as *corrales*, where anyone could pay to watch a repeat performance.[17]

Some scholars have concluded that the transplanting of this sacred drama into a secular context was ultimately responsible for the death of the genre.[18] For one thing, the Eucharistic centerpiece would by neces-

---

[15] Price, 24–26.

[16] Ibid., 26.

[17] On the question of audiences for the *autos*, see Pedro Ruiz Pérez, "Calderón y su público: La recepción de los autos sacramentales," in *Hacia Calderón: Décimo Coloquio Anglo-germano (Passau 1993)*, ed. Hans Flasche and Klaus Dirscherl (Stuttgart, 1994), 45–53.

[18] Price, 27.

sity have been absent from these secular performances after-the-fact. In the older formulation, the Eucharist had been more than simply a convenient excuse for dramatic production: "No matter the subject of the *auto sacramental*, each play would end with the actors presenting to the audience a monstrance containing the Eucharist.... [P]eople kneeled when the Eucharist was presented, just as they did when the consecrated host was carried through the streets during the Corpus Christi parade."[19] At its height, then—before it was transplanted into the unfertile soil of the *corrales*—the *auto sacramental* flourished not only as popular entertainment, but also as a form of worship. In the conception of Martin Vincent, the *autos* served as an "illuminative bridge" between the mass and the popular procession.[20]

III. *What We Know About Actual Costumes for the Autos*

Elaborate costumes were prescribed in the dramatic theory of the period, such as José de Pellicer's *Idea de la comedia*, precept 17, which states that "finery and adornment in actors is mute eloquence heard by the eyes."[21] Evidently in this case theory was connected to practice from early on, for King Ferdinand I of Aragon, favorably impressed with the Corpus Christi celebrations he had seen in Valencia in 1413, requested in a letter to the city councilors the loan of the angel costumes for use at his coronation.[22] This tradition of elaborate costumes for the *autos* clearly continued, with new costumes being ordered every year for the productions commissioned in honor of the feast of Corpus Christi.[23]

With the annual design of new costumes and the sale of old ones to raise funds for the theater companies (sometimes the costumes were sold second-hand to members of the audience), "theatres functioned

---

[19] Ibid., 23.

[20] Martin Vincent, *El concepto de "representación" en los autos sacramentales de Calderón* (Pamplona and Kassel, 2002), 201.

[21] "la gala y el adorno en los que representan es elocuencia muda que escuchan los ojos" (F. Sánchez Escribano and Alberto Porqueras Mayo, *Preceptiva dramática española del Renacimiento y el Barroco* [Madrid, 1972], 271); cited in Ignacio Arellano, *Estructuras dramáticas y alegóricas en los autos de Calderón* (Pamplona and Kassel, 2001), 195.

[22] John E. Varey, "Los autos sacramentales como celebración regia y popular," *Revista Canadiense de Estudios Hispánicos* 17,2 (1993): 358.

[23] Bruce W. Wardropper, *Introducción al teatro religioso del Siglo de Oro (Evolución del auto sacramental: 1500–1648)* (Madrid, 1953), 59.

as engines of fashion."[24] Various inventories exist for actual costumes used during this period.[25] Furthermore, Parker confirms that Calderón himself was responsible for the descriptions of costumes prescribed in the stage directions for his plays.[26] We know the exact positions of the wardrobes within the functioning of the scenery in several *autos* of Calderón such as *El primer refugio del hombre* and *El nuevo hospicio de pobres*.[27] Normally the wardrobe was kept in the hollow compartment underneath the portable stage,[28] although sometimes the hollow compartment was built behind a throne or other large piece of scenery. The inverisimilitude of the costumes called for in the *autos sacramentales* was actually part of the eighteenth century's criticism of this earlier genre. For example, the critic José de Clavijo y Fajardo found it absurd that the Samaritan in Calderón's *Tu prójimo como a ti* could appear onstage dressed as a Frenchman.[29] As a representative sampling of costumes for the genre as a whole,[30] let us examine the costumes prescribed for use by one or more of the Seven Deadly Sins in the *autos*. Evidence will be drawn from 20 works by Calderón as well as *autos* by Lope de Vega, Mira de Amescua, Tirso de Molina, and José de Valdivielso.

IV. *Typologies of the Vices: Evidence from Specific Plays*

The Seven Deadly Sins appear together onstage as a hydra with seven heads in Calderón's *El primer refugio del hombre*, *A María el corazón*, *El año santo en Madrid*, and *El jardín de Falerina*. Sandra Delgado and other scholars have suggested that perhaps the hydra corresponds to the

---

[24] Stallybrass, "Properties," 186.

[25] Vicenta Esquerdo, "Indumentaria con la que los cómicos representaban en el siglo XVII," *Boletín de la Real Academia Española* 58 [215] (1978): 447–554.

[26] Parker, 97.

[27] For the first *auto* see N. D. Shergold and John E. Varey, *Los autos sacramentales en Madrid en la época de Calderón (1637–1681): Estudio y documentos* (Madrid, 1961), 151; for the second, see *Memorias y apariencias y otros documentos sobre los autos de Calderón de la Barca*, ed. Lara Escudero and Rafael Zafra (Pamplona and Kassel, 2003), 155.

[28] José Sánchez Arjona, *El teatro en Sevilla en los siglos XVI y XVII* (Madrid, 1887), 63.

[29] Parker, 22.

[30] Manuel Ruiz Lagos, "Estudio y catálogo del vestuario escénico en las personas dramáticas de Calderón," *Anales del Instituto de Estudios Madrileños* 7 (1971): 181–214, attempted a broader study of costume in Calderón's *autos sacramentales*, and he has compiled a valuable catalogue of 142 recurring characters and allegorical figures; but unfortunately, his study remains somewhat incomplete. For example, his catalogue covers only three out of the Seven Deadly Sins.

tarasca, the dragon used in the popular Corpus Christi parade.[31] The Seven Sins also appear together as "proud" giants in Mira de Amescua's *Pedro Telonario*. The Affects (or sinful passions) representing the Seven Sins appear together as Hebrews complaining to Moses in the desert in Calderón's *La serpiente de metal*.[32] In most of the *autos*, however, the Vices are dressed differently from each other, even if they appear onstage together. Their costumes and stage descriptions are listed in the table below.

GLUTTONY

COSTUME / DESCRIPTION	*AUTO*	AUTHOR
innkeeper	*El gran mercado del mundo*	Calderón de la Barca
blind man	*El gran mercado del mundo*	Calderón de la Barca
gypsy man	*El gran mercado del mundo*	Calderón de la Barca
with basket of fruit	*El año santo en Madrid*; *El indulto general*	Calderón de la Barca
"lost" adulteress with hands bound	*El primer refugio del hombre*	Calderón de la Barca
female innkeeper dancing	*A María el corazón*	Calderón de la Barca
with cup (implying inebriation)	*A María el corazón*; *El jardín de Falerina*	Calderón de la Barca
male prisoner	*La universal redención*	Calderón de la Barca
hungry and thirsty	*El primer refugio del hombre*; *El hospital de los locos*	Calderón de la Barca; José de Valdivielso
crazy man	*El hospital de los locos*	José de Valdivielso

---

[31] Sandra Delgado, "La función de los pecados capitales en los autos sacramentales de Calderón de la Barca," Ph.D. diss., Univ. of Illinois at Urbana-Champaign, 1993, 109.

[32] The Affects correspond to the Seven Sins in several *autos sacramentales*, most notably Calderón's *La serpiente de metal* and his *loa* for *El indulto general*. Sandra Delgado, 107, explains the relationship between the Affects and the Sins: "Los afectos, en algunas ocasiones, acompañan a los pecados capitales. Ellos representan la inclinación, la pasión del hombre hacia el pecado correspondiente.... Los Afectos, por lo general, actúan con un pecado capital con el cual comparten las características propias del pecado."

Table *(cont.)*

COSTUME / DESCRIPTION	*AUTO*	AUTHOR
whore embraced by Flesh	*El hospital de los locos*	José de Valdivielso
makes altar of stomach	*El hospital de los locos*	José de Valdivielso
dances without restraint, whipped by Madness	*El hospital de los locos*	José de Valdivielso
ignorant nurse who prescribes eating and drinking as a remedy	*El hospital de los locos*	José de Valdivielso

ANGER

COSTUME / DESCRIPTION	*AUTO*	AUTHOR
with a sword	*El año santo en Madrid*	Calderón de la Barca
armed, with wings (bird-beast)	*La semilla y la cizaña*	Calderón de la Barca
with musical instruments, dancing and singing	*La semilla y la cizaña*	Calderón de la Barca
carries stems with no stalks (result of locust plague)	*La semilla y la cizaña*	Calderón de la Barca
male bandit with gun belt and pistol	*A María el corazón*	Calderón de la Barca
Gentiles persecuting the early church	*A María el corazón*	Calderón de la Barca
carries breastplate	*El indulto general*	Calderón de la Barca
Roman who helps Jews to crucify Christ	*El primer refugio del hombre*	Calderón de la Barca
Herod slaying the infants	*El primer refugio del hombre*	Calderón de la Barca
Saint Paul before conversion	*El primer refugio del hombre*	Calderón de la Barca

AVARICE

COSTUME / DESCRIPTION	*AUTO*	AUTHOR
with jewels	*El año santo en Madrid*	Calderón de la Barca
a violent woman with hands bound, led by Lucifer	*La primer flor del Carmelo*	Calderón de la Barca
peasant woman	*La primer flor del Carmelo*	Calderón de la Barca
waitress	*La primer flor del Carmelo*	Calderón de la Barca
with basket of fruit and flowers	*La primer flor del Carmelo*	Calderón de la Barca
fighting	*A María el corazón*	Calderón de la Barca
thirsty gallant with beard	*El nuevo hospicio de pobres*	Calderón de la Barca
carries on a tray a golden chain,[33] from which hangs a heart	*El indulto general*	Calderón de la Barca
gambles away a gold *Agnus Dei* in a card game	*Los hermanos parecidos*	Tirso de Molina
Turk	*Pedro Telonario*	Mira de Amescua
deaf publican	*El primer refugio del hombre*	Calderón de la Barca
swollen and thirsty	*El primer refugio del hombre*	Calderón de la Barca

---

[33] Delgado, 145, notes that gold is the metal and color most frequently associated with Avarice.

PRIDE

COSTUME / DESCRIPTION	*AUTO*	AUTHOR
sells a plumed hat[34]	*El gran mercado del mundo*	Calderón de la Barca
wears a plumed hat	*El año santo en Madrid*	Calderón de la Barca
holds flag decorated with royal coat of arms	*El año santo en Madrid*	Calderón de la Barca
carries red cloak	*El indulto general*	Calderón de la Barca
gypsy woman (specifically from Egypt)	*La siega*	Lope de Vega
Jewish king who fears infant king will take away power (allusion to Herod)	*El primer refugio del hombre*	Calderón de la Barca
unrepentant thief on left side of Christ's cross	*El primer refugio del hombre*	Calderón de la Barca
Mary Magdalene (proud of her beauty)	*El primer refugio del hombre*	Calderón de la Barca
Pirate with his ship, identified as a Muslim from Africa or Asia, who is making slaves on the Catholic coast	*A María el corazón*	Calderón de la Barca

SLOTH

COSTUME / DESCRIPTION	*AUTO*	AUTHOR
old man with a staff	*El año santo en Madrid*	Calderón de la Barca
leper covered with sores	*El nuevo hospicio de pobres*	Calderón de la Barca
paralytic cured by Jesus	*El nuevo hospicio de pobres*	Calderón de la Barca

---

[34] Delgado, 130, postulates that these feathers represent the wings by which the prideful person distances himself from mere commoners.

Table *(cont.)*

COSTUME / DESCRIPTION	*AUTO*	AUTHOR
goes 6 hours without getting dressed	*La amistad en el peligro*	José de Valdivielso
phlegmatic	*La amistad en el peligro*	José de Valdivielso
eats like a Lutheran	*La amistad en el peligro*	José de Valdivielso
walks like a turtle	*La amistad en el peligro*	José de Valdivielso
male gypsy robber who takes Innocence hostage	*La amistad en el peligro*	José de Valdivielso
too lazy to fly; has a headache	*La amistad en el peligro*	José de Valdivielso

ENVY

COSTUME / DESCRIPTION	*AUTO*	AUTHOR
with cloak to hide jealousy	*El año santo en Madrid*	Calderón de la Barca
with flag bearing coats of arms of the military orders	*El año santo en Madrid*	Calderón de la Barca
wears mask	*Loa* for *No hay más fortuna que Dios*	Calderón de la Barca
fighting	*A María el corazón*	Calderón de la Barca
prisoner	*La universal redención*	Calderón de la Barca
perched on the main mast of a black ship with a serpent at the prow and dragons on the sails, sailing through waves of fire	*El laberinto del mundo*	Calderón de la Barca
asleep	*El laberinto del mundo*	Calderón de la Barca
gypsy woman from Egypt	*La siega*	Lope de Vega
crazy old man who won't stop pacing	*El hospital de los locos*	José de Valdivielso

Table *(cont.)*

COSTUME / DESCRIPTION	*AUTO*	AUTHOR
desecrator of graves (exhumes the dead and buries the living)	*El hospital de los locos*	José de Valdivielso
eats own heart out	*El hospital de los locos*	José de Valdivielso
injects poison into cup of glory	*La amistad en el peligro*	José de Valdivielso
dances without restraint, whipped by Madness	*El hospital de los locos*	José de Valdivielso
fire	*La amistad en el peligro*	José de Valdivielso
face of a lobster	*La amistad en el peligro*	José de Valdivielso
male gypsy robber who takes Innocence hostage	*La amistad en el peligro*	José de Valdivielso
wants to commit suicide by throwing self into the sea	*La amistad en el peligro*	José de Valdivielso
repentant thief on right side of Christ's cross who does enter heaven	*El primer refugio del hombre*	Calderón de la Barca
male bandit / thief who enters house at night to steal gold and life (is murdered by stabbing)	*El primer refugio del hombre*	Calderón de la Barca

LUST

COSTUME / DESCRIPTION	*AUTO*	AUTHOR
maid	*El gran mercado del mundo*	Calderón de la Barca
woman who sells flowers[35]	*El gran mercado del mundo*	Calderón de la Barca
waitress	*Los encantos de la culpa*	Calderón de la Barca

---

[35] Delgado, 208, notes that flowers signify deception and the brevity of beauty.

Table *(cont.)*

COSTUME / DESCRIPTION	*AUTO*	AUTHOR
carries a tray and a silver glass (fire comes out of the glass after man drinks from it)	*La primer flor del Carmelo*	Calderón de la Barca
wife of the World	*El año santo de Roma*	Calderón de la Barca
with a golden cup	*El año santo de Roma*	Calderón de la Barca
dragged by Chastity and Honor	*El año santo de Roma*	Calderón de la Barca
with mirror	*El año santo en Madrid*	Calderón de la Barca
violent woman, hands bound, led by Lucifer	*La primer flor del Carmelo*	Calderón de la Barca
carries basket of fruit and flowers	*La primer flor del Carmelo*	Calderón de la Barca
peasant woman with a pitcher	*El primer refugio del hombre*	Calderón de la Barca
blind Samaritan woman	*El primer refugio del hombre*	Calderón de la Barca
Prodigal Son	*El nuevo hospicio de pobres*	Calderón de la Barca
female pilgrim with timbrel, dancing	*A María el corazón*	Calderón de la Barca
male beggar	*El nuevo hospicio de pobres*	Calderón de la Barca
female bandit, with French cape, waistcoat, cloth "peasant" cap and pistols	*A tu prójimo como a ti*	Calderón de la Barca
half-naked, disheveled hair (damsel in distress)	*A tu prójimo como a ti; Tu prójimo como a ti*	Calderón de la Barca
male bandit	*A tu prójimo como a ti; Tu prójimo como a ti*	Calderón de la Barca

Table *(cont.)*

COSTUME / DESCRIPTION	*AUTO*	AUTHOR
woman fleeing in fear	*Tu prójimo como a ti*	Calderón de la Barca
comes out of a cloud	*La nave del mercader*	Calderón de la Barca
afraid	*La nave del mercader*	Calderón de la Barca
carries a basket of flowers; wears an arm-band like those worn by military officers to denote country of origin by color of band	*El indulto general*	Calderón de la Barca

Certain costumes in this inventory are precisely what we would expect to see. Arellano notes that the depiction of Lust as a woman was simply one of the standard conventions of the new comedy (i.e., the *comedia* as first envisioned by Lope de Vega).[36] The soldier costume was usually appropriate for demons or demonic agents, although demons were also often characterized as bandits.[37]

Some of these costumes send more complex signals. For example, we might think that a rustic garment would be, in some sense, degrading to the figure wearing it.[38] Thus, scholars have assumed that Gluttony and Sloth, two of the figures most often dressed in peasant clothes, are identified with the lower class and also treated more with humor.[39] But in fact, from inventories we know that peasant costumes were often quite luxurious. Arellano concludes from Esquerdo's inventory and other sources that peasant women on the stage often wore aprons, but these were coupled with ornate frocks, so these costumes are perhaps more complicated than they might seem.[40]

---

[36] Arellano, 201.
[37] Ibid., 214, 208.
[38] Marco Presotto, "Vestir y desvestir: Apuntes sobre la indumentaria en la dramaturgia del primer Lope de Vega," *Annali di Ca' Foscari: Rivista della Facoltà di Lingue e Letterature Straniere dell'Università di Venezia* 34,1–2 (1995): 373.
[39] Delgado, 194, 221.
[40] Arellano, 196, 202n17.

Other costumes require a very specific knowledge of period conventions in order to be visualized. For instance, a costume for a crazy
person would probably have resembled the outfit of a clown or a buf-
foon. Its mixture of brightly-colored fabrics would have signaled to the
audience immediately that this character was mentally unbalanced. Still
other costumes might seem ambivalent in their choice of accessories;
for example, feathers were understood to symbolize pride, but could
also simply indicate the office of a soldier. In an even more complex
example, Gluttony appears as a blind peasant in Calderón's *El nuevo
hospicio de pobres*, while Lust is a blind Samaritan woman in his *El primer
refugio del hombre*. From this evidence we might conclude that blindness
is usually indicative of moral depravity. But as Arellano reminds us,
another figure who is often pictured as blind is Faith.[41] So apparently
it is impossible to conclude that a given costume or accessory always
means the same thing in every context.

V. *Ambiguity*

Alison Lurie notes that "[b]etween cliché and madness in the language
of dress are all the known varieties of speech,"[42] while Alexandra
Warwick and Dani Cavallaro remind us that "[d]isparate discourses
criss-cross over the territory of dress."[43] Especially on the stage, "fashion
signs are endlessly commutable and permutable,"[44] lending themselves
to what can only be termed "an epistemology of ambiguity."[45] In current theoretical formulations, fashion is viewed quite rightly as a visual
code,[46] but what happens when that code is undecipherable? In the
autos sacramentales, the actors' costumes ("clothes of polyvalent uses"[47])
could border on "sartorial . . . illegibility," especially when an actor
"sacrilegiously combined items borrowed from several different social

---

[41] Ibid., 203, 197, 207.
[42] Alison Lurie, *The Language of Clothes* (New York, 1981), 21.
[43] Cavallaro and Warwick, xvii.
[44] Sheringham, 151.
[45] Susan Kaiser, "Minding Appearances: Style, Truth and Subjectivity," in *Body Dressing*, ed. Joanne Entwistle and Elizabeth Wilson (Oxford and New York, 2001), 89.
[46] Guillermo Carrascón, "Disfraz y técnica teatral en el primer Lope," *Edad de Oro*
16 (1997): 129.
[47] Arellano, 205.

groups. . . . The meaner sort reinscribed the ambivalence produced within the dominant rules of recognition as symbolic insubordination."[48] It was perhaps this social—rather than religious—sacrilege that would have proven most disturbing to elites in the audience; although in essence, the social vs. religious distinction cannot even be made with any clarity, given "the seventeenth century's concern with fashion as a morally confusing factor that obscured social boundaries."[49] This moral confusion in fact reflects the ambiguity of the vices themselves during this time period, as for example when anger could be viewed as both "righteous" and sinful, or avarice might be seen merely as "thrift."[50] This ambiguity in turn replicates a social hierarchy in which privileged social groups were permitted to indulge in vices which were then recast as virtues. Let us see how, in the context of costume, social and moral elements became inextricably intertwined.

VI. *Satire of Social Groups*

Perhaps it is this conflation of the moral sphere with the theological one that leads to our first category for uses of costume in the *autos sacramentales*—namely, to satirize social groups. One factor that immediately becomes apparent from even a cursory examination of the table above is that costumes are used on the stage to satirize marginal figures in Spanish society. In a less politically correct era, this xenophobic outlook was viewed merely as patriotism: "[t]he opposition Spaniard / foreigner, which responds frequently in the universe of the *autos* to the opposition faith / heresy, manifests itself equally on the level of costume."[51] Here we find Pride, Sloth, Envy, and Gluttony all appearing

---

[48] Amanda Bailey, " 'Monstrous Manner': Style and the Early Modern Theater," *Criticism: A Quarterly for Literature and the Arts* 43,3 (2001): 261–62, 273.

[49] Beatrix Bastl, "Clothing the Living and the Dead: Memory, Social Identity and Aristocratic Habit in the Early Modern Habsburg Empire," *Fashion Theory: The Journal of Dress, Body, & Culture* 5,4 (2001): 361.

[50] On the inherent ambiguity of the vices, see Richard Newhauser, "Zur Zweideutigkeit in der Moraltheologie: Als Tugenden verkleidete Laster," in *Der Fehltritt: Vergehen und Versehen in der Vormoderne*, ed. Peter von Moos, (Köln, Weimar, Wien, 2001), 377–402.

[51] Arrellano, 201: "La oposición español / extranjero, que responde en el universo de los autos a menudo a la oposición fe / herejía, se manifiesta igualmente en el plano del vestido."

as gypsies, Avarice as a Turk, Anger as a Roman, and Lust as a wild French woman. Sometimes the playwrights have their characters speak lines explaining the various associations of their outfits. For example, in Calderón's *El gran mercado del mundo*, Gluttony says, "I am pleasure, / gypsy of the senses, for I can / rob them with my drinks."[52] Likewise, in Mira de Amescua's *Pedro Telonario*, Charity asks Avarice why he presents himself as a Turk: "How, Avarice, do you put on / that suit and that form?" Avarice responds: "I am a Turk, for neither pity nor human pleading move me."[53] Finally, in Calderón's *A María el corazón*, Pride presents himself as a Muslim pirate: "For in me the African sect / henceforth is represented / when it goes making slaves / on the Catholic coasts." He explains the connection between Muslims and Pride later on: "the African sect, / that today is haughty Pride, / with the triumphs it has won."[54]

We see here that in Baroque Spain, costumes could also parody heterodox religious affiliations: Sloth eats like a Lutheran, while Pride is dressed variously as a Muslim pirate or a Jew. Costumes can even reveal sly political commentary, as when Envy bears a standard embossed with the military orders' coats of arms, or Pride holds a flag decorated with the royal crest. A similar purpose may have been served by the arm bands worn by certain characters such as Lust; these were devices used by military officials at the time to designate which country a soldier was fighting for. These seemingly innocuous details—flags, arm bands, and the like—could have been agents of extreme subversion in performance, if by implication the powerful religio-military orders were being criticized as envious[55] and the king was being caricatured as proud. This point serves as a reminder that performance techniques, even on what would appear to be a microscopic level, can shed much

---

[52] Pedro Calderón de la Barca, *Obras completas. Tomo III: Autos sacramentales*, ed. Ángel Valbuena Prat, 2nd ed. (Madrid, 1967), 240: "Yo soy el placer, gitano de los sentidos, pues puedo robarlos con mis bebidas."

[53] Antonio Mira de Amescua, *Pedro Telonario*, in *Autos sacramentales (El auto sacramental antes de Calderón)*, ed. Ricardo Arias (Mexico City, 1988), 434: Caridad: "¿Cómo, Avaricia, te vistes / ese traje y esa forma?"; Avaricia: "Turco soy, que no me rinden / piedad ni ruegos humanos."

[54] Calderón, 1141–42: "Que en mí la secta africana / desde aquí se representa, / cuando haciendo esclavos anda, / en las católicas costas"; Calderón, 1146: "la secta africana, / que hoy es la Soberbia ufana, / con los triunfos que ha ganado."

[55] Delgado, 180, offers the opposite interpretation, that military orders were immune to envy because they already possessed the highest honors awarded by their society.

light on the larger culture as a whole. This "superficial" trivia should
be recovered as completely and as often as possible to ensure that we
are not missing out on valuable information about a society's deepest
prejudices and concerns.

VII. *Clothes in the Bible*

Along with the ample social commentary we find in costumes for
the *autos sacramentales*, there is of course a plethora of Biblical figures
appearing as ghosts to haunt the Spanish Baroque stage. This should
come as no surprise, considering that clothing is a theme which appears
repeatedly in the Bible itself. Genesis even begins with Adam, Eve, and
the fig leaves, an episode which some scholars of fashion have come
to see as "an extraordinary meditation upon clothes."[56] It should be
remembered that in this story, God actually reclothes the pair in animal
skins, a fact which Jewish commentators interpreted as a remnant of
animal sacrifice, but which Renaissance Christian interpreters viewed
as a *memento mori* as well as a prefiguration of Christ clothed with our
sins.[57] The Old Testament contains many more examples of stories
which hinge upon clothing. Jacob "becomes" Esau to trick his father
by dressing up in his brother's clothes (Genesis 27:15). Joseph's coat
of many colors occasions the jealousy of his brothers and in many
ways serves as a catalyst in his saga of loss and redemption (Genesis
37:3). The New Testament continues and even heightens this emphasis.
Romans 13:14 instructs Christians to "put on the Lord Jesus Christ,"
Colossians 3:12 tells them to clothe themselves with compassion, 1 Peter
5:5 reminds them to clothe themselves with humility, and Ephesians
6:10–17 exhorts them to don the armor of faith.

The *autos sacramentales*, not surprisingly, often identify one or more
of the Vices with one or several Biblical figures. For example, Pride
appears as a Jewish king who fears a new infant king will take away his
power (this is a transparent allusion to Herod and his slaughter of the
innocents). Pride is also readily identifiable as Mary Magdalene, who
is proud of her beauty, as well as the unrepentant thief hanging on
the left side of Christ's cross. Sloth is the paralytic cured by Jesus, who

---

[56] Jones and Stallybrass, 269.
[57] Ibid., 271.

tells him to take up his mat and walk. Anger is depicted as four different Biblical personages or groups of people: Herod slaying the infants,
Saint Paul before conversion, a Roman who helps the Jews to crucify
Christ, and the Gentiles persecuting the early church. Finally, Lust is
a blind Samaritan woman or, in a different iteration, the Prodigal Son.
The authors of the *autos sacramentales*, almost all of whom were priests,
were clearly familiar with Holy Scripture. They did not hesitate to use
it to illustrate moral theology, even on the level of costume.

VIII. *Emblem Books*

In addition to the Holy Scriptures, playwrights turned to emblem books
for inspiration for designing costumes. Parker suggests that Calderón
looked to theologians such as Thomas Aquinas for his definitions of
the virtues and the vices,[58] but usually sources like this would not have
proven helpful for determining what the Seven Deadly Sins were supposed to wear. For this information, dramatists frequently turned to
popular emblem books, which pictured the vices, virtues, and other
figures dressed in "signifying" ways.[59] In fact, Manuel Ruiz Lagos has
identified the specific emblem book, Cesare Ripa's *Iconologia* (1618),
upon which Calderón de la Barca modeled the designs for costumes
of at least three of the Deadly Vices: Pride, Anger, and Gluttony.[60] I
have examined the 1611, 1618 and 1644 editions of this emblem book
and believe a strong case could be made for connecting Calderón's
costume for Avarice to this emblem book as well. See the accompanying figures for images of the Vices reproduced from this important
source (fig. 1–3).

---

[58] Parker, 70.
[59] For the relationship of emblem books to theatrical costumes, see DeLong and
Hemmis.
[60] Manuel Ruiz Lagos, "Interrelación pintura / poesía en el drama alegórico
calderoniano: El caso imitativo de la *Iconología* de C. Ripa," *Goya* 161,2 (1981): 288.
Unfortunately, Ruiz Lagos does not specify exactly which *autos sacramentales* he is using
for this comparison, offering instead a composite list which includes several of the same
autos examined in this essay.

Figure 1: Avarice. From Cesare Ripa, *Iconologia, overo descrittione d'imagini delle virtù, vitij, affetti, passioni humane, corpi celesti, mondo e sue parti* (Padua, 1611), 35.

Figure 2: Gluttony. From Ripa, *Iconologia* (Padua, 1611), 209.

Figure 3: Wrath. From Ripa, *Iconologia* (Padua, 1611), 263.

IX. *Relation of Fashion to the Seven Deadly Sins*

We have now examined various sources for, and allusions created by, the costumes for the Vices in the *autos sacramentales*. But why would playwrights necessarily choose costume as the vehicle for all of this moral-theological as well as social commentary? Upon closer inspection we discover a firm connection between the Seven Deadly Sins and clothes. Beginning with Saint Peter's objections to fine clothing or jewelry for women (1 Peter 3:3), the fear has persisted that fancy "vestments would poison the wearer, corrupting his inner faith."[61] Through the ages dress has been associated with sin.[62] Moralists such as Tertullian (in *De pallio*) associated fancy dress with pride. Continuing this tradition, the concept of fashion was intimately bound up with the discourse of the Seven Deadly Sins during the Spanish Baroque period. The anonymous *Respvesta theologica acerca del abvso de los escotados* (*Theological Response Regarding the Abuse of Décolletage*), whose author identifies himself simply as "a reader of theology," launches this lengthy vituperation against a concern for fashion as fostering all the sins:

> And who doubts that the passion for adorning oneself with excess, for painting oneself and exposing one's breasts among women is the daughter of pride? Then the woman who would be very given to the profanity of adornments will remain full of curses and sins. The first, vanity, because all the concern of those women who adorn themselves in excess is that others celebrate them as beautiful. The second, of envy, because such women tarnish themselves and eat themselves alive, thinking that others equal or surpass them. The third, of anger, because they become annoyed easily toward the women who stand out the most in beauty and

---

[61] Jones and Stallybrass, 4.

[62] On the general connection of clothes to the sins, and in particular Pride to courtly clothing, see Richard Newhauser, *The Treatise on Vices and Virtues in Latin and the Vernacular* (Turnhout, 1993); see also Maria Grazia Profeti, "Storia di O: Sistema della moda e scrittura sulla moda nella Spagna del Secolo d'Oro," in *Identità e metamorfosi del barocco ispanico*, ed. Giovanna Calabrò, (Naples, 1987), 135: "Moda significa Corruzione." Some kinds of dress are associated not just with vice, but also with virtue; for more on "l'étroite alliance de la vertu et de la mode," see Louise Godard de Donville, "Mode et sentiment de culpabilité au XVIIe siècle," *Travaux de Litterature* 8 (1995): 158. Specific garments such as the whaleboned doublet and the stayed corset were seen as both living moral metaphors for "upright" living and instruments of social control; see Ronnie Mirkin, "Performing Selfhood: The Costumed Body as a Site of Mediation Between Life, Art and Theatre in the English Renaissance," in *Body Dressing*, ed. Entwistle and Wilson, 155. In the early modern period, "[v]irtue is figured as a garment that can be put on. . . . The costume of custom habituates one to the habits (both dress and customary behavior) of good and evil alike" (Jones and Stallybrass, 267).

in finery. The fourth, of avarice, because to maintain their finery they guard what they have too much and covet what they do not have. The fifth, of gluttony, because to pacify beauty they easily attend too much to gift-giving. The sixth, of lust, because this is cultivated among delicacies, and is fomented with decoration and finery; and a woman who is much attached to finery will not hesitate to sell her honesty so as not to lack decoration. The seventh, laziness, because as Saint Augustine says, the women who are very diligent in the adornment of the body are usually negligent in the adornment of the soul.[63]

So we see that when playwrights were left to describe costumes to be designed for their Vices, what better mechanism did they have to denote evil behavior than a fancy outfit? We shall see, however, that this prejudice against finery—sanctioned by long tradition—was not one which playwrights accepted unproblematically. They used costumes in surprisingly complicated ways to open up larger questions of theology and subjectivity.

We shall now explore themes of dressing, undressing, and changing clothes as they appear in the plays, taking as our point of departure specific lines in which we find meditations on these themes. It will become clear that clothes should be central to any future poetics of how the *auto sacramental* works as a genre.

X. *Dressing and Disguise*

In the case of theatrical costume, there is a sense (by definition) in which "the breach between surface and substance . . . marked the sar-

---

[63] "Y quién duda que la passión de adornarse con excesso, de pintarse y escotarse las mujeres es hija de la soberbia? Luego la mujer que fuere muy dada a la profanidad de los adornos quedará llena de maldiciones y pecados. Lo primero, de vanidad, porque, las que con demasía se adornan, toda su ansia es que las celebren por hermosas. Lo segundo de embidia, porque las tales se carcomen y tiznan de que otras las aventajen o igualen. Lo tercero de ira, porque fácilmente se enojan contra las más sobresalientes en hermosura y gala. Lo quarto de avaricia, porque para mantener la gala guardan con demasía lo que tienen y codician lo que no tienen. Lo quinto de gula, porque por conciliar hermosura fácilmente atienden con demasía al regalo. Lo sexto de luxuria, porque ésta se cría entre las delicias, y se fomenta con el aliño y con la gala; y muger muy asida a las galas, porque éstas no le falten, no reparará en vender su honestidad. Lo séptimo de pereza, porque como dize San Agustín las que son muy diligentes en los adornos del cuerpo, suelen ser negligentes en el adorno del alma" (*Respvesta theologica acerca del abvso de los escotados* [Santiago: Antonio Fraiz Pineiro, 1673], 60–61, quoted in Profeti, 140).

torial mode,"[64] and where clothing appeared "as a kind of sacrifice of truth."[65] By virtue of the very function of theatrical costume,

> the plays themselves revolve around and thematize instances of counterfeiting as they demonstrate that pretence does not function as a mask or disguise but rather that affect has entirely replaced authenticity.... Subjectivity is realized as the theatrical, not as an expression of an inner core, but as the effect of a sartorial fantasy played out on the surface of the body.[66]

This theatrical fantasy is in fact sometimes not too far from what happens with clothing in everyday life. The psychoanalyst Jacques Lacan writes that the infamous "mirror stage" manufactures a "succession of phantasies," ultimately leading to the "assumption of the armour of an alienating identity."[67] But especially on the stage, the deliberate intent to disguise, to appear as other than one "is," makes it especially difficult to determine how a playwright is trying to speak through the language of clothes: "If a complete grammar of clothing is ever written it will have to deal not only with these forms of dishonesty, but with many others that face linguists and semioticians: ambiguity, error, self-deception, misinterpretation, irony and framing."[68]

The *autos sacramentales* express this aspect of fashion, as when Pride says in *A María el corazón*: "I try to put on unfaithful disguises."[69] Likewise, in *El gran mercado del mundo*, Fault describes her origin in a tissue of deceitful cloth: "for Fault / was born from a lie; / moved in various forms, / dressed in various suits... / knitting cloths of deceits / for men to wear."[70] But the Vices are not the only ones in the *autos* who get to play dress-up. There are other memorable scenes of robing, as when Free Will dresses Man in Calderón's *El año santo en Madrid*. Free Will accepts each of the garments proffered by the Seven Deadly Sins in an ironic reversal of the Pauline injunction to put on the armor

---

[64] Bailey, 272.

[65] John Vignaux Smyth, *The Habit of Lying: Sacrificial Studies in Literature, Philosophy, and Fashion Theory* (Durham, NC, 2002), 156.

[66] Bailey, 272.

[67] Jacques Lacan, "The Mirror Stage as Formative of the Function of the I as Revealed in Psychoanalytic Experience," in *Écrits*, trans. Alan Sheridan (New York, 1977), 4.

[68] Lurie, 25.

[69] Calderón, 1148: "intento vestir infieles disfraces."

[70] Ibid., 230: "pues nació / la Culpa de la mentira; / en varias formas mudada, / en varios trajes vestida... / urdiendo telas de engaños / de que los hombres se vistan."

of Christ. With each new layer, Man repeats, "Give me clothes."[71] Appropriately, Pride presents him with a plumed hat, Avarice with jewels, Envy with a cape, and Anger with a sword. Lust and Gluttony complete the picture with a mirror and a basket of fruit. Man again confirms his request: "Give me, I beg you, / what has been lacking for my adornment."[72]

The association of clothing with deceit or disguise in the *autos* should not be surprising, given their Scriptural background. It must be remembered that the devil can appear as an angel of light, or as a snake in the Garden of Eden. In the Christian life, sin appears in a multiplicity of disguises. It should also be noted that disguise was not always so menacing, or even associated with evil: witness the popular masked festivities during Carnival season. Nonetheless, there is an insistent thread running through the *autos* in which clothes are presented as deceitful and therefore disturbing. After all, "dress . . . atomizes the subject into a plethora of alternative masks," and clothes are "emphatically exposed rhetorical structures capitalizing on repeated dislocations of identity."[73]

XI. *Undressing / Layers*

There is also a sense in the *autos sacramentales* in which successive layers of clothing are associated with morality or immorality. The process of layering was seen to continue even after clothes had been stripped away, for clothes were thought to cover the body as the body covers the soul. An interesting fact of social history may help to illuminate this point of view: "in the late European Renaissance . . . it was mystifyingly common for revelers to wear a double mask, so that when the first layer came off, others would think they were beholding the true face." Evidently, then, in the early modern period "[f]ashion's text . . . is essentially a palimpsest" where layers of writing may be erased or added at will.[74]

The motivation for stripping away these layers is that deceitful clothes will bring downfall; the devil will use clothing to catch humans and cast them down. Thus, in Calderón's *loa* for *El indulto general* a Demon

---

[71] Calderón, 543, 544–45: "Dadme de vestir."
[72] Ibid., 545: "dadme, os pido, / lo que a mi adorno ha faltado."
[73] Cavallaro and Warwick, 53, 134.
[74] Ibid., 137, 153.

disrobes the Affect of Pride onstage, tearing off a red cloak of fine cloth. Pride immediately falls to the ground, asking, "Do you use the cape / to cast me to the ground?"[75] The Demon asks in return, "Who is not cast down by Pride's own adornment?"[76] The Demon proceeds to choke the Affect of Avarice using his own golden chain. Avarice begs, "I'm choking, let go, let go."[77] The Demon replies, conflating two of the Deadly Sins, "Which Avarice and Envy / is not choked by its own wealth?"[78] The stripping continues as the Demon burns the Affect of Lust with her own flame-colored sash; she falls to the ground, and the Demon throws the sash onto the pile of other clothes. In the same way, the Demon uses her own sword against the Affect of Anger to weigh her down and make her fall to the ground. Clothes are seen here to weigh down the wearer, to bring about a literal as well as spiritual downfall.

Man realizes this in Calderón's *El año santo en Madrid*, where he strips himself of his finery in repentance for his negative choices. He explains his actions as he takes off one garment at a time:

> Take, Pride, those plumes, / for I no longer want your wings; / take, Avarice, your jewels; / take, Anger, your daggers; / you take, Envy, the disguise / that was the cloak of my jealousies; / take, Gluttony, the fasts / that I offer from this moment on; / and you, Sloth, these steps / with which I draw near to Grace; / you, Lust, take (it only / hurts me to uproot your affection), / take your affection, and let your cry / be my repentance, / because naked of all / my passions, I go fleeing / from seeing that I am the evil one, / where so many are good.[79]

In a variation of this paradigm, Lust, Fault, World, and Demon undress Man in Calderón's *A tu prójimo como a ti*. Fault takes off his cloak, saying, "Now that he fell to the ground / I first of all despoil him / of his adornments, / for nakedness was the punishment / of his first error."[80] Then Lust removes a jeweled brooch from his chest (signifying

---

[75] Calderón, 1718: "¿De la púrpura te vales / para dar conmigo en tierra?"

[76] Ibid., 1718: "¿A quién no derriba el mismo adorno de su Soberbia?"

[77] Ibid., 1719: "Que me ahogas, suelta, suelta."

[78] Ibid., 1719: "¿A qué Avaricia y Envidia / no ahoga su misma riqueza?"

[79] Ibid., 555: "Toma, Soberbia, esas plumas, / que ya tus alas no quiero; / toma, Avaricia, tus joyas; / toma, Ira, tus aceros; / toma tú, Envidia, el disfraz, / toma, Gula, los ayunos, / que desde este instante ofrezco; / y tú, Pereza, estos pasos / con que a la Gracia me acerco; / tú, Lascivia, toma (sólo / me duele arrancar tu afecto), / toma tu afecto, y tu llanto / sea mi arrepentimiento, / porque desnudo de todas / mis pasiones, vaya huyendo, / de ver, que yo soy el malo, / adonde tantos son buenos."

[80] Ibid., 1899: "Ya que en la tierra caio / despojole io primero / que todos de sus adornos / Pues de su primero yerro / fue la desnudez castigo."

the removal of free will from his heart), World removes the rings from his fingers (signifying the loss of memories), and Demon steals the jewel from his hat (signifying a loss of understanding and the ability to reason). So we see that the devil both undresses the believer and at the same time uses his clothing as a trap. This ambivalence relates to the ambiguous discourse of clothing in general: "clothes both enable ('abiliments') and enslave. . . ."[81] Either way, the result is nakedness, a state which might at first seem equally ambivalent in the sartorial language of the *autos sacramentales*.

XII. *The Sacredness of Nakedness*

Few states have aroused more contradictory responses in the course of art history than nudity. To illustrate this predicament, Cavallaro and Warwick give the example of Titian's painting *Sacred and Profane Love*, in which no one is sure which type of love the naked (vs. the clothed) woman is supposed to represent.[82] On the one hand, "the shame of death in the Renaissance was intimately connected to the disgrace of nakedness."[83] With this line of reasoning, "[n]*aked* implies the unidealized figure, often depicting human frailty." Nudity can even be construed as indicative of savagery, by a signifying system in which "clothing connotes culture, breeding, and superiority; nudity here implies the opposite, i.e., the primitive, the savage, or at best, unbridled opportunity."[84]

But on the other hand, nakedness can imply "universal" virtues such as innocence or truth: "[i]n Christian mythology, we acquire our clothes in losing our 'natural' innocence and coming into knowledge of good and evil."[85] Profeti concludes, "Nudity, as one can see, thus almost becomes Truth."[86] It should be remembered in this context that Christ was stripped naked for the crucifixion. It is this more positive sense of nudity that we see most often presented in the *autos sacramentales*.

In a remarkable scene of Calderón's *loa* for *El indulto general*, the Pilgrim Jesus tramples on a pile of clothing thrown down by the demon

---

[81] Jones and Stallybrass, 231. As they continue here, ". . . the Italian *spogliare* means both to undress and to despoil."
[82] Cavallaro and Warwick, 128.
[83] Jones and Stallybrass, 270.
[84] DeLong and Hemmis, 121, 120.
[85] Kate Soper, "Dress Needs: Reflections on the Clothed Body, Selfhood and Consumption," in *Body Dressing*, ed. Entwistle and Wilson, 17.
[86] Profeti, 138: "[l]a Nudità come s'è visto diventa così Verità."

and then proceeds to strip off his own clothes in preparation for the spiritual battle he is about to undertake:

> Pilgrim (Christ): For this battle they are of no use, / for first I must divest myself / of profane riches.
> Demon: You take off the tunics?
> Pilgrim (Christ): Yes.
> Demon: But look how you spoil and affront / the royal purple you trample.
> Pilgrim (Christ): To enter this battle / Humility must trample / the pomp of Pride.
> Demon: Does your foot despise the jewels / of Avarice and Envy?
> Pilgrim (Christ): *Largesse* and Mildness know / how to pass over them.
> [The Pilgrim (Christ) passes over the pile of clothes without stepping on the sash of Lust.]
> Demon: So the favor of Lust, / how do you not step on [it]?
> Pilgrim (Christ): It is a garment / that does not even deserve, by way of my feet / contact with my purity.[87]

In the scene that unfolds, the Demon literally cannot catch the Pilgrim because he has no clothes to grab hold of. The Demon says: "As you fight so naked / of the passions of Pride, / Lust, Anger, Envy, and Gluttony, / when I go to make you a prisoner / I do not find anything to grab hold of."[88] Christ then throws the Demon to the ground, saying to Man: "This, mortal, is so that you will see / that in the battles of the Demon, / [when] he finds nothing to grab hold of, / you will vanquish him, if you enter / naked of human Affects."[89] As we will see, the *autos sacramentales* teach the sacredness of nakedness, especially in preparation for a spiritual change of clothes.

---

[87] Calderón, 1720:
Peregrino: Para esta lid no aprovechan, / que antes me he de desnudar / de las profanas riquezas.
Demonio: ¿Las túnicas quitas?
Peregrino: Sí.
Demonio: Pues mira que ajas y afrentas / la real púrpura que pisas.
Peregrino: Para entrar a esta pelea / ha de pisar la Humildad / las pompas de la Soberbia.
Demonio: ¿De la Avaricia y Envidia / las joyas tu pie desprecia?
Peregrino: Largueza y Templanza saben / pasar por encima de ellas.
(Pasa el Peregrino sin pisar la banda de la Lascivia.)
Demonio: Pues de Lascivia el favor, / ¿cómo no pisas?
Peregrino: Es prenda / que aun no merece en mis plantas / contactos de mi pureza."
[88] Ibid., 1721: "Como lidias tan desnudo / de pasiones de Soberbia, / Lascivia, Ira, Envidia y Gula, / que al ir a hacer en ti presa / no hallo de qué pueda asirte."
[89] Ibid.: "Esto es, mortal, porque adviertas / que en las lides del Demonio / no hallando de qué te prenda, / le vencerás, si desnudo / de humanos Afectos entras."

XIII. *Re-Dressing / Change of Clothes*

Theater critics have long noted that "a change of costume ... can indicate an important change in the status of the individual."[90] A change of costume may signify conversion or corruption.[91] Thus, Lucifer says to Avarice and Lust in *La primer flor del Carmelo*: "reclothe yourselves with my envy."[92] Presumably, this change of clothing leads to a sort of morphing of one vice into another, as Avarice and Lust "become" Envy by trying on its clothes: "in Renaissance drama, the changing of clothes leads to a changing of name.... Dressing and undressing are embodied forms of naming and unnaming."[93]

Changes of costume often occurred quite rapidly on the Golden Age stage: "the speed of the change of costume was evidently designed to have a considerable impact on the audience. The actor is given twenty lines in which to effect the change.... Calderón has, therefore, played upon the use of costume as indicative of ... the swiftness of his change of status."[94] Changes of costume were viewed during this period through the lens of linguistic terminology, which when we realize how it is actually used in the period will at once seem familiar and alien to us: "This redressing is an act of 'translation'—the technical term in Renaissance England both for linguistic metamorphosis and for the act of reclothing."[95] In Covarrubias' *Tesoro de la lengua castellana* (1611), we find at least the recognition that the verb *traducir* (to translate) could have analogous meanings.[96]

Costume changes in the *autos* are frequently encountered in the context of a Vice turning into a Virtue. They also often appear in a scene where a morally neutral or as-yet "undecided" or "uncommitted" figure makes a choice between garments with positive valences and those with negative ones. For example, Atheism says to Faith in Calderón's *El nuevo*

---

[90] John E. Varey, "The Use of Costume in Some Plays of Calderón," in *Calderón and the Baroque Tradition*, ed. Kurt Levy, Jesús Ara, and Gethin Hughes (Waterloo, 1985), 110.

[91] For the first signification, see the essays in *Undressing Religion: Commitment and Conversion from a Cross-Cultural Perspective*, ed. Linda B. Arthur (Oxford and New York, 2000); for the second, Arellano, 217.

[92] Calderón, 652: "de mi envidia os revestid."

[93] Jones and Stallybrass, 273, 13.

[94] Varey, "The Use of Costume," 113.

[95] Jones and Stallybrass, 220.

[96] Sebastián de Covarrubias Orozco, *Tesoro de la lengua castellana o española* (Madrid, 1611), ed. Felipe C. R. Maldonado, rev. ed. Manuel Camarero (Madrid, 1995), 930.

hospicio de pobres: "the rarity of your beauty, / the strangeness of your costume, / uplift and astound me so much / that if I believed there was a Deity, / I would believe it was you."[97] Presumably it is possible at any point to put on the "strange" and "rare" costume of Faith. The same is true for the similarly-depicted garment of Humility. In one exchange in Calderón's *El gran mercado del mundo*, Innocence, Ingenuity, and Fault discuss the garment of Humility:

> Ingenuity: Take, Innocence.
> Fault: This robe, / more than for a wedding, is for a funeral.
> Ingenuity: Not because of this is it worse to seek alive that which serves, being dead.
> Innocence: The fabric is outmoded, for it has the same thing outside as inside.
> (Music plays:) Congratulations, / let it be in a good hour, / dress yourselves with / the poor fabrics of Humility.[98]

The most important costume change, however, is seen repeatedly in the *autos sacramentales* to take place within the context of the Wedding Feast of Christ.

XIV. *The Wedding Feast of Christ*

In fact, Calderón's auto *El nuevo hospicio de pobres* dramatizes the Scriptural passages alluding to the wedding feast of Christ (Matthew 22:2–14, Revelation 19:7–9). The king (representing God the Father) is outraged that his wedding invitations have been refused by the nobility (allegorized as the four corners of the world). He tells his servants to go into the streets to gather up the refuse of society to attend the celebration instead. They find marginalized figures who represent Deadly Vices: Gluttony appears as a blind peasant, Lust as a poor beggar (a reference to the widely-held view that the poor were guilty

---

[97] Calderón, 1191: "lo raro de tu belleza, / lo no usado de tu traje, / tanto me admiras y elevas, / que si creyera que había / Deidad, serlo tú creyera."

[98] Ibid., 237:
Buen Genio: Toma, Inocencia.
Culpa: Esa gala, / más que de boda, es de entierro.
Buen Genio: No por eso es peor buscar vivo / lo que sirve muerto.
Inocencia: Tela es, pasada, pues tiene / lo mismo fuera que dentro.
(Música): Norabuena sea, / sea norabuena, / de Humildad vestiros / las pobres telas.

of sexual immorality[99]), Sloth as a leper, and Greed as a gallant young
man suffering from the dropsy.[100] The King (God the Father) says to
Wisdom, "You, eternal Wisdom, / have for everyone white garments,
/ that would be wedding clothes, / so that their nakedness / does not
create dissonance at the table, / sitting down with stains / of current
failing."[101] The King then orders all the marginal figures to "exchange
the rough garment / for a long nuptial robe."[102] When he sees the poor
scoundrels transformed into proper guests, he is gratified and expresses
his satisfaction to Wisdom: "Seeing them / with white garments, / you
having dressed them, / they signify the interior / purity of their Affects."[103]
In contrast, when he catches Atheism without the proper garment, the
King flies into a rage: "I intend / to give punishment to such bold /
sacrilegious audacity / as to sit at that table / without stripping oneself
first / of the garment of the old man / and putting on the garment
of the new."[104]

Various critics have plumbed the theological depths of signification
inherent in this elaborate allegory. For example, Calderón may have
drawn upon the writings of Gregory the Great or a sermon by John of
Avila for additional connotations of the alban wedding garments:

> This nuptial clothing is a paradigmatic example in Calderón's *autos* of the
> fusion of theatrical visuality with the motifs and senses of allegory. . . . Saint
> Gregory (*Homilies on the Gospels*) writes . . . that the wedding suit is the
> virtue of charity, and therefore the one who has faith in the Church,
> but does not possess charity, is the one who enters the wedding without
> the [appropriate] garment: What therefore should we understand the
> nuptial garment to be but charity? [. . .] Rightly therefore is charity
> called the nuptial garment, that which our Leader had in himself, while
> he came to the wedding of the Church for the purpose of associating
> it with himself. . . .

---

[99] Price, 192.

[100] On the connection between dropsy and avarice, see Richard Newhauser, "The
Love of Money as Deadly Sin and Deadly Disease," in *Zusammenhänge, Einflüsse, Wirkun-
gen. Kongressakten zum ersten Symposium des Mediävistenverbandes in Tübingen, 1984*, ed. J. O.
Fichte et al., 315–26 (Berlin, New York, 1986).

[101] Calderón, 1199: "Tú, eterna Sabiduría, / ten a todos vestes blancas, / que
nupciales ropas sean; / porque no hagan disonancia / su desnudez en la mesa, /
sentándose a ella con manchas / de actual achaque."

[102] Ibid., 1202: "trocadle el tosco vestido / en talar veste nupcial."

[103] Ibid., 1205: "De verlos / con las albas vestiduras, / que habiéndoselas tú puesto,
/ significan la interior / pureza de sus afectos."

[104] Ibid.: "pretendo / dar castigo a tan aleve / sacrílego atrevimiento, / como
sentarse a esa mesa, / sin desnudarse primero / del hábito de hombre antiguo, / y
vestido el de hombre nuevo."

The blessed John of Avila dedicates part of a sermon for Sunday, the nineteenth day after Pentecost, to explain what the wedding dress is: And this I say is the wedding dress: to be clothed in the imitation of Jesus Christ. . . .

As one can see, complex aspects of religious doctrine express themselves through costume, and many uses of the same in the *autos* are not understood well without appealing to doctrinal elements.[105]

Here we see how the special wedding clothes may be seen to signify charity, without which faith is meaningless, or the imitation of Christ, which again emphasizes the practical aspect of the faith / works equation.

XV. *Immutability / Fashion as a Readable Code*

As we have seen, it is important not to underestimate the "rhetorical power of costume" in the *autos sacramentales*.[106] In spite of the ambiguity surrounding some specific outfits or accessories, in general fashion constituted "a very familiar though wordless language . . . in early modern times."[107] Even in our postmodern age which values indeterminacy, we should not mistake our ignorance for an earlier era's unknowability. Early moderns demonstrated a persistent faith in the "metamorphosing powers of dress, . . . a means of translating the material body into a symbolic system."[108] Unlike other more amorphous aspects of Spanish Baroque culture, fashion in the *autos sacramentales* is a readable figurative code, if only we as critics can become literate in this language. Especially within a religious context, "[f]ashion . . . still has the form

---

[105] Arellano 217–18: "Esta ropa nupcial es un ejemplo paradigmático en los autos calderonianos de fusión de la visualidad teatral con los motivos y sentidos alegóricos de la alegoría. . . . San Gregorio (*In Evangelia homiliae*) escribe . . . que el traje de bodas es la virtud de la caridad, y por tanto entra a las bodas sin el vestido quien tiene fe en la Iglesia, pero no posee la caridad: Quid ergo debemus intelligere nuptialem vestem nisi charitatem? [. . .] Recte enim charitas nuptialis vestis vocatur, quia hanc in se Conditor noster habuit, dum ad sociandae sibi Ecclesiae nuptias venit. . . .

El beato Juan de Ávila dedica parte de un sermón para el domingo 19 después de Pentecostés a explicar qué es la vestidura de boda: Y esta digo que es vestidura de boda, estar vestido a la imitación de Jesucristo. . . . Como se ve, aspectos complejos de la doctrina religiosa se expresan a través del indumento, y muchos usos del mismo en los autos no se comprenden bien sin apelar a elementos doctrinales."

[106] Mirkin, 155.

[107] Bastl, 362.

[108] Cavallaro and Warwick, 136.

of sacred mimetism. . . . Fashion thus proceeds to a kind of immediate sacralization of the sign."[109]

The theme of immutability is emphasized repeatedly with respect to clothing in the *autos sacramentales*. For example, in Calderón's *El gran mercado del mundo*, Ingenuity states with confidence, "Now I know who you are, Fault, because although you change suits, you do not change inclination."[110] Similarly, Man says in *El año santo en Madrid*: "what does it matter / if the costume changes, / if always the same being / does not change Nature."[111] Joined to this theme is the failure of disguise, as in the same *auto* when Man realizes, "Now I see that they have wanted / to disguise themselves with the cloak of Envy, / and have not been able to."[112]

Ironically, a different type of immutability was possible in a world in which costumes could be recycled.[113] As Peter Stallybrass notes, "[i]t is . . . because the costume can endure after the performance is ended that it takes on a curious precedence to the actor, as if through the donning of a costume alone the actor puts on Christ, or Satan, or a Roman soldier. . . ."[114] Thus, the costume takes on a thoroughly material aura of immutability. The production may change, the location may change, the actor or actress may change, and even the script may change—but the costume of a Deadly Vice might endure as mute testimony to an enduring theological concept.

---

[109] Smyth, 160, 175.

[110] Calderón, 232: "Ahora / conozco quién eres, Culpa, / porque aunque mudes de traje, / no mudas de inclinación."

[111] Ibid., 543: "qué importa que mude / el traje, si siempre el mismo / no muda Naturaleza."

[112] Ibid., 545: "Ahora veo que han querido / con la capa de la Envidia / disfrazarse, y no han podido."

[113] This was more true of the English stage than the Spanish one, particularly for the genre of the *autos sacramentales*, where (at least when the genre was at its height) new costumes tended to be ordered every year. In the period of decline of the genre, however, costumes began to be recycled as production companies would have gone bankrupt otherwise—the costumes for an *auto* comprising the single greatest proportion of the total expense.

[114] Peter Stallybrass, "Worn Worlds: Clothes and Identity on the Renaissance Stage," in *Subject and Object in Renaissance Culture*, ed. Margreta de Grazia, Maureen Quilligan, and Peter Stallybrass, (Cambridge, Eng., 1996), 294.

XVI. *Real-life Parallels*

It is indicative of this early modern attitude toward clothing that we find accounts from the period in which real-life people wore "signifying" garments. The then-fashionable study of physiognomy had been founded on the principle that appearance was somehow transparently indicative of the qualities or characteristics of the soul.[115] It was customary during this period for young courtiers to possess at least as many three-piece suits as there were days in the week, each of a different color to reflect the mood or state of the soul.[116] One of the central conflicts of Elizabethan England was the vestiarian controversy over what clothes Anglican priests should wear.[117] Layers of clothing were also used in real life to designate concepts like outer or public appearance versus inner or spiritual reality. In England, the Spanish-born Queen Katherine of Aragon (first wife of Henry VIII) wore the coarse habit of the third order of Franciscans under her court dress.[118] And it must not be forgotten that during a different kind of *auto*, the *auto de fe*, the Inquisition forced penitents to wear a *sanbenito* or garment of reconciliation which they were then required to hang in the church with their names attached as lasting signs of their disgrace.

To comprehend fully the function of costume on the Renaissance stage, we must first understand the concepts of livery and investiture:

> [I]t was investiture, the putting on of clothes, that quite literally constituted a person as a monarch or a freeman of a guild or a household servant.... It is through the coronation service—the putting on of a crown and of coronation robes—that the monarch becomes a monarch. It is through the eldest son's ritual inheritance, publicly staged in church, of his father's armor, sword and shield that the son "becomes" his father.... Investiture was ... the means by which a person was given a form, a shape, a social function, a "depth."[119]

Investiture takes on even greater significance when we realize that "[p]rofessional actors, those most notorious of shape-shifters, were also liveried members of aristocratic households," although this livery was

---

[115] Joanne Finkelstein, *The Fashioned Self* (Philadelphia, 1991).

[116] Manuel Comba, "A Note on Fashion and Atmosphere in the Time of Lope de Vega," *Theatre Annual* 19 (1962): 46.

[117] Jones and Stallybrass, 4.

[118] Ibid., 237.

[119] Ibid., 2.

in fact something of a legal fiction.[120] By and large, during this period clothing was viewed not only as indicative but as constitutive of identity, and finally it is to this function of clothing that we shall turn.

XVII. *The Power of Clothing to Change the Soul*

"Clothes . . . inscribe themselves upon a person who comes into being through that inscription. . . . Fashion fashions, because what can be worn can be worn deeply."[121] In other words, there is a paradoxical "depth" to the apparently superficial: "[t]he material of cloth matters so much because it operates on, and undoes, the margins of the self."[122] This was more true in the Baroque period even than it is today, for then people still read enough Latin to be attuned to the root of the word *fashion* in the Latin *facio, facere* meaning "to shape" or "to make." Jones and Stallybrass comment upon the significance of this etymology: "it was in the late sixteenth century that the word 'fashion' first took on the sense of restless change. . . . [t]he modern sense of 'fashion' no longer captures the root sense of clothes as the making or fashioning of a person."[123] The etymological derivation is also apparent in other words we still use for clothing: for example, there is an obvious allusion to monastic spiritual "habits" when we refer to monks' vestments by the same term. Ironically, "[d]ress clothes the body from the inside as a self-fashioning discourse."[124] This involves a mapping of the exterior on the interior and vice versa.[125] Lest these theoretical formulations seem anachronistic, Calderón himself identifies "hábitos villanos" with "afectos humanos" in *El año santo de Roma*.[126] In this sense clothing may be seen as shamanistic:

> Both dress and the body could be said to play a shamanistic role: if it is the case that the body is figuratively decarnalized by its subjection to linguistic codes and conventions, of which sartorial and vestimentary ones are no negligible part, it also seems to be the case that this dismemberment ushers in new powers, specifically connected with the assumption

---

[120] Ibid., 175.
[121] Ibid., 2–3.
[122] Ibid., 202.
[123] Ibid., 1, 269.
[124] Cavallaro and Warwick, 15.
[125] Ibid., 38.
[126] *Amor* speaks, p. 500.

of an enunciative position. The body, in this respect, is a shaman of sorts, emptied of individuality and stripped of carnality to make room for the acquisition of alternative faculties. At the same time, it is dress that enacts the part of the shaman, by allowing itself to be possessed by a body, whose animal energies may give both literal shape and rhetorical means of expression to an otherwise limp casing.[127]

The power of dress to inscribe character qualities upon the wearer is one with which Baroque people were intimately familiar. We have lost this notion of fashion, so it is vitally important that we regain it in order to understand the *autos sacramentales* more fully.

XVIII. *Conclusion*

In current theoretical debates about fashion, one finds such statements as: "Fashion demonstrates clearly that morality is not a set of fixed absolutes stating a monolithic culture's unchanging standards of acceptability but, rather, constantly shifting beliefs that can be moulded and challenged."[128] A similarly postmodern example would be: "truth resembles appearance style; both are individual constructions that must in turn be collectively interpreted and reinterpreted so as to produce knowledge and fashion, respectively."[129] But the *autos sacramentales* have shown us that in Baroque Spain, fashion was used as a readable figurative code by playwrights trying to demonstrate clearly that morality *was* a set of fixed, immutable absolutes. Did they fail in this endeavor?

We cannot escape the fact that for Baroque people, "truth" was not some sort of postmodern, individual construction. The records of costumes we have for the *autos sacramentales* reveal eloquent—if competing—discourses of theology and morality, articulated through the language of clothing. It is our responsibility to learn this language in the same way that we would study French or Latin in order to "read" these encoded messages passed down to us through the ages.

But just as every translation is also an act of creation, and every act of interpretation is by its very nature presumptuous, so too our attempts to "read" Baroque costume will not always yield a univocal message.

---

[127] Cavallaro and Warwick, 129.
[128] Rebecca Arnold, *Fashion, Desire and Anxiety: Image and Morality in the 20th Century* (New Brunswick, NJ, 2001), xiii.
[129] Kaiser, 81.

What about the cases, as we have seen, where blindness in a character may be said to symbolize either depravity or faith? Or where nudity could imply both shame and sanctity?

Unfortunately, Baroque playwrights' use of costume is not so transparent to us as we might wish. This ambiguity may in turn derive organically from a long moral-theological tradition of ambiguity concerning the Vices themselves. The Seven Deadly Sins have always made fashion statements, but we have never been fully sure how to interpret them.

INDIVIDUALS

"BLESSED ARE THEY THAT HUNGER AFTER JUSTICE": FROM VICE TO BEATITUDE IN DANTE'S *PURGATORIO*

V. S. Benfell III
Brigham Young University

Abstract: As a virtuous system opposed to the seven deadly sins, the beatitudes were understood to imply a narrative of spiritual progress in which the concatenation of blessed states mirrors or opposes prominent virtues or vices. Dante draws on this tradition in the *Purgatorio*. Though he organizes part of the realm according to disorders of love reflected in the seven capital vices identified and elaborated by Gregory the Great and others, he signals the defeat of each vice by reference to one of the beatitudes. His use of the beatitudes, however, is not as straightforward as this account implies; he mixes up their ordering (a factor held to be very important in the exegetical tradition) and omits one of them. In this essay, I explore the reasons for Dante's unexpected mix of both the system of the seven deadly sins, where avarice emerges as a particularly decisive vice, and the beatitudes.

The seven deadly sins provided a convenient index of immoral behavior in the Middle Ages. These deadly sins, or—to be more precise—capital vices,[1] were frequently seen to form a narrative of moral degeneration. Hugh of St.-Victor, for example, referred to the capital vices as "the source of the dark abyss, from which the rivers of Babylon flow," and he summarized the progressive corruption induced by them in the following way:

> There are therefore seven [capital vices], and of these, three [pride, envy, and wrath] plunder man; the fourth [sadness or sloth] scourges the plundered man; the fifth [avarice] casts the scourged man out; the sixth [gluttony] seduces the man who has been cast out; the seventh [lust] subjects him to slavery.[2]

---

[1] Typically, medieval theologians defined sins as specific acts, while vices were held to be settled habits of sinful behavior. In most Latin discussions, the "seven deadly sins" were correspondingly referred to as *vitia*. For a brief discussion of the differences between sin and vice, see Patrick Boyde, *Human Vices and Human Worth in Dante's "Comedy"* (Cambridge, Eng., 2000), 149–53.

[2] *De quinque septenis*, 2, ed. Roger Baron, in Hugues de Saint-Victor, *Six Opuscules Spirituels*, SC 155 (Paris, 1969), 104: "Septem ergo sunt, et ex his tria hominem exspoliant; quartum, exspoliatum flagellat; quintum, flagellatum eicit; sextum, eiectum

In order to combat these vices, virtuous qualities were often opposed to particular sins in order to reverse the process initiated by the vices. These opposing entities varied and could include the seven gifts of the Holy Spirit, the theological and cardinal virtues, the Ten Commandments, or various lists of remedial virtues.[3] Prominent among these virtuous qualities were the Beatitudes found in the Sermon on the Mount, in which many moral theologians saw a narrative of moral ascent that formed a positive counterpart to the descent described by the vices.

It comes as no surprise, then, that Dante views these inverted narratives as a way of organizing his own narrative of moral ascent in the *Purgatorio*. He structures Mount Purgatory according to the most wide-spread ordering of the capital vices, allocating one to each of the seven terraces, starting with pride and ascending through envy, wrath, sloth, avarice, gluttony, and lust.[4] Conversely, a Beatitude signals the completion of each terrace, thus implying a remedial force that corresponds to the vice purged on that terrace. This dual narrative of the progressive liberation from vice and the moral ascent toward blessedness, however, is complicated by Dante's refusal to follow the standard ordering and interpretation of the Beatitudes. In this essay, I will explore the relationship between vice and Beatitude in the second canticle of the *Comedy*, though in order to understand Dante's idiosyncratic use of the Beatitudes it is first necessary to understand the interpretive context in which Dante read them.

I. *The Beatitudes in Medieval Thought*

The Beatitudes open Christ's Sermon on the Mount (Matthew 5:3–10), for many medieval commentators the central sermon of his life; they attracted, therefore, a great volume of commentary, as exegetes sought to uncover the multi-layered meaning they found under the surface of

---

seducit; septimum, eductum servituti subicit." All unattributed translations, including this one, are my own.

[3] For a concise overview of the relationship between virtues and vices in the Middle Ages, see Richard Newhauser, "Virtues and Vices," in *Dictionary of the Middle Ages, Supplement 1*, ed. William Chester Jordan (New York, 2004), 628–33.

[4] This ordering is often referred to, using the first letter of the Latin names of the vices, as SIIAAGL (superbia, invidia, ira, accedia, avaritia, gula, luxuria). As Richard Newhauser notes, this version of the capital vices had become the most common by the twelfth century. See *The Treatise on Vices and Virtues in Latin and the Vernacular* (Turnhout, 1993), 190–91.

the text. Each Beatitude contains two parts. In the first, the macarism, Christ declares members of a particular group (defined by its behavior) to be blessed (or *makarioi* in Greek). In the second, he identifies the reward awaiting that group. Both parts were important to medieval interpreters, and some of their exegetical efforts were directed toward elucidating the relationship between macarism and reward.

Another major crux for exegetes centered on the ordering of the Beatitudes. In what seems to be the earliest extended treatment, Gregory of Nyssa assumed that Christ purposefully numbered and ordered the Beatitudes. In his *Homilies on the Beatitudes* (c. 375), Gregory finds a narrative of ascent, which he illustrates by comparing them to a ladder: "I think the arrangement of the Beatitudes is like a series of rungs, and it makes it possible for the mind to ascend by climbing from one to another."[5]

For Augustine of Hippo the ordering is important because through the concatenation of the Beatitudes, he argued, Christ actually intended to teach us how to attain perfection, which we achieve by passing through humility and the other steps implicit in the Beatitudes until we gain the kingdom of God. Furthermore, he invoked another issue that became important in the exegetical history of this text: the numbering of the Beatitudes. Gregory counted eight, although the Sermon on the Mount commences with nine successive sayings that begin with the phrase "blessed are." Augustine, on the other hand, found only seven, arguing that the eighth Beatitude, "Blessed are they that suffer persecution," actually summarizes the first seven, a fact signaled by the return of its reward to that of the first Beatitude ("the kingdom of heaven"). The ninth macarism ("Blessed are ye when they shall revile you") should not be considered a Beatitude at all, Augustine maintained, since Christ identifies no reward in it and speaks directly to his disciples, not following the impersonal structure of the eight Beatitudes. Augustine's identification of seven Beatitudes allows him to find a correspondence between them and the "sevenfold operation of the Holy Ghost."[6]

---

[5] Gregory of Nyssa, *Homilies*, 2.1, in *Homilies on the Beatitudes. An English Version with Commentary and Support Studies*, ed. Hubertus R. Drobner and Alberto Viciano (Leiden, 2000), 32. See also in the same volume, Judith L. Kovacs, "Clement of Alexandria and Gregory of Nyssa on the Beatitudes," 311–29, who notes that for the earlier Clement as well, "the Beatitudes both enjoin and symbolize this graduate pursuit of perfection" (323).

[6] Augustine of Hippo, *De sermone Domini in monte libri ii*, 1.1.2–4.12, ed. Almut Mutzenbecher, CCSL 35 (Turnhout, 1967), 2–13.

Most later treatments of the Beatitudes follow the precedent set by Augustine and emphasize one or more of the issues treated in his exegesis. The relationship of the Beatitudes to various vices or prominent elements of Christian theology was one of the most frequent of these topics. Many writers were determined to follow Augustine in locating parallels between the Beatitudes and other scriptural teachings. William Peraldus, for example, in his extremely popular *Summa virtutum* from the mid-thirteenth century, juxtaposed the Ten Commandments received by Moses on Mount Sinai with the new law preached by Christ and encapsulated within eight Beatitudes, which, like the Mosaic law, was preached upon a mountain.[7]

Many others, however, sought to oppose the Beatitudes and the vices. A Latin poem from the Carolingian period represents one of the earliest juxtapositions of the Beatitudes with prominent vices. It alternates three-line stanzas; one restates a Beatitude (each stanza begins with "blessed is the man"), and the other articulates an equivalent cursing ("cursed is he"). These pairings are based, though not without variation, on the list of the vices found in the works of John Cassian (gluttony, lust, avarice, wrath, sadness, acedia, vainglory, pride).[8] The first stanza, for instance, restates the first Beatitude, "Blessed is the man who is poor in spirit," but the second stanza curses the man "given over to food,"[9] rather than cursing the man of pride as one would expect if the vices were based on the order found in Gregory the Great's *Morals on Job* (that is: pride as the source of all vices; vainglory, envy, wrath, sadness, avarice, gluttony, lust).

Later authors became much more systematic in their attempts to link the Beatitudes to other significant lists in Christian doctrine, a trend exemplified in the previously cited Hugh of St.-Victor's *On the Five Sevens*, in which Hugh lines up five groups of seven important theological concepts and shows how they relate to each other. Thus, the seven capital vices are seen to correspond to the seven petitions

---

[7] William Peraldus, *Summa virtutum*, 5.2 ("de beatitudinibus tractatus") (Antwerp, 1588), 225.

[8] Newhauser provides a general history of the various systems of the capital vices in *The Treatise on Vices and Virtues*, 181–93, with a helpful schematic comparison of the systems of Cassian and Gregory at 187–88. See also now Carole Straw, "Gregory, Cassian, and the Cardinal Vices," in *In the Garden of Evil. The Vices and Culture in the Middle Ages*, ed. Richard Newhauser (Toronto, 2005), 35–58.

[9] "Versus de octo vicia et octo beatitudines," ed. Karl Strecker, MGH Poetae Latini Aevi Carolini, 4,2 (Berlin, 1923; reprint, 1964), 585–87 [title as it appears in the MGH].

of the Lord's Prayer, the seven gifts of the Holy Spirit, seven virtues, and the seven Beatitudes. These sevens emphasize the Beatitudes to a degree not immediately apparent, since the "virtues" to which Hugh refers are not remedial virtues, nor the traditional cardinal and theological virtues, but instead the macarisms that constitute the first half of each Beatitude.

Bernard of Clairvaux, on the other hand, while not providing a systematic treatment of the Beatitudes, in an early work, *On the Steps of Humility and Pride* (c. 1125), provides one example of an exegete looking to the Beatitudes to discover a key to spiritual progress. He finds their ordering important in his attempt to trace the "three steps" of the ladder of our knowledge of truth, since they teach us that meekness comes before mercy, which precedes purity of heart, thus pointing to the three steps of truth: the difficulty of humility (*laborem humilitatis*), the affect of compassion (*affectum compassionis*), and finally the flight of contemplation (*excessum contemplationis*).[10] Similarly, in the widely read exegesis of Matthew 5 contained in the *Glossa ordinaria*, much is made of the fact that one can come to the later Beatitudes only by having passed through the earlier ones. When discussing Matthew 5:7, for example, "Blessed are the merciful," the *Gloss* reads: "Mercy is born from the preceding [Beatitudes], because if true humility has preceded, and the mind becomes meek and laments its own misfortunes and those of others and hungers for justice, afterward true mercy is born."[11]

The final end of blessedness or beatitude that exegetes and theologians found promised in the Biblical text also increasingly became a topic of interest. Most early medieval exegetes followed Augustine in seeing the promised beatitude occurring primarily in the life to come, but nevertheless being anticipated and to some degree achieved in this life, as was the case with Christ's apostles (*De sermone Domini*, 1.4.12, 11–13). Another tradition identified particular Beatitudes with degrees of holiness, which writers correlated with particular types of saints or grades of celestial creatures.[12]

---

[10] *Liber de gradibus humilitatis et superbiae*, 4.13–6.19, in *Sancti Bernardi opera*, ed. Jean Leclercq and H. M. Rochais (Roma, 1963), 3:13–59.

[11] *Biblia Latina cum Glossa ordinaria. Facsimile reprint of the Editio Princeps, Adolph Rusch of Strassburg 1480/81*, intro. Karlfried Froehlich and Margaret T. Gibson (Turnhout, 1992), 4:17–18: "Misericordia nascitur de praecedentibus, quia si praecesserit vera humilitas et animus mansuescat, et suos et aliorum casus fleat, et justitiam esuriat, post nascitur vera misericordia."

[12] For an account of this tradition, see Louis Jacques Bataillon, "Béatitudes et types de sainteté," *Revue Mabillon*, n. s. 7 (1996): 79–104.

The Beatitudes, then, were frequently seen as a locus for questions of moral theology, especially the question of how one can overcome vice and proceed toward the moral perfection implicit in the ultimate beatitude. It should not surprise us that the Beatitudes became a text of some interest with the rediscovery of Aristotle's *Nichomachean Ethics*, as philosophers and theologians sought ways of reconciling the newly authoritative views of Aristotle and traditional Christian ethics.[13] Three topics in particular discussed in the history of the exegesis of the Beatitudes relate directly to the issues of moral theology raised by the recovery of Aristotelian ethical thought.

First, Aristotle considers happiness only as it applies to this earthly life, whereas for Christians ultimate beatitude is possible only in the life to come. The debate concerning blessedness or happiness is well illustrated in an important text composed before the complete translation of Aristotle's *Ethics*, namely, Abelard's *Dialogue of a Philosopher with a Jew and a Christian* (c. 1136). Here, Abelard has his Christian convince the philosopher that one must look to the life to come in order to gain true blessedness, since all of the goods promised in this life reach their perfection only in "the supreme good of man or . . . the goal of the good, in the blessedness of a future life (*finem boni, future vite beatitudinem*), and the route thereto in the virtues." This teaching was set down by Jesus himself, "where he encouraged contempt for the world and the desire for this beatitude as well, saying, 'Blest are the poor in spirit, for theirs is the kingdom of heaven' . . . all prosperity is to be held in contempt or adversities tolerated out of hope for that highest and eternal life."[14] It is telling that Abelard's Christian cites a Beatitude in order to "prove" that ultimate blessedness resides only in the beatitude of the kingdom of heaven.

---

[13] Serious debate surrounding the *Ethics* begins in the second half of the thirteenth century, as there was no complete translation of the text into Latin until Robert Grosseteste's translation of 1246–47, though Latin translations of the first three books did circulate prior to that time. For an overview of the reception and translation of the *Ethics* during this period, see R. A. Gauthier, *Introduction*, vol. 1 of R. A. Gauthier and J. Y. Jolif, *L'Éthique à Nicomaque: Introduction, Traduction, et Commentaire* (Louvain, 1970), 111–34; Georg Wieland, "The Reception and Interpretation of Aristotle's *Ethics*," in *The Cambridge History of Later Medieval Philosophy from the Rediscovery of Aristotle to the Disintegration of Scholasticism: 1100–1600*, ed. Norman Kretzmann, Anthony Kenny, and Jan Pinborg (Cambridge, Eng., 1982), 657–672; and Bonnie Kent, *Virtues of the Will: The Transformation of Ethics in the Late Thirteenth Century* (Washington, D. C., 1995), 39–93.

[14] Peter Abelard, *Dialogue of a Philosopher with a Jew and a Christian*, trans. Pierre J. Payer (Toronto, 1979), 95–96.

Second, Christian theology traditionally held that charity, which is infused in the Christian soul by grace and not by any effort of the individual, is necessary for any virtuous action. For Aristotle, however, virtues can be learned through the development of habits and the education of the mind. Augustine of Hippo was perhaps most influential in insisting that pagan virtue was no virtue at all since it was not based on charity, for actions that appear virtuous but lack charity actually consist of one vice (usually pride) overcoming another vice. "Therefore, then only may we consider vices overcome when they are overcome by love for God. This love is granted only by God himself, and only through the mediator between God and men, the man Christ Jesus."[15]

Finally, Aristotle held that virtue was best defined as a mean between extremes. Dante, following Aristotle, states the idea in his philosophical treatise, the *Convivio*: "Each of these virtues has two collateral enemies, that is vices, one in excess and another in deficiency; and these virtues are the means between those extremes."[16] This "moderate virtue" (or "golden mean") seems to contradict the ethics taught by Christ in the New Testament, which in many cases seem to embrace extreme notions of virtue.[17]

Medieval Aristotelianism, then, began to influence the ways in which exegetes read the Beatitudes well before Dante wrote the *Comedy*. A thorough attempt at reconciling the Beatitudes with the new Aristotelian moral philosophy can be found in Thomas Aquinas, who devotes a question with four articles to the consideration of the Beatitudes in the *Summa theologiae*. Aquinas, like many before him, counts seven Beatitudes, but he begins to depart from previous commentators in the third article of the question, where his Aristotelian assumptions come to the fore. Here, in order to clarify why the "list of Beatitudes is altogether appropriate," he notes that "there are three kinds of beatitude" after

---

[15] Augustine of Hippo, *The City of God Against the Pagans*, 21.16, trans. William M. Green (Cambridge, MA, 1984), 7:91: "Tunc itaque victa vitia deputanda sunt cum Dei amore vincuntur, quem nisi Deus ipse non donat nec aliter nisi per mediatorem Dei et hominum, hominem Christum Iesum."

[16] Dante, *Convivio*, 4.17.7, ed. Cesare Vasoli and Domenico de Robertis, in *Dante Alighieri: Opere Minori*, vol. 2, parts 1 and 2 (Milan, 1988; reprint, 1995), 727: "E ciascuna di queste vertudi ha due inimici collaterali, cioè vizii, uno in troppo e un altro in poco; e queste tutte sono li mezzi intra quelli."

[17] In the Sermon on the Mount, for example, Jesus tells his disciples: "Love your enemies; do good to them that hate you; and pray for them that persecute and calumniate you," a teaching that is certainly at variance with the spirit of Aristotle's ethical thought.

which people seek: the beatitude of a life of pleasure (*vita voluptuosa*),
that of an active life (*vita activa*), and that of a contemplative life (*vita
contemplativa*), a tripartite division derived from the beginning of the
Nichomachean Ethics where Aristotle identifies the three most common
perceptions of happiness as the life of pleasure (*vita voluptuosa*), the civic
life (*vita civilis*), and the contemplative life (*vita contemplativa*).[18] Thomas
incorporates the standard interpretation of the Beatitudes as narrative ascent into this Aristotelian framework. Rather than reversing the
progressively degenerative effects of sin, Aquinas sees the Beatitudes
as counteracting the negative influence of incorrect notions of happiness. The first three "eliminate the obstacle created by the happiness
of pleasure." The fourth and fifth teach the happiness of the active
life, while the final two address the contemplative life, or the "final
beatitude itself," which is the direct vision and contemplation of God
enjoyed after this life.

Aquinas, further, weighs in on the issue of whether happiness can
be obtained in this life, as Aristotle held; in an earlier article of this
question, he writes, "Beatitude is the last end of human life, as was
said above. However, a person is said to have hold of the end already
because of his hope of obtaining it. Hence according to Aristotle, boys
are called happy out of hope; and Saint Paul says, 'In hope we have
been saved.'"[19] The conjunction of Paul and Aristotle provides an apt
illustration of the Scholastic project of reconciliation, though Aquinas's
use of Aristotle is problematic here. In the *Ethics*, Aristotle argues that
children cannot be considered happy, because their youth prohibits
them from engaging in the activities that lead to happiness, and if we
do call children happy, it is by way of congratulation on their future
promise.[20] Aquinas interestingly misreads him here, but he does so in

---

[18] *Summa theologiae*, 1a 2ae, 69.3. I cite the Blackfriars edition and translation (London
and New York, 1964–81), 24:50–53. Latin text of Aristotle taken from *Ethica Nicomachea,
translatio Roberti Grosseteste Lincolniensis, recensio pura*, ed. R. A. Gauthier (Leiden, 1972),
145–46; English translation taken from Aristotle, *The Nichomachean Ethics*, trans. J. A. K.
Thompson, rev. Hugh Tredennick (London, 2004), 8–9 (1095b–1096a); though I cite
this translation of the Greek, I have checked it against Grosseteste's Latin translation
and note where there are important differences.

[19] *Summa theol.*, 1a 2ae, 69.1 (24:44–45): "beatitudo est ultimus finis humanae vitae.
Dicitur autem aliquis jam finem habere, propter spem finis obtinendi: unde et Phi-
losophus dicit, in *Ethic.*, *quod pueri dicuntur beati propter spem*; et Apostolus dicit, *Rom.*, *Spe
salvi facti sumus.*"

[20] Aristotle, *Nichomachean Ethics*, 1100a (21); *Ethica Nichomachea*, 155: "...neque puer

order to support an Aristotelian idea—that happiness or beatitude can be found in this life.

Aquinas moves further in an Aristotelian direction by arguing for the intermediary validity of the earthly notion of happiness found in the active life. For while the beatitude of the life of pleasure is "false and contrary to reason," the beatitude of the active life "disposes one for the beatitude which is to come."[21] Elsewhere in the *Summa*, Aquinas argues, against Augustine, that non-Christians can possess true moral virtues. As Bonnie Kent has shown, "toward the end of the thirteenth century it became standard to distinguish between natural *moral* goodness, which makes one an admirable member of human society in the present life, and supernatural, *meritorious* goodness, which makes one eligible for the perfect happiness of the afterlife."[22] Aquinas uses this distinction to reconcile the ideas of happiness and moral virtue in Aristotle and those of Augustine and the earlier Christian tradition.

Dante, then, inherited a rich interpretive tradition surrounding the Beatitudes, one that had fairly well defined contours and limits but also some degree of variety based upon the theological and philosophical contexts in which the Biblical text was interpreted. Most interpreters took great interest in the ordering of the blessings, finding in them a series of stages moving toward the ultimate beatitude of salvation and the contemplation of God. These stages were frequently seen to correspond to opposing lists of vices or equivalent lists of virtues, spiritual gifts, or other Scriptural texts. But there was sufficient variety in the tradition to allow for a new Scholastic interpretation that could accommodate the Beatitudes in the context of medieval Aristotelian moral thought. We will see evidence of all of these aspects of the interpretive tradition in Dante's *Purgatorio*, though we will also see that Dante frequently draws on that tradition in original ways, ultimately making use of the Beatitudes so that they serve his own poetic purposes.

---

felix est. Nondum enim operator talium propter etatem. Dicti autem, propter spem beatificantur."

[21] *Summa theol.*, 1a 2ae, 69.3 (24:52–53): "Nam beatitudo voluptuosa, quia falsa est et rationi contraria, impedimentum est beatitudinis futuræ. Beatitudo vero activæ vitæ dispositiva est ad beatitudinem futuram."

[22] *Virtues of the Will*, 30 (emphasis Kent's). See *Summa theol.*, 2a 2ae, 10.4 (32:48–51); 2a 2ae, 23.7 (34:26–31).

II. *The Beatitudes in Dante's* Purgatorio

The ascent of Dante the pilgrim up Mount Purgatory is configured largely in liturgical terms, with a set ritual governing his progress through each terrace. Upon entering, he encounters positive and negative examples; souls chanting a hymn, psalm, or prayer based on a Biblical text; and angels who guard the transitions to the following terraces and who sing Beatitudes that signal the soul's freedom from the vices of each terrace.[23] Although the Beatitudes had no place in the medieval liturgy, Dante places them within this liturgical context, providing them with the function of marking the soul's progress toward God.[24] As we have seen, this use fits into the medieval interpretive tradition, which frequently saw in the Beatitudes a narrative of moral ascent. This same tradition, however, leads us to expect a careful ordering of the Beatitudes, while Dante's own use and ordering proves to be more complex.[25]

Dante's freedom with the ordering of the Beatitudes can be illustrated by comparing it to Hugh of St.-Victor's more traditional ordering in *De quinque septenis*. While both employ the same ordering of the vices derived from Gregory the Great and both associate the first Beatitude ("Blessed are the poor in spirit") with the first and foundational vice of pride, their juxtaposition of Beatitude to vice does not coincide in any other case. Hugh takes care to use each of the Beatitudes in proper Biblical order, associating the second Beatitude with the second vice, the third Beatitude with the third vice, and so on. Dante, however, disregards

---

[23] For a fuller exposition of the moral structure of the canticle, see Edward Moore, "Unity and Symmetry of Design in the *Purgatorio,*" *Studies in Dante: Second Series* (Oxford, 1899; reprint, 1968), 246–267. There is no hymn on the fourth terrace, where the vice of sloth or acedia is purged. All citations of the *Comedy* refer to the Petrocchi text as reproduced in Dante Alighieri, *The Divine Comedy*, trans. Charles S. Singleton (Princeton, 1970–75). Translations of the *Comedy*, though, are my own.

[24] The fact that the Beatitudes are not included in the liturgy is noted by Evelyn Birge Vitz, "The Liturgy and Vernacular Literature," in *The Liturgy of the Medieval Church*, ed. Thomas J. Heffernan and E. Ann Matter (Kalamazoo, 2001), 591–92.

[25] There has been comparatively little work on the Beatitudes in Dante. See the following: Frederigo Tollemache's entry "Beatitudini evangeliche" in *Enciclopedia Dantesca*, ed. Umberto Bosco (Rome, 1970–78), 1:540–41; Richard Lansing's entry on "Beatitudes" in the *Dante Encyclopedia*, ed. Richard Lansing (New York, 2000), 89; the extended treatments of the question include Anna Maria Chiavacci Leonardi, "Le beatitudini e la struttura poetica del *Purgatorio,*" *Giornale storico della letteratura Italiana* 101 (1984): 1–29; Sergio Cristaldi, "Dalle beatitudini all'*Apocalisse*: il Nuovo Testamento nella *Commedia,*" *Letture classensi* 17 (1988): 23–67; Mark Cogan, *The Design in the Wax* (Notre Dame, 1999), 94–119; Peter S. Hawkins, *Dante's Testaments* (Stanford, 1999), 45–49; Boyde, *Human Vices*, 106–10.

the traditional ordering completely; following his citation of the first
Beatitude, he uses the others in the following order: the fifth, seventh,
third, fourth, the fourth again, and the sixth Beatitude. He never makes
use of the second Beatitude ("Blessed are the meek"). He thus does
not see in the ordering of the Beatitudes a concatenation of ascent,
although the fact that the souls on Purgatory are literally ascending
toward the blessed life would seem to call for an ordered use of them.
It is worth noting, however, that neither does Dante accept the notion
that the vices are linked by the typical notion of concatenation. (Dante
declares on the terrace of envy that although he sins greatly through
pride, he is not very envious [see 13.133–38 (138)].) Furthermore, he is
not averse to making additions, subtractions, and alterations to the text
of the Beatitudes, which he does to four of the seven that he cites. And
indeed, the best way of gaining an understanding of why and how
Dante employs the Beatitudes in the second canticle may be to examine
those that he alters. I will therefore consider in some detail the Beatitudes
found at the conclusion of the fourth, fifth, and sixth terraces.

On the fourth terrace, souls purge the vice of sloth, which Dante
terms "little love" (*poco amor*), "negligence" (*negligenza*), and "acedia"
(*accidia*), employing the Greek word for sloth that had become standard
in the Middle Ages. As Dante and Virgil leave this terrace, they hear
the angel pronounce the third Beatitude, though Dante recounts the
Angel's words indirectly: "Then he moved his feathers and fanned us, /
affirming those *who mourn* (*Qui lugent*) to be blessed, / for their souls
will be possessed of consolation" (19.49–51 [204]).[26] This Beatitude
has typically troubled commentators, as it—unlike the previous Beatitudes—does not suit its context; there is little correspondence to be
seen between the blessed mourners and the sin of sloth. The most
common way of tying the two together is to argue that the mourners will find consolation because they mourn precisely for their sin
of sloth. This reading has precedents in the exegetical tradition, with
Aquinas, for example, suggesting that those who forsake their sins must
willingly mourn for them, "taking on voluntary sorrow."[27] When read
in this way, however, the Beatitude can apply equally well to all of
the repentant souls on Mount Purgatory, not simply the slothful. The

---

[26] "Mosse le penne poi e ventilonne, / '*Qui lugent*' affermando esser beati, / ch'avran
di consolar l'anime donne."
[27] *Summa theol.*, 1a 2ae, 69.3 (24:54–55): "voluntarium luctum assumendo."

Beatitude's relation to the sin of sloth is not, then, immediately apparent, but if we note its broader context—it is surrounded by Dante the pilgrim's second purgatorial dream—we may begin to understand its place within the poem.

Canto 19 opens with Dante's dream of the *femina balba*—the stuttering, lame woman who is transformed by Dante's gaze into a "sweet siren" (19 [202]) and who enraptures Dante just as she claims to have entranced Ulysses. Her spell is broken, however, by the appearance of a "holy woman" (*donna . . . santa*), who calls Virgil twice and asks him "Who is this woman?," before exposing the siren's belly. The resultant smell awakens Dante, who follows Virgil up to the terrace of the avaricious. There, immediately following the angel's words of beatitude, we return to a discussion of the dream, with Virgil instructing Dante to learn from it how to free himself from the "ancient witch" by looking to the heavens for guidance. Dante's subsequent colloquy with Pope Adrian V reinforces this meaning of the dream; we discover that Adrian learned to desire God only after becoming pope and realizing that all earthly things fail to satisfy:

> My conversion, alas, was late;
> but as I was made the Roman pastor
> I discovered that life is deceitful.
> I saw there that my heart could not come to rest,
> nor could I ascend further in that life;
> so for this life love was ignited in me (19.106–11 [206–08]).[28]

Adrian's narrative further serves as an apt illustration of the discourse that Virgil provides to the pilgrim in cantos 17 and 18 on human motivation, sin, and virtue, in which Virgil explains that all human action derives from love of some perceived good. The way to virtue and to God is to learn to place love or desire on the proper goods. There are human goods that may be properly desired, but they are not the ultimate good, and all desires must finally be directed toward God. Thus, Virgil describes the moral logic of the sequence of vices (according to the wide-spread SIIAAGL ordering) that Dante encounters as he ascends the mountain; the first three terraces of Purgatory (dealing with pride, envy, and wrath) are dedicated to purging desires directed toward false

---

[28] "La mia conversïone, omè!, fu tarda; / ma, come fatto fui roman pastore, / così scopersi la vita bugiarda. / Vidi che lì non s'acquetava il core, / né più salir potiesi in quella vita; / per che di questa in me s'accese amore."

goods; the middle terrace corrects the insufficient love for the ultimate good that characterizes sloth; and the final three terraces (devoted to avarice, gluttony, and lust) redirect desires for earthly things that are good but not the good that "makes man happy" (17.133 [186]). Adrian initially sought peace in an earthly good, and only on discovering that it failed to satisfy did he turn his love to God. Dante's dream in turn illustrates the process of desire in allegorical form. It is only through Dante's gaze that the stuttering woman becomes the sweet siren—only, that is, when Dante directs his desire to her does he actually transform her into an apparently eloquent and beautiful woman, a point Dante makes clear in the language he employs ("my gaze made straight / her tongue" [19.12–13 (200)]).[29] Another point worth emphasizing, however, is that neither Dante nor Virgil is able to free Dante from the siren without the help of the "holy woman" who comes and reprimands Virgil and exposes the siren. We later learn that Virgil had called Dante "at least three times" before Dante awakened from his dream, a reference, perhaps, to Virgil's inability to free Dante from the siren.

Dante held that certain moral virtues, the "cardinal virtues," as well as the happiness proper to this life could be obtained solely through earthly means, specifically through "philosophical teachings" (documenta phylosophica), as he states it in the Monarchia. We attain to eternal happiness, however, though "spiritual teachings that transcend human reason."[30] While Dante, then, sided with the moderate Aristotelians such as Aquinas in arguing that real moral virtues are possible for non-Christians, he also maintained that certain virtues can be attained only through an infusion of grace that actually transforms our will, which, because of its fallen nature, cannot reform itself. With this context, and a reading of the "holy woman" of Dante's dream as an agent of grace, a more complete allegorical interpretation of the dream emerges. Dante's fallen desires transform evils into apparent goods, so much so that he begins to follow after them. Virgil (or unaided reason?) is unable to free him from the grip of these desires, despite his attempts to call Dante back to himself. Only the "holy woman," or divine grace, can unmask the true nature of the apparent goods for the evils they are

---

[29] "lo sguardo mio le facea scorta / la lingua."

[30] Dante, Monarchia, 3.15.7–9, ed. Bruno Nardi, Dante Alighieri: Opere Minori, vol. 3, part 1 (Milan, 1979; reprint, 1996), 498: "documenta spiritualia que humanam rationem transcendent." translation from Dante Alighieri, On World-Government, trans. Herbert W. Schneider (New York, 1957), 78.

by correcting Dante's gaze so that he comes to see her rightly again. This sense of grace is reinforced by Dante when he has Virgil say to the pilgrim following his dream, "Rise and come" (*Surgi e vieni* [19.35 (202)]), words that echo Christ's words in the Gospels to a paralytic man whom he heals: "Rise . . . and go" (see Matthew 9:6). Indeed, in this Gospel episode Christ had first forgiven the sins of the lame man, a statement that aroused the anger of the scribes. Christ healed the man specifically to demonstrate the reality of the grace that he brings: ". . . that you may know that the Son of man hath power on earth to forgive sins. . . ." Dante, that is, associates himself with the paralytic from the Gospel episode, portraying himself as the recipient of miraculous, healing grace. His dream illustrates both the process of sinfully attaching our desires to false goods and the fact that grace is often necessary to change those desires.

Canto 19, then, occupies a central place in the moral order of the *Purgatorio*, illustrating both through Dante's dream and through his encounter with Pope Adrian V the nature of human motivation, sin, and reformation. The Beatitude that is spoken near the middle of the canto reinforces its message, as it declares blessed those who mourn for their sins. The Beatitude is ideally suited to this canto (if not to the particular sin of sloth) that portrays the dangerous seduction of worldly goods, and it also prepares the way for the final three terraces of Purgatory, which, as Virgil tells Dante, are devoted to the love that "too much abandons itself" (17.136 [186]) to worldly goods. Critics have not known what to make of this Beatitude because they have assumed that it must function according to the system established by the previous three Beatitudes. As I have argued, however, this Beatitude provides an exception to that system; rather than summarizing the vice purged on the preceding terrace, it serves primarily to introduce the next stage in the process of purgation.

The Beatitudes that are spoken at the end of the fifth and sixth terraces are actually different parts of the same Beatitude, the fourth that Jesus speaks in the Sermon on the Mount: "Blessed are they that hunger and thirst after justice." Dante divides the hunger from the thirst, and has thirst conclude the terrace of the avaricious, while hunger ends the terrace of the gluttonous. The choice of the fourth Beatitude is obviously appropriate for the sixth terrace, as gluttony involves immoderate hungering and thirsting, but it also proves suitable for the fifth terrace, since avarice was often described in terms of thirsting and hungering. In Richard of St.-Victor's words, it involves thirsting and hungering after "gold, silver, clothing, estates, lands, vineyards, houses, horses, and innumerable possessions."[31] Souls on these terraces who have immoderately desired worldly gain or food and drink must now learn to desire the things of God, a longing which is summarized as the hungering and thirsting for justice. From the perspective of medieval moral philosophy, this Beatitude is particularly interesting, since justice is one of the four cardinal virtues (along with prudence, fortitude, and temperance) not exclusive to Christians, and one discussed at length by Aristotle in book five of the *Ethics*. It was held by Aristotle and his Scholastic followers to be a virtue that was fully attainable by human beings without supernatural aid. In fact, before discussing the eleven Aristotelian virtues—including justice—in the *Convivio*, Dante suggests that the "fruits most proper to us are the moral virtues, since they are in every respect within our power."[32] As we have just seen, however, Dante took some pains in canto 19 to suggest that grace was essential for finally overcoming certain vices and attaining virtue. One of the key questions we will need to ask, therefore, is to what degree the justice proclaimed in the fourth Beatitude is compatible with an Aristotelian conception of justice and the beatitude that Dante's angels proclaim at the end of the fifth and sixth terraces.

Dante creates an Aristotelian fifth terrace by including both avaricious and prodigal souls—those whose attitudes toward wealth were so extreme either in desiring it or in caring nothing for it that they must learn the proper mean between them. As we move through the terrace, however, the portrayal seems completely one sided. We meet only two figures (Adrian V and the king Hugh Capet), both of whom were avaricious; we hear positive examples of those happy with virtuous poverty (Mary and the Roman consul Gaius Fabricius) and negative examples of avarice punished. There is one other positive example, however—Saint Nicholas—who is praised for his legendary generosity in providing dowries for a nobleman's three daughters. This example begins to hint at something like an Aristotelian virtue, because unlike

---

[31] *Allegoriae in Novum Testamentum*, PL 175:764: "Alii etenim esuriunt et sitiunt aurum, argentum, vestes pretiosas, praedia, terras, vineas, domos, equos et possessiones innumeras." Richard Newhauser identifies earlier uses of "thirst" and "hunger" as imagery to describe avarice; Evagrius uses both thirst and hunger to describe the vice; Chrysostom uses thirst. See *The Early History of Greed: The Sin of Avarice in Early Medieval Thought and Literature* (Cambridge, Eng., 2000), 136, 140.

[32] Dante, *Convivio*, 4.17.2 (720–721): "propiissimi nostri frutti sono le morali vertudi, però che da ogni canto sono in nostra podestate."

the previous instances of individuals who are content to be poor but virtuous, Nicholas is praised for using wealth generously and properly. Dante seems here to be strongly influenced by the Aristotelian virtue of liberality, which Aristotle describes at the beginning of book four of the *Ethics*, and which Dante defines in the *Convivio* as "the mean between our giving and our receiving temporal goods."[33] Nicholas, in other words, provides an example of Aristotelian liberality, positioned between the opposite extremes of avarice and prodigality.

Prodigality as a sin punished on the fifth terrace is mentioned only at the beginning of the sixth terrace, when Statius reveals to Dante and Virgil that the sin for which he spent so much time on the fifth terrace was not avarice, but prodigality. Furthermore, Statius' description of his sin as a "lack of measure" (*dismisura*) that placed him too far from avarice (*avarizia fu partita / troppo da me* [22.34–35; 236])—and thus too far from the mean between his own sin and that of the opposite extreme) reinforces the Aristotelian nature of the virtue that he as a prodigal needed to learn while on the fifth terrace. What is wanted is not an extreme embracing of poverty, it seems, such as many Christians including Francis of Assisi would have engaged in, but a proper appetite for material goods, one that recognizes that they are good but does not mistake them for our final Good.

Following, then, the terrace of the avaricious and the prodigal, another Beatitude is spoken, though Dante reports this one indirectly as well. "Those that have justice as their desire / [the angel] declared blessed, and his words / with '*they thirst*,' without the rest, concluded" (22.4–6 [234]).[34] The justice that the blessed desire must be understood here in its Aristotelian sense, which in the *Convivio* Dante summarizes as "loving and following rectitude (*dirittura*) in all things."[35] Aristotle associates injustice with unfairness and inequality, and we have the implication that by thirsting for justice, the souls cured of avarice and prodigality now hunger fairly for material things, in a way that recognizes their worth without over- or under-estimating them, as well as the further implication that they will, as did Saint Nicholas, expend

---

[33] Dante, *Convivio*, 4.17.4 (723): "moderatrice del nostro dare e del nostro ricevere le cose temporali."

[34] "e quei c'hanno a giustizia lor disiro / detto n'avea beati, e le sue voci / con '*sitiunt*', sanz'altro, ciò forniro."

[35] Dante, *Convivio*, 4.17.6 (727): "amare e operare dirittura in tutte cose."

their riches fairly, giving to each person his or her due.[36] One cannot help noticing, however, that the virtue thereby achieved is a resolutely earthly one, since riches, and the ability to distribute them, are not to be found in the afterlife. In addition, nowhere does Dante insist on the necessity of grace for the attaining of this virtue of justice. Indeed, when Statius tells Virgil and Dante how he came to repent of his prodigality, we learn that it was through reading Virgil's *Aeneid* that he began to appreciate that there was a proper or "sacred" hunger for gold that should restrain his spending.[37] If we think back to Virgil's inability to unmask the siren in Dante's dream, Statius' learning of virtue through the study of the *Aeneid* presents a telling contrast. We seem, then, on the fifth terrace suddenly to be moving within an Aristotelian universe, a perhaps surprising development given Dante's emphasis on grace on the previous terrace.

Gluttony is the subject of the sixth terrace, and here too we have an Aristotelian virtue that can be seen to correct the vice in question: temperance. In the *Convivio*, temperance is listed among the Aristotelian virtues, and Dante defines it as the "rule and bridle (*freno*) of our gluttony (*gulositade*) and of our excessive abstinence from things that are necessary to life (*che conservano la nostra vita*)."[38] Implicit in this definition is the Aristotelian mean: we must restrain our gluttony, but we must also avoid excessive asceticism and endeavor to act like Aristotle's temperate man: "such pleasures as conduce to health and bodily fitness he will try to secure in moderation."[39] Coming as we have from the

---

[36] Newhauser notes that this definition of justice, as "a virtue allotting to each person that which is his / hers," was very common in texts of the High Middle Ages. See "Justice and Liberality: Opposition to Avarice in the Twelfth Century," in *Virtue and Ethics in the Twelfth Century*, ed. István P. Bejczy and Richard G. Newhauser (Leiden, 2005), 295–316 (citation on 297).

[37] See *Purg.*, 22.40–41 (236): "Per ché non reggi tu, o sacra fame / de l'oro, l'appetito de' mortali?" My translation of "sacra fame" as "sacred hunger," while not unprecedented, is somewhat controversial. A majority of critics would translate the phrase as "cursed hunger," since that is what the phrase in the *Aeneid* means (see 3.56–57). My own sense of the context of the phrase in the *Comedy* as well as the fact that "sacro" means "sacred" in all its other appearances in the poem lead me to support the translation I have provided. My larger point, however, that Statius' reform resulted from the study of a pagan text, holds irrespective of how the phrase is translated. For a careful analysis of the episode that explores the meaning of the phrase as I have translated it here, see Teodolinda Barolini, *Dante's Poets: Textuality and Truth in the Comedy* (Princeton, 1984), 256–69.

[38] Dante, *Convivio*, 4.17.4 (723): "regola e freno de la nostra gulositade e de la nostra soperchievole astinenza ne le cose che conservano la nostra vita."

[39] Aristotle, *Nichomachean Ethics*, 1119a (79); *Ethica Nicomachea*, 199: "Quecumque

fifth terrace, we may well expect an Aristotelian virtue of temperance to be advocated on the sixth terrace and to see both gluttons and the excessively ascetic, just as we saw, at least in retrospect, the avaricious and the prodigal on the previous terrace. Instead, only the gluttonous are shown, and they purge their vice by desiring fruit that emits a sweet odor but hangs on an inaccessible, inverted tree. The result of their unrequited longing is complete emaciation. Dante tells us that the gluttonous are able to move rapidly because of their leanness as well as their "light wills" (24.69 [260]). Of course, this method of purgation can also be read as having a kind of Aristotelian force. The extreme of one vice (gluttony) is purged and balanced by forcing the gluttonous over to the other extreme of complete abstinence from food, hoping thereby to create a properly temperate disposition.[40] In addition, it is possible to view the purgative processes of all of the terraces of Mount Purgatory, with their repetitive actions that are aimed at correcting the will, as fundamentally Aristotelian in that they are directed toward the establishment of virtuous habits. Nevertheless, we do not see any examples of the opposite vice, and in fact certain famous ascetics (such as John the Baptist) are explicitly praised.

We do find, however, that when we come to the pronouncement of the Beatitude at the end of the terrace, Dante transforms the fourth Beatitude into one that declares the temperate blessed: "Blessed the ones / whom grace illumines so that the love of taste / does not cause too much desire in their breast, / always hungering as much as is just!" (24.151–54 [266]).[41] The emphasis on hungering in just measure (*quanto è giusto*) identifies the virtue being praised here as temperance, even though it is not explicitly named. Nevertheless, two details indicate that the temperance that Dante praises both is and is not *Aristotelian* temperance.

First, by proclaiming blessed those who *always* desire in the proper

---

autem ad sanitatem sunt vel ad bonam habitudinem delectabilia existencia, hec appetet mensurate."

[40] There is some Aristotelian precedent for this idea; at the end of the second book of the *Ethics*, Aristotle suggests that, since "one of the extremes is always more erroneous than the other," a good rule of conduct is to "choose the lesser of the evils." See Aristotle, *Ethics*, 1109a (48). This point is made even more strongly in Grosseteste's Latin translation where "more erroneous" is rendered as "the greater sin" (*peccatum magis*). *Ethica Nichomachea*, 177: "Extremorum enim, hoc quidem est peccatum magis, hoc autem minus."

[41] "Beati cui alluma / tanto di grazia, che l'amor del gusto / nel petto lor troppo disïr non fuma, / esurïendo sempre quanto è giusto!"

measure, the angel identifies the temperance of the blessed as Aristotelian temperance. The thirteenth century witnessed a debate about the nature of temperance and the possibility of attaining it in this life. Aristotle made an important distinction between the temperate and the continent man; both behave the same, but only the temperate man is truly virtuous. For Aristotle, the truly temperate man follows his own desires, but because his desires are virtuous, he perpetually acts in accordance with virtue. The continent man, however, has both good and evil desires, but because he is able to recognize the difference between the two, he refuses to act on his evil desires. Augustine of Hippo had defined temperance in terms that resemble Aristotle's conception of continence; that is, for Augustine, the temperate man may still have disordered desires. In fact, for Augustine, human desires are necessarily disordered, since our fallen nature prohibits us from becoming temperate (in an Aristotelian sense) in this life. When Aristotle's *Ethics* was recovered, some of the more radical Aristotelians adopted Aristotle's view that continence is not essentially a virtue, a position that opposed the teachings of Augustine and so was specifically targeted by Etienne Tempier, the bishop of Paris, in his Condemnation of 1277, which was aimed at radical Aristotelian teachings.[42]

Dante, then, identifies the temperance that the blessed learn on the sixth terrace as fully Aristotelian in that it constitutes a correction of their wills so that they no longer will or hunger in any measure but a just one. It is also, however, a Christian virtue, because the souls attain it only through an infusion of divine grace. Thus, whereas the Beatitude pronounced after the previous terrace made no mention of the necessity of grace in regulating the desires of the blessed, this Beatitude requires grace in order to gain a supernatural virtue not attainable in this life and thus suitable only for the life to come.

The reason for the dissimilar Beatitudes of these two terraces (even though, we should remind ourselves, each is derived from the same Biblical Beatitude) may well lie in Dante's conception (or—to be more accurate—conceptions) of happiness. As noted above, a debate arose following the rediscovery of Aristotle whether happiness was attainable in this life, as Aristotle held, or could be found only in the world to come (as the Beatitudes themselves seem to imply). Dante followed

---

[42] See Kent, *Virtues of the Will*, 68–72, 209–210. For Augustine's views, see *The City of God*, 19.4 (6:123–39).

those such as Aquinas who sought to find a way to reconcile the two conceptions. Thus, after detailing the Aristotelian virtues in the fourth book of the *Convivio*, Dante asserts that there are "two happinesses, according to two different paths, one good and one best, that lead to them. One is the active life, and the other is the contemplative."[43] This passage first of all shows us how shrewdly Dante reconciles the Christian view with the Aristotelian, since Aristotle too associates a real happiness with the active life that is inferior to the ultimate happiness of the contemplative life;[44] Dante, though, adapts Aristotle's discussion so that the happiness of the contemplative life becomes perfected only in the complete beatitude of the life to come, which consists in the contemplation of God.[45] Nevertheless, for Dante the happiness of the active life is crucially important, more important than for many other Christian thinkers, since Dante, unlike Augustine, considers the beatitude of this life important for God's providential ordering of history. In both the *Monarchia* and *Paradiso* 6–7, Dante argues that the divine ordering of the spiritual and that of the temporal aspects of human history are thoroughly intertwined. His devotion to what he took to be the divinely ordained political order found in the Roman empire is well known,[46] and it perhaps helps to explain why Dante creates an Aristotelian terrace for the avaricious and the prodigal.

In Dante's ordering of the vices that structure Mount Purgatory, pride has preeminence as the first and foundation of all the other vices. While this ordering follows a medieval tradition inscribed in Gregory's *Moralia*, it is also true that in the later Middle Ages avarice become a much more prominent vice. Lester Little has argued that due to political and social change avarice had displaced pride as the root of all evil by Dante's day, because it was seen as particularly damaging to the political and social order of late medieval Europe.[47] While Dante

---

[43] *Convivio*, 4.17.9 (730): "due felicitadi, secondo due diversi cammini, buono e ottimo, che a ciò ne menano: l'una è la vita attiva, e l'altra la contemplativa."

[44] See the *Ethics*, 1095b–1096a, 1177a–1178a (8–9, 270–74).

[45] In this same passage of the *Convivio*, though, Dante refers to these two happinesses as possible "in this life": "noi potemo avere in questa vita due felicitadi, secondo...."

[46] See, for example, Hawkins, *Dante's Testaments*, 197–212.

[47] Lester K. Little, "Pride Goes before Avarice: Social Change and the Vices in Latin Christendom," *The American Historical Review* 76 (1971): 16–49. Little as well as Alexander Murray, in *Reason and Society in the Middle Ages* (Oxford, 1978), 59–80, argue that the increased attention paid to avarice was linked to the rise of a money economy in the later Middle Ages. Newhauser, though, has shown that avarice was viewed as

keeps pride as the pre-eminent vice, he also spends a good deal of time criticizing avarice in all three canticles of the *Comedy*, largely because it upsets what he understands to be the divinely ordained order between church, empire, and local rulers.[48] Indeed, given Dante's abhorrence of avarice, the balanced, Aristotelian nature of the fifth terrace may come as something of a surprise. If we look ahead to the life of Francis of Assisi recounted in *Paradiso* 11.43–117 (120–26), we will recall that Dante there places particular emphasis on Francis' marriage to Lady Poverty who had remained a widow since the death of Christ.[49] Indeed, Dante frequently and explicitly condemns popes and other ecclesiastical leaders who pervert the proper, spiritual role of the church by seeking after worldly things, a fact dramatized by Dante in his portrayal of the damned simonists in *Inferno* 19, among other places. Nevertheless, Dante does not hold up poverty as an ideal for all Christians.[50] In fact, the active life, which, as we have seen, Dante praises as a "good" road to happiness, requires the proper, liberal use of wealth. Social problems arise when wealth is used improperly, either through avarice or prodigality, the results of which can be seen in certain local leaders, who, grasping as much as they can, make it more difficult for the divinely ordained political ruler of Christendom, the Roman Emperor, to gain his rightful place. Furthermore, these rulers also abuse ecclesiastical leaders inappropriately, imprisoning and persecuting, for example, Boniface VIII in Anagni. Hugh Capet describes both of these corruptions on the terrace of the avaricious (see 20.43–90 [214–18]).

Avarice, that is, becomes for Dante not just a private vice for the individual soul to overcome, but an ecclesiastical and a political vice. The ecclesiastical vice of avarice requires an extreme solution—the church's willing divestment of worldly goods, after the manner of

---

the pre-eminent vice as early as the fifth-century by a group of bishops in northern Italy. See *The Early History of Greed*, 70–95.

[48] Murray argues that we should distinguish between the social prominence of a vice and its importance in the psychology of a Christian. He thus notes that although Dante found more people damned for avarice than for any other sin (*Inf.*, 7.25 [70]), he nevertheless retained pride as the foundational vice in the moral organization of Purgatory. See *Reason and Society*, 436n62.

[49] For a consideration of this episode, see Nick Havely, *Dante and the Franciscans: Poverty and the Papacy in the "Commedia"* (Cambridge, Eng., 2004), 130–52.

[50] Richard Newhauser traces the attempts, and ultimate failure, by the Spiritual Franciscans to make voluntary poverty a universal ideal of the Christian life in "*Avaritia* and *Paupertas*: On the Place of the Early Franciscans in the History of Avarice," in *In the Garden of Evil*, ed. Newhauser, 324–48.

Francis of Assisi. Political avarice, however, requires a social remedy that can be achieved only through an Aristotelian virtue: justice. This virtue is appropriate for the active, earthly life in which we live, and is not limited to the life beyond, because our essential beatitude here on earth depends upon it.

In general, then, Dante represents the transition from vice to Beatitude as one from earthly sin to heavenly blessedness; the grace and the Beatitudes that the souls in Purgatory receive prepare them for their life beyond, when their wills will be, as Virgil describes Dante's corrected will, "free, upright, and sound" (*Purg.*, 27.140 [300]).[51] Dante's Beatitudes present, for the most part, images of a Christian blessedness brought about by a grace that enables the souls that receive it to ascend to the contemplation of God. On the terrace of avarice, however, Dante avoids descriptions of grace, instead proposing an Aristotelian virtue of justice that we can follow in our life here, insisting—as he does even in the *Paradiso*—on the necessity of our beatitude on earth as well as in heaven. Souls that pass through Purgatory will have their vices purged and their wills corrected through grace as they prepare to embark on the path that will lead them to the final happiness. We on earth, though, must learn to follow justice in order to conquer avarice and follow the path of Aristotelian virtue to our properly terrestrial beatitude.

---

[51] "libero, dritto e sano."

GREED AND ANTI-FRATERNALISM IN CHAUCER'S "SUMMONER'S TALE"

Derrick G. Pitard
Slippery Rock University

Abstract: In the "Summoner's Tale," the erudite friar/confessor's avarice compromises his ability to gain alms from a "cherl," Thomas. Thomas gives him a fart instead, a *reductio ad absurdum* of his avarice. The fart grounds the satire because it reduces the exchange to a bodily, vulgar utterance in which the friar finally hears Thomas' refusal to confess. As in the "Pardoner's Tale," a cleric's rhetorical power is stymied because of his commodification of the immaterial.

In the Lollard sermon "Omnis plantacio," the speaker argues to his congregation that "in couetise" clerics "sell and buy from you with deceitful words, for they sell their prayers or good deeds and buy your worldly welfare with them; and in this way they engage in commerce [doen marchaundise] with you or for you with deceitful [feyned] words."[1] They sell their words of forgiveness to you with other, "feyned wordis." This traffic in words, the Lollard writer says (invoking Saint Peter), is precisely how you will know them for the hypocrites they are. They commodify words, the means of salvation, and by extension they commodify your souls. To use the classic, Marxist definition, a commodity has value not in terms of what it can do (i.e., use value), but in terms of the money or other goods for which it can be traded (exchange value).[2] The clerics' ability to perform confession or preach has a specific economic exchange value in that it can be converted into cash. To the Lollard writer, then, clerics conceive of the process of penance as an economy in which spiritual values become useful for

---

[1] *The Works of a Lollard Preacher: The Sermon Omnis plantacio, the Tract Fundamentum aliud nemo potest ponere and the Tract De oblacione Iugis Sacrificii*, ed. Anne Hudson, EETS os, 317 (Oxford, 2001), Egerton Tract, 473–75: "sillen and bien of 3ou in fayned wordis, for þei sillen her suffragiis or meritis, and bien þerwiþ 3oure worldi good; and þus doen marchaundise wiþ 3ou or of 3ou in feyned wordis."

[2] "Commodity," in *A Dictionary of Marxist Thought*, ed. Tom Bottomore, 2nd ed. (Oxford, 1991), 86–87.

the profit they can turn. The "suffragis or meritis" in this economy, which clerics sell with "fayned wordis," in fact have no cash value in and of themselves, though clerics deceive you into thinking so. This critique, which as we will see also appears in Chaucer's "Summoner's Tale," makes language the keystone of an anti-clerical argument: clerical avarice is the conjoined twin of linguistic hollowness. Both the Friar and the Summoner (and the summoner and the friar in their tales) rely upon what Janette Richardson has called the "art of glibness" to victimize the laity.[3] They do not take language, or their words, very seriously, and so they empty them to deceive.

What Chaucer believed about English that the Lollards did not was that it did not have to be an academic language to gain authority. In fact, he frequently made fun of academic pretension. Chaucer loved the quotidian—the dialects, the anger, the curses, even the farts—which made English a vernacular, and he used all of these aspects of language to lend linguistic authority to his characters. These forms of speech are not academic, but malleable, ephemeral, and often downright disrespectful. One key aspect of vernacularity is that it defies the linguistic stability which universities and other institutions need to survive. The problem for Chaucer is that these institutional forms become fossilized, emptied of meaning, and need the pressure of new forms to revivify them. This process can be rebellious, but the vernacular does not necessarily foment outright violence. Instead, the constant, creative upwelling of new linguistic forms, and of new (or at least the perception of new) images and ideas, always puts pressure on older linguistic forms, bending or forcing them to accommodate new meaning.

Satire is one way in which this pressure can be exerted, and Chaucer and Lollard writers were at times bitterly satiric. Satire is not composed just in the vernacular, of course, but if vernacularity implies resistance, this includes a mockery of what is resisted. Nor does this necessarily imply a fundamental disagreement with the object of satire, since it is also often accompanied by a sense of the object's absurdity, or humor. And this indicates an instructive aspect of Chaucer's work: his humor implies an ironic distance from a subject, even as he loves the subject. With Chaucerian satire, this perspective is always vital.

---

[3] Janette Richardson, "Friar and Summoner, the Art of Balance," *The Chaucer Review* 9,3 (1975): 231.

One way in which Chaucer represents clerical investment, or over-investment, in the church is by portraying them as greedy. The Pardoner is the classical example, a man who can tell a story demonstrating that "radix malorum est cupiditas," that "greed is the root of all evil," while being badly infected with the vice himself.[4] Other examples come to mind: the Monk, who loves hunting and fine food, the corrupt Monk in the "Shipman's Tale," and the guileful canon in the "Canon's Yeoman's Tale" all exemplify the vice. These characters are profoundly divided from themselves—what Marshall Leicester has called "disenchanted." As Leicester uses the term, a "disenchanted perspective constitutes the world as a tissue of institutions rather than natures."[5] For these clerics, disenchantment means a complete evacuation of the self—their highest value has become how to use the institutional church for personal gain. The corrupt friar in the "Summoner's Tale" is also disenchanted, but he adds a dimension to this: he is a friar, and anti-fraternal writings were a particularly nasty strain of anti-clerical literature.

The reasons for this nastiness make him an instructive instance of Chaucer's vernacularity. Friars were, on the one hand, deeply invested in maintaining the institution of the church. Following the examples of Bonaventure of Balneoregio (a Franciscan) and Thomas Aquinas (a Dominican), one of the most important of fraternal vocations was an intellectual pursuit. The study of the Scriptures was vital to the maintenance of the ecclesiastical hierarchy. Describing their use by the Church Fathers, Berryl Smalley said that the Scriptures had two purposes:

> First and foremost the Scriptures were a means to holiness. *Lectio divina* formed one side of the ascetic triangle: reading, prayers, and contemplation. Equally important was its role in upholding the faith. The long line of commentators who developed the spiritual senses were not only contemplatives but men of action. They built up the Church, defending her doctrines against pagans, Jews, and heretics. They rallied her to the defence of the Christian state under Charlemagne. They supported the Gregorian reform against the secular power. They set forth the duties of the clergy and laity.[6]

---

[4] The Pardoner's tagline is adapted from 1 Tim. 6:10: "radix enim omnium malorum est cupiditas."

[5] H. Marshall Leicester, *The Disenchanted Self: Representing the Subject in the Canterbury Tales* (Berkeley, 1990), 27. I use Leicester's term pejoratively, though it does not have to be taken so.

[6] Beryl Smalley, *The Study of the Bible in the Middle Ages*, 2nd ed. (Oxford, 1952), 358.

Commentary on the Bible supported the political institution of the
church—and even Christian states. After the millennium, the work of
"building up the Church" reached new levels of intensity, and new
institutions, the universities, grew for the sole purpose of studying the
Scriptures. The Bible's interpretation was the ultimate guide to "the
duties of clergy and laity," and academics became the most knowledgeable of interpreters. As Gordon Leff has described:

> With Innocent III (1198–1216) [the Church's] administrative, political,
> and financial unity under the curia at Rome had been finally established.
> It was the culmination of the policy begun by the Gregorian reform-
> ers in the eleventh century: papal jurisdiction in all important disputes,
> elections to bishoprics, the despatch of legates, the hearing of appeals,
> had all become enshrined in canon law.....Innocent, in helping to bring
> papal government to a new pitch...set the tone for the lawyer statesmen
> who succeeded him.[7]

The Church became the most developed bureaucracy of the high
Middle Ages, and friars during the thirteenth century became a key
part of its development.

While on the one hand, then, friars had a deep investment in the
church, on the other their origins, especially in the example of Francis
of Assisi, spoke of a reaction against investment.[8] One sign of this was
Francis's fanatical disgust for money. Francis was, famously, the son of
an Assisi merchant family who abandoned his father and the family's
cloth-making business by stripping himself naked in the marketplace in
front of his father and the Bishop of Assisi.[9] Both Dominic and Francis

---

[7] Gordon Leff, *Heresy in the Later Middle Ages: The Relation of Heterodoxy to Dissent, c. 1250–c. 1450* (Manchester, 1967), 1:22.

[8] I make little differentiation between the different orders because Chaucer does not either, and because anti-fraternal satire often conflated them. See *The Riverside Chaucer*, ed. Larry D. Benson et al., 3rd ed. (New York, 1987), 807–08 for a discussion here. This conflation, I would argue, makes sense because satire often relies on pejoratively stereotyping its targets by lumping together groups which, in fact, might not at all be similar. All quotations from Chaucer are from *The Riverside Chaucer*.

[9] For the story of his clothes, see *Francis of Assisi: Early Documents*, ed. Regis J. Armstrong, J. A. Wayne Hellman, and William J. Short (New York, 1999) 1:192–94 (in ch. 6 of the "Life of Saint Francis" by Thomas of Celano). For discussions of the origins of the friars within this new mercantile culture, see especially Lester Little, *Religious Poverty and the Profit Economy in Medieval Europe* (London, 1978), and Alexander Murray, *Reason and Society in the Middle Ages* (Oxford, 1978). Their thesis that avarice was the new and greatest vice has been significantly altered by Richard Newhauser, *The Early History of Greed: The Sin of Avarice in Early Medieval Thought and Literature* (Cambridge, Eng., 2000), but their narrative of the contradiction between Franciscan poverty and the society which enabled it is still compelling.

insisted on poverty, but Francis forbade his followers from even touching money. One of the stories from his biography tells of followers who found a bag of coins on a roadway; when he was asked if they could give the money to the poor, Francis told them it was a temptation from the devil, and to leave it be. When one of the followers returned to get the money, a snake crawled out of the bag.[10] In the light of such aversion to money and the standards Francis set, any falling away from these ideals became fodder for satire. And a falling away was inevitable when the orders of friars grew—as grow they did, immensely—and found themselves with novices, aged to care for, bequests, property, and a hierarchy to oversee it all.[11] The friars needed money to sustain their churches—which is precisely, as we will see, what Friar John admits to Thomas in the tale.

Because vernacularity critiques investment, and becomes for Chaucer a remedy for disenchantment, a comparison between the satire of fraternal over-investment in the church and the vernacular world of Chaucer's tale provides the key to how Chaucer's satire works. But what is only partially clear, as yet, is why I should call this a "vernacular" world. That is the subject of this paper. It is an ironic twist of literary history that the tropes of anti-fraternal satire which Chaucer uses have their origin in the highest echelons of the academic establishment, in the arguments which broke out in the 1250s in the university in Paris between friars and secular priests over fraternal privileges. William of St. Amour, then a secular master at Paris, wrote a series of tracts taking the friars to task for their apostolic pretensions. A short analysis of his highly erudite work will occupy the first part of this paper, to examine both the points he made, which Chaucer took up, and his scholastic discourse, which Chaucer mocked. An examination of Chaucer's "Summoner's Tale" will form the second part of the paper. Where William's erudition gave his points authority, Chaucer rewrites them from a vernacular, rather than an elite and Latinate, perspective. To

---

[10] *Francis of Assisi: Early Documents*, 2:579–80 (ch. 7 of the "Major Legend of Saint Francis," by Bonaventure of Balneoregio). On avarice and the Franciscans, now also see Richard Newhauser, "*Avaritia* and *Paupertas*: On the Place of the Early Franciscans in the History of Avarice," in *In the Garden of Evil: The Vices and Culture in the Middle Ages*, ed. Richard Newhauser (Toronto, 2005), 324–48.

[11] As a measure of the problem within the fraternal orders, in the 1260 Constitutions of Narbonne Bonaventure passed a set of regulations to deal with money which precluded friars from, among other things, accepting money as a form of penance; on this see John Moorman, *A History of the Franciscan Order from Its Origins to the Year 1517* (Oxford, 1968), 148–51.

Chaucer, financial and academic investments mesh. He turns William's pretension on its head by showing that it, too, becomes complicit with the desire for money, and that one way to expose greed is to expose elitist erudition. Chaucer is not just writing an anti-fraternal satire; he is *re*writing it by moving it entirely into the discursive realm of the vernacular. The central argument of this paper is that Chaucer uses greed as a linguistic trope in order to amplify his readers' understanding of the importance of language, and to argue for the vitality of vernacularity.

I. *William of St. Amour*

William of St. Amour was a Paris secular who wrote several seminal anti-fraternal tracts, the most important of which was his *Tractatus brevis de periculis novissimorum temporum*, "A Short Tract on the Perils of the End of Times," published in 1254 in the midst of fights over the academic status of the friars in the university. In part, these arguments were about fraternal privileges, both academic and pastoral.[12] Friars refused to be part of the *consortium magistrorum*, the conference of masters who set university policies, which prevented the university from acting as a unit to resist policies it felt against its best interest. Yet they were permitted to run their own schools outside of the university's jurisdiction. They could give confession, preach, and bury people on their own land—privileges which, many argued, took money from parish priests. In December, 1254, in an effort to quell unrest in Paris, Pope Innocent IV issued the bill *Etsi animarum* which greatly restricted the rights of mendicants.[13] This victory for the seculars, however, was short-lived: Innocent died within the month, and his successor, Alexander IV, immediately revoked the bull.[14] In response, the university

---

[12] On the background for the debates, William, and his tract, see Gordon Leff, *Paris and Oxford Universities in the Thirteenth and Fourteenth Centuries* (New York, 1968); Moorman, *A History*, esp. 124–131; James Doyne Dawson, "William of St. Amour and the Apostolic Tradition," *Mediaeval Studies* 40 (1978): 223–38; Penn R. Szittya, *The Antifraternal Tradition in Medieval Literature* (Princeton, 1986), esp. ch. 1; Kathryn Kerby-Fulton, *Reformist Apocalypticism and Piers Plowman* (Cambridge, Eng., 1990), esp. ch. 4.

[13] Moorman, *A History*, 122. A copy of the bull appears in William of St. Amour, *Opera omnia* (Constance, 1632). All citations from William of St. Amour are from this early printing; no modern edition exists.

[14] Hastings Rashdall, *The Universities of Europe in the Middle Ages*, ed. A. B. Emden (Oxford, 1936), 1:383; Moorman, *A History*, 127–28.

took the remarkable step of dissolving itself completely.[15] This extreme reaction signals how consequential the issues in the dispute were. What was at stake here, Rashdall emphasizes, "was the autonomy of the society.... [B]y the issue of the present controversy it was placed beyond dispute that henceforth the university was as much a part of the ecclesiastical system, as much subject to papal regulation, as the older capitular body whose authority it had by papal favour nearly succeeded in shaking off."[16]

The quarrel, then, must be understood as part of the thirteenth-century process by which the friars came increasingly under the direct protection of the Holy See. Francis and Dominic had both received their blessing directly from the Pope to preach throughout Christendom. This caused intense resentment within both the monastic and secular orders since they were perceived to curtail the control that local curates, bishops, and other officials had over them within their domains. Greater than this worry was the increasingly centralized power of the papacy, which depended upon theological arguments for justification. This was a fight over how power was allocated. Who can disagree with the See of Peter? *Can* it be disagreed with? The university found itself in a difficult position since it acted both as the support for and entry point to the establishment, and in conflict with the Pope at its summit. This problem had developed because orthodox belief, which Paris helped to define, and the bureaucratic power of the Church, represented by the Pope, were inseparable. To use the former to disagree with the latter—as William discovered—was to risk excommunication.

William never loses sight of the fact that this is an argument over ecclesiastical authority. To avoid a direct affront to the Papacy, then, he never refers to the friars directly. His readings of Scripture instead talk about "predicatores," "seductores," and "phariseos"; the subtitle of his *Collectiones* refers to "Hypocritas, Pseudo-predicatores, & Penetrantes domos, & Otiosos, & Curiosos, & Gyrovagos."[17]

Each of these terms allows him to place the friars within a different context for condemnation.

---

[15] Rashdall, *The Universities of Europe*, 1:384, Moorman, *A History*, 128.
[16] Rashdall, *The Universities of Europe*, 1:379.
[17] William of St. Amour, *Opera omnia*, 111. For a recent account of his work and editions of it, see Andrew G. Traver, "Thomas of York's Role in the Conflict between Mendicants and Seculars at Paris," *Franciscan Studies* 57 (1999): 179–202. The "distinctions" he makes between these various names form the structure of the five divisions which make up the *Collectiones*.

This process depends wholly on the conventions of scholastic commentary. In his excellent analysis of the effect of William's work on the later Middle Ages, Penn Szittya observes that "the most salient feature of all William's writings is their exegetical character."[18] He argues that "William's exegesis of scripture is sufficiently complex and internally consistent to give it an imaginative and intellectual validity lacking in 'mere rhetoric.' Insofar as it serves as an exploration of the shape of history and not as ornament or propaganda, Biblical exegesis is primary, not rhetorical or secondary, in William's writings."[19] Szittya's point, by extension, can be applied to much exegesis during the Middle Ages. William used the academic method learned while students progressed through the study of the arts before incepting in the *studium generale* to become part of the consortium of masters. His method exemplifies the interpretive foundation the Church relied upon to justify all of the larger institutional structures which it had created.

Yet Szittya reduces the concept of "rhetoric" here to its most simplistic meaning. Rhetorical devices such as commentary suggest or forge connections between ideas. Users rely on these connections to make arguments based on those ideas: justifications for tithing, for preaching, for confession, for burial rights, for marriage—all of these central events in the laity's lives depended upon clerical interpretations of Scripture. William himself wished to use this exegetical method to effect a bureaucratic change in the structure of the Church: to dispense with the orders of friars. His commentary is a rhetorical practice which connects his apocalyptic theology to its articulation, the condemnation of the friars. This is far from "mere rhetoric"; it is the very way in which commentators created ecclesiastical authority. William himself describes this connection in the Prologue of his *Collectiones*, which he subtitles "For the defense of the Ecclesiastical hierarchy, and for the instruction and preparation of the simple faithful of Christ."[20]

William begins the *De periculis* with an analysis of 2 Timothy 3:2, which begins: "there will be men who love themselves." This self-love is a root of other sins, notes William: "Now from this perverse love of themselves, as if from some evil root, those men 'loving themselves' will

---

[18] Szittya, *The Antifraternal Tradition*, 18.

[19] Ibid., 20.

[20] William of St. Amour, *Opera omnia*, 111: "Ad defensionem Ecclesiasticae Hierarchiae, & ad instructionem, & praeparationem simplicium fidelium Christi."

fall into various kinds of sin...."²¹ These men, he says quoting Augustine, love themselves more than God. This then leads to a catalog of sins which William takes up in order. These men will also be "greedy, haughty, proud, blasphemous, disobedient to their parents, ungrateful, wicked, without affection, criminals, disparagers, intemperate, without kindness, traitors, violent, shameless, inflated [with pride], lovers of pleasure more than God."²² The first of these William specifically describes as greedy, "*cupidi* pecuniae, vel mundanae gloriae" (lovers of money or of worldly glory). These are the "penetrantes domos," those who "penetrate houses" to seduce the gullible.

To accuse the friars, however obliquely, of such sins was to assault the basic rationale for the orders' existence. Weren't they—like many of the wandering preachers throughout Europe at the time—deliberately making themselves the lowest of the low? How could one call them greedy? Begging, in fact, was especially annoying to William. William published several *quaestiones* on this issue, including the *De quantitate eleemosynae* ("On the Amount of Alms") and the *De valido mendicante* ("On Legitimate Mendicancy") in which he quotes Scriptural arguments given in favor of begging (such as the beatitude "Blessed are the poor in spirit," and various other Gospel passages, especially from Luke), and then refutes them with an array of other quotations from Scripture and patristic authors, with commentary. The quotations flush out several issues, including the crucial question of whether Christ and his apostles had any possessions. Many others, however, revolve around the concept of work, and whether a beggar who chose to be a beggar, even though he could work, should be countenanced. William's answer was that he should not be, that in fact it was permissible not to be poor, and that keeping money for oneself was sanctioned if not encouraged by the Gospel. He responds, for instance, to Luke 14:33, which he quotes as an argument for voluntary poverty ("So likewise,

---

²¹ Ibid., 22: "Ex hoc autem peruerso amore sui, quasi ex mala quadam radice, incident illi homines seipsos amantes in varia genera peccatorum...."

²² This is 2 Tim 3:2–4, the terms of which are used in William of St. Amour, *Opera omnia*, 22: "...cupidi...elati...superbi...blasphemi...inobedientes parentibus...ingrati...scelesti...sine affectione...criminatores...detractores...incontinentes...sine benignitate...proditores...proterui...procaces...tumidi...voluptatum amatores magis quam Dei." For Szittya's discussion of this passage, see Szittya, *The Antifraternal Tradition*, 57–61.

every one of you who does not forsake all that he has cannot be my disciple")[23] by quoting the *Glossa ordinaria*:

> The *Glossa ordinaria* responds, "The difference between renouncing (*renuntiare*) all things and relinquishing (*relinquere*) all things is that 'to renounce' is appropriate for all people, who legitimately use the worldly goods they possess so they can then turn their minds to higher things; 'to relinquish,' however, belongs only to the perfect, who lay aside all temporal things and gaze upon eternal things alone."[24]

"To relinquish" all goods is such an extreme rejection of property that only the rare and solitary saint is expected to do it. His definition of "to relinquish" here is telling, as it alludes to the collection of property for ownership by a group—that is, to the creation of a monastic community, a cenobitic form of spiritual worship. J. D. Dawson's discussion of the ecclesiastical stakes here notes that William's argument about manual labor "was part of the larger problem of the relation between priestly and monastic status.... William insisted that the *vita apostolica* had always meant the common ownership of property... and hence the friar's practice of poverty individual *and* common had no place in the tradition of the Church."[25] To William it was clear that monastic communities did not embrace absolute poverty on an institutional level because the Gospel did not in fact require it.

William even carries the implications of the argument one step further in his *quaestio* entitled *De valido mendicante*. Much of his argument here revolves around passages from Paul's letter to the Thessalonians. These verses have a clear and common thread; just one might be taken as an example. 2 Thessalonians 3:8–9 reads:

> Nor did we eat of anyone's bread for free, but instead by working with labor and fatigue night and day that we might not be a burden to you—not because we have no power, but to make ourselves an example to you to follow us.[26]

---

[23] "Sic ergo omnis ex vobis, qui non renuntiat omnibus quae possidet, non potest meus esse discipulus."

[24] *De quantitate eleemosynae*, in *Opera omnia*, 79: "Respondet Glos. Haec differentia est inter Renuntiare omnibus, & Relinquere omnia; quod Renuntiare conueniat omnibus, qui ita licite vtuntur mundanis, quae possident, vt tum mente tendant ad superiora; Relinquere autem est tantummodo perfectorum, qui omnia temporalia postponunt, & solis aeternis inhiant."

[25] Dawson, "William of St. Amour and the Apostolic Tradition," 229–30.

[26] "Neque gratis panem manducavimus ab aliquo, sed in labore, et in fatigatione, nocte et die operantes, ne quem vestrum gravaremus. Non quasi non habuerimus

We should work to earn a living; we should, if at all possible, have a vocation. No one, William argues from these passages, should deliberately put himself into a state of poverty in order to be admired, and then beg.[27] This is, in fact, an occasion for avarice: "But asking for money, or goods, is an occasion for avarice; therefore, to ask is contrary to Paul's teaching; therefore, one should not give to those who ask."[28] And elevating the pressure on begging even more, he argues of preachers that "he who begs, when he is able to live from manual labor, neglects justice, because he acts contrary to Paul's teaching, and he ought to be excommunicated...."[29] This is a powerful statement to say the least. The fraternal imitation of the apostles is actually an invitation to sin, to greed. William is, as Szittya observes, questioning the friars' "very right to exist as they did. If their apostolic claims were accepted as valid, then they were entitled to all the privileges of the apostolic clergy, including the lucrative rights of preaching and confession. If not, they had no right to live either 'from the Gospel,' as the clergy did, or from the mendicancy which made their own way of life distinct."[30]

The immediate context for this denunciation applies it to beggar-preachers. But William makes it within an argument which relies upon a categorical denunciation for its authority. These arguments, as we have seen, are always framed within a very earnest exploration of Biblical texts on the best way to "live by the Gospel." To make his case, William quotes Biblical and patristic texts as authorities which in the rhetorical structure of his argument only incidentally apply to his case against the friars. Anyone who is voluntarily poor—including all of the unattached beguines, Humiliati, Waldensians, and various other wandering preachers who covered Europe at the time—might very well

---

potestatem, sed ut nosmetipsos formam daremus vobis ad imitandum nos." Other close passages are 1 Thess 4:11, and 1 Thess 5:12.

[27] *De quantitate eleemosynae*, in *Opera omnia*, 76: "Sed nemo debet se ponere in tali statu, vt aduletur; Ergo nec omnia dare, vt mendicitate sibi victum quaerat."

[28] *De valido mendicante*, in *Opera omnia*, 85: "Sed in petendo pecuniam, vel sumptus, est occasio auaritiae; Ergo petere est contra doctrinam Apostoli; Ergo non est dandum eis petentibus." This is a gloss he gives to 1 Thess 2:5, and he repeats this warning again at the conclusion to the his treatise: "Quod quaeritur de Praedicatoribus, vtrum possint petere, credo quod non, ne videatur esse occasio auaritiae" (87).

[29] *De valido mendicante*, in *Opera omnia*, 86: "Sed qui mendicat, cum possit viuere de labore corporis, iustitiam negligit, quia facit contra doctrinam Apostoli et excommunicari debet...."

[30] Szittya, *The Antifraternal Tradition*, 50–51.

be included in William's argument.[31] This opens up larger issues which might be explored. For the present, though, it is enough to say that the absolute nature of his reference to Scripture—part of his rhetorical method—helps him to argue that mendicancy in whatever form was a cause of sin and cultural decay. His arguments were influential, and fueled the anger of much anti-fraternal criticism in later authors, including Chaucer.

II. *Chaucer's Vernacular Anti-Fraternalism*

The fart which Thomas donates to the grasping friar in the "Summoner's Tale" makes for wonderful comedy. It is not just explosive humor, however, but also an explosive semiotic event. Peter Travis, taking his cue from the thirteen emission points—twelve spokes and the hub—from which the friars will partake of the fart in Jankyn's solution to the churl John's *insolubile*, gives thirteen "ways of listening to" the fart.[32] It is perhaps not necessary to go further than Travis's list to make the point that this pre-, or proto-, linguistic moment, far from being unmeaningful, is polyvalent because it stands at the nexus (that is, the hub) of a range of associations which more articulate language would only reduce to make more precise. This range is, I take it, part of what Fiona Somerset means to indicate when she calls the fart a "vernacular utterance."[33] It is a primal outburst of Thomas's churlish anger, as elemental as a child's scream, and at least as justifiable, given his provocation by the friar. Lee Patterson's argument that Thomas's rebellion invokes the paradigmatic rebellion of Chaucer's lifetime, the 1381 Peasants' Revolt, is well taken, and it is amplified by both Somerset's and Travis's analyses.[34] Yet to understand the fart as a vernacular utterance, the point need not be metaphorized so specifically.

---

[31] For discussions of William of St. Amour within the context of the wandering religious poor of the 13th century see Leff, *Heresy in the Later Middle Ages*, 167–255; Ernest W. McDonnell, *The Beguines and Beghards in Medieval Culture* (New Brunswick, NJ, 1954).

[32] Peter W. Travis, "Thirteen Ways of Listening to a Fart: Noise in Chaucer's Summoner's Tale," *Exemplaria* 16,2 (Fall, 2004): 323–48.

[33] Fiona Somerset, "'As just as is a squyre': The Politics of 'Lewed Translacion' in Chaucer's *Summoner's Tale*," *Studies in the Age of Chaucer* 21 (1999): 187.

[34] Lee Patterson, *Chaucer and the Subject of History* (Madison, 1991), 317–21.

The vernacular is rebellious because it is "churlish," loud, and does not know its social place. For this reason, Somerset's comment also, surely, alludes to Thomas's crudity. The vernacular is often rude, and scatological utterances are a crude extreme.

One specific pun which the fart makes is of course the old association between money and filth: the friar wanted money, and, crudely put, that's what he got. Thomas has reduced John's desires to its fundamentals. He sees that penance is, to John, a business. With her close reading of the first part of the tale, Linda Georgianna is one of the only critics to illustrate his mercantile approach to penance. "From the very beginning of the tale," she argues, "the friar establishes his mode of free enterprise, with its strong emphasis on accounting procedures and competitive markets."[35] By his "accounting procedures," Georgianna means his close reckoning of the process of exchange. The friar, for instance, "... above all things / he excited the people in his preaching / to endow trentals, and to give [alms], for God's sake, / from which men could construct sacred buildings" (III.1715–19).[36] Trentals are a requiem series of thirty masses which could be sung for a soul in purgatory, and they had to be paid for. Here, the money goes to building programs for the friars and not to help members of the clergy "live, thanks be to God, in plenty and prosperity" (III.1723).[37] The friar posits a form of exchange: we get buildings, you get prayers.

This is also a competitive market, as the friar competes with the local parish priest. Chaucer gives him a speech which connects him back to William's critiques. When Friar John says to Thomas' wife that he'd like to meet with Thomas a bit, to hear his confession, John denigrates the local curates:

> These local curates are too negligent and lazy
> To delve into [grope] a conscience tenderly
> During confession; my expertise is in preaching
> And the study of Peter's and Paul's words.
> I go about and fish for the souls of Christian men
> To pay to [yelden] Christ his proper dues [rente];

---

[35] Linda Georgianna, "Lords, Churls, and Friars: The Return to Social Order in the Summoner's Tale," in *Rebels and Rivals: The Contestive Spirit in the Canterbury Tales*, ed. Susanna Greer Fein, David Raybin, and Peter C. Braeger (Kalamazoo, 1991), 156.

[36] "...aboven every thyng, / Excited he the peple in his prechyng / To trentals, and to yeve, for Goddes sake, / Wherwith men myghte hooly houses make" (III.1715–19).

[37] "lyve / Thanked be God, in wele and habundaunce" (III.1723).

> My purpose [entente] is set solely on spreading his word
> (III.1816–22).[38]

John notes here that his education is a real advantage compared to local priests, who, lacking his knowledge, are unable to confess as effectively. The distinction here refers to ongoing arguments between the fraternal orders and parish priests. Local priests were, from the middle of the thirteenth century, upset about the intrusion of friars into their parishes, both for the money they took and for the disruption of the local harmony of the parish.[39] And, in fact, friars were often highly educated, since fraternal regulations mandated age and educational requirements for those who heard confessions by those outside the order.[40] It was an important responsibility; if a confessor did not know the sins well enough, or how to examine a confessant well enough to extract the sins, they would remain to sully a penitent's soul at death. This friar's eagerness to trade his knowledge for money, however, stretches his rhetoric beyond his erudition. He ends this quotation with a mixed metaphor—he will "walk and fish," as if he were a fisherman, but will also collect "rent," as if he were a landlord. He is fishing for money by spreading the word.

This mixed metaphor serves a purpose for the friar, though, as it allows him to move quickly from confession to preaching. He associates himself with the apostles: he studies "in Peter's words and Paul's"; and like the apostles, he is a "fisher of men" (Matth 4:19). The friar's elision does have some authority behind it. Bonaventure defended confession and preaching as parallel obligations, as it was intended to spur the conscience of audiences to confess, and friar preachers would, during tours, stay behind to hear the confessions of an audience after a sermon.[41] At the same time, however, this association intensely irritated William of St. Amour, who argued that the friars' voluntary poverty was a false imitation of the apostles, and that one should not give money to

---

[38] "Thise curatz been ful necligent and slowe / To grope tendrely a conscience / In shrift; in prechyng is my diligence, / And studie in Petres wordes and in Poules. / I walke and fisshe Cristen mennes soules / To yelden Jhesu Crist his propre rente; / To sprede his word is set al myn entente" (III.1816–22).

[39] The literature on this conflict is vast. For a general history of the disputes see Moorman, *A History*, passim. For a recent discussion in the context of fraternal education see Bert Roest, *A History of Franciscan Education (c. 1210–1517)* (Leiden, 2000), chapter 7, "Preaching."

[40] Roest, *A History of Franciscan Education*, 317.

[41] Ibid., 315–16.

any undeserving poor, of which the voluntary poor were certainly an example. Seculars also argued that preaching, along with confession and burials, were what the friars pursued most avidly because, they were the most lucrative sacraments.[42] Friars were, it should be said, very early on in their history explicitly prohibited from asking for money in exchange for penance.[43] John follows only the letter of this law, not the spirit. He does not ask directly for payment in return for confession, but by imbricating the imagery of apostleship and fundraising Chaucer clearly indicates that Friar John thinks of the two interchangeably.

Whether Chaucer read William or not, this is an example of Chaucer's vernacular version of what had been a Latinate criticism—that friars preached in exchange for money. Both William and Chaucer construct this with reference to a Biblical text. Yet they differ in crucial ways. Each writer is blunt about some issues, but leaves others for the reader to infer. William is blunt about the theological and ecclesiological stakes; he describes how mendicancy is an invitation to vices, including greed; he applies the range of sins he has quoted from 2 Timothy to the behavior they inspire—sins which, as Paul's letter describes, augur the end of times; he describes how the very ecclesiastical hierarchy is threatened by the presence of the "pseudo-apostles." He is in all ways categorical—but he never names the friars. This he leaves up to his readers' imaginations.

Chaucer, however, inverts this. He tells the story of one grasping, greedy friar trying to take money from a sick, bereaved old man. His story is the opposite of categorical—it is the narrowest of portraits of greed, as most of his tale is constructed from the personal conversation between John and Thomas. Yet here, too, implications are made. The friar's distended rhetoric, his "fayned wordis," commodify penance. He has a facility with language, and his goal with words is to gain money. Understanding this lets us also understand a larger context for the economy of penance. Chaucer's narrative constantly hints that we see here not just the activities of the friar, but the culture of "enterprise" which a number of friars had set up to assure themselves of an income. Masses have been endowed for Thomas's illness; John's order

---

[42] This was argued by, for instance, Archbishop Fitzralph; see Katherine Walsh, *A Fourteenth-Century Scholar and Primate: Richard Fitzralph in Oxford, Avignon, and Armagh* (Oxford, 1981), 370–74, 402–03.

[43] See note 11, above.

has a building program underway; Thomas is a member of a confraternity, a group of lay brothers connected to a friary; there are other
groups of friars in town who are also asking for money; and they all
spend time learning their *exempla* and speeches as well as saying masses.
The fingers of this enterprise stretch deeply into local lives. But any
application of these examples to the greater categories of ecclesiology,
theology, and eschatology, about which William is so explicit, remain
implicit in Chaucer. This is precisely the inverse of William's strategy.
The difference indicates a key difference between William's Latinity
and Chaucer's vernacularity.

The reason why, then, the fart is vernacular is that it is at once the
most intimate picture of John's greed in the story and also the moment
most suggestive of the sweeping consequences of sin described by William. Chaucer's choice of words here again moves the narrative to its
climax, but generates images which are far from random. Thomas is
speaking:

> "Now, then, put your hand in, down by my back,"
> Said the man, "and grope around behind.
> There beneath my buttock you will find
> A thing that I have hidden in secrecy [pryvetee]" (III.2140–43).[44]

This image of grabbing, groping, or grasping is suggestive because it
is a classic, iconographic image of avarice in penitential treatises and
analyses of the seven sins, where Greed is often personified with a hand
that grasps. In one classic early medieval example from Prudentius's
Psychomachia, for instance, "Greed...crooked her hand and seized on
everything of price that gluttonous Indulgence left behind....Her
quick right hand is busy scraping up the plunder and plies nails hard
as brass in gathering up the booty."[45] The image becomes popular in
later literature as well. In the collection of preachers' texts known as
the *Fasciculus morum*, the preacher—a Dominican friar, in fact, quoting
Innocent III—says that "[a]n avaricious person is naturally eager in

---

[44] "Now thanne, put in thyn hand doun by my bak," / Seyde this man, "and grope
wel bihynde. / Bynethe my buttok there shaltow fynde / A thyng that I have hyd in
pryvetee" (III.2140–43).
[45] Prudentius, *Psychomachia*, ed. and trans. by H. J. Thomson, in *Prudentius* (Cambridge, MA, 1949), 1:311; this is his translation. On the movement of Avaritia's hands
in Prudentius, see Newhauser, *The Early History of Greed*, 81–82. Alternatively, an open
hand is often a sign of generosity; see for instance Guillaume de Lorris and Jean de
Meun, *The Romance of the Rose*, trans. Charles Dahlberg (Hanover, 1983), 45–46 (vv.
1127–90).

grasping" ("*naturaliter ad petendum*").[46] The verb he uses here, *petere*, also means "to beg"; Siegfried Wenzel's translation is not literal, but captures very well the contemporary image for the sin.

Friar John's grasp, then, crystallizes the range of satiric images which Chaucer has deployed. The image of "groping" has also been used earlier in the tale, by the friar, to describe the process of confession: "These local curates are too negligent and lazy / To delve into [grope] a conscience tenderly / During confession": "To grope," we can see now more clearly, is a pun: while a common use of the word meaning "to examine for shrift" died out in the seventeenth century, both this meaning and "to grasp" were available to Chaucer.[47] His attempts to grope Thomas's conscience have come to naught, frustrated by Thomas's intransigence. Thomas has flatly refused his requests, and so John has been reduced to simply demanding the money: "Give me then some of your gold, to build our cloister" (III.2099).[48] Here is the desire for gold at its most naked. No exchange is implied or promised any more; he is simply in debt:

> ...for many a mussel and many an oyster,
> While other men have been well at ease,
> Has been our food, in order to build our cloister.
> And yet, God knows, barely the foundation has
> Been completed, nor has even one tile
> Of the floor been laid within our dwelling.
> By God, we owe forty pounds for stones (III.2100–06).[49]

Nobody appreciates all of the work that goes into begging: the argument flies in the face of William's condemnation of mendicancy as a refusal to work. Begging here has become an invitation to institutionalized avarice. To the friar, it is Thomas's own fault that he is sick, and

---

[46] *Fasciculus morum: A Fourteenth-Century Preacher's Handbook*, ed. and trans. Siegfried Wenzel (University Park and London, 1989) 313: "Avarus, inquit, naturaliter ad petendum est promptus, ad dandum tardus, ad negandum frontuosus." I quote Wenzel's translation.

[47] "Grope, *v.*" 4c. *Oxford English Dictionary*, 2nd ed. (1989). This is also noted in Geoffrey Chaucer, *The Friar's, Summoner's, and Pardoner's Tales from the Canterbury Tales*, ed. N. R. Havely (London, 1975), 139.

[48] "Yif me thanne of thy gold, to make oure cloystre" (III.2099).

[49] "...for many a muscle and many an oystre, / Whan othere men had ben ful wel at eyse, / Hath been oure foode, our cloystre for to reyse. / And yet, God woot, unnethe the fundement / Parfourned is, ne of our pavement / Nys nat a tyle yet withinne oure wones. / By God, we owen fourty pound for stones" (III.2100–06).

it is apparently everyone else's fault that the friary can't pay its bills. Chaucer's satire opens up an interesting perspective on mendicant culture. Because the only means which they have to earn money is by showing others that they deserve pity, it follows that if people don't buy their arguments, they are selfish, or insensate to their suffering. Friar John does not just think of his income in economic terms. Rather, money is a right which he deserves. And the friar, then, is not merely greedy. His greed is a manifestation of a fundamental selfishness. This in fact leads us to think of his sin in terms of 1 Timothy 2:3, with which William had begun his *De periculis*: the sinful, the *penetrantes domos*, are ultimately "*homines seipsos amantes*," men who love themselves.

Chaucer's vernacular perspective, however, amplifies this sin beyond what was possible for William because Friar John's sin is also a fault of his academic arrogance. This was implicit in his denigration of the "local curates," but here at the end of the tale it becomes explicit. When he goes to the local lord to seek some recompense for his insult, the lord begins "Now maister...," but the friar rapidly interrupts:

> Not Master, sir, he said, but servant,
> Though I have received that degree in school.
> It displeases God that men call us 'rabbi':
> Not in the market, and not in your great hall (III.2185–88).[50]

The reference touches one of the most sensitive areas of anti-fraternal criticism. Francis of Assisi, according to Etienne Gilson, "never condemned learning for itself, but...he had no desire to see it developed in his Order. In his eyes it was not in itself an evil, but its pursuit appeared to him unnecessary and dangerous."[51] Poverty was to be the mark of the Franciscan apostolic mission, not learning. Szittya notes that friars had taken to heart the injunction in Matthew 23:6–7, where Christ says that Pharisees—false teachers, rather than true apostles—"love...to be called by men "Rabbi." Friar John's allusion is therefore, in Szittya's words, a "clear cut allusion to the apostles" which "cap[s] the apostolic pattern and bring[s] it boldly to our attention before the cartwheel

---

[50] "No maister, sire," quod he, "but servitour, / Thogh I have had in scole that honour. / God liketh nat that 'Raby' men us calle, / Neither in market ne in youre large halle" (III.2185–88).
[51] Quoted in Moorman, *A History*, 123.

joke."[52] William had turned the image of the Pharisee back on the friars, however, especially in his sermon *De Pharisaeo et publicano* ("On the Pharisee and the Publican"). William compares them to the Pharisee in Luke 18:9–14, who prays, "I thank you that I am not as other men are," while the publican could not even lift his head for shame. His pride in his education leads him to sin.[53]

To avoid this shame, John denies the phrase, but he praises himself here with faint humility. We know he is proud of his learning because he has disparaged the local curates. And what is more, he had, in fact, been called master earlier. When he first met Thomas's wife, she had said to him: "Hello, Master, you are welcome, by Saint John! / ... How fare you, well?" (III.1800–01).[54] At that point, he had placed himself at their service: "... very well, / As one who is your servant in every way" (III.1805–06), but he did not argue against or erase the distinction in learning between himself and the family.[55] She refers to him as "Master" again a few lines later, and he again lets it stand (III.1836). Friar John had also explained to Thomas that "... we see more of Christ's secret things / Than ignorant [burel] people"—"burel" meaning, very explicitly, uneducated (III.1871–72).[56] From Thomas's wife he had received the title gladly, as an acknowledgement of his academic accomplishments which authorized him to be in their home. His education is a commodity. But in front of the "man of greet honour" (III.2163) from whom he wants a favorable judgment, he properly denigrates his academic achievement. The distinction, however, clearly illustrates his smooth-tongued toadyism.

It simultaneously, therefore, exposes his elitism. The fart has exposed his institutional investment in all its hypocrisy. If it signifies rebellion, as Lee Patterson has argued, it does this by leveling the difference in academic knowledge between John and Thomas. John's fury is a sign of how seriously he takes this. The Lady's response tries to contain his reaction:

> I say a churl has done a churl's deed.
> What should I say? God never let him prosper!

---

[52] Szittya, *The Antifraternal Tradition*, 241.

[53] "De Pharisaeo et publicano," in *Opera omnia*, 7–16.

[54] "Ey, maister, welcome be ye, by Seint John! / ... How fare ye, hertely?" (III. 1800–01).

[55] "... right weel, / As he that is youre servant every deel" (III.1805–06).

[56] "... moore we seen of Cristes secree thynges, / Than burel folk" (III.1871–72).

His sick head is full of vanity;
I suppose him to be crazy (III.2206–09).[57]

John, however, like William, envisions immense implications. The "odi-
ous" mischief has been perpetrated not against him, but his order "and
so, *per consequens*, to ech degree / of holy chirche" (III.2192–93). It is
not a personal insult, but an institutional one. The Friar clarifies this
again to the Lady. No—it is not the fart alone. It is this:

> "Madam," he said, "by God, I shall not lie,
> Unless I can be revenged in some way,
> I shall slander him wherever I open my mouth,
> This false blasphemer who has asked me
> To divide that which will not be divided
> For each person in equal shares....! (III.2210–15).[58]

The insult to his order is that he has been stumped by a puzzle, which
Roy Pearcy many years ago identified as an example of the academic
genre called "impossibilia."[59] An "insolubile" or "impossibile" is a
deliberate sophism concocted to educate students in logic. A professor
would make up an answer which proves that, for instance, "God does
not exist" or "the Trojan War is still in progress." The purpose of these
sophisms "was evidently to give students practice in recognizing and
refuting false arguments."[60] The churl's vernacularity has defeated all
his learning.

Chaucer's vernacular satire in the tale centers on the fart, but the
satire is not that the fart is disgusting. The satire happens because it is
hilarious that the friar is *not* insulted by the fart. He has disembodied it;
it becomes an intellectual puzzle of how a "ferthyng" can be departed
evenly into twelve. John's greed, which he feeds with his investment in
Latinity, leads him into an un-fraternal elitism so profound that he cannot even perceive a personal insult. The satire of the tale is precisely

---

[57] I seye a cherl hath doon a cherles dede. / What shold I seye? God lat hym
nevere thee! / His sike heed is ful of vanytee; / I holde hym in a manere frenesye
(III.2206–09).

[58] "Madame," quod he, "by God, I shal nat lye, / But I on oother wyse may be
wreke, / I shal disclaundre hym over al ther I speke, / This false blasphemour
that charged me / To parte that wol nat departed be / To every man yliche...!"
(III.2210–15).

[59] Roy J. Pearcy, "Chaucer's 'An Impossible' ('Summoner's Tale III.2231)," *Notes and
Queries* n. s. 14 (Sept., 1967): 322–25.

[60] Pearcy, "Chaucer's 'An Impossible,'" 323.

that the Friar's immense learning is frozen by the uneducated, the "burel" churl.

This is the distinction for Chaucer between the vernacular and the fossilized discourse he pejoratively identifies with Friar John. Thomas does not have the academic fluency to make an impression on John's narcissism—perhaps no-one does. Faced with this inability, Thomas finally seeks simply to shut him up. Friar John may be multi-lingual—he speaks in French and Latin as well as English in the tale—but he cares to speak only to the (moneyed) elite; he cannot comprehend the vernacular of the laity whom he is enjoined to serve. The "vernacular" Thomas resorts to is not a language, but a linguistic mode defined by its self-conscious lack of cultural authority. By this time in the *Canterbury Tales* we have seen several examples of the vernacular's power to stymie established discourses: the Miller's crudity and the Wife of Bath's vernacularization of her blatantly feminist agenda are affronts to established traditions of romance and academic commentary, and more are to come. In this religious context, because commentary defines ecclesiastical power, empty words signify the impoverishment of clerical authority. Chaucer, I suspect, thought this fact was tragic, though he indicates it with humor.

SOCIAL STATUS AND SIN: READING BOSCH'S PRADO *SEVEN DEADLY SINS AND FOUR LAST THINGS* PAINTING

Laura D. Gelfand
The University of Akron

Abstract: Bosch's painting, erroneously called the "tabletop" of the Seven Deadly Sins, seems instead to have served as a meditative device for a devout layman, or perhaps laywoman. Like most of Bosch's work, this painting may be read on a number of different levels simultaneously. The great circle in its entirety may represent an eye and/or a mirror, such as the Mirror of Human Salvation, and it is also related to the wheel of Fate. The figures who illustrate the sins show that these vices are committed by members of every level of society, from the aristocracy to the lowest of disenfranchised wanderers. Some of the images include subtexts related to proverbs or warnings about societal breakdown. I will address the levels of meaning and focus specifically on the social status of the figures depicted in the scenes of the vices, connecting these figures to contemporary ideas about class and behavior.

Upon encountering Hieronymus Bosch's painting, *The Seven Deadly Sins and the Four Last Things*, in the Prado in Madrid,[1] we are placed in the remarkable position of looking at a painting that, somewhat confrontationally, looks back at us, with a great unblinking eye (fig. 1).[2] This unique representation of the Seven Deadly Sins, probably painted around 1490, features a large central circle with four smaller circles in the corners showing scenes of the Four Last Things: the initial judgment following death, also called the Particular Judgment; the Last Judgment; Heaven; and Hell.[3] The central circle resembles an eye that

---

[1] The oil on panel painting measures 47 × 59 inches. The most recent technological studies were published by Roger Van Schoute and M. C. Garrido, "Les péches capitaux de Jérôme Bosch au Musée du Prado à Madrid. Étude technologique. Premièrs considérations," in *Le dessin sous-jacent dans la peinture, Colloque VI. 12–14 septembre 1985. Infrarouge et autres techniques d'examen*, ed. Helene Verougstraete-Marcq and Roger Van Schoute (Louvain-la-Neuve, 1987), 103–6.

[2] My thanks go to James Elkins whose book, *The Object Stares Back: On the Nature of Seeing* (San Diego, 1997), supplied the idea for this introduction.

[3] The identification of the scene in the upper left hand corner as the Particular Judgment was made by Walter Gibson. Ideas related to this are explored in his article

Figure 1: Hieronymus Bosch, *Tabletop of the Seven Deadly Sins*, Madrid, Prado.
Photo: Museo Nacional del Prado.

simultaneously observes the viewer while acting as a mirror to reflect his or her sins and the foolish behavior of all human beings who sin.[4] In the center of the "pupil" is an image of Christ as the Man of Sorrows, or an *Imago pietatis*, displaying His wounds while standing in His sepulcher. Beneath Him is the inscription, "Cave, cave, D[omi]n[u]s videt," or, "Beware, beware, the Lord is watching." The yellow ring beyond this black center is filled with radiating lines that lead to the outermost ring, or the "iris." Here the Seven Deadly Sins are shown in genre-like scenes with each sin clearly labeled in Latin.

Above and below the central circle are two banderoles with Latin texts from Deuteronomy. When translated, the upper inscription reads, "For they are a nation void of council. Neither is there any understanding in them. O that they were wise, that they understood this, that they would consider their latter end." The banderole below the circle reads, "I will hide my face from them, I will see what their end will be."[5] These inscriptions, along with the scenes of the sins, the Four Last Things, and the *Imago pietatis* in the center of the "eye," indicate that this painting was intended to provide for its commissioner, and perhaps a larger group of viewers, a nexus of visual stimulus that would inspire an appropriately contrite state, one in which the contemplation of one's sins and their punishments was devoutly desired. As we shall see such contemplation was prescribed by pastoral literature, such as confessor's manuals, and was an essential part of confession.

Hieronymus Bosch, the artist to whom most have attributed this work,[6] was a high-ranking member of the Confraternity of Our Lady

---

"The Once and Future Judgments: Two Enigmatic Miniatures in the Salting Hours," *Acta Historiae Artium* 44 (2003): 161–70.

[4] This painting has been the subject of relatively few iconographic or other studies. Some of the most recent include Walter S. Gibson, "Hieronymus Bosch and the Mirror of Man," *Oud Holland* 87 (1973): 205–26; Nathalie Bibot, "'Les sept péchés capitaux' de Jérôme Bosch. Étude iconographique. Un état de la question," *Revue des archéologues et historiens d'art de Louvain* 17 (1984): 302–3; Laurinda Dixon, *Bosch* (London, 2003), 42–55. Although it is commonly known as the *Tabletop of the Seven Deadly Sins* because the composition around the eye makes it seem as if one would have to walk around it, rather than displaying it on a wall, there is no evidence that it was ever used as a table. The scenes of the Four Last Things line up to a single point of view, as does the central portion of the eye, so it is also possible that it was always displayed vertically. Marijnissen suggested that the painting might have been built into the ceiling of a small room, but there is little evidence to support this; see Roger H. Marijnissen, *Hieronymus Bosch: The Complete Works* (Antwerp, 1987), 334.

[5] The first is Deuteronomy 32:28–29, and the second is Deuteronomy 32:20.

[6] See Gibson, "Mirror of Man," 207, and Marijnissen, *Complete Works*, 329, on the attribution of this painting.

in his home town of 's-Hertogenbosch, and he may have been working
for a member of his immediate religious circle when completing this
work.[7] However, as is true for most of Bosch's paintings, the original
commissioner of the work is unknown. The iconography of the work is
derived in part from lay spiritual movements whose ideas were circulating in and around the Netherlands at the end of the fifteenth century.
Although much of Bosch's work is seen to have a surreal or fantastic
aspect by modern viewers, his paintings are the product of a deeply
religious man working for equally pious patrons.

This essay will examine the representation of social status in the
scenes illustrating the sins that fill the outer ring of the central circle
of the Prado painting.[8] The representations of individuals within the
scenes show people from all classes, ages, and both genders engaged in
committing one or more of the sins. This representation of all classes
of society is not unlike the popular Dance of Death images from the
late Middle Ages and Renaissance which showed a skeletal figure of
Death claiming young and old, rich and poor, and laymen and clerics
alike. Bosch's image, however, is more than a reminder of the inevita-
bility of death. Here, the viewer confronts not only the idea of death,
judgment and the ultimate state of the soul, as spelled out in the Four
Last Things, but also the central idea of Christ's sacrifice, the pain that
our sins inflict upon Him and the explicit warning that He watches
and will judge all that we do. In this way the painting presents a far
more layered set ideas than the Dance of Death.

A description of this painting dating from around 1605 by Fray José
de Sigüenza, a monk in the El Escorial where it formed part of Philip
II's collection, stresses the mirroring function of this work and how it
reflects the viewer's soul.[9] The concept of mirrors and mirroring in

---

[7] In addition to being a deeply religious man, Bosch was also a very successful artist
who had the good fortune to marry well. See Bruno Blondé and Hans Vlieghe, "The
Social Status of Hieronymus Bosch," *Burlington Magazine* 131 (1989): 699–700.

[8] I would like to thank Susan Dudash, whose work on the social status of various
sins in the work of Christine de Pizan inspired my own approach to this painting. A
number of aspects of the painting's appearance and iconography remain to be inves-
tigated; these will be the subject of a future essay.

[9] Jaco Rutgers, "Hieronymus Bosch in El Escorial, Devotional Paintings in a Monastery," in *Hieronymus Bosch. New Insights into his Life and Work*, ed. Jos Koldwewij and
Bernard Vermet (Rotterdam, 2001), 34. It is not known when the painting entered
Philip's collection, but it was moved to the Escorial in 1574. It has been on display at
the Prado since 1939. See M. C. Garrido and Roger Van Schoute, *Bosch at the Museo
del Prado, Technical Study* (Madrid, 2001), 77.

the Middle Ages has been the subject of a great deal of scholarship.[10] Deborah Shuger observed that, "What Renaissance persons do see in the mirror...are saints, skulls, offspring, spouses, magistrates, Christ. The mirror reflects these figures because they are images of oneself; one encounters one's own likeness only in the mirror of the other. Renaissance texts and emblems consistently describe mirroring in these terms, which suggests that early modern selfhood was not experienced reflexively, but, as it were, relationally."[11] Most of the mirrors that would have been used by Bosch and his contemporaries were quite small, often dark and frequently convex so that the reflections that appeared in them would have been distorted. Certainly one of the most well-known Renaissance mirrors is found in Jan van Eyck's *Arnolfini Wedding Portrait* from 1434 in the National Gallery, London (fig. 2).[12] In the reflection we see not only the backs of the couple who appear as the main subject of the painting but, famously, two figures who stand in a doorway, as well as the rest of the room in reverse. The distortions of this bulls-eye reflection allow for the inclusion of the entirety of the room, including those things which are not visible within the highly illusionistic scene recorded in the painting. Like several of Bosch's paintings, the *Seven Deadly Sins and Four Last Things* reflects, or displays, the nature of human folly.[13] But the resemblance of the circular eye-like form to a

---

[10] Susan K. Hagen, *Allegorical Remembrance: A Study of the Pilgrimage of Life of Man as a Medieval Treatise on Seeing and Remembering* (Athens, GA, 1990), includes a well-reasoned approach to the idea of the mirror in literature and visual culture. See also Hans Leisegang, "La conaissance de Dieu au miroir de l'ame et de la nature," *Revue d'histoire et de philosophie religieuses* 17 (1937): 145–71; Heinrich Schwarz, "The Mirror of the Artist and the Mirror of the Devout: Observations on some Paintings, Drawings and Prints of the Fifteenth Century," in *Studies in the History of Art Dedicated to William E. Suida on his Eightieth Birthday* (London, 1959), 90–105; and Herbert Grabes, *The Mutable Glass: Mirror-Imagery in Titles and Texts of the Middle Ages and English Renaissance* (Cambridge, Eng., 1982).

[11] Debora Shuger, "The 'I' of the Beholder: Renaissance Mirrors and the Reflexive Mind," in *Renaissance Culture and the Everyday*, ed. Patricia Fumerton and Simon Hunt (Philadelphia, 1999), 21–41.

[12] Jan van Eyck's painting has been the subject of a large number of studies, but the recent catalogue by Lorne Campbell is an important contribution that has altered our understanding of the painting: *The Fifteenth Century Netherlandish Paintings* (London, 1998), 174–211.

[13] Sigüenza divided the works by Bosch in the Escorial into three groups: devotional paintings, variations on the theme of the Temptation of Saint Anthony, and "maca-ronic" paintings such as the *Garden of Earthly Delights*. See Jaco Rutgers, "El Escorial," 34. Recently, scholars have associated the *Haywain Triptych* by Bosch, also in the Prado, with the Seven Deadly Sins; see Anne M. Morganstern, "The Rest of Bosch's 'Ship of Fools,'" *Art Bulletin* 66 (1984): 295–302. Additionally, the *Death of the Miser* in The

Figure 2: Jan van Eyck, *Arnolfini Wedding Portrait*, London, National Gallery.
Photo: National Gallery, London.

mirror, something that would have been immediately recognized by late medieval viewers, allows for a complicated and polysemous type of vision, one that provides the viewer with a visual checklist of sins organized within an intrinsically memorable composition.

The eye and the mirror were closely linked during the Middle Ages. Among the many descriptions that relate the eye of God to the mirror, one that has been most felicitously connected with this particular painting appears in the work of Nicolas of Cusa, whose *Vision of God* states: "O Lord, You see and You have Eyes. Therefore, You are an eye, because Your having is being. Accordingly, You behold within Yourself all things.... Moreover, the angle of Your eye is a circle—or better, an infinite sphere—because Your sight is an eye of sphericity and of infinite perfection. Therefore, Your sight sees—roundabout and above and below—all things at once."[14] It is important to recognize the visual complexity of Bosch's composition. When standing before the painting, the viewer is simultaneously being observed by God, but also sharing in God's vision of the viewer's world, a vision that includes the viewer him- or herself. Sharing God's view of the world and recognizing oneself within this view would certainly have aided in inspiring simultaneous self-examination while emphasizing God's external, and eventually eternal, scrutiny and judgment as well.

The vivid display of the sins may have acted as a stimulus for a number of important religious activities including self-examination prior to confession and as a prompt to help remember each of the Seven Deadly Sins. The *Imago pietatis* in the "pupil" of the central circle was a devotional image par excellence (fig. 3). Its emphasis on Christ's sacrifice was intended to inspire an appropriately contrite devotional

---

National Gallery in Washington, D.C., has been connected with the Louvre *Ship of Fools*, the New Haven *Allegory of Intemperance*, and the Rotterdam *Wayfarer*. In its original state it seems likely that this triptych would have been a commentary on the Seven Deadly Sins, as well. See Dixon, *Bosch*, 69–79.

[14] *De visione Dei*, 8.32, in *Nicolas of Cusa's Dialectical Mysticism: Text, translation and Interpretive Study of De visione Dei*, ed. and trans. Jasper Hopkins (Minneapolis, 1985), 152–53: "Domine, tu vides et habes oculos. Es igitur oculus, quia habere tuum est esse. Ob hoc in te ipso omnia specularis.... Quod enim oculus noster se ad obiectum flectit, ex eo est quia visus noster per angulum quantum videt. Angulus autem oculi tui, deus, non est quantus, sed est infinitus, qui est et circulus, immo et sphaera infinita, quia visus est eculus sphaericitatis et perfectionis infinitae. Omnia igitur in circuitu et sursum et deorsum simul videt. "There are many additional examples linking the eye of God with the mirror and a number of these have been discussed in regard to this painting. For a summary of some of these, see Dixon, *Bosch*, 44–46. The first scholar to explore some of these links was Walter S. Gibson, in "Mirror of Man," 209–18.

Figure 3: Hieronymus Bosch, *Tabletop of the Seven Deadly Sins*: detail, *Imago Pietatis*. Photo: Museo Nacional del Prado.

state in whose who gazed upon it.[15] The symbols of the Four Last Things in the corners take the viewer through a dramatic depiction of the processes that follow death and the eternity to which they lead. They would have motivated the viewer to consider his or her decisions and their consequences in the next world. The contrite state this would produce was thought necessary prior to an efficacious confession. Prior to confession, one was to engage in serious soul searching, recalling any and all sins for which confession and penance were necessary. Even the most devout person could be punished in the afterlife for failing to recall and do penance for every sin she or he had committed. Bosch's genre scenes showing the seven sins rotating around the figure of the Man of Sorrows may have helped to prod the memory and aid in this process.

The display of the sins in the circular format does not recall simply an eye and/or a mirror. A number of important ideas and systems were illustrated in the form of the wheel. As Mary Carruthers has explained, "The metaphors buried within the English word 'rote' ('wheel' and 'route', both from Latin *rota*) imply the orderly disposition of the various 'bits' of memory: the 'things' of a culture are learned within repeated patterned sequences, the 'little forms' of formulae—a bit of text and/or picture—with which meditation began. These provide structured/structuring 'backgrounds' or 'places,' the 'habits' (as in habitation) of one's own thinking mind."[16] The genre-like scenes painted by Bosch would provide the viewer with distinct and memorable images with which to recall each of the sins. As we shall see below, the ways in which each sin leads to others created patterns of looking and additional associations that aided in the retention and understanding of the number and nature of the sins.

Bosch was not alone in his use of the circle or wheel in the depiction of the Seven Deadly Sins. A roughly contemporary woodcut is one of many such images produced throughout the Middle Ages (fig. 4).[17] A number of other common medieval themes were shown in the form of a wheel. These include depictions of the Seasons, Labors

---

[15] A recent, interesting discussion of this important iconographic sign is found in Alexander Nagel, *Michelangelo and the Reform of Art* (Cambridge, Eng., 2000), 49–70.

[16] Mary Carruthers, "Reading with Attitude: Remembering the Book," in *The Book and the Body*, ed. Dolores Warwick Frese and Katherine O'Brien O'Keefe (Notre Dame, IN, 1997), 7.

[17] This is found in Dixon, *Bosch*, 49, ill. 17.

238   LAURA D. GELFAND

Figure 4: Anonymous (single-leaf woodcut) from Munich, about 1490–1500:
The Four Christian Ages (panel with the virtues and vices), woodcut, 35.4 × 19 cm.
Basel, Kupferstichkabinett des Kunstmuseums Basel (Inv. X.1877).
Photo: Kunstmuseum Basel.

and Zodiac; scenes of the Seven Virtues and Seven Sins in the Medieval City from Augustine's *City of God*;[18] the illustration of Hugh of
St.-Victor's *De quinque septenis*; and other concentric portrayals of catechetical matter such as that in the *Speculum theologie* by John of Metz.[19]
The Wheel of Fortune was naturally shown as a *rota* and its conceptual
significance is not entirely unrelated to Bosch's Prado painting.[20] The
Wheel of Fortune is a multivalent symbol, most frequently representing the impermanence and temporality of earthly wealth, but during
the fourteenth and fifteenth centuries it took on a somewhat altered
meaning. In a period in which instability in the maintenance of the
social class structure began to cause ripples in the increasingly urban
landscape, the Wheel of Fortune served as a reminder that the desire
to move outside the class in which one was born was a vainglorious
wish. Such messages were created for members of the upper classes
who were threatened by the rise of the merchant class and the shifting
fabric of late medieval society.[21]

The representation of social classes in the Prado painting has not
previously been the subject of study, but the work clearly indicates that
the members of different social classes were associated with specific sins
and Bosch uses this widely understood set of conceptions to characterize the foibles commonly associated with these classes and genders.
Additionally, such an approach allows him to draw attention to the
ways in which the sins undermine concepts of civic responsibility and
appropriate social constructions. Bosch depicts the sins of *Luxuria* and
Superbia as those committed by the aristocracy. Additionally, the obviously
wealthy, fashionably-dressed man with the falcon serves as an object of
Envy while members of the merchant class are shown committing the
sin itself. Members of this merchant class are also shown as guilty of
Avaritia and *Accidia*, while the poor are shown in scenes of *Ira* and *Gula*.
The social status of these three groups is made recognizable by Bosch
thanks to the ways in which he dresses his figures and the settings into

---

[18] Found in an illustrated, fifteenth-century manuscript: The Hague, Rijksmuseum
Meermanno-Westreenianum MS. 11, fol. 6r., illustrated in Dixon, *Bosch*, 48, ill. 16.
[19] See Lucy Freeman Sandler, *The Psalter of Robert De Lisle in the British Library* (London,
1983; reprint 1999), 23–26.
[20] See Hans-Joachim Raupp, "Visual Comments on the Mutability of Social Positions and Values in Netherlandish and German Art of the Fifteenth and Sixteenth
Centuries," in *Showing Status: Representation of Social Positions in the Late Middle Ages*, ed.
Wim Blockmans and Antheun Janse (Brepols, 1999), 282.
[21] Ibid.

which they are placed. Those intended to represent members of the upper classes are dressed in up-to-date, expensive fashions that clearly indicate their wealth and status. The poor, especially in the scene of *Gula*, are shabbily attired with holes in their shoes and torn clothing. Those of the merchant classes wear the long robes and hats, or chaperons, associated with their class. The bourgeois man depicted in the scene showing *Accidia* is in a middle-class interior with a tiled floor and large fireplace—in sharp contrast to the figures in the scene of *Gula* who inhabit the room of a house or a tavern in which the dirt floor serves as a place for the small fire over which sausages roast. Again, this is in stark contrast to the scene of *Superbia* in which opulent objects and furniture decorate the richly appointed domestic interior.

When the scenes are examined in terms of gender, we find that men are far more likely to be shown engaged in sinful activities. The only sin shown committed by a woman alone is *Superbia*, but women are shown together with male sinners in the activities depicted in *Luxuria* and *Invidia*. Men alone are shown committing the sins of *Ira*, *Gula*, *Accidia* and *Avaritia*. In fact, women appear in the scenes of *Accidia* and *Ira*, but in both scenes they seem to attempt to stop the men from committing the sins, and a female tavern keeper is shown as a seemingly helpless accessory who feeds the rapacious gluttons in the scene of *Gula*.

Bosch's depictions of the sins do far more than provide a simple catalogue of sinful behaviors. Rather than showing representations of the personifications of the sins, as had been standard in earlier medieval depictions, additional layers of meaning are accrued through the depiction of narratives. Details included in the scenes point out the destructiveness to society of each of the sins. Each scene supplies a specific example of the negative impact of the sins: for instance, the woman looking in the mirror in *Superbia* is setting a bad example for the servants, and poor parenting is evident in the scene of *Gula*.[22] The man sleeping in his chair before the fire in *Accidia* is not contributing to society and is neglecting his religious duties and the health of his soul. The sins committed in *Luxuria* flout socially approved behaviors and clearly break the sacrament of marriage. *Ira* shows men who are out

---

[22] The club and ball in the foreground by the boy may be elements of a game called *kolf* which was extremely popular with children and adults during this period. See Annemarieke Willemsen, "Playing with Reality. Games and Toys in the Oeuvre of Hieronymus Bosch," in *Hieronymus Bosch. New Insights*, ed. Koldwewij and Vermet, 195.

of control because of their anger, and it includes intimations of sexual behavior and/or violence occurring between a man and a woman. The judge taking bribes in *Avaritia* shows the break-down of governmental systems and, finally, among other things the scene of *Invidia* shows the naked envy of members of the lower classes for those above them. These members of the merchant class are inappropriately wishing to rise above their God-given social rank.

In addition to conveying the effects that the sins have on society, there is also an indication that committing one of the sins may lead to committing others, which is similar to the concatenation of sins described by Cassian and other early church fathers.[23] It has not previously been observed that the sins depicted are not confined to their own pie-shaped parts of the circle. Rather, each of the scenes includes an element that alludes to another sin. Most prominently, the money bags which are most commonly associated with *Avaritia* are found in every scene but *Ira*. Clearly, avarice must have been of particular importance to the commissioner of this work. The scene of *Luxuria* shows fruit and wine, common accompaniments in illustrations of this sin, but objects that are also associated with the sin of gluttony. The angry man who grapples with the woman in the scene of *Ira* holds a mug of beer indicating that in becoming drunk and belligerent he too has committed the sin of gluttony. The scene of Avarice shows a tavern in the background with a woman in the doorway, a common symbol of lust. And the hat with the arrow through it and the knife on the wall of the room with the gluttons indicates the anger and violence that often accompany drunkenness.

Bosch's painting reveals some of the ways in which he and his contemporaries thought of the seven deadly sins. But, perhaps equally revealing, the representation of members of specific social classes within the narrative scenes illustrates contemporary conceptions of the relationship between an individual's position in society and specific sins. *Ira* (fig. 5) is appropriately placed beneath the *Imago pietatis* and, although there is no sense of anger in the passive figure of Christ, His righteous anger is promised in the Last Judgment in the upper right corner. The scene of *Ira* depicts two men, who are dressed as peasants, engaged in a terrible brawl before a run-down inn. The man on the left, in the

---

[23] John Cassian, *De institutis coenobiorum*, 5.1–2, ed. and trans. Jean-Claude Guy, SC 109 (Paris, 1965), 191–93.

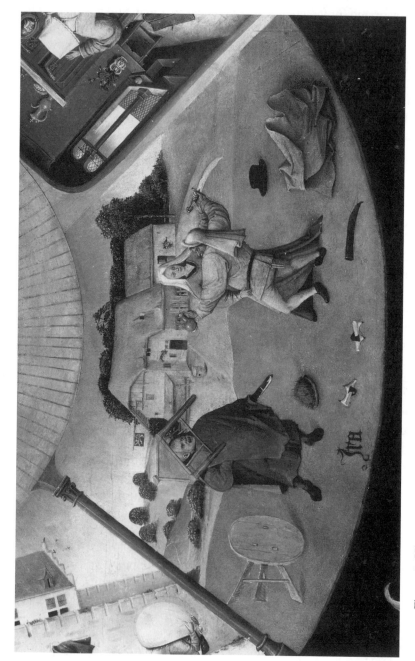

Figure 5: Hieronymus Bosch, *Tabletop of the Seven Deadly Sins*, Madrid, Prado: Ira (detail). Photo: Museo Nacional del Prado.

brown cloak, has already been clobbered by a three-legged stool and his head is bleeding freely, but the knife in his hand and the look on his face makes it clear that the fight is far from over. A woman tries to intervene and stop the man in the short jacket who holds a beer stein in one hand and a large knife in the other. Shoes and clothing are strewn across the field of battle and it is clear that these are men with very little to lose. Their actions place them on the outskirts of society as do the clothes they wear.

The pleasant domestic interior into which we peer to observe *Superbia* reveals a woman who is so busy admiring herself that she doesn't even recognize the devil who holds the mirror in which she adjusts her foolishly large hat (fig. 6). The dresser in front of her is laden with opulent objects including imported ceramics, gold and silver vessels and other luxury items.[24] The large mirror itself would have been an expensive object that few, other than the wealthiest people, could have owned. Although we cannot see this woman's face, we do see her distorted profile reflected in the mirror before her. The devil who holds the mirror is the only demonic figure to appear in the central circle. A connection between the devil and mirrors was well established in Bosch's lifetime and illustrations linking the two even appear on the inexpensive lead-tin badges that were commonly worn on hats and clothing. One found in Reimerswaal, in the Netherlands, illustrates the proverb "when you look in the mirror, you are looking up the devil's arse."[25]

The fourteenth-century English confessor's manual, the *Memoriale presbiterorum*, like many other such texts, divides potential penitents by social status and instructs confessors on the specific questions each of these groups should be asked. Such manuals indicate the particular sins that were associated with various social or gender groups. For example, the confessor is instructed to inquire of married women, "if they have worn extravagant, vainglorious, outlandish and inordinate apparel on their heads, because they go about wearing horns and looking outlandish, which is a category of pride."[26] The fancy hat worn by the woman

---

[24] Hans Janssen, Olaf Goubitz, and Jaap Kottman, "Everyday Objects in the Paintings of Hieronymus Bosch," in *Hieronymus Bosch. New Insights*, ed. Koldwewij and Vermet, 174. The authors identify the two-handled blue and white majolica vase as Italian, dated to around 1500.

[25] Hans van Gangelen and Sebastiaan Ostkamp, "Parallels between Hieronymus Bosch's Imagery and Decorated Material Culture from the Period Between 1450–1525," in *Hieronymus Bosch. New Insights*, ed. Koldwewij and Vermet, 166.

[26] Michael Haren, "The Interrogatories for Officials, Lawyers and Secular Estates

Figure 6: Hieronymus Bosch, *Tabletop of the Seven Deadly Sins*, Madrid, Prado:
Superbia, (detail). Photo: Museo Nacional del Prado.

in *Superbia* is also singled out for mockery by the devil who sports a similar one, thus emphasizing the wicked nature of those who care more about their appearance than their eventual salvation.

The woman's skirt is held up behind her by her belt revealing the garment's luxuriant fur lining. This arrangement probably helped to keep the skirt from dragging on the floor behind her. Extra long skirts and trains were frequently the subject of sumptuary laws as well as supplying fodder for the sermons of preachers who identified women as being more inclined to commit the sins of pride and vanity.[27] Bernardino of Siena (1380–1444) was particularly vexed by this practice and in one of his sermons compared women with long trains to serpents or demons who act as snares for men. He also told a story of a woman whose trailing skirts raised so much dust that it filled her lungs and she defiled the house with her spit.[28] Threats of purgatorial and infernal torments accompanied these descriptions, but this did little to stop the progress of fashion or the desire of women for long trains, luxurious fabrics and new styles. In Bosch's scene of *Superbia*, the room adjacent to the main room in which the woman stands has a fireplace, a cat and another woman within it. This woman's hair falls over her shoulders and she is also admiring herself in a mirror. The woman of the house and her sinful behavior has clearly set a bad example for others in the household.

Luxuria (fig. 7) features two amorous couples in a Venus tent accompanied by a fool who is having his bottom spanked with a wooden spoon.[29] The couples are well-dressed, with the men in fashionably short tunics and leggings and the women wearing expensive, brocaded fabrics. The

---

of the *Memoriale presbiterorum*: Edition and Translation," in *Handling Sin: Confession in the Middle Ages*, ed. Peter Biller and A. J. Minnis (Woodbridge, Eng., 1998), 157. The text is analyzed by the author in his essay in the same volume entitled, "Confession, Social Ethics and Social Discipline in the *Memoriale presbiterorum*," 109–22.

[27] There are many fine studies on sumptuary laws, particularly in Florence; see Romand Rainey, "Dressing Down the Dressed-Up: Reproving Feminine Attire in Renaissance Florence," in *Renaissance Society and Culture: Essays in Honor of Eugene F. Rice*, ed. J. Monfasani and R. G. Musto (New York, 1991), 217–38.

[28] Thomas M. Izbicki, "Pyres of Vanities: Mendicant Preaching on the Vanity of Woman and Its Lay Audience," in *De Ore Domini*, ed. Thomas L. Amos, Eugene A. Green, and Beverly Mayne Kienzle (Kalamazoo, MI, 1989), 211–34, esp. 216 and 222 respectively.

[29] It has been suggested that the recorder, drum, and harp are included here to provide examples of wind, percussion, and stringed instruments. See Kees Vellekoop, "Music and Dance in the Paintings of Hieronymus Bosch," in *Hieronymus Bosch. New Insights*, ed. Koldwewij and Vermet, 203.

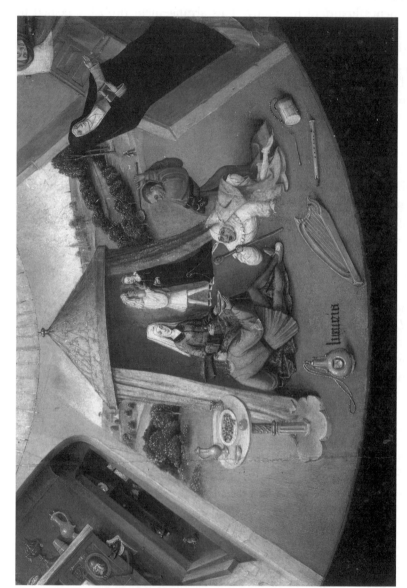

Figure 7: Hieronymus Bosch, *Tabletop of the Seven Deadly Sins*, Madrid, Prado: Luxuria (detail). Photo: Museo Nacional del Prado.

couple inside the tent seems to be intent on their love-making while a seduction occurs in the foreground. The male figure, who we see from behind, is actually reclining within the long folds of the woman's dress. Again, we recall San Bernardino and other mendicant preachers railing against the seductive intent of long gowns worn by women. Surrounding this merry company are the common accoutrements of such encounters, musical instruments and fruit. Bosch frequently included these elements in scenes illustrating the sin of *Luxuria*; they are particularly prominent in the Hell panel of the *Garden of Earthly Delights*.[30] The fool himself is seen as a symbol of lust and the obscene gesture of having his bared bottom spanked with a large wooden spoon illustrates the saying "door de billen slaan," ("to strike through the buttocks"), an allusion to profligate, dissolute behavior.[31] Fools appear only twice in Bosch's work and both times in relation to the sin of *Luxuria*.[32] In addition to his inclusion in the Prado painting a fool appears prominently in the *Ship of Fools* in the Louvre, Paris. The musical instruments that appear in the foreground of the scene of *Luxuria* probably belong to the fool who was commonly shown with such instruments.[33]

The scene depicting *Accidia* (fig. 8) is one of the simplest and most straight-forward. Here, we see a middle-class gentleman asleep before a warm fire in a nicely appointed, yet not luxurious interior. The gentleman is dressed in a green robe with a red chaperon wrapped around his head and he clutches the money bag that rests in his lap. This costume is quite similar to that worn by Chancellor Nicolas Rolin in the famous presentation scene illuminated by Rogier van der Weyden in the *Chroniques de Hainaut*.[34] Nicolas Rolin's robe is blue, but the costumes are otherwise identical, even to the inclusion of the money bag. However,

---

[30] Bosch, c. 1510, Prado Museum, Madrid. Numerous scholars have addressed the meaning of Bosch's iconography in this respect. See Walter S. Gibson, "The Strawberries of Hieronymus Bosch," *Cleveland Studies in the History of Art* 8 (2003): 24–33.

[31] Van Gangelen and Ostkamp, "Parallels," 162.

[32] Ibid.

[33] A final detail of interest is to be found near the text on the wine bottle in the foreground. The bottle is decorated with a coat of arms, white with a simple red chevron, and the same coat of arms appears in the *Invidia* scene. The appearance of the arms in this scene has previously been mentioned, but its owner is yet to be identified. Marijnissen, *Complete Works*, 334, correctly noted that the coats of arms in Bosch's work deserve further study.

[34] Brussels, Bibliothèque royale de Belgique MS. 9242, fol. 1r, illustrated in Thomas Kren and Scot McKendrick's marvelous catalogue for the exhibition, *Illuminating the Renaissance; The Triumph of Flemish Manuscript Painting in Europe* (Los Angeles, 2003), 90–93 (cat. no. 3).

Figure 8: Hieronymus Bosch, *Tabletop of the Seven Deadly Sins*, Madrid, Prado: Accidia (detail).
Photo: Museo Nacional del Prado.

Rogier's illumination has been dated around 1450, about forty years before Bosch's painting was completed. This marks the gentleman's costume as notably out-of-date and such a fashion faux pas would have been immediately recognizable to Bosch's contemporaries. I believe the distinctly unfashionable costume is intended to indicate that this man, who could certainly afford new clothing, is too slothful to update his look. Such behavior is associated with the sin of avarice, especially in connection with misers, as found in the *Romance of the Rose*, in which the image of Avarice on the garden wall is shown wearing a robe that was "ten years old, at least."[35] Fashion changed quickly among the upper classes during the Late Middle Ages and those who would have seen Bosch's painting probably would have recognized and understood the symbolic elements in this choice of costume.

Returning to the scene, we see daylight sky outside the window revealing that this is an inappropriate time for sleep. A dog curls up between the napping man and the fire while a woman in a black robe and head-covering holds out a rosary and a book that is most likely a devotional text of some sort. On the wooden bench behind the man is a larger black book which is closed and which, like the woman and her religious paraphernalia, he also ignores. It is possible that the book is an account book, a ledger, or some other work-related text and, like his religious observations, the slothful man's business is also being neglected while he sleeps. The identity of the woman is intriguing since she appears in the painting again near the bedside of the dying man in the scene of the Particular Judgment. She cannot be a nun, as there is no order that wears red lining beneath their black robes, but she may be a member of some confraternity.

Gula (fig. 9) shows a far different interior and members of the lower class engaged in sin. The dirt floors of this room, which is probably an inn or tavern, are strewn with objects including, from left to right, a potty training seat, the ball and stick for the game of *kolf*, a sausage on a skewer that would be roasted over the fire in the center of the floor, a cooking pot and an overturned stool. The four figures in this interior are equally untidy, with holes in their shoes, torn and dirty

---

[35] Guillaume de Lorris and Jean de Meun, *Le Roman de la Rose*, v. 218, ed. Félix Lecoy (Paris, 1974), 1:8: "Bien avoit sa robe X anz"; *The Romance of the Rose*, trans. Harry W. Robbins (New York, 1962), 7, line 59. On the miser's poor clothing, see Richard Newhauser, *The Early History of Greed: The Sin of Avarice in Early Medieval Thought and Literature* (Cambridge, Eng., 2000), 32.

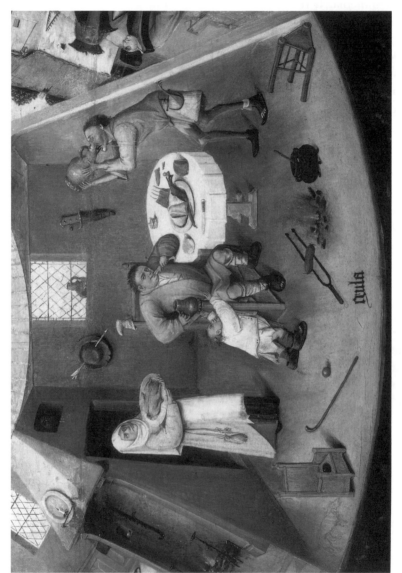

Figure 9: Hieronymus Bosch, *Tabletop of the Seven Deadly Sins*, Madrid, Prado: Gula (detail). Photo: Museo Nacional del Prado.

clothing, and grotesque bodies. The money bag and key that hang from the belt of the woman entering the room indicate that she is the proprietor of this disreputable establishment. An owl sits in a niche just above the door and it has clearly been living there for some time as evidence of its own filthy habits may be seen dripping down the wall. Owls were symbols of evil during Bosch's time and were associated with drunkenness because when owls were seen during the daytime they often exhibited behaviors resembling that of a drunk.[36]

The men who crowd the table represent two different aspects of gluttony, one associated with food and the other with drink. The seated man, whose child stubbornly begs for food, as discussed above, is seen bursting out of his clothing as he shovels food into his mouth. He holds a beer mug in one hand and the cooked leg of some animal in the other. His companion, a thin drunken man, focuses on nothing but the rapidly emptying flask he lifts above his head as he struggles to drain every drop. His torn stockings and ragged tunic reveal that he is probably a marginalized member of society and the money bag he wears may mark him as a peddler. Bosch represented peddler's twice, both on the exterior wings of triptychs, and the men in these depictions share a number of attributes with the man in the Prado painting.[37] Peddlers were held in deep suspicion because of their itinerant lifestyles, and they were known to frequent taverns, inns and other places of disrepute. Peddlers were also known for their drinking, lechery and dishonesty. The inclusion of this figure in the representation of the sin of gluttony emphasizes both the social status of those most frequently associated with this sin, but also that excessive drinking was a type of gluttony equal to the sin of overindulgence in food.[38]

Avaritia (fig. 10) shows a bailiff, who holds the symbol of his office (a *baljuwroede*) with one hand and accepts a bribe with the other. This sin was long associated with bailiffs and the instructions to confessors in the *Memoriale presbiterorum* states: "Confessor, if it chances that you hear from time to time [a bailiff] in confession, you must strive manfully to extract the truth, because such people are exceedingly caviling and

---

[36] The association of evil with owls in Bosch's work is found in Jakob Rosenberg, "On the Meaning of a Bosch Drawing," in *De Artibus Opuscula XL: Essays in Honor of Erwin Panofsky*, ed. M. Meiss (New York, 1961), 1:422–26.

[37] Eric de Bruyn, "Hieronymus Bosch's So-called Prodigal Son Tondo: The Pedlar as Repentant Sinner," in *Hieronymus Bosch. New Insights*, ed. Koldwewij and Vermet, 133–43.

[38] See Augustine, *Confessions*, 10.31, ed. James O'Donnell (Oxford, 1992), 1:136.

Figure 10: Hieronymus Bosch, *Tabletop of the Seven Deadly Sins*, Madrid, Prado: Invidia (detail). Photo: Museo Nacional del Prado.

altogether given to avarice and falsity and led by blind greed which is
the root of all evils; nor do they care for God or for holy church or its
ministers, but only for securing profits and rewards."[39] Two gentlemen
of middle class status watch from a bench and, although they must
see the activity taking place before them, they do nothing to stop it,
making them accomplices to the sin.

The scene of *Invidia* (fig. 11) includes the most explicit references to
social status and sin. A number of individuals gather at the windows
of a house with large windows and a half-door, a couple and a woman
who may be their daughter are within the building. The windows of
this building show two coats of arms, one is impossible to decipher,
but the other is identical to that on the wine flask in the foreground
of *Luxuria*. Outside the home, a young man in red stares fixedly at
the young woman inside. These figures have been the subject of some
speculation.[40] The young man in red with a money bag holds a flower
in his hand that he wishes to present to the young woman inside;
however, she already has a flower of her own, and a headdress, probably indicating that she is either married or affianced, and his wish to
court her will be unfulfilled. His intensity as he pushes himself toward
the woman indicates that he is gripped by envy of the man who has
bested him in his pursuit. The dapper figure of a falconer in white with
a large money bag stands outside the house while the brutish male of
the couple and his wife gaze at him with a mixture of unbridled envy
and curiosity. The man looking at the falconer holds a bone in his
hand and the two dogs beneath him echo his envy as they beg for his
bone rather than gnaw on those already on the ground before them.
As discussed above, the poorer man and his wife represent the sinful

---

[39] See Haren, "Confession, Social Ethics and Social Discipline," 135.

[40] Marijnissen describes some of the interpretations of this scene, including that of
Reutersward who believed that the man and woman were comparing their flowers to
see which was better. He also cites Bax who initially believed that the man was showing a tulip to the woman and she was showing him a carnation. However, following
restoration of the painting Bax renounced this belief and asserted that the man actually holds nothing in his hand. See Marijnissen, *Complete Works*, 332n472. In detailed
photos it appears as if the man does hold a flower in his hand, but this may be a
misreading of the image or the product of overpaint. In any case, the carnation held
by the woman is a symbol of betrothal and is found in the *Hours of Mary of Burgundy*,
Vienna, Österreichische Nationalbibliothek MS. 1857, fol. 14v, and in Jan van Eyck's
Portrait of a Man with a Pink of c. 1435 in the Staatliche Museen, Gemäldegalerie-
Dahlem, Berlin.

Figure 11: Hieronymus Bosch, Tabletop of the Seven Deadly Sins, Madrid, Prado: Invidia (detail). Photo: Museo Nacional del Prado.

behavior associated with the desire to rise from the social class into which one is born.

To the right of the falconer, a man in patched clothing carries off a large sack. His face is mostly hidden and he escapes the notice of the rest of the figures. This figure has been interpreted in a number of ways. Marijnissen proposed that the falconer is a profiteer and the sack carried by the man contains grain that the falconer would sell at a profit following a crop failure.[41] However, it is not altogether clear to me that the falconer and the man with the sack are traveling together. In fact, it seems more likely that he is stealing the sack and its contents from the falconer. Perhaps this is a symbolic representation of the topos, current in Bosch's time, that sinners bear the burden of their sins like a sack or a pack, i.e., that a lifetime of sin creates a heavy burden.[42] Finally, it is possible that this figure may be an "everyman" whose movement from the scene of Envy towards that of Anger represents the common progression made by all who engage in this sin.

I hope that this description of the painting and its details will allow for a clearer picture of the ways in which it might have been used by its original owner. The multivalent interpretations of the sins, cast as they are around the all seeing eye of God with its mirror-like aspect, creates a wheel promoting memory and forging connections between the sins themselves as well as those who commit them. The ways in which the sinners are characterized in terms of their social status reflects contemporary ideas of class and the sins associated with particular groups, as evidenced in confessor's manuals. Thus, we see a correlation between Bosch's painting and instructions for interrogators in Raymond of Penaforte's *Summa de poenitentia*, in which he instructs: "Item, with princes ask about the maladministration of justice; with knights ask about pillage; with merchants, and officials, and those practicing the mechanical arts, ask about perjury, lying, theft, fraud, and suchlike; with burgesses and citizens generally, ask about usuries and securities; with peasants, ask about envy, theft—especially about tithes, first-fruits, dues and taxes."[43] To paraphrase Peter Biller, the need for a penitential

---

[41] Marijnissen, *Complete Works*, 334.

[42] Eric de Bruyn, "Hieronymus Bosch's So-called Prodigal Son Tondo," 139–40.

[43] S. Raimundus de Pennaforte, *Summa de paenitentia*, 3.34.35, ed. Xaverio Ochoa and Aloisio Diez (Roma, 1976), 834: "Item, circa principes de iustitia; circa milites, de rapina; circa mercatores necnon et officiales artes mechanicas exercentes, de periurio, mendacio, furto dolo, et similibus. Circa burgenses et cives communiter, de usuris et pignoribus. Circa rusticos, de invidia, furto maxime circa decimas, primitias, tributa

process created a sort of moral sociography.[44] Such a system is readily displayed in Bosch's painting and it is important to note that ecclesiastics, who are the subject of extensive discussion in the confessor's manuals, are not found in Bosch's painting at all. This may, perhaps, provide some evidence for the identity of the original owner, who was presumably not a cleric, and about the audience for whom this work was intended. Further inquiry into the representation of social status in the work of Bosch and his contemporaries could reveal equally telling aspects of the ways in which late-medieval people thought about those around them as well as themselves.

---

et census." Translation by Peter Biller, "Confession in the Middle Ages: Introduction," in *Handling Sin*, ed. Biller and Minnis, 17.
   [44] Ibid. 18.

FREUD AS VIRGIL: THE ANTHROPOLOGIES OF PSYCHOANALYSIS AND THE *COMMEDIA*

Thomas Parisi
Saint Mary's College

Abstract: This essay explores the "existential cosmologies" of Freud and Dante. I highlight the use of autobiography in Freud's body of work and the *Commedia*, and discuss why autobiography is thought to fundamentally weaken Freud's claims while enriching Dante's. I argue that the overlap in their existential cosmologies suggests that we take Freud's claims more seriously, but that this will entail re-characterizing the nature of his epistemological and moral enterprise. After describing some examples of convergence between Dante and Freud that have not been explored before, including the central place of pride for Dante and narcissism for Freud, I suggest an analogy between Freud and Dante's Virgil, with Freud as a pivotal figure on the frontier of the "creaturely" and the "soul-ful," unaware of the limits of the positivism he vigorously espoused, but pointing the way, as Jonathan Lear has put it, toward re-imagining what an epistemology of the soul might look like.

Freud as Virgil? Readers of the *Commedia* soon come to appreciate the developmental aspects of the relationship between Virgil and the pilgrim. At the start of the journey, Virgil serves as a reliable, knowledgeable, and confident guide to a lost pilgrim who is psychologically and existentially immature. As the journey continues, however, things change gradually but dramatically. In Purgatory, it is Virgil who is not at home, and the pilgrim who grows into his task. At the very center of the poem, after he offers his discourse on love, Virgil fades into the background as the baton is passed to Statius. The pilgrim continues to venerate Virgil as teacher and master, but from the time Statius appears on the scene, Virgil is reduced to a gentle shade who must be superseded by other guides who know the terrain of faith. In one of the more moving scenes in the *Commedia*, Statius describes Virgil as "the first who, after God, enlightened me. / You did as he who goes by night and carries / the light behind him—he is of no help / to his own self but teaches those who follow."[1]

Within the interdisciplinary context of biological psychology, psychiatry, and the neurosciences, and in a metaphorical sense of course, I see Freud as Statius saw Virgil, as someone who illuminated a path for others to follow, even though he was himself somewhat in the dark, particularly in his stubborn insistence that psychoanalysis is science in the usual sense. Freud was a revolutionary, and as Jonathan Lear has put it, "it is in the nature of things that one cannot both give birth to a revolution and then be there at the end of the process to appreciate its consequences."[2] My aim in discussing Dante and Freud together (always keeping in mind that Freud's claims are problematic from an empirical point of view), is to consider those ways in which we can use his anthropology as a springboard for the consideration of ethical issues which arise from the ongoing revolutions in neuroscience and biological psychiatry, research communities which are in turn the source of influential critiques of that anthropology.

That there are surface correspondences between Freud and Dante—that the Freudian world and the Freudian project are in some sense Dantean—has been often noticed. For example, one picks up the central psychoanalytic text, *The Interpretation of Dreams*, and notices the epigraph from book seven of the *Aeneid: Flectere si nequeo, Acheronta movebo*.[3] One is also struck by how Freud envisioned the book when it

---

[1] One of the goals of our seminar was for a fruitful engagement of the medieval and the modern. As he said in his invitation to the seminar, Richard Newhauser is committed to transmitting the ways in which our concepts about what it means to be human are historically constructed, and thus worthy of humanistic study. In specific terms, this comes down to having medievalists talk to non-medievalists (and vice versa) more than they evidently do. Newhauser's goals converged with my own. I am a teacher of biological psychology with a scholarly interest in Freud. For several years, I have been reading Dante and taking notes—in the margins of my books, in growing electronic files—of the correspondences I see between the anthropologies of Freud and Dante. This essay explores some of these connections. I am grateful to Richard Newhauser for including me in the seminar and for his support of this project.

Purgatorio, 22.65–69, in *The Divine Comedy of Dante Alighieri*, trans. Allen Mandelbaum (Berkeley, 1980–82), 2:203. I use Mandelbaum's translation throughout the essay.

[2] Jonathan Lear, *Love and Its Place in Nature: A Philosophical Interpretation of Psychoanalysis* (New York, 1990), 3.

[3] Freud's translators render this as: "If I cannot bend the higher powers, I will move the infernal regions." See Sigmund Freud, *The Interpretation of Dreams*, in *The Standard Edition of the Complete Psychological Works of Sigmund Freud*, trans. James Strachey et al. (London, 1957–74), 4:ix.

was still in the making. To his crackpot-confidante Wilhelm Fliess, he described it this way:

> The whole thing is planned on the model of an imaginary walk. At the beginning, the dark forest of authors (who do not see the trees), hopelessly lost on the wrong tracks. Then a concealed pass through which I lead the reader—my specimen dream...and then suddenly the high ground and the view and the question: which way do you wish to go now?[4]

The two most often noted parallels between Dante and Freud have to do with love and conversion. First, in the Dantean world, love moves the sun and the stars; for Freud, love is the motor of psychological life. Of course, as soon as one notices this parallel, the many differences between Dante and Freud also begin to ask for attention. For example, in this case we notice that the variety of love to which the pilgrim in the end aspires is not the brute erotic desire that Freud characterizes as instinctual.[5] But sexual instinct is not the end of Freud's discussion either. Sexual desire, for Freud, is the cause of our moving into the world, developing as social beings, forming attachments, and building social and civic institutions. And if the whole plan of Dante's Purgatory is based on the idea of love disordered or perverted, one can say much the same about Freud's scheme of psychological development.

But the connection between the two thinkers is not so surprising, after all, since Dante and Freud share a culturally unavoidable reliance on Aristotelianism. And since Freud imbibed his Aristotle through the lectures of Franz Brentano and in formative conversations with him, one may even begin to wonder about the ways Freud may be considered something of a closet Thomist.[6] In any event, this thread that runs from Aristotle and Aquinas through Dante and Freud has sensitized me to the ways in which a commitment to developmentalism in the natural sciences and psychology are deeply embedded in history, to the fact that the very categories of mind / brain / psyche / soul which we choose

---

[4] Letter of August 6, 1899, in *The Complete Letters of Sigmund Freud to Wilhelm Fliess, 1887–1904*, ed. J. M. Masson (Cambridge, MA, 1985), 365.

[5] But see F. Regina Psaki, "Love for Beatrice: Transcending Contradiction in the *Paradiso*," in *Dante for the New Millenium*, ed. Teodolonda Barolini and H. Wayne Storey (New York, 2004), 115–30.

[6] On Freud's relationship with Brentano, see *The Letters of Sigmund Freud to Eduard Silberstein, 1871–1881*, trans. Arnold J. Pomerans, ed. Walter Boelich (Cambridge, MA, 1990). See also James R. Barclay, "Franz Brentano and Sigmund Freud," *Journal of Existentialism* 5 (1964): 1–36.

to explore are deeply constrained not only by nature, as moderns use that word, but by our intellectual, moral, and cultural traditions.

If the first parallel relies on Aristotle and Aquinas, the second is broadly Augustinian. Freud said famously that the task of psychoanalysis is to transform neurotic misery into common unhappiness. In the letter to Can Grande, Dante says his purpose in the *Commedia* is "to remove those living in this life from the state of misery, and lead them to a state of felicity."[7] For both, the process or journey that is undertaken, if successful, will remove the pilgrim from forms of bondage—for Dante, the bondage of sin; for Freud, the bondage of neurosis—and result in a kind of existential freedom. For both, the journey is abreactive: we cannot simply be told what our problem is; we must experience it in all its full-blown emotionality and intensity. The existential muck that we find ourselves in is of the sort that we must go through it if we are to have any chance of being free of it.

For both Freud and Dante, the freedom so hard won is of a decidedly unsentimental kind. Freud says often that he can offer no consolation, only strength and a kind of reconciliation to a harsh world. Dante is for the most part quite different on this point, offering the very face of God as the end point of the journey. However, that end point is famously, one might say frustratingly, ineffable. Furthermore, along the way in Dante's narrative, the pilgrim learns—and the reader learns along with him—that the existential pot at the end of the rainbow, after the parade has gone by, is mixed with a good deal of reconciliation to the ways of the universe. I am thinking here especially of the pilgrim's long-awaited reunion with Beatrice—she turns out to be quite a hard lover—and his encounter with Piccarda in the sphere of the Moon: *E'n la sua volontade è nostra pace.*[8] In the Dantean as well as the Freudian world, whatever is achieved depends on reconciliation to the rules of the existential game. Transformation is a basic Freudian theme: the eventually healthy individual has achieved some success in changing instinctual desire into radically different forms of psychological life. Dante-pilgrim undergoes a similar process: at the start he was looking for love in the wrong places; at the end of the journey, the paradisiacal

---

[7] Freud's statement can be found in Josef Breuer and Sigmund Freud, *Studies on Hysteria*, in Freud, *Standard Edition*, 2:305; Dante's letter to Can Grande is quoted in Francis Fergusson, *Dante's Drama of the Mind. A Modern Reading of the Purgatorio* (Princeton, 1953), 3.
[8] *Paradiso*, 3.85.

love he discovers is essentially incommensurate with his more primal and earth-bound desire.

I am interested in going beyond these surface correspondences and systematically exploring the deeper correspondences in the anthropologies of Dante and Freud. In this essay, I explore three such correspondences that as far as I know have not been discussed before. The themes of these correspondences are: (1) prophecy and citizenship; (2) inheritance, development, fate, and character; and (3) language, desire, and materialism.

What the anthropologies of Freud and Dante share is a concern for the human soul, how the soul is organized, the ways in which the soul is held in bondage, and finally, the possibilities for redemption. Of course, these words—soul, bondage, redemption—have in many respects different connotations for Dante and Freud, but there is also significant overlap in their concerns, and this overlap bears directly on the construction, on our conceptions, of sinfulness. Although the Dantean and Freudian anthropologies are to some degree incommensurable, most importantly perhaps because they reside within incompatible views of human history, they nevertheless reinforce the truth value—a loaded term, I know—of each. I believe this discussion will be helpful in appraising the Freudian anthropology which competes with the anthropology emanating from the disciplines of neuroscience and biological psychiatry, while it will also begin to move us toward the absorption of that Freudian anthropology into something else. My own view as a scholar of Freud's enterprise is that it has several core elements that are essentially fictive rather than empirically demonstrable, verifiable, or falsifiable. But of course this is quite different from saying that they are untrue or wrong.

Dante loved Virgil. He loved him as a poet and for what he represented in terms of classical pagan values, but at the same time, Dante's journey is directed toward a new ontology, one which Virgil could not understand. And yet Dante needed Virgil. Any parallels between Dante's situation and our own can be taken only so far, of course, but I want to explore what happens when we moderns, being informed by neurobiology and psychiatry about matters of the soul and therefore taking ontological naturalism as a given, nevertheless see yearning all around us in our secular age. Just as the pilgrim comes to supersede Virgil, what I am striving for in this essay is some insight about what it means to take seriously the idea of the bondage of the human soul—that is, *sin*—as well as the idea of the soul's redemption. In all of this I am committed to ontological naturalism, but I also strive to avoid the pitfalls that awaited Freud because of his staunch positivism.

Before considering the three correspondences, however, we need to take a detour.

Over the course of a distinguished career, the historian of science Gerald Holton has developed the concept of the thematic origins of scientific thought.[9] Holton distinguishes between internal and external commitments. Internal commitments are identifiable in the daily routines of science, be it laboratory, clinical, or theoretical work, as well as in documents, published articles, and notebooks. External or thematic commitments, on the other hand, are the background assumptions which the scientist brings to the work. Holton is not in the business of doing psychology, nor does he have in mind anything like Jungian archetypes or "irreducibly intuitive apprehensions."[10] Nevertheless, these thematic commitments, these unacknowledged presuppositions, are unconscious in the sense that they influence the work both in its practice and in the shape and content of the hypotheses it puts forward, and are invisible from the standpoint of the public reception of the scientist's work in the form of published articles and even in journals and laboratory notebooks.

The domain of thematic commitments can be ignored when evaluating scientific claims. Yes, our appreciation of Einstein's life, work, and imagination is deepened when we understand his discomfort with the implications of quantum mechanics or his refusal to believe that God plays dice with the universe. Similarly, we know better who Newton was and the forces that shaped his work when we appreciate the connection between his laws of motion and his commitment to the idea of an orderly universe. In the most important case within the biological sciences, our understanding and appreciation of Darwin's work is enhanced when we know things about his psyche that, it is fair to say, he did not know himself.[11] However, in none of these cases do we need to take account of these thematic commitments in order to evaluate the claims that emerge from the work.

---

[9] Gerald Holton, *Thematic Origins of Scientific Thought: Kepler to Einstein* (Cambridge, MA, 1973; revised 1988). Holton's work has focused on Einstein and other prominent theoreticians in the physical sciences.

[10] Holton, *Thematic Origins*, 17.

[11] Darwin studies are a whole other industry. See Howard E. Gruber, *Darwin on Man. A Psychological Study of Scientific Creativity*, 2nd ed. (Chicago, 1981).

Freud's case is different. It is impossible to make sense of the empirical domain in Freud's enterprise without considering the thematic commitments he brought to his work, because those thematic commitments are to a significant degree the subject of his work. For example, the dreams at the center of the discussion in *The Interpretation of Dreams* are Freud's own. More generally, the central claims that Freud puts forward about human motivation—e.g., about Oedipal dynamics or about dreams as the disguised fulfillment of wishes—arise first from his own life. The criticism that has been leveled at Freud for over fifty years regarding problems in his methodology has in good part to do with the fact that he came to certain conclusions about the nature of the psychological world on the basis of his own early experience and then fatally overgeneralized.

I have found it helpful to keep Holton's framework in mind when reflecting on what distinguishes science from art, specifically literary art. With respect to Freud, the problem is not that he had the audacity to make his own depth-psychological themes the subject of his own work, but that he claimed, while doing so, to be hewing to an inductive ideal. Unlike the cases of Newton, Einstein, or Darwin, Freud's enterprise doesn't make sense without understanding his thematic commitments, because those commitments are really the subject of his work. When this happens in science, when the thematic commitments become, not the motivator of the work, but the work itself, we have a problem, and the paradigmatic example of this problem is Freud.

In literary art, on the other hand, we expect that the empirical domain will be largely replaced by the domain of thematic commitments. What distinguishes literary art which comes to be considered great—literature with a capital L—is that the artist's imagination has moved him to present the substance and details of his own imaginative world in a way that transcends the merely personal. If, on the other hand, a literary venture begins with personal motivation but ends only in the description of the empirical domain, it fails as art.

I have heard many Dantists say that Dante was the first poet to have the audacity to make himself both the author and the hero of his poem. This audacity is something else that Freud and Dante share. For both, an understanding of the author's life is central to an understanding of the author's work. As I have just argued, this is a problem for Freud, while of course it is not for Dante. But there is an interesting wrinkle that, I think, strengthens the case for considering Dante and Freud together.

The wrinkle is that the author of the *Commedia* wishes his readers to believe not only that the poem is true in religious, theological, philosophical, and existential senses, but also in an "empirical" sense, in the sense that the pilgrim, who is the poet, actually made the trip.[12] Keeping Holton's framework in mind, we may be right in thinking that the *Commedia* begins from and reflects the poet's deepest thematic commitments. But it is interesting to remember that we don't actually know this. All we know is what is in the poem and Dante's other works. From these, we can guess how the poet felt about the world, but to the extent that we are confident in our guesses, this is because of the way the poem fills out, in Holton's language, the empirical domain. What we know about the Dante the man—the mundane details of his life, who he knew, who he hated—we know only through the work.

So we are left in the following situation. In the case of Dante—the artist—we have a work that transcends the mundane events that contributed to its creation, but its value depends in an unusual, even unique, way on that empirical domain. In the case of Freud—the so-called scientist—we have a body of work that purports to be about the empirical domain, but because it originates so much from its author's thematic concerns, raises profound questions about its value. Keeping all this in mind, let us now proceed to the three correspondences: prophecy and citizenship; inheritance, development, fate and character; language, desire and materialism.

I. *Prophecy and Citizenship*

Throughout the *Commedia*, especially in the invectives against cities, Italy, emperors, and popes, Dante articulates what he believes to be the right relationship between the individual and the larger spheres of which the individual is a part.[13] For Dante, these spheres are separate

---

[12] Charles Singleton's statement that "the fiction of the *Divine Comedy* is that it is not a fiction" becomes confusing on repetition. I have found Teodolinda Barolini, *The Undivine Comedy: Detheologizing Dante* (Princeton, NJ, 1992), chapter 1, helpful on this point.

[13] With the word "individual" we are reminded of the incommensurability between the Dantean and Freudian worlds. Some historians argue that the idea of the individual—even the sense of individual consciousness—does not emerge until Dante has left the stage. While I am not equipped to survey this cultural and literary history, it is evident that intrapsychic conflict—the central concern of psychoanalysis—is an important motivator of the pilgrim's journey in the poem. But see note 19.

and distinct. He believes that human history will be set right if the proper relationship can be established between the Church and the Empire. In Freud's anthropology, on the other hand, the individual is a collection of overlapping and interacting spheres, and is in turn embedded in other ones, concentrically arranged. So, we have first of all the tensions and interactions between the id—the source of desire and therefore movement into the world—and the ego as well as the superego. A second important view of the Freudian cosmos is from the perspective of the ego, which, as Freud said, cannot even be the master of its own house because it is striving to meet the demands not only of the id and the superego, but also of those in the world outside the psyche. Finally, the Freudian individual is surrounded by concentrically arranged spheres of influence and conflict—lovers, family members, and social institutions.

From these views of the relationship between the individual and the larger world, some conclusions follow from Dante and Freud about obligation and justice. First, in both schemes, there is a central place for what Freud called renunciation. In the pilgrim's journey from the dark wood to the beatific vision, we see one form of love—eros—given up for other forms. I am reminded once again of Piccarda Donati: the paradise she has achieved depends on the total renunciation of desire. It is interesting as well to note that renunciation is at the very center of Freud's anthropology even though he doesn't see the individual going anywhere. Dante-pilgrim's journey takes place within a providential view of history, whereas the Freudian story is all about the threshing floor.[14] For Dante, renunciation gets the individual home; for Freud, renunciation is essential too, but only because of existential necessity. Because of these differences—the purposeful role of renunciation in Dante's scheme, its merely functional role in Freud's—their views of justice and citizenship differ as well.

In the Dantean world, renunciation—the move to higher forms of love—is consistent with what justice demands, and there is no ambivalence on this point. The pilgrim's redemption depends on seeing that his earlier ways of loving the world—his sympathy for Francesca, for example—must be totally renounced, as indeed they have been over the course of the journey. In the Freudian world, too, renunciation is

---

[14] *L'aiuola che ci fa tanto feroci*—"The little threshing floor / that so excites our savagery"—is earth; *Paradiso* 22.150–51.

consistent with the demands of justice. However, the transformation of sexual desire into other forms of erotic attachment as well as sublimated and aim-inhibited love is merely necessary, not part of a transcendent process. Furthermore, in the Freudian scheme, because these renunciatory transformations are inevitably experienced, in part, as loss, there is a mournful and deeply ambivalent aspect to the accomplishment of justice, to the establishment of codes by which a culture will attempt to mature and legitimate itself.[15]

Freud has been described as a humane pessimist.[16] He is pessimistic in the sense that he cannot offer the kind of consolation that the pilgrim finds in paradise. But Freud nevertheless hopes that people will find consolation, perhaps through the process of analysis. Since renunciation in his scheme is merely functional, earthly joy—fun on the threshing floor—is to be embraced wherever it can be found, however fleetingly. Dante, on the other hand, is finally an optimist, but, in a way, inhumane. While Freud's writings on the topic of justice wind up being more about mercy and, despite his protestations, consolation, Dante's justice has a harsh quality that can only be defended because it is carried out within a providential context.

II. *Inheritance, Development, Fate, and Character*

Cantos 17 and 18 of the *Purgatorio*—the central cantos of the *Commedia*—are devoted to Virgil's description of the plan of Purgatory and to his discourse on love. As I have already mentioned, while there are many differences between Dante's and Freud's views on love, there is an impressive amount of common ground, and I want to explore that common ground in more detail here.

Dante's Purgatory is organized around the many ways that love can and does go wrong. The most serious sins, purged on the steepest

---

[15] In this passage from *Civilization and Its Discontents* (in Freud, *Standard Edition*, 21:104), Freud highlights the connection between justice on a cultural level and injustice at the level of the individual: "A cultural community is perfectly *justified*, psychologically, in starting by proscribing manifestations of the sexual life of children, for there would be no prospect of curbing the sexual lusts of adults if the ground had not been prepared for it in childhood. But...the requirement, demonstrated in these prohibitions, that there shall be a single kind of sexual life for everyone...cuts off a fair number of them from sexual enjoyment, and so becomes the source of serious *injustice*" (my emphases).

[16] Peter D. Kramer, *Listening to Prozac* (New York, 1993), 76.

terraces, are pride, envy, and wrath. In Dante's scheme, it is not possible, at least for any of the shades in Purgatory, to truly hate God or hate themselves, and so it follows that these three most serious sins are forms of "ill love," that is, wishing one's neighbor ill. In the case of pride, the sinner, "through abasement of another, / hopes for supremacy." Envy, in turn, involves one's fear of "loss of fortune, fame, power." Finally, anger, which seeks the harm of one's neighbor, grows out of resentment.[17]

Dante's plan takes the form it has for a good reason: it is firmly anchored in Thomism. To the modern reader, for whom Freud is "inescapable,"[18] what is odd about Dante's scheme is the claim that pride, envy, and anger are first directed outward toward other people. What seems to be missing in the rationale for the plan of Purgatory is a concept of inwardness, which we moderns take for granted. Our tacit assumption is that pride, envy, and anger begin with inner turmoil; we then see the consequences of that inner turmoil in its outward manifestations.[19] The important point, though, is that, even for Dante, these three most serious sins are actually forms of love. And Freud would agree. Once we add the dimension of inwardness to the discussion, we can see that all three of these sins—especially pride—have to do with self-love. The difference between Freud and Dante concerns the object of love. For Dante, love seeks the good, and the good is "somewhere, out there." For Freud, love moves the subject to objects beyond itself, but the aim is inner satisfaction, however fleeting. These attempts at inner satisfaction are what move the individual into the world.

Virgil tells the pilgrim that "love is the seed in you of every virtue / and of all acts deserving of punishment."[20] These lines are a prelude to the discourse on love in canto 18. Virgil's story is a developmental one, and tightly congruent with Freud's story of human development. The soul, Virgil tells the pilgrim, initially responds with pleasure to the world; eventually, it fixes on objects in the world and moves, "never

---

[17] *Purgatorio*, 17.112–23.

[18] The word belongs to Peter Gay, describing Freud's legacy for modern consciousness.

[19] In note 13, though, I said that the pilgrim's journey is motivated by intra-psychic conflict. I think we can have it both ways. At the start of the poem—the mid-life crisis, the dark wood, losing the path that does not stray—we have what from our perspective seems a true description of inner conflict. Here, as the plan of Purgatory unfolds, the emphasis is on the relationship between God and his creation.

[20] *Purgatorio*, 17.104–05.

resting / till the beloved thing has made it joyous."[21] But the impulse to love usually leads us into error, because not all objects of love that seem worthy actually are. And (Freud would appreciate this in particular:)[22] "man does not know the source of his...tending toward desire's primal object...[it] is in you just as in bees there is the honey-making urge; such primal will deserves no praise, and it deserves no blame." Everything we do, good and bad, is motivated by the attempt to love. But the impulse to love is itself neither praiseworthy nor blameworthy.

In Freud's account, what moves us into the world is the search for satisfaction. Out of various levels of necessity, from the ecological niche in which we find ourselves to the inner demands of the developing psyche and the outer demands of the culture in which the psyche is nested, this search is destined—fated—to go awry: we will at times be narcissistically self-involved, we will at times be unable to love completely because we have fetishized some aspect of our love object. For some of us, this may be closer to a permanent than a temporary condition, and others of us will move from one form of misdirected love to another; few of us will ever get it right for very long. But it will be love, as Freud defined it, just the same.[23] Freud once said that all men are deserving of punishment,[24] but his whole project—this is the compassionate aspect of Freud often missed—was directed at finding freedom from those various forms of punishment.

At the end of his speech in the Valley of the Rulers, Sordello remarks on "how seldom human worth ascends from branch to branch."[25] The

---

[21] *Purgatorio*, 18.32–33.

[22] "Why do our relatives, the animals, not exhibit any such cultural struggle? We do not know. Very probably some of them—the bees, the ants, the termites—strove for thousands of years before they arrived at the State institutions, the distributions of functions and the restrictions on the individual, for which we admire them today" (Freud, *Civilization and Its Discontents*, in Freud, *Standard Edition*, 21:123). Freud is not being entirely tongue-in-cheek in talking about the "State institutions" of the social insects, and in this passage we see yet another way in which Freud's theory is anchored in Aristotle: his functionalism is complicated by a teleological view of evolution. This teleological leaning may well be another reason for seeing Dante in Freud: Freud is one of the authors of modernity, of the view which says humankind has "no particular place to go" (E. O. Wilson, *On Human Nature*, [Cambridge, MA, 1978]). But the Freudian creature is a yearning creature, in an existential sense looking for home; the Freudian creature is a pilgrim (see Ernest Becker, *The Denial of Death* [New York, 1973]).

[23] W. H. Auden put it this way: "You shall love your crooked neighbor / With your crooked heart." "As I Walked Out One Evening," in *The Norton Anthology of Modern Poetry*, ed. Richard Ellmann and Robert O'Clair, 2nd ed. (New York, 1988), 738–39.

[24] Adam Phillips, *Darwin's Worms* (New York, 2000).

[25] *Purgatorio*, 7.121.

comment highlights an important feature of the Dantean afterlife, namely, how family members are distributed through its three realms. For Dante, it is simply wrong that the apple doesn't fall far from the tree, because virtue must be hard-won over the course of a life; it cannot be possessed simply because of family membership.[26] Over the course of a life, hurdles will be thrown in front of an individual. Until the life is over, we cannot tell how it will turn out, and the fate of the soul will be determined by its own efforts to use its reason and free will in the best way.

For Freud, of course, there is no such thing as free will, nor for that matter reason either, at least not the kind of God-given good of the intellect that Dante had in mind, which can be unambivalently relied upon to produce a good outcome. But where Freud agrees with Dante, and this is reflected in their convergence on how love goes awry, is that the loving impulse, which Freud called instinct, undergoes many vicissitudes over the course of a life. Implicit in "vicissitudes"—Freud used *Triebschicksale* in his native German—is the idea that an instinct has a fate or a destiny. Would Freud say, then, in disagreement with Dante, that "by their seeds shall ye know them," referring not to offspring but to the motivating predispositions that move us in the world? Actually, no. Rather, what Freud wants to convey in his emphasis on the vicissitudes as much as on instinct itself is that over the course of a life an individual will make many adjustments and decisions as he makes his way in the world. While Freud was committed to psychological determinism, it is also true that the Freudian future is open to possibility. Indeed, without this openness, the psychoanalytic process makes no sense.

This convergence of Dante and Freud on the subject of inheritance, development, and fate can be useful as we negotiate our way through the ethical and philosophical implications of biological psychiatry and the neurosciences. In *Listening to Prozac*, Peter Kramer makes an important distinction between two conceptions of human motivation that compete for our attention. On the one hand, there is "history-laden character," the idea that what we become, we become slowly; character accrues as we make our way through the vicissitudes of life. On the other hand, we have "biologically-given temperament."[27] This

---

[26] This is Paolo Cherchi's point in "*Purgatorio* VII," in *Dante's Divine Comedy. Introductory Readings, II: Purgatorio*, ed. Tibor Wlassics (Charlottesville, VA, 1993), 111.

[27] *Listening to Prozac*, xv.

is the idea, more likely the worry, that the vicissitudes of life do not make much difference, that what we become is tightly constrained by the hand we are dealt.

Up through the heyday of psychoanalysis in the 1950s, the idea of character as history-laden dominated our conceptions. But as psychiatry and basic neuroscience continue to develop ever more specific, safer, and, it must be added, ever more effective drugs for the treatment of psychiatric disorders, we are forced to rethink things. Here is how Dante and Freud, taken together, can help.

For all their differences in how they make use of what is basically an Aristotelian idea of psychological and moral development, Dante and Freud both acknowledge the fact of our biological creatureliness. They both agree that we begin with basic responses to the world, and that these involve a search for pleasure. They also agree that, because of intrinsic human frailty, we can expect a certain regularity to the kind of difficulties we fall into. At the top of the list of these difficulties is what Dante called pride and Freud called narcissism. And they would agree, I think, that on the one hand it is more accurate to say we fall into such ways of being rather than create them for ourselves, but that on the other hand we have the responsibility to correct these ways of being. While we are biological creatures with biological temperament, character is nonetheless accomplished in the ongoing history of our daily lives. There is no advice implicit here about what to do with the opportunity or challenge or threat represented by drugs such as Prozac. Except, perhaps, the advice to appreciate that our creatureliness—powerfully affected by these drugs—does not cancel out the "vicissitudinal" nature of our lives.

I have before me a reader compiled by the President's council on bioethics,[28] an anthology of canonical sources as well as more contemporary writings, organized under headings such as "Are we bodies?," "Many stages, one life," "Vulnerability and suffering," and "Living immediately." There are many good things about this anthology; with nearly 100 entries, representing authors and genres as diverse as Francis Bacon and Galway Kinnell, it will serve well in seminars and discussion groups as a stimulus to good work in the teaching of bioethics. What worries me, though, is Sordello's message. The anthology was compiled by a group of scholars and scientists who, I must assume,

---

[28] *Being Human. Readings from the President's Council on Bioethics* (Washington D.C., 2003).

are committed to the conception of character as history-laden. Any virtue that is created by this anthology will come out of active reading and debate. But is there also a tacit position operating in the work of this compilation and others like it, namely, that virtue can be so simply possessed and transmitted?[29]

III. *Language, Desire, and Materialism: Aphasic Giants*

In her commentary on *Inferno* 31, Dorothy Sayers says that while allegorically the giants signify pride, they may also "be taken as the images of the blind forces which remain in the soul, and in society, when the 'general bond of love' is dissolved and the 'good of the intellect' wholly withdrawn."[30] The bottom of the Dantean universe is not in any way the functional equivalent of the Freudian id, but this is nonetheless language that has a Freudian resonance.

There are many places in the *Commedia* where the poet pauses to share his creative struggles with the reader. We read double invocations; we read small craft warnings, urging us to shore. For my own purposes in reading Dante together with Freud, it is interesting to note that there are two locations where Dante especially focuses on the role of language in the unfolding drama. The first is in the Empyrean. Admittedly, language is not the only human faculty which fails Dante here; memory is equally insufficient to the task. But in the Empyrean, the failure of language and memory are tied in with the whole theme of ineffability.

At the bottom of the universe, on the other hand, the subject of language serves a different function. Here, too, Dante tells us that he has a hard time finding the words, a hard time devising "the crude and scrannel rhymes to suit / the melancholy hole."[31] But in contrast to *Paradiso* 33, in *Inferno* 31 and 32 he focuses on the linguistic difficulty in order to emphasize that language is implicated in the sins that are punished here. While the poet tells us that the rhymes are hard to find,

---

[29] In addition to the anthology from the council on bioethics, headed up by Leon Kass, I am thinking here especially of volumes cobbled together by William Bennett and Lynne Cheney, both of whom led the NEH during previous Republican administrations. If I were to give myself the assignment often given to students, to populate the realms of the afterlife with contemporary figures, well....

[30] *Inferno*, trans. Dorothy L. Sayers (New York, 1949), 269.

[31] *Inferno*, 32.1–2 and 7–8.

he succeeds nonetheless. Things are ugly down here, but ineffability is not an issue.

The issue, rather, is existential and moral stupidity of the most egregious and unforgivable kind. At the base of Hell we find those who have committed treacherous fraud, and it is more than symbolic to have this ultimate subversion of the good of the intellect eternally punished with the loss of language, because language and intellect are inseparable, for Dante, and for Freud as well. In Dante's universe, the gift of language is inextricably tied to the use of reason, and it is reason and language which are misused when the sin of fraud is committed. For those sins punished at the base of hell, language is especially implicated in the turning of the soul away from God. But here at the bottom of hell are found not only the most serious sins; this is also the location, as it were, of the beginning of sin, the place where Dante represents sin's origin.

Freud was seldom at a loss for words. But neither was he a poet. As an empiricist (as we have seen, he thought of himself in this way), he used analogies, not similes. And in a way that is reminiscent of Dante, from time to time, and without bothering with invocations, he stopped to remind his reader about the limits of analogies. His construct of the id does not describe a fallen state; nor is it an analog of Dante's hell. Rather, it is the source of all things psychological and existential, the stuff out of which language and reason grow. But the id, like Dante's heaven, is fundamentally unknowable in terms of language. "We approach the id with analogies," Freud says; "we call it a chaos, a cauldron full of seething excitations…it produces no collective will, but only a striving to bring about the satisfaction of the instinctual needs…."[32] Like Dante's heaven, the Freudian id is a bit ineffable.

Years before he self-consciously undertook the task of describing his own underworld,[33] before he settled on the central tension between reason and instinct, Freud confronted the relationship between language and the material world in his monograph, *On Aphasia*. Published nearly a decade before *The Interpretation of Dreams*, at a time when Freud still

---

[32] Sigmund Freud, *New Introductory Lectures on Psychoanalysis*, in Freud, *Standard Edition*, 22.

[33] Valerie D. Greenberg, *Freud and His Aphasia Book: Language and the Sources of Psychoanalysis* (Ithaca, NY, 1997). This is in line with the idea of Jonathan Lear that Freud could not fully anticipate the implications of the work he was doing, the frontiers he was pushing into.

considered himself a neurologist, *On Aphasia* is now recognized as the first psychoanalytic text. Freud had a specific goal in this monograph: to demonstrate that the relationship between language and brain function was more dynamic and functional than his mentors in neurology and physiology had made it out to be. He was interested in how word-presentations (*Vorstellungen*) arise out of neural processes. At the time he wrote the monograph, the dominant way of articulating the relationship between the aphasias and their presumptive underlying brain pathology was in localizationalist terms, that is, in terms of neural centers and the pathways connecting them. Freud's thesis is that this localizationalist approach does not do justice to the rich dynamic and functional relationship between brain function and the linguistic life of the individual. His functional, dynamic approach anticipated a central tenet of psychoanalysis, namely, that when considering the relationship between brain events and psychological events, the causal arrows run in both directions: ideas can cause physiological symptoms just as physiological events can cause ideas.[34] Furthermore, the relationship between word-presentations and motivational states cannot be separated out neatly. Dante on the giants reminds me of Freud because Freud, too, saw the melding of the creaturely with the linguistic as arguably the essential move toward humanity. And, while Freud of course is famous for arguing that at the root of everything one will find sexual and aggressive motivations, when things come apart, it is evidenced by this linguistic-motivational rupture.

Why does this convergence of Dante and Freud on the connection between desire and language matter? One way of looking at the contrapasso that the giants suffer—the way they are reduced to babbling, stupid souls—is that the theme of language represents the more central property of God-given reason and free will. But I think this is insufficient. As we read the *Purgatorio*, the canticle in which Dante most fully develops an anthropology, we are forced to think about the relationship between our biological natures and those characteristics—essentially fabricative and linguistic—that mark us as human.[35]

---

[34] J. F. Rychlak, "Freud's Confrontation with the Telic Mind," *Journal of the History of the Behavioral Sciences* 59 (1981): 176–83.

[35] On the whole question of human beings as *makers*, the relationship between creation and representation, and how these intersect in the poem with the dimension of humility/pride, see Marianne Shapiro, "Purgatorio X," and Rebecca West, "Purgatorio XI," both in *Dante's Purgatorio: Introductory Readings*, ed. Wlassics: 158–68 and 169–82.

Dante, in his straightforward use of Aristotelianism, could construct this anthropology teleologically, without apology. Freud, on the other hand, while he had a quite similar existential anthropology, wants to anchor the human being securely on the threshing floor. But he also sees that somehow this will not suffice, that being human entails the emergence of qualities much like the ones Dante deems as central, qualities that will not so neatly be limited to that threshing floor.

IV. *Conclusion*

Reading Dante while thinking about Freud has helped me delineate some problems with the reductive and materialist emphases of the neurosciences and biological psychiatry, problems which arise when the disciplines, implicitly mostly but sometimes explicitly, carve out an anthropology, or as one might say in terms of the humanities, attempt to transmit concepts about what it means to be human. This is not to say that neuroscientists and psychiatrists should stop speaking in this way, but only that there is something to be learned from Freud's case. In the development of his anthropology, he pushed back frontiers, but was himself unaware of the implications of what he was doing. While himself mostly in the dark about the limits of scientific materialism when dealing with the human soul, his work gives us a multilayered and deeply dynamic framework of human psychological and existential affairs that captures our creatureliness without denying our soulfulness. To call Freud's enterprise science, as he did himself, is to mischaracterize it. Perhaps it is closer to the truth to say that Freud, too, has given us a fiction that is not a fiction.[36]

---

[36] See note 12.

BIBLIOGRAPHY

Primary Sources

Manuscripts

Brussels. Bibliothèque royale de Belgique MS. 9242.
Cambridge. Jesus College MS. 13.
The Hague. Rijksmuseum Meermanno-Westreenianum MS. 11.
London. Lambeth Palace MS. 352.
Paris. Bibliothèque Mazarine MS. 794.
Vienna. Österrichische Nationalbibliothek MS. 1857.
Würzburg. Universitätsbibliothek MS. M.p.th.f.149a.

Printed Works

Abelard, Peter. *Dialogue of a Philosopher with a Jew and a Christian*. Translated by Pierre
    J. Payer. Toronto: Pontifical Institute of Mediaeval Studies, 1979.
———. *Historia calamitatum, texte critique avec une introduction*. Edited by J. Monfrin. Paris:
    J. Vrin, 1959.
———. *Historia calamitatum*. Translated by Betty Radice. In *The Letters of Abelard and
    Heloise*. New York: Penguin, 1974.
Albert the Great. *Super Ethica*. In *Opera omnia*. Vol. 14. Edited by W. Kübel. Münster:
    Aschendorf, 1968.
Alcuin. *Adversus Elipandum Toletanum libri*. PL 101:243B–70D.
———. *Epistolae*. Edited by Ernst Dümmler. In *Epistolae Karolini aevi*, 2:1–493. MGH
    Epistolae, 4. Berlin: Weidmann, 1895; reprint, 1994.
———. *De virtutibus et vitiis liber ad Widonem comitem*. PL 101:613C–38D.
Aldhelm. *Opera*. Edited by Rudolf Ehwald. MGH, Auctores Antiquissimi, 15. München:
    Monumenta Germaniae Historica, 1919; reprint 1984.
———. *Prosa de uirginitate cum glosa Latina atque Anglosaxonica*. Edited by Scott Gwara. CCSL
    124A. Turnholt: Brepols, 2001.
———. *The Poetic Works*. Translated by Michael Lapidge and James L. Rosier. Dover,
    NH: D. S. Brewer, 1985.
———. *The Prose Works*. Translated by Michael Lapidge and Michael Herren. Totowa,
    NJ: Rowman & Littlefield, 1979.
Alexander of Hales. *Summa theologica*. 4 vols. Quaracchi: Ex Typographia Collegii
    S. Bonaventurae, 1924–79.
Alighieri, Dante. *Convivio*. Edited by Cesare Vasoli and Domenico de Robertis. Volume
    2, parts 1 and 2. In *Dante Alighieri: Opere Minori*. 3 vols. in 6 parts. Milan: Mondadori,
    1988; reprint, 1995.
———. *The Divine Comedy of Dante Alighieri*. Translated by Allen Mandelbaum. 3 vols.
    Berkeley: Univ. of California Press, 1980–82.
———. *The Divine Comedy*. Translated by Charles S. Singleton. 3 vols. Bolingen Series,
    80. Princeton: Princeton Univ. Press, 1970–75.
———. *Inferno*. Translated by Dorothy L. Sayers. New York: Penguin, 1949.
———. *Monarchia*. Edited by Bruno Nardi. Volume 3, part 1. In *Dante Alighieri: Opere
    Minori*. 3 vols. in 6 parts. Milan: Mondadori, 1979; reprint, 1996.
———. *On World-Government*. Translated by H. W. Schneider. New York: Macmillan,
    1957.

Aristotle. *Ethica Nicomachea, translatio Roberti Grosseteste Lincolniensis sive "Liber Ethicorum,"* *recensio pura.* Edited by R. A. Gauthier. Aristoteles Latinus 26, 1–3, fasc. 3. Leiden: Brill, 1972.

———. *The Nichomachean Ethics.* Translated by J. A. K. Thompson. Revised by Hugh Tredennick. London: Penguin, 2004.

Augustine of Hippo. *Confessions.* Edited with Commentary by James O'Donnell. 3 vols. Oxford: Clarendon, 1992.

———. *The City of God Against the Pagans.* Edited and translated by R. W. Dyson. Cambridge, Eng.: Cambridge Univ. Press, 1998.

———. *The City of God Against the Pagans.* Translated by William M. Green. 7 vols. Cambridge, MA: Harvard Univ. Press, 1984.

———. *De civitate Dei libri XXII.* Edited by B. Dombart and A. Kalb. 2 vols. 5th ed. Stuttgart: Teubner, 1981; reprint München, K. G. Saur, 1993.

———. *Contra mendacium.* Edited by Josephus Zycha. CSEL 41:469–528. Vienna: Tempsky, 1900.

———. *De doctrina christiana.* Edited and translated by R. P. H. Green. Oxford: Clarendon, 1995.

———. *Enarrationes in Psalmos.* Edited by E. Dekkers and J. Fraipont. 3 vols. CCSL 38–40. Turnhout: Brepols, 1956.

———. *Epistulae LVI—C.* Edited by K. D. Daur. CCSL 31A. Turnhout: Brepols, 2005.

———. *De Genesi ad litteram. La Genèse au sens littéral.* Edited by J. Zycha, Translated by P. Agaësse and A. Solignac. 2 vols. Bibliothèque Augustinienne, 48–49. Paris: Desclée de Brouwer, 1972.

———. *De mendacio.* Edited by Josephus Zycha. CSEL 41:413–65. Vienna: Tempsky, 1900.

———. *De sermone Domini in monte libri ii.* Edited by Almut Mutzenbecher. CCSL 35. Turnhout: Brepols, 1967.

———. *De trinitate libri xv.* Edited by W. J. Mountain and Fr. Glorie. 2 vols. CCSL 50–50A. Turnhout: Brepols, 1968.

Autos sacramentales (El auto sacramental antes de Calderón). Edited by Ricardo Arias. Mexico City: Porrúa, 1988.

Baudri of Bourgueil. *Poèmes.* Edited and translated by Jean-Yves Tilliette. 2 vols. Paris: Les Belles Lettres, 1998–2002.

Bede. *Historia ecclesiastica gentis Anglorum.* Edited and translated by Bertram Colgrave and R. A. B. Mynors. Oxford: Clarendon Press, 1969.

Bernard of Clairvaux. *Liber de gradibus humilitatis et superbiae.* In *Sancti Bernardi opera,* 3:13–59. Edited by Jean Leclercq and H. M. Rochais. Roma: Editiones Cistercienses, 1963.

Biblia Latina cum Glossa ordinaria. Facsimile Reprint of the Editio Princeps, Adolph Rusch of Strassburg 1480/81. Introduction by Karlfried Froehlich and Margaret T. Gibson. 4 vols. Turnhout: Brepols, 1992.

Bonaventure of Balneoregio. *Opera omnia iussu et auctoritate.* Edited by Patres Collegii a S. Bonaventura. 10 vols. Ad Claras Aquas (Quaracchi): Ex Typographia Collegii S. Bonaventura, 1882–1902.

Breuer, Josef, and Sigmund Freud. *Studies on Hysteria, 1893–1895.* In Sigmund Freud. *Standard Edition.* Vol. 2.

Brinton, Thomas. *The Sermons of Thomas Brinton, Bishop of Rochester (1373–1389).* Edited by Mary Aquinas Devlin. 2 vols. Camden Third Series, 85. London: Offices of the Royal Historical Society, 1954.

Calderón de la Barca, Pedro. *Obras completas. Tomo III: Autos sacramentales.* Edited by Ángel Valbuena Prat. 2nd ed. Madrid: Aguilar, 1967.

Cambridge Middle English Lyrics. Edited by Henry A. Person. Seattle: Univ. of Washington Press, 1953.

Cassian, John. *Collationes patrum*. Edited and translated by E. Pichery. 3 vols. SC 42 [New ed., 1966], 54 [New ed., 1967], 64. Paris: Cerf, 1955–59.

———. *The Conferences*. Translated by Boniface Ramsey. Ancient Christian Writers, 57. New York: Paulist Press, 1997.

———. *Conlationes patrum*. Edited by Michael Petschenig. CSEL 13. Vienna: Geroldi, 1886.

———. *The Institutes*. Translated by Boniface Ramsey. Ancient Christian Writers, 58. New York: Paulist Press, 2000.

———. *De institutis coenobiorum*. Edited and translated by Jean-Claude Guy. SC 109. Paris: Cerf, 1965.

———. *De institutis coenobiorum et de octo principalium vitiorum remediis libri xxi*. Edited by Michael Petschenig. CSEL 17. Vienna: F. Tempsky, 1888.

Chaucer, Geoffrey. *The Friar's, Summoner's, and Pardoner's Tales from the Canterbury Tales*. Edited by N. R. Havely. London: Univ. of London Press, 1975.

———. *The Riverside Chaucer*. Edited by Larry D. Benson et al. 3rd ed. New York: Houghton Mifflin, 1987.

Conrad of Hirsau. *Dialogus super auctores*. In *Accessus ad auctores. Bernard d'Utrecht. Conrad d'Hirsau, Dialogus super auctores*. Edited by R. B. C. Huygens. 2nd ed. Leiden: E. J. Brill, 1970.

Covarrubias Orozco, Sebastián de. *Tesoro de la lengua castellana o española*. First published Madrid: Luis Sánchez, 1611. Edited by Felipe C. R. Maldonado, rev. ed. by Manuel Camarero. Madrid: Castalia, 1995.

Cyprian of Carthage. *De zelo et livore*. Edited by M. Simonetti. In *Sancti Cypriani Episcopi Opera II*, 75–86. CCSL 3A. Turnhout: Brepols, 1976.

David of Augsburg. *De institutione novitiorum*. In Bonaventure of Balneoregio. *Opera omnia*. Edited by A. C. Peltier. Vol. 12. Paris: Vivès, 1868.

A Descriptive Index of the English Lyrics in John of Grimestone's Preaching Book. Edited by Edward Wilson. Medium Ævum Monographs, New Series 2. Oxford: Blackwell for the Society for the Study of Mediaeval Languages and Literature, 1973.

Downame, John. *A Treatise Against Lying*. London, 1636.

Eberhard the German. *Laborintus*. Edited by Edmond Faral. In *Les Arts poétiques du XIIe et XIIIe siècle*, 337–77. Paris: Champion, 1924.

Einhard. *Vita Caroli Magni*. In *Vie de Charlemagne*. Edited and translated by Louis Halphen. Paris: Librairie Éd. Champion, 1923.

Evagrius Ponticus. *Praktikos*. In *Évagre le Pontique: Traité pratique ou le moine*. Edited and translated by Antoine Guillaumont and Claire Guillaumont. 2 vols. SC 170–71. Paris: Cerf, 1971.

———. *The Praktikos*. Translated by John Eudes Bamberger. Kalamazoo, MI: Cistercian Publications, 1981.

———. *De vitiis quae opposita sunt virtutibus*. PG 79:1139–44.

Fasciculus morum: A Fourteenth-Century Preacher's Handbook. Edited and translated by Siegfried Wenzel. University Park and London: The Pennsylvania State Univ. Press, 1989.

Francis of Assisi: Early Documents. Edited by Regis J. Armstrong, J. A. Wayne Hellman, and William J. Short. 3 vols. New York: New City Press, 1999.

Freud, Sigmund. *Civilization and Its Discontents*. In Sigmund Freud. *Standard Edition*. Vol. 21. [originally published in 1930]

———. *The Complete Letters of Sigmund Freud to Wilhelm Fliess, 1887–1904*. Edited by Jeffrey M. Masson. Cambridge, MA: Harvard Univ. Press, 1985.

———. *The Interpretation of Dreams*. In Sigmund Freud. *Standard Edition*. Vols. 4–5. [originally published in 1900]

———. *The Letters of Sigmund Freud to Eduard Silberstein, 1871–1881*. Translated by Arnold J. Pomerans. Edited by Walter Boelich. Cambridge, MA: Harvard Univ. Press, 1990.

———. *New Introductory Lectures on Psycho-Analysis*. In Sigmund Freud. *Standard Edition*. Vol. 22. [originally published in 1933]

———. *On Aphasia: A Critical Study*. Translated and with an Introduction by E. Stengel. New York: International Universities Press, 1953. [originally published in 1891]

———. *The Standard Edition of the Complete Psychological Works of Sigmund Freud*. Translated from German and edited by James Strachey; in collaboration with Anna Freud, Alix Strachey, and Alan Tyson. 24 vols. London: Hogarth, 1957–74.

Godescalc of Orbais. *Œuvres théologiques et grammaticales de Godescalc d'Orbais*. Edited by C. Lambot. Spicilegium Sacrum Lovaniense. Études et Documents, 20. Louvain: Spicilegium Sacrum Lovaniense, 1945.

The Goodman of Paris: A Treatise on Moral and Domestic Economy by a Citizen of Paris. Translated with Introduction and Notes by Eileen Power. Avon, Eng.: The Bath Press, 1992.

Gregory of Nyssa. *Homilies on the Beatitudes. An English Version with Commentary and Supporting Studies: Proceedings of the Eighth International Colloquium on Gregory of Nyssa*. Edited by Hubertus R. Drobner and Alberto Viciano. Supplements to *Vigiliae Christianae*, 52. Leiden: Brill, 2000.

Gregory of Tours. *Libri Historiarum X*. Edited by Bruno Krusch. 2nd ed. MGH Scriptores Rerum Merovingicarum, 1. Hanover: Hahn, 1951.

Gregory the Great. *Moralia in Iob*. Edited by M. Adriaen. 3 vols. CCSL 143–143B. Turnhout: Brepols, 1979–85.

———. *Morals on the Book of Job*. Translated with Notes and Indices by J. Bliss. In *A Library of the Fathers of the Holy Catholic Church*. 3 vols. in 4. Oxford: John Henry Parker, 1844–50.

———. *Règle pastorale*. Edited by Floribert Rommel, translated by Charles Morel. 2 vols. SC 381–382. Paris: Éditions du Cerf, 1992.

Guillaume de Lorris and Jean de Meun. *Le Roman de la Rose*. Edited by Félix Lecoy. 3 vols. Les Classiques Français du Moyen Age, 92, 95, 98. Paris: Honoré Champion, 1970–74.

———. *The Romance of the Rose*. Translated by Harry W. Robbins. New York: Dutton, 1962.

———. *The Romance of the Rose*. Translated by Charles Dahlberg. Hanover: Univ. Press of New England, 1983.

Hildebert of Lavardin. *Carmina minora*. Edited by A. B. Scott. 2nd ed. München: G. Saur, 2001.

Hildegard of Bingen. *On Natural Philosophy and Medicine, Selections from "Cause et Cure"*. Translated and edited by Margaret Berger. Cambridge, Eng.: D. S. Brewer, 1999.

Hilton, Walter. *The Scale of Perfection*. Edited by Evelyn Underhill. London: John M. Watkins, 1923.

Hincmar of Reims. *De cavendis vitiis et virtutibus exercendis*. Edited by Doris Nachtmann. MGH Quellen zur Geistesgeschichte des Mittelalters, 16. München: Monumenta Germaniae Historica, 1998.

Hugh of St.-Victor. *De quinque septenis*. In Hugues de Saint-Victor. *Six Opuscules Spirituels*. Edited by Roger Baron, 100–119. SC 155. Paris: Éditions du Cerf, 1969.

Humbert of Romans. *De eruditione praedicatorum*. In *De vita regulari*. Edited by Joachin Joseph Berthier. Vol. 2. Rome: A. Befani, 1889.

"The Interrogatories for Officials, Lawyers and Secular Estates of the *Memoriale presbiterorum*: Edition and Translation." Edited by Michael Haren. In *Handling Sin*, ed. Biller and Minnis, 123–63.

Jacob's Well, An English Treatise on the Cleansing of Man's Conscience. Edited by Arthur Brandeis. EETS os 115. London: Kegan, Paul, Trench Trübner & Co., Ltd., 1900.

Jacobus de Voragine. *The Golden Legend: Readings of the Saints*. Translated by William Granger Ryan. 2 vols. Princeton, N.J.: Princeton Univ. Press, 1993.

Iohannis de Caulibus Meditaciones vite Christi: olim S. Bonaventuro attributae. Edited by M. Stallings-Taney. CCCM 153. Turnhout: Brepols, 1997.

John Duns Scotus. *Duns Scotus on the Will and Morality*. Selected and translated by Allan B. Wolter. Washington, D.C.: Catholic Univ. of America Press, 1986.

——. *In librum tertium sententiarum*. In *Opera Omnia*. Edited by Luke Wadding. New ed. Vol. 25. Paris: Vivès, 1894.

John of Salisbury. *Metalogicon*. Edited by J. B. Hall. CCCM 98. Turnhout: Brepols, 1991.

Los autos sacramentales en Madrid en la época de Calderón (1637–1681): Estudio y documentos. Edited by N. D. Shergold and John E. Varey. Madrid: Edhigar, 1961.

Ludolph of Saxony. *Vita Jesu Christi*. Edited by L. M. Rigollot. 4 vols. Paris: Palme, 1870.

Mannyng, Robert. *Roberd of Brunne's Handlyng Synne (Written A.D. 1303); with the French treatise on which it is founded, Le Manuel des Pechiez by William of Wadington*... Edited by F. J. Furnivall. London: Printed for the Roxburghe Club, 1862.

Marbod of Rennes. *Carmina Varia*. Edited by A. Beaugendre. In *Venerabilis Hildeberti... Opera tam edita quam inedita...*, 1615–34. Paris: Laurentius LeConte, 1708.

Martial. *Epigrammata*. Edited by D. R. Shackleton Bailey. Stuttgart: Teubner, 1990.

Matthew of Vendôme. *The Art of Versification*. Translated by Aubrey E. Galyon. Ames, IA: Iowa State Univ. Press, 1980.

——. *Opera*. Edited by Franco Munari. 3 vols. Storia e Letteratura Raccolta di Studi e Testi, 144, 152, 171. Roma: Storia e Letteratura, 1977–88.

Memorias y apariencias y otros documentos sobre los autos de Calderón de la Barca. Edited by Lara Escudero and Rafael Zafra. Pamplona: Univ. de Navarra; Kassel: Reichenberger, 2003.

Nicolas of Cusa's Dialectical Mysticism: Text, Translation and Interpretive Study of De visione Dei. Edited and translated by Jasper Hopkins. Minneapolis: A. J. Banning Press, 1985.

Of Shrifte and Penance: The ME Prose Translation of Le Manuel des Péchés. Edited by Klaus Bitterling. Middle English Texts, 29. Heidelberg: Winter, 1998.

Ovid. *Carmina amatoria: Amores, Medicamina faciei femineae, Ars amatoria, Remedia amoris*. Edited by Antonio Ramirez de Verger. München: Saur, 2003.

Peraldus, William. *Summa virtutum*. Antwerp: Martinus Nutius, 1588.

——. *Summae virtutum ac vitiorum*. 2 vols. Antwerp, 1571.

Peter Lombard. *Magistri Petri Lombardi Parisiensis episcopi Sententiae in IV libris distinctae*. 2 vols. 3rd ed. Spicilegium Bonaventurianum, 4–5. Grottaferrata: Collegium S. Bonaventurae, 1971–81.

Plato. *Republic*. In *Platonis opera*. Vol. 4. Edited by J. Burnet. Oxford Classical Texts. Oxford: Clarendon, 1982.

——. *The Republic of Plato*. Translated with Notes, an Interpretive Essay, and a New Introduction by Allan Bloom. 2nd ed. New York: Basic Books, 1991.

Poetry of the Carolingian Renaissance. Edited by Peter Godman. Norman: Univ. of Oklahoma Press, 1985.

Prudentius. *Psychomachia*. Edited and translated by H. J. Thomson. In *Prudentius*, 1:274–343. The Loeb Classical Library, 387. Cambridge, MA: Harvard Univ. Press, 1949.

S. Raimundus de Pennaforte. *Summa de paenitentia*. Edited by Xaverio Ochoa and Aloisio Diez. Universa Bibliotheca Iuris, 1B. Roma: Commentarium pro religiosis, 1976.

Religious Lyrics of the XIVth Century. Edited by Carleton Brown. Oxford: Clarendon Press, 1924.

Religious Lyrics of the XVth Century. Edited by Carleton Brown. Oxford: Clarendon Press, 1939.

Respvesta theologica acerca del abvso de los escotados. Santiago: Antonio Fraiz Pineiro, 1673.

Richard of St.-Victor. *Allegoriae in Novum Testamentum*. PL 175:750–923.

Ripa, Cesare. *Iconologia, overo descrittione di diverse imagini cavate dall'antichità, e di propria inventione*. Roma, 1603. Facsimile ed. with intro. by Erna Mandowsky. Hildesheim and New York: Georg Olms, 1970.

———. *Iconologia, overo descrittione d'imagini delle virtù, vitij, affetti, passioni humane, corpi celesti, mondo e sue parti.* Padua: Pietro Paolo Tozzi, 1611. Facsimile ed with preface by Stephen Orgel. New York and London: Garland, 1976.

Se7en. Directed by David Fincher. Written by Andrew Kevin Walker. New Line Cinema, 1995.

Seneca the Younger. *Ad Lucilium Epistulae morales.* Edited by L. D. Reynolds. 2 vols. Oxford: Clarendon Press, 1965.

———. *Dialogorum libri duodecim.* Edited by L. D. Reynolds. Oxford: Clarendon Press, 1977.

Summa Virtutum de Remediis Anime. Edited and translated by Siegfried Wenzel. Athens, GA: Univ. of Georgia Press, 1984.

Thomas Aquinas. *Summa theologiae.* 9 vols. In *Sancti Thomae Aquinatis doctoris angelici opera omnia iussu impensaque Leonis XIII P. M. edita,* vols. 4–12. Rome: Typographia Polyglotta S. C. de Propaganda Fide, 1888–1906.

———. *Summa theologiae.* Blackfriars edition. 61 vols. London: Eyre & Spottiswoode; New York: McGraw-Hill, 1964–81.

"Versus de octo vicia et octo beatitudines [*sic*]." Edited by Karl Strecker. MGH Poetae Latini Aevi Carolini, 4,2:585–87. Berlin: Weidmann, 1923; reprint, 1964.

Virgil. *The Aeneid of Virgil.* Translated by Allen Mandelbaum. New York: Bantam Books, 1981.

William of Malmesbury. *The Deeds of the Bishops of England (Gesta Pontificum Anglorum).* Translated by David Preest. Rochester, NY: Boydell, 2002.

———. *Gesta pontificum Anglorum libri quinque.* Edited by N. E. S. A. Hamilton. Rerum Britannicarum Medii Aevi Scriptores, 52. London: Treasury, 1870.

William of St. Amour. *Opera Omnia.* Constance, 1632.

The Works of a Lollard Preacher: The Sermon Omnis plantacio, the Tract Fundamentum aliud nemo potest ponere and the Tract De oblacione iugis sacrificii. Edited by Anne Hudson. EETS os, 317. Oxford: Oxford Univ. Press, 2001.

Wyclif, John. *Sermones.* Edited by Iohann Loserth. 4 vols. London: Trübner & Co., 1890.

Secondary Texts

Adkin, Neil. "Pride or Envy? Some Notes on the Reason the Fathers Give for the Devil's Fall." *Augustiniana* 34 (1984): 349–51.

Albala, Ken. "Weight Loss in the Age of Reason." In *Cultures of the Abdomen: Diet, Digestion and Fat in the Modern World.* Edited by Christopher Forth and Ana Carden-Coyne, 169–83. New York: Palgrave Macmillan, 2005.

Allon, Natalie. "The Stigma of Overweight in Everyday Life." In *Psychological Aspects of Obesity.* Edited by Benjamin B. Wolman, 130–74. New York: Van Nostrand Reinhold Co., 1982.

Amory, Frederic. "Whited Sepulchres: The Semantic History of Hypocrisy to the High Middle Ages." *Recherches de Théologie ancienne et médiévale* 53 (1986): 5–39.

Anger's Past: The Social Uses of an Emotion in the Middle Ages. Edited by Barbara Rosenwein. Ithaca and London: Cornell Univ. Press, 1998.

Arellano, Ignacio. *Estructuras dramáticas y alegóricas en los autos de Calderón.* Teatro del Siglo de Oro. Estudios de literatura, 62. Pamplona: Univ. de Navarra; Kassel: Reichenberger, 2001.

Arnold, Rebecca. *Fashion, Desire and Anxiety: Image and Morality in the 20th Century.* New Brunswick, NJ: Rutgers Univ. Press, 2001.

Arthur, Linda B. "Dress and the Social Control of the Body." In *Religion, Dress, and the Body.* Edited by Linda B. Arthur, 1–7. Oxford and New York: Berg, 1999.

Bailey, Amanda. "'Monstrous Manner': Style and the Early Modern Theater." *Criticism: A Quarterly for Literature and the Arts* 43,3 (2001): 249–84.

Barclay, James R. "Franz Brentano and Sigmund Freud." *Journal of Existentialism* 5 (1964): 1–36.

Barolini, Teodolinda. *Dante's Poets: Textuality and Truth in the Comedy*. Princeton: Princeton Univ. Press, 1984.

———. *The Undivine Comedy. Detheologizing Dante*. Princeton: Princeton Univ. Press, 1992.

Barthes, Roland. *The Fashion System*. Translated by Matthew Ward and Richard Howard. New York: Hill and Wang, 1983.

Barton, Richard E. "Gendering Anger: *Ira, Furor*, and Discourses of Power and Masculinity in the Eleventh and Twelfth Centuries." In *In the Garden of Evil*, ed. Newhauser, 371–92.

Bastl, Beatrix. "Clothing the Living and the Dead: Memory, Social Identity and Aristocratic Habit in the Early Modern Habsburg Empire." *Fashion Theory: The Journal of Dress, Body, & Culture* 5,4 (2001): 357–88.

Bataillon, Louis Jacques. "Béatitudes et types de sainteté." *Revue Mabillon*. n. s. 7 (1996): 79–104.

Becker, Ernest. *The Denial of Death*. New York: The Free Press, 1973.

Beller, Anne Scott. *Fat and Thin: A Natural History of Obesity*. New York: Farrar, Strauss, & Giroux, 1977.

Bériou, Nicole. "Latin and Vernacular. Some Remarks about Sermons Delivered on Good Friday during the Thirteenth Century." In *Die deutsche Predigt im Mittelalter*. Edited by Volker Mertens and Hans-Jochen Schiewer, 268–84. Tübingen: Niemeyer, 1992.

Bestul, Thomas H. *Texts of the Passion: Latin Devotional Literature and Medieval Society*. Philadelphia: Univ. of Pennsylvania Press, 1996.

Bibot, Nathalie. "'Les sept péches capitaux' de Jérôme Bosch. Étude iconographique. Un état de la question." *Revue des archéologues et historiens d'art de Louvain* 17 (1984): 302–3.

Biller, Peter. "Confession in the Middle Ages: Introduction." In *Handling Sin*, ed. Biller and Minnis, 3–33.

Blondé, Bruno, and Hans Vlieghe. "The Social Status of Hieronymus Bosch." *Burlington Magazine* 131 (1989): 699–700.

Bloomfield, Morton W. *The Seven Deadly Sins: An Introduction to the History of a Religious Concept, with Special Reference to Medieval English Literature*. [East Lansing, MI:] Michigan State Univ. Press, 1952. Reprint, 1967.

Bodies Out of Bounds: Fatness and Transgression. Edited by Jana Evans Braziel and Kathleen LeBesco. Berkeley: Univ. of California Press, 2001.

Body Dressing. Edited by Joanne Entwistle and Elizabeth Wilson. Oxford and New York: Berg, 2001.

Bok, Sisella. *Lying: Moral Choice in Public and Private Life*. New York: Pantheon, 1978.

The Book and the Body. Edited by Dolores Warwick Frese and Katherine O'Brien O'Keeffe. Notre Dame: Univ. of Notre Dame Press, 1997.

Bosco, Umberto, ed. *Enciclopedia Dantesca*. 6 vols. Rome: Istituto della Enciclopedia Italiana, 1970–78.

Bossy, John. "Moral Arithmetic: Seven Sins into Ten Commandments." In *Conscience and Casuistry in Early Modern Europe*. Edited by Edmund Leites, 214–34. Cambridge, Eng.: Cambridge Univ. Press, Paris: Editions de la maison des sciences de l'homme, 1988.

Boyde, Patrick. *Human Vices and Human Worth in Dante's "Comedy."* Cambridge, Eng.: Cambridge Univ. Press, 2000.

Brakke, David. "The Problematization of Nocturnal Emissions in Early Christian Syria, Egypt, and Gaul." *Journal of Early Christian Studies* 3,4 (1995): 419–60.

Breward, C. *The Culture of Fashion*. Manchester: Manchester Univ. Press, 1995.

Brown, Peter. *Augustine of Hippo: A Biography*. New ed. London: Faber and Faber, 2000.

Bullough, Donald A. *Alcuin: Achievement and Reputation*. Leiden: Brill, 2004.

Burns, E. Jane. *Bodytalk: When Women Speak in Old French Literature*. Philadelphia: Univ. of Pennsylvania Press, 1993.

Burton-Cristie, Douglas. *The Word in the Desert*. New York: Oxford Univ. Presss, 1993.

Bynum, Caroline Walker. *Fragmentation and Redemption: Essays on Gender and the Human Body*. New York: Zone Books, 1992.

Campbell, Lorne. *The Fifteenth Century Netherlandish Paintings*. London: National Gallery, 1998.

Carrascón, Guillermo. "Disfraz y técnica teatral en el primer Lope." *Edad de Oro* 16 (1997): 121–36.

Carruthers, Leo. "'And what schall be the ende': an Edition of the Final Chapter of *Jacob's Well*." *Medium Ævum* 61:2 (1992): 289–97.

——. "'Know Thyself': Criticism, Reform and the Audience of *Jacob's Well*." In *Medieval Sermons and Society: Cloister, City, University*. Edited by Jacqueline Hamesse, et al., 219–40. Texts et Études du Moyen Age, 9. Louvain-la-Neuve: Fédération Internationale des Instituts d'Etudes Médiévales, 1998.

Carruthers, Mary. "Reading with Attitude: Remembering the Book." In *The Book and the Body*. Edited by Dolores Warwick Frese and Katherine O'Brien O'Keefe, 1–33. Notre Dame, IN: Univ. of Notre Dame Press, 1997.

Casagrande, Carla, and Silvana Vecchio. "La classificazione dei peccati tra settenario e decalogo (secoli XIII–XV)." *Documenti e studi sulla tradizione filosofica medievale* 5 (1994): 331–95.

——. *I peccati della lingua: Disciplina ed etica della parola nella cultura medievale*. Rome: Istituto della Enciclopedia Italiana, 1987.

——. "Péché." In *Dictionnaire Raisonné de l'Occident Médiéval*. Edited by Jacques Le Goff and Jean-Claude Schmitt, 877–91. Paris: Fayard, 1999.

——. *Les péchés de la langue: discipline et éthique de la parole dans la culture médiévale*. Translated from the Italian into French by Philippe Baillet. Paris: Les editions du Cerf: 1991.

——. *I sette vizi capitali: Storia dei peccati nel Medioevo*. Saggi, 832. Turin: Giulio Einaudi, 2000.

Cavallaro, Dani, and Alexandra Warwick. *Fashioning the Frame: Boundaries, Dress and Body*. Oxford and New York: Berg, 1998.

Chadwick, Owen. *John Cassian: A Study in Primitive Monasticism*. Cambridge, Eng.: Cambridge Univ. Press, 1950.

Chenu, Marie Dominique. *Toward Understanding Saint Thomas*. Translated and corrected by A. M. Landry and D. Hughes. Chicago: H. Regnery, 1964.

Cherchi, Paolo. "Purgatorio VII." In *Dante's Purgatorio: Introductory Readings, II*, 98–114.

Clanchy, M. T. *Abelard: A Medieval Life*. Oxford: Blackwell, 1997; reprint, 1999.

Clark, Elizabeth A. "Foucault, the Fathers, and Sex." *Journal of the American Academy of Religion* 56 (1988): 619–41.

——. *Reading Renunciation: Asceticism and Scripture in Early Christianity*. Princeton: Princeton Univ. Press, 1999.

Clopper, Lawrence M. *Drama, Play, and Game: English Festive Culture in the Medieval and Early Modern Period*. Chicago and London: Univ. of Chicago Press, 2001.

Cogan, Marc. *The Design in the Wax: The Structure of the Divine Comedy and its Meaning*. Notre Dame: Notre Dame Univ. Press, 1999.

Colish, Marcia. "Another Look at the School of Laon." *Archives d'histoire doctrinale et littéraire du moyen âge* 53 (1986): 7–22.

——. "Rethinking Lying in the Twelfth Century." In *Virtue and Ethics in the Twelfth Century*. Edited by István P. Bejczy and Richard G. Newhauser, 155–73. Brill's Studies in Intellectual History, 130. Leiden: Brill, 2005.

——. "St. Augustine's Rhetoric of Silence Revisited." *Augustinian Studies*, 9 (1978): 15–24.

———. "The Stoic Theory of Verbal Signification and the Problem of Lies and False Statements from Antiquity to St. Anselm." In *Archéologie du signe*. Edited by Lucie Brind'Amour and Eugène Vance, 17–43. Recueils d'études médiévales [Papers in Mediaeval Studies], 3. Toronto: Pontifical Institute of Mediaeval Studies Press, 1982.

Comba, Manuel. "A Note on Fashion and Atmosphere in the Time of Lope de Vega." *Theatre Annual* 19 (1962): 46–51.

Craun, Edwin D. *Lies, Slander, and Obscenity in Medieval English Literature: Pastoral Rhetoric and the Deviant Speaker*. Cambridge Studies in Medieval Literature, 31. Cambridge, Eng.: Cambridge Univ. Press, 1997.

Cristaldi, Sergio. "Dalle beatitudini all'*Apocalisse*: il Nuovo Testamento nella *Commedia*." *Letttture classensi* 17 (1988): 23–67.

Cross, Richard. "Duns Scotus on Goodness, Justice, and What God Can Do." *Journal of Theological Studies* 48 (1997): 48–76.

———. *Duns Scotus*. Oxford: Oxford Univ. Press, 1999.

Daniélou, Jean. *From Shadows to Reality: Studies in the Biblical Typology of the Fathers*. Translated by Wulstan Hibberd. London: Sheed and Ward, 1960.

The Dante Encyclopedia. Edited by Richard Lansing. New York: Garland, 2000.

Dante's Purgatorio: Introductory Readings, II: Purgatorio. Edited by Tibor Wlassics. Lectura Dantis, 12, Supplement. Charlottesville, VA: Univ. of Virginia Press, 1993.

Davis, David Brion. *The Problem of Slavery in the Age of Revolution, 1770–1823*. Ithaca, NY: Cornell Univ. Press, 1975.

Dawson, James Doyne. "William of St. Amour and the Apostolic Tradition." *Mediaeval Studies* 40 (1978): 223–38.

de Bruyn, Eric. "Hieronymus Bosch's So-called Prodigal Son Tondo: The Pedlar as Repentant Sinner." In *Hieronymus Bosch. New Insights*, ed. Koldwewij and Vermet, 133–43.

de Certeau, Michel. *The Mystic Fable, Volume One: The Sixteenth and Seventeenth Centuries*. Translated by Michael B. Smith. Chicago: Univ. of Chicago Press, 1995.

Delgado, Sandra. "La función de los pecados capitales en los autos sacramentales de Calderón de la Barca." Ph.D. Dissertation. Univ. of Illinois at Urbana-Champaign, 1993.

DeLong, Marilyn R., and Patricia A. Hemmis. "Historic Costume and Image in Emblem Analysis." In *The Telling Image: Explorations in the Emblem*. Edited by Ayers L. Bagley, Edward M. Griffin, and Austin J. McLean, 117–38. New York: AMS, 1995.

Demyttenaere, Albert. "The Cleric, Women and the Stain." In *Frauen in Spätantike und Frühmittelalter. Lebensbedingungen, Lebensnormen, Lebensformen: Beiträge zu einer internationalen Tagung am Fachbereich Geschichtswissenschaften der Freien Universität Berlin, 18. bis 21. Februar 1987*. Edited by Werner Affeldt and Ursula Vorwerk, 141–65. Sigmaringen: Jan Thorbecke, 1990.

Denery II, Dallas G. *Seeing and Being Seen in the Later Medieval World: Optics, Theology and Religious Life*. Cambridge Studies in Medieval Life and Thought, 4th ser., 63. Cambridge, Eng.: Cambridge Univ. Press, 2005.

A Dictionary of Marxist Thought. Edited by Tom Bottomore. 2nd ed. Oxford: Blackwell, 1991.

Diekstra, F. N. M. "The Art of Denunciation: Medieval Moralists on Envy and Detraction." In *In the Garden of Evil*, ed. Newhauser, 431–54.

Dixon, Laurinda. *Bosch*. London: Phaidon, 2003.

Dondaine, Antoine. "Guillaume Peyraut: Vie et oeuvres." *Archivum Fratrum Predicatorum* 18 (1948): 162–236.

Douglas, Mary. "Culture and Food." In *The Pleasures of Anthropology*. Edited by Morris Freilich, 74–101. New York: NAL, 1983.

———. *Purity and Danger: An Analysis of Concepts of Pollution and Taboo*. With a New Preface by the Author. London: Routledge, 2000.

Dunbabin, K. M. C., and M. W. Dickie. "Invida rumpantur pectora. The Iconography of Phthonos/Invidia in Graeco-Roman Art." *Jahrbuch für Antike und Christentum* 26 (1983): 7–37.

Elkins, James. *The Object Stares Back: On the Nature of Seeing.* San Diego: Harcourt Brace, 1997.

Elliott, Dyan. "Pollution, Illusion, and Masculine Disarray: Nocturnal Emissions and the Sexuality of the Clergy." In *Constructing Medieval Sexuality.* Edited by Karma Lochrie, Peggy McCracken, and James A. Schultz, 1–23. Minneapolis: Univ. of Minnesota Press, 1997.

Elliott, John. *A Home for the Homeless: A Sociological Exegesis of 1 Peter, Its Situation and Strategy.* Minneapolis: Fortress Press, 1990.

Elshtain, Jean Bethke. *Augustine and the Limits of Politics.* Notre Dame, IN: Univ. of Notre Dame Press, 1995.

Esquerdo, Vicenta. "Indumentaria con la que los cómicos representaban en el siglo XVII." *Boletín de la Real Academia Española* 58 [215] (1978): 447–554.

Euben, Peter. *Corrupting Socrates: Political Education, Democratic Culture, and Political Theory.* Princeton: Princeton Univ. Press, 1997.

Eve and Adam: Jewish, Christian and Muslim Readings on Genesis and Gender. Edited by Kristen E. Kvam, Linda S. Schearing, and Valarie H. Ziegler. Bloomington: Indiana Univ. Press, 1999.

Fairlie, Henry. *The Seven Deadly Sins Today.* Washington, D.C.: New Republic Books, 1978.

Fergusson, Francis. *Dante's Drama of the Mind. A Modern Reading of the Purgatorio.* Princeton, NJ: Princeton Univ. Press, 1953.

Finkelstein, Joanne. *The Fashioned Self.* Philadelphia: Temple Univ. Press, 1991.

Fleming, John V. "The Antifraternalism of the *Summoner's Tale.*" *Journal of English and Germanic Philology* 65 (1966): 688–700.

Foucault, Michel. "About the Beginning of the Hermeneutics of the Self: Two Lectures at Dartmouth." Edited by Mark Blasius. *Political Theory* 21,2 (1993): 198–227.

——. "The Battle for Chastity." In *Western Sexuality: Practice and Precept in Past and Present Times.* Edited by Philippe Ariès and André Béjin. Translated by Anthony Forster, 14–25. Oxford: Basil Blackwell, 1985.

——. *The History of Sexuality,* Vol. I: *An Introduction.* Translated by Robert Hurley. New York: Vintage, 1990.

Garrido, M. C., and Roger Van Schoute. *Bosch at the Museo del Prado, Technical Study.* Madrid: Museo del Prado, 2001.

Gauthier, R. A. *Introduction.* Volume 1 of R. A. Gauthier and J. Y. Jolif. *L'Éthique à Nicomaque: Introduction, Traduction, et Commentaire.* 4 vols. Louvain: Publications Universitaires, 1970.

Georgianna, Linda. "Lords, Churls, and Friars: The Return to Social Order in the Summoner's Tale." In *Rebels and Rivals: The Contestive Spirit in the Canterbury Tales.* Edited by Susanna Greer Fein, David Raybin, and Peter C. Braeger, 149–72. Kalamazoo: Medieval Institute, 1991.

Gergen, Kenneth J. "Constructionism and Realism: How Are We to Go On?" In *Social Constructionism, Discourse and Realism.* Edited by Ian Parker, 147–55. London: SAGE, 1998.

——. "The Social Constructionist Movement in Modern Psychology." *American Psychologist* 40 (1985): 266–75.

Gibson, Walter S. "Hieronymus Bosch and the Mirror of Man." *Oud Holland* 87 (1973): 205–26.

——. "The Once and Future Judgments: Two Enigmatic Miniatures in the Salting Hours." *Acta Historiae Artium* 44 (2003): 161–70.

——. "The Strawberries of Hieronymus Bosch." *Cleveland Studies in the History of Art* 8 (2003): 24–33.

Gneuss, Helmut. *Handlist of Anglo-Saxon Manuscripts: A List of Manuscripts and Manuscript Fragments Written or Owned in England up to 1100*. Medieval and Renaissance Texts and Studies, 241. Tempe: Arizona Center for Medieval and Renaissance Studies, 2001.

Godard de Donville, Louise. "Mode et sentiment de culpabilité au XVIIᵉ siècle." *Travaux de Litterature* 8 (1995): 151–69.

Godman, Peter. "The Anglo-Latin *Opus Geminatum*: From Aldhelm to Alcuin." *Medium Ævum* 50,2 (1981): 215–29.

Grabes, Herbert. *The Mutable Glass: Mirror-Imagery in Titles and Texts of the Middle Ages and English Renaissance*. Cambridge, Eng.: Cambridge Univ. Press, 1982.

Grant, Edward. *The Foundations of Modern Science in the Middle Ages: Their Religious, Institutional, and Intellectual Contexts*. Cambridge, Eng.: Cambridge Univ. Press, 1996.

Greenberg, Valerie D. *Freud and His Aphasia Book: Language and the Sources of Psychoanalysis*. Ithaca, NY: Cornell Univ. Press, 1997.

Gruber, Howard E. *Darwin on Man. A Psychological Study of Scientific Creativity*. 2nd ed. Chicago: Univ. of Chicago Press, 1981.

Hadot, Pierre. *Philosophy as a Way of Life*. London: Blackwell Pub., 1995.

Hagen, Susan K. *Allegorical Remembrance: A Study of the Pilgrimage of Life of Man as a Medieval Treatise on Seeing and Remembering*. Athens, GA: Univ. of Georgia Press, 1990.

Handling Sin: Confession in the Middle Ages. Edited by Peter Biller and A. J. Minnis. York Studies in Medieval Theology, 2. Woodbridge, Suffolk, and Rochester, NY: York Univ. Press, 1998.

Haren, Michael. "Confession, Social Ethics and Social Discipline in the *Memoriale presbiterorum*." In *Handling Sin*, ed. Biller and Minnis, 109–22.

Harpham, Geoffrey Galt. *The Ascetic Imperative in Culture and Criticism*. Chicago: Univ. of Chicago Press, 1987.

Harré, Rom. "An Outline of the Social Constructionist Viewpoint." In *The Social Construction of Emotions*. Edited by Rom Harré, 2–14. Oxford: Blackwell, 1982; reprint 1988.

Harwood, Britton J. "Chaucer on 'Speche': *House of Fame*, *The Friar's Tale*, and the *Summoner's Tale*." *The Chaucer Review* 26,4 (1992): 343–49.

Havely, Nick. *Dante and the Franciscans: Poverty and the Papacy in the "Commedia"*. Cambridge, Eng.: Cambridge Univ. Press, 2004.

Hawkins, Peter S. *Dante's Testaments: Essays in Scriptural Imagination*. Stanford: Stanford Univ. Press, 1999.

Hieronymus Bosch. New Insights into his Life and Work. Edited by Jos Koldwewij and Bernard Vermet. Rotterdam: Museum Boijmans Van Beuningen, 2001.

Hollis, Stephanie. *Anglo-Saxon Women and the Church: Sharing a Common Fate*. Rochester, NY: Boydell, 1992.

Holton, Gerald. *Thematic Origins of Scientific Thought: Kepler to Einstein*. Rev. ed. Cambridge, MA: Harvard Univ. Press, 1988.

Howland, Jacob. *The Republic: The Odyssey of Philosophy*. New York: Twayne Publishers, 1993.

Iggers, Jeremy. "Innocence Lost: Our Complicated Relationship With Food." *The Utne Reader* 60 (November/December 1993): 54–60.

In the Garden of Evil: The Vices and Culture in the Middle Ages. Edited by Richard Newhauser. Papers in Mediaeval Studies, 18. Toronto: Pontifical Institute of Mediaeval Studies Press, 2005.

Izbicki, Thomas M. "Pyres of Vanities: Mendicant Preaching on the Vanity of Woman and Its Lay Audience." In *De Ore Domini*. Edited by Thomas L. Amos, Eugene A. Green, and Beverly Mayne Kienzle, 211–34. Studies in Medieval Culture, 27. Kalamazoo, MI: Medieval Institute Publications, 1989.

James, Montague Rhodes. *Two Ancient English Scholars: St Aldhelm and William of Malmesbury*. Glasgow: Jackson, Wylie & Co., 1931.

———, and Claude Jenkins. *A Descriptive Catalogue of the Manuscripts in the Library of Lambeth Palace*. 5 parts in 1 vol. Cambridge, Eng.: Cambridge Univ. Press, 1930–32.

Janssen, Hans, Olaf Goubitz, and Jaap Kottman. "Everyday Objects in the Paintings of Hieronymus Bosch." In *Hieronymus Bosch. New Insights*, ed. Koldwewij and Vermet, 171–92.

Jehl, Rainer. "*Acedia* and Burnout Syndrome: From an Occupational Vice of the Early Monks to a Psychological Concept in Secularized Professional Life." Translated by Andrea Németh-Newhauser. In *In the Garden of Evil*, ed. Newhauser, 455–76.

Johnson, Holly. "Preaching the Passion: Good Friday Sermons in Late-Medieval England." Ph.D. Dissertation. Univ. of North Carolina, 2001. Ann Arbor: UMI, 2001. ATT 3031854.

Jolivet, Jean. "Poésie et philosophie au XIIème siècle." *Perspectives médiévales* 17 (1991): 51–70.

Jones, Ann Rosalind, and Peter Stallybrass. *Renaissance Clothing and the Materials of Memory*. Cambridge Studies in Renaissance Literature and Culture, 38. Cambridge, Eng.: Cambridge Univ. Press, 2000.

Jonsen, Albert R., and Stephen Toulmin. *The Abuse of Casuistry: A History of Moral Reasoning*. Berkeley: Univ. of California Press, 1988.

Jordan, Mark. "Words and Word: Incarnation and Signification in Augustine's *De doctrina Christiana*." *Augustinian Studies* 11 (1980): 177–96.

Kaiser, Susan. "Minding Appearances: Style, Truth and Subjectivity." In *Body Dressing*, ed. Entwistle and Wilson, 79–102.

Karras, Ruth Mazo. "The Latin Vocabulary of Illicit Sex in English Ecclesiastical Court Records." *Journal of Medieval Latin* 2 (1992): 1–17.

———. "The Lechery that Dare Not Speak its Name: Sodomy and the Vices in Medieval England." In *In the Garden of Evil*, ed. Newhauser, 371–92.

———. "Two Models, Two Standards: Moral Teaching and Sexual Mores." In *Bodies and Disciplines: Intersections of Literature and History in Fifteenth-Century England*. Edited by Barbara A. Hanawalt and David Wallace, 123–38. Medieval Cultures, 9. Minneapolis: Univ. of Minnesota Press, 1996.

Kaster, Robert. "*Invidia* and the End of *Georgics* 1." *Phoenix* 56 (2002): 257–95.

———. "Invidia, Νέμεσις, Φθόνος, and the Roman Emotional Economy." In *Envy, Spite and Jealousy: The Rivalrous Emotions in Ancient Greece*. Edited by David Konstan and N. Keith Rutter, 253–76. Edinburgh Leventis Studies, 2. Edinburgh: Edinburgh Univ. Press, 2003.

Katzenellenbogen, Adolf. *Allegories of the Virtues and Vices in Mediaeval Art from Early Christian Times to the Thirteenth Century*. Translated by Alan J. P. Crick. London: The Warburg Institute, 1939. Reprint, Toronto: Univ. of Toronto Press, 1989.

Kent, Bonnie. *Virtues of the Will: The Transformation of Ethics in the Late Thirteenth Century*. Washington, D.C.: Catholic Univ. of America Press, 1995.

Kerby-Fulton, Kathryn. *Reformist Apocalypticism and Piers Plowman*. Cambridge Studies in Medieval Literature, 7. Cambridge, Eng.: Cambridge Univ. Press, 1990.

Kloppenborg, John. "Ideological Texture in the Parable of the Tenants." In *Fabrics of Discourse: Essays in Honor of Vernon K. Robbins*. Edited by David Gowler, L. Gregory Bloomquist, and Duane Watson, 64–88. Harrisburg, PA: Trinity Press International, 2003.

Koselleck, Reinhart. "Begriffsgeschichte und Sozialgeschichte." In *Soziologie und Sozialgeschichte*, ed. P. Lutz. *Kölner Zeitschrift für Soziologie und Sozialpsychologie*, Sonderheft 16 (1972): 116–31. English translation: "Begriffsgeschichte and Social History." In Reinhart Koselleck. *Futures Past: On the Semantics of Historical Time*. Translated by Keith Tribe, 73–91. Cambridge, MA and London: MIT Press, 1985.

Kovacs, Judith L. "Clement of Alexandria and Gregory of Nyssa on the Beatitudes." In Gregory of Nyssa. *Homilies on the Beatitudes*, 311–29.

Kramer, Peter D. *Listening to Prozac*. New York: Penguin, 1993.

Kren, Thomas, and Scot McKendrick. *Illuminating the Renaissance; The Triumph of Flemish Manuscript Painting in Europe.* Los Angeles: Getty Museum, 2003.

Lacan, Jacques. "The Mirror Stage as Formative of the Function of the I as Revealed in Psychoanalytic Experience." In *Écrits.* Translated by Alan Sheridan. New York: Norton, 1977.

Laistner, M. L. W. *Thought and Letters in Western Europe, A.D. 500 to 900.* Revised ed. Ithaca, NY: Cornell Univ. Press, 1957.

Lake, Stephen. "The Influence of John Cassian on Early Continental and Insular Monasticism to c. A.D. 817." Ph.D. Dissertation. Cambridge Univ., 1996.

Lear, Jonathan. *Love and Its Place in Nature: A Philosophical Interpretation of Psychoanalysis.* New York: Farrar Strauss and Giroux, 1990.

Leff, Gordon. *Heresy in the Later Middle Ages: The Relation of Heterodoxy to Dissent, c. 1250–c. 1450.* 2 vols. Manchester: Manchester Univ. Press, 1967.

———. *Paris and Oxford Universities in the Thirteenth and Fourteenth Centuries.* New York: John Wiley & Sons, 1968.

Leicester, H. Marshall. *The Disenchanted Self: Representing the Subject in the Canterbury Tales.* Berkeley: Univ. of California Press, 1990.

Leisegang, Hans. "La conaissance de Dieu au miroir de l'ame et de la nature." *Revue d'histoire et de philosophie religieuses* 17 (1937): 145–71.

Leonardi, Anna Maria Chiavacci. "Le beatitudini e la struttra poetica del *Purgatorio.*" *Giornale storico della letteratura Italiana* 101 (1984): 1–29.

Little, Lester K. "Pride Goes before Avarice: Social Change and the Vices in Latin Christendom." *The American Historical Review* 76 (1971): 16–49.

———. *Religious Poverty and the Profit Economy in Medieval Europe.* London: Paul Elek, 1978.

Lochrie, Karma. *Covert Operations: The Medieval Uses of Secrecy.* Philadelphia: Univ. of Philadelphia Press, 1999.

Lurie, Alison. *The Language of Clothes.* New York: Random House, 1981.

Marijnissen, Roger H. *Hieronymus Bosch: The Complete Works.* Antwerp: Mercatorfonds, 1987.

Markus, R. A. "St. Augustine on Signs." *Phronesis* 2 (1960): 60–83.

Matthews, Thomas. *The Clash of the Gods: A Reinterpretation of Early Christian Art.* Revised and Expanded Edition. Princeton: Princeton Univ. Press, 1999.

Mayr-Harting, Henry. "The West: the Age of Conversion, 700–1050." In *The Oxford Illustrated History of Christianity.* Edited by John McManners, 101–10. Oxford: Oxford Univ. Press, 1996.

McDaniel, Rhonda. "Male and Female He Created Them: Ælfric's *Lives of Saints* and Patristic Theories of Gender." Ph.D. Dissertation. Western Michigan Univ., 2003.

McDonnell, Ernest W. *The Beguines and Beghards in Medieval Culture.* New Brunswick, NJ: Rutgers Univ. Press, 1954.

Mews, Constant. *The Lost Love Letters of Heloise and Abelard: Perceptions of Dialogue in Twelfth-Century France.* New York: St. Martin's Press, 1999.

Miller, William Ian. "Gluttony." In *Wicked Pleasures: Meditations on the Seven Deadly Sins.* Edited by Robert C. Solomon, 19–49. Lanham, MD: Rowman and Littlefield, 1999.

Mirkin, Ronnie. "Performing Selfhood: The Costumed Body as a Site of Mediation Between Life, Art and Theatre in the English Renaissance." In *Body Dressing*, ed. Entwistle and Wilson, 143–64.

Momigliano, Arnaldo. "Christianity and the Decline of the Roman Empire." In *Paganism and Christianity in the Fourth Century.* Edited by Arnaldo Momigliano, 1–16. Oxford: Oxford Univ. Press, 1963.

Moore, Edward. "Unity and Symmetry of Design in the *Purgatorio.*" In *Studies in Dante: Second Series*, 246–67. Oxford: Oxford Univ. Press, 1899; reprint, 1968.

Moorman, John. *A History of the Franciscan Order from its Origins to the Year 1517.* Oxford: Clarendon, 1968.

Morganstern, Anne M. "The Rest of Bosch's 'Ship of Fools.'" *Art Bulletin* 66 (1984): 295–302.

Morrison, Karl F. "The Gregorian Reform." In *Christian Spirituality: Origins to the Twelfth Century*. Edited by Bernard McGinn and John Meyendorff, 177–93. World Spirituality: An Encyclopedic History of the Religious Quest, 16. New York: Crossroad, 1997.

Munari, Franco. *Ovid im Mittelalter*. Zürich: Artemis, 1960.

Murray, Alexander. *Reason and Society in the Middle Ages*. Oxford: Clarendon, 1978.

Nagel, Alexander. *Michelangelo and the Reform of Art*. Cambridge, Eng.: Cambridge Univ. Press, 2000.

Nagy, Gregory. *The Best of the Achaeans*. Baltimore: The Johns Hopkins Univ. Press, 1981.

Nehamas, Alexander. *The Art of Living: Socratic Reflections from Plato to Foucault*. Berkeley: Univ. of California Press, 1998.

Newhauser, Richard. "*Avaritia* and *Paupertas*: On the Place of the Early Franciscans in the History of Avarice." In *In the Garden of Evil*, ed. Newhauser, 324–48.

——. "Capital Vices." In *Laster im Mittelalter. Freiburger Kolloquium vom 20. bis 22. Februar 2006*. Edited by Ch. Flüeler and M. Rohde. Fribourg, CH. Forthcoming.

——. *The Early History of Greed: The Sin of Avarice in Early Medieval Thought and Literature*. Cambridge Studies in Medieval Literature, 41. Cambridge, Eng.: Cambridge Univ. Press, 2000.

——. "From Treatise to Sermon: Johannes Herolt on the *novem peccata aliena*." In *De ore domini: Preacher and Word in the Middle Ages*. Edited by T. L. Amos, Eugene A. Green, and Beverly Mayne Kienzle, 185–209. Studies in Medieval Culture, 27. Kalamazoo, MI: Medieval Institute Publications, 1989.

——. "Justice and Liberality: Opposition to Avarice in the Twelfth Century." In *Virtue and Ethics in the Twelfth Century*. Edited by Istán P. Bejczy and Richard G. Newhauser, 295–316. Brill's Studies in Intellectual History, 130. Leiden: Brill, 2005.

——. "The Love of Money as Deadly Sin and Deadly Disease." In *Zusammenhänge, Einflüsse, Wirkungen. Kongressakten zum ersten Symposium des Mediävistenverbandes in Tübingen, 1984*. Edited by J. O. Fichte et al., 315–26. Berlin, New York: Walter de Gruyter, 1986.

——. "Towards a History of Human Curiosity: A Prolegomenon to its Medieval Phase." *Deutsche Vierteljahrsschrift* 56 (1982): 559–75.

——. *The Treatise on Vices and Virtues in Latin and the Vernacular*. Typologie des sources du moyen âge occidental, 68. Turnhout: Brepols, 1993.

——. "Virtues and Vices." In *Dictionary of the Middle Ages, Supplement 1*. Edited by William Chester Jordan, 628–33. New York: Charles Scribner's Sons, 2004.

——. "Zur Zweideutigkeit in der Moraltheologie: Als Tugenden verkleidete Laster." In *Der Fehltritt: Vergehen und Versehen in der Vormoderne*. Edited by Peter von Moos, 377–402. Norm und Struktur, 15. Köln, Weimar, Wien: Böhlau, 2001. Revised and expanded English version as "On Ambiguity in Moral Theology: When the Vices Masquerade as Virtues." Translated by Andrea Németh-Newhauser. In Richard Newhauser. *Sin: Essays on the Moral Tradition in the Western Middle Ages*. Variorum Collected Studies Series. Aldershot: Ashgate, 2007. Forthcoming.

Nichols, Mary. *Citizens and Statesmen: A Study of Aristotle's Politics*. Lanham, MD: Rowman & Littlefield Pub., 1992.

The Norton Anthology of Modern Poetry. Edited by Richard Ellmann and Robert O'Clair. 2nd ed. New York: Norton, 1988.

O'Sullivan, Sinéad. *Early Medieval Glosses on Prudentius' Psychomachia: The Weitz Tradition*. Mittellateinische Studien und Texte, 31. Leiden, Boston: Brill, 2004.

Owst, G. R. *Literature and Pulpit in Medieval England*. 2nd rev. ed. New York: Barnes and Noble, 1961.

——. *Preaching in Medieval England: An Introduction to Sermon Manuscripts of the Period c. 1350–1450*. Cambridge, Eng.: Cambridge Univ. Press, 1926.

Pangle, Lorraine Smith. *Aristotle and the Philosophy of Friendship*. Cambridge, Eng.: Cambridge Univ. Press, 2002.

Pantin, William A. *The English Church in the Fourteenth Century*. Cambridge, Eng.: Cambridge Univ. Press, 1955.

Parker, Alexander A. *The Allegorical Drama of Calderón: An Introduction to the Autos Sacramentales*. Oxford: Dolphin, 1968.

Patterson, Lee. *Chaucer and the Subject of History*. Madison: Univ. of Wisconsin Press, 1991.

Payer, Pierre. *The Bridling of Desire: Views of Sex in the Later Middle Ages*. Toronto: Univ. of Toronto Press, 1993.

Pearcy, Roy J. "Chaucer's 'An Impossible' ('Summoner's Tale III.2231)." *Notes and Queries* n. s. 14 (Sept., 1967): 322–25.

Penchansky, David. "Up for Grabs: A Tentative Proposal for Doing Ideological Criticism." *Semeia* 59 (1992): 35–41.

Peters, Edward. "*Vir inconstans*: Moral Theology as Palaeopsychology." In *In the Garden of Evil*, ed. Newhauser, 59–73.

Petruccione, John. "The Persecutor's Envy and the Martyr's Death in *Peristephanon* 13 and 7." *Sacris Erudiri* 32 (1991): 69–70.

Phillips, Adam. *Darwin's Worms*. New York: Basic Books, 2000.

President's Council on Bioethics. *Being Human. Readings from the President's Council on Bioethics*. Washington, D.C., 2003.

Presotto, Marco. "Vestir y desvestir: Apuntes sobre la indumentaria en la dramaturgia del primer Lope de Vega." *Annali di Ca' Foscari: Rivista della Facoltà di Lingue e Letterature Straniere dell'Università di Venezia* 34,1–2 (1995): 365–83.

Price, Todd Arthur. "The Stage in the Streets: Calderón de la Barca's autos sacramentales in the Urban Landscape of Madrid." Ph.D. Dissertation. Univ. of Virginia, 2004.

Profeti, Maria Grazia. "Storia di O: Sistema della moda e scrittura sulla moda nella Spagna del Secolo d'Oro." In *Identità e metamorfosi del barocco ispanico*. Edited by Giovanna Calabrò, 113–48. Naples: Guida, 1987.

Psaki, F. Regina. "Love for Beatrice: Transcending Contradiction in the *Paradiso*." In *Dante for the New Millenium*. Edited by Teodolinda Barolini and H. Wayne Storey, 115–30. New York: Fordham Univ. Press, 2004.

Radding, C. M., and F. Newton. *Theology, Rhetoric, and Politics in the Eucharistic Controversy, 1078–1079: Alberic of Monte Cassino Against Berengar of Tours*. New York: Columbia Univ. Press, 2003.

Rahe, Paul A. *Republics Ancient & Modern*. Vol. 1. Chapel Hill, NC: Univ. of North Carolina Press, 1994.

Rainey, Romand. "Dressing Down the Dressed-Up: Reproving Feminine Attire in Renaissance Florence." In *Renaissance Society and Culture: Essays in Honor of Eugene F. Rice*. Edited by J. Monfasani and R. G. Musto, 217–38. New York: Italica Press, 1991.

Rakoczy, Thomas. *Böser Blick, Macht des Auges und Neid der Götter: Eine Untersuchung zur Kraft des Blickes in der griechischen Literatur*. Classica Monacensia, 13. Tübingen: Gunter Narr, 1996.

Ramsey, Boniface. "Two Traditions on Lying and Deception in the Ancient Church." *The Thomist* 49 (1985): 504–33.

Rashdall, Hastings. *The Universities of Europe in the Middle Ages*. Edited by A. B. Emden. 3 vols. Oxford: Oxford Univ. Press, 1936.

Raum, Otto. *Chaga Childhood*. New York: Oxford Univ. Press, 1940.

Raupp, Hans-Joachim. "Visual Comments on the Mutability of Social Positions and Values in Netherlandish and German Art of the Fifteenth and Sixteenth Centuries." In *Showing Status: Representation of Social Positions in the Late Middle Ages*. Edited by Wim Blockmans and Antheun Janse, 277–306. Turnhout: Brepols, 1999.

Reyes, Alfonso. "Los autos sacramentales en España y América." *Boletín de la Academia Argentina de Letras* 5 (1937): 349–60.

Richardson, Janette. "Friar and Summoner, the Art of Balance." *The Chaucer Review* 9,3 (1975): 227–36.

Robbins, Vernon. *The Tapestry of Early Christian Discourses: Rhetoric, Society, and Ideology.* London: Routledge, 1996.

Roest, Bert. *A History of Franciscan Education (c. 1210–1517).* Education and Society in the Middle Ages and Renaissance, 11. Leiden: Brill, 2000.

Rose, Christine M. "What Every Goodwoman Wants: The Parameters of Desire in *Le Menagier De Paris/The Goodman of Paris.*" *Studia Anglica Posnaniensia* 38 (2002): 393–410.

Rosenberg, Jacob. "On the Meaning of a Bosch Drawing." In *De Artibus Opuscula XL: Essays in Honor of Erwin Panofsky.* Edited by Millard Meiss, 422–26. New York: New York Univ. Press, 1961.

Roy, Bruno, and Hugues Shooner. "Querelles de maîtres au XIIᵉ siècle: Arnoul d'Orléans et son milieu." *Sandalion* 8–9 (1985–1986): 315–41.

Ruiz Lagos, Manuel. "Estudio y catálogo del vestuario escénico en las personas dramáticas de Calderón." *Anales del Instituto de Estudios Madrileños* 7 (1971): 181–214.

———. "Interrelación pintura/poesía en el drama alegórico calderoniano: El caso imitativo de la *Iconología* de C. Ripa." *Goya* 161,2 (1981): 282–89.

Ruiz Pérez, Pedro. "Calderón y su público: La recepción de los autos sacramentales." In *Hacia Calderón: Décimo Coloquio Anglogermano (Passau 1993).* Edited by Hans Flasche and Klaus Dirscherl, 45–53. Stuttgart: Steiner, 1994.

Rutgers, Jaco. "Hieronymus Bosch in El Escorial, Devotional Paintings in a Monastery." In *Hieronymus Bosch. New Insights,* ed. Koldwewij and Vermet, 33–40.

Rychlak, J. F. "Freud's Confrontation with the Telic Mind." *Journal of the History of the Behavioral Sciences* 59 (1981): 176–83.

Sabini, John, and Maury Silver. *Moralities of Everyday Life.* Oxford: Oxford Univ. Press, 1982.

Sánchez Arjona, José. *El teatro en Sevilla en los siglos XVI y XVII.* Madrid: Estab. Tip. de A. Alonso, 1887.

Sánchez Escribano, F., and Alberto Porqueras Mayo. *Preceptiva dramática española del Renacimiento y el Barroco.* Madrid: Gredos, 1972.

Sandler, Lucy Freeman. *The Psalter of Robert De Lisle in the British Library.* London: H. Miller, 1983; reprint 1999.

Schiwietz, Stefan. *Das morgenländische Mönchtum.* 3 vols. Mainz: Kirchheim & Co.; Mödling: Missionsdruckerei Sankt Gabriel, 1904–1938.

Schwarz, Heinrich. "The Mirror of the Artist and the Mirror of the Devout: Observations on some Paintings, Drawings and Prints of the Fifteenth Century." In *Studies in the History of Art Dedicated to William E. Suida on his Eightieth Birthday,* 90–105. London: Samuel Kress Foundation, 1959.

Shapiro, Marianne. "Purgatorio XI." In *Dante's Purgatorio: Introductiory Readings, II,* 158–68.

Sheringham, Michael. "Fashion, Theory, and the Everyday: Barthes, Baudrillard, Lipovetsky, Maffesoli." *Dalhousie French Studies* 53 (2000): 144–54.

Shuger, Debora. "The 'I' of the Beholder: Renaissance Mirrors and the Reflexive Mind." In *Renaissance Culture and the Everyday.* Edited by Patricia Fumerton and Simon Hunt, 21–41. Philadelphia: Univ. of Pennsylvania Press, 1999.

Smalley, Beryl. *The Study of the Bible in the Middle Ages.* 2nd ed. Oxford: Blackwell, 1952.

Smith, Thomas W. *Revaluing Ethics: Aristotle's Dialectical Pedagogy.* Albany, NY: State Univ. of New York Press, 2001.

Smyth, John Vignaux. *The Habit of Lying: Sacrificial Studies in Literature, Philosophy, and Fashion Theory.* Durham, NC: Duke Univ. Press, 2002.

Social Construction: A Reader. Edited by Mary Gergen and Kenneth J. Gergen. London: SAGE, 2003.

Somerset, Fiona. "'As just as is a squyre': The Politics of 'Lewed Translacion' in Chaucer's *Summoner's Tale*." *Studies in the Age of Chaucer* 21 (1999): 187–207.

Soper, Kate. "Dress Needs: Reflections on the Clothed Body, Selfhood and Consumption." In *Body Dressing*, ed. Entwistle and Wilson, 13–32.

Spade, Paul Vincent. "The Semantics of Terms." In *The Cambridge History of Later Medieval Philosophy*. Edited by Norman Kretzman et al., 188–96. Cambridge, Eng.: Cambridge Univ. Press, 1982.

Spence, Sarah. "Double Vision: Love and Envy in the *Lais*." In *In Quest of Marie de France, a Twelfth-Century Poet*. Edited by Chantal Maréchal, 262–79. Lewiston, NY: Edwin Mellen, 1992.

Spencer, H. Leith. *English Preaching in the Late Middle Ages*. Oxford: Clarendon Press, 1993.

Stallybrass, Peter. "Properties in Clothes: The Materials of the Renaissance Theatre." In *Staged Properties in Early Modern English Drama*. Edited by Jonathan Gil Harris and Natasha Korda, 177–201. Cambridge, Eng.: Cambridge Univ. Press, 2002.

———. "Worn Worlds: Clothes and Identity on the Renaissance Stage." In *Subject and Object in Renaissance Culture*. Edited by Margreta de Grazia, Maureen Quilligan, and Peter Stallybrass, 289–320. Cambridge, Eng.: Cambridge Univ. Press, 1996.

Stauffer, Devin. *Plato's Introduction to the Question of Justice*. Albany, NY: State Univ. of New York Press, 2001.

Stevenson, Jane Barbara. "Theodore and the *Laterculus Malalianus*." In *Archbishop Theodore*. Edited by Michael Lapidge, 204–21. Cambridge, Eng.: Cambridge Univ. Press, 1995.

Stewart, Columba. *Cassian the Monk*. New York: Oxford Univ. Press, 1999.

Stone, Martin W. F. "In the Shadow of Augustine: The Scholastic Debate on Lying from Robert Grosseteste to Gabriel Biel." In *Herbst des Mittelalters? Fragen zur Bewertung des 14. und 15. Jahrhunderts*. Edited by J. A. Aertsen and M. Pickavé, 277–317. Miscellanea mediaevalia, 31. Berlin: De Gruyter, 2004.

Strauss, Leo. *The City and Man*. Chicago: Univ. of Chicago Press, 1964.

Straw, Carole. "Gregory, Cassian, and the Cardinal Vices." In *In the Garden of Evil*, ed. Newhauser, 35–58.

Szittya, Penn R. *The Antifraternal Tradition in Medieval Literature*. Princeton: Princeton Univ. Press, 1986.

Tessitore, Aristide. *Reading Aristotle's Ethics: Virtue, Rhetoric, and Political Philosophy*. Albany, NY: State Univ. of New York Press, 1996.

Theunissen, Michael. *Vorentwürfe der Moderne: Antike Melancholie und die Acedia des Mittelalters*. Berlin and New York: de Gruyter, 1996.

Tilliette, Jean-Yves. "Savants et poètes du moyen âge face à Ovide: les débuts de l'*aetas Ovidiana* (v. 1050–v. 1200)." In *Ovidius redivivus: von Ovid zu Dante*. Edited by Michelangelo Picone and Bernhard Zimmermann, 63–104. Stuttgart: M & P, 1994.

Tollemache, Frederigo. "Beatitudini evangeliche." In *Enciclopedia Dantesca*, 1:540–41. Edited by Umberto Bosco. 6 vols. Rome: Istituto della Enciclopedia italiana, 1970–78.

Traver, Andrew G. "Thomas of York's Role in the Conflict Between Mendicants and Seculars at Paris." *Franciscan Studies* 57 (1999): 179–202.

Travis, Peter W. "Thirteen Ways of Listening to a Fart: Noise in Chaucer's *Summoner's Tale*." *Exemplaria* 16,2 (Fall, 2004): 323–48.

Undressing Religion: Commitment and Conversion from a Cross-Cultural Perspective. Edited by Linda B.Arthur. Oxford and New York: Berg, 2000.

van Gangelen, Hans, and Sebastiaan Ostkamp. "Parallels between Hieronymus Bosch's Imagery and Decorated Material Culture from the Period Between 1450–1525." In *Hieronymus Bosch. New Insights*, ed. Koldwewij and Vermet, 153–70.

Van Schoute, Roger, and M. C. Garrido. "Les péches capitaux de Jérôme Bosch au Musée du Prado à Madrid. Étude technologique. Premièrs considérations." In *Le dessin sous-jacent dans la peinture, Colloque VI. 12–14 septembre 1985. Infrarouge et autres techniques d'examen*. Edited by Helene Verougstraete-Marcq and Roger Van Schoute, 103–6. Université Catholique de Louvain, Institut Supérieur d'Archéologie et d'Histoire de l'Art. Document de travail, 23. Louvain-la-Neuve: Collége Erasme, 1987.

Varey, John E. "Los autos sacramentales como celebración regia y popular." *Revista Canadiense de Estudios Hispánicos* 17,2 (1993): 357–71.

———. "The Use of Costume in Some Plays of Calderón." In *Calderón and the Baroque Tradition*. Edited by Kurt Levy, Jesús Ara, and Gethin Hughes, 109–118. Waterloo: Wilfrid Laurier Univ. Press, 1985.

Vecchio, Silvana. "Mensonge, Simulation, Dissimulation." In *Vestigia, Imagines, Verba: Semiotics and Logic in Medieval Theological Texts (XIIth–XIVth century)*. Edited by Constantine Marmo, 117–32. Semiotic and Cognitive Studies, 4. Turnhout: Brepols, 1997.

Vellekoop, Kees. "Music and Dance in the Paintings of Hieronymus Bosch." In *Hieronymus Bosch. New Insights*, ed. Koldwewij and Vermet, 201–6.

Villa, Dana. *Socratic Citizenship*. Princeton: Princeton Univ. Press, 2001.

Vincent, Martin. *El concepto de "representación" en los autos sacramentales de Calderón*. Pamplona: Univ. de Navarra; Kassel: Reichenberger, 2002.

Vincent-Cassy, Mireille. "Between Sin and Pleasure: Drunkenness in France in the Late Middle Ages." Translated by Erika Pavelka. In *In the Garden of Evil*, ed. Newhauser, 393–430.

———. "L'Envie en France au Moyen Age." *Annales E.S.C.* 35 (1980): 253–71.

———. "La *gula* curiale ou les débordements des banquets au début du règne de Charles VI." In *La Sociabilité à table: Commensalité et convivialité à travers les âges*. Edited by Martin Aurell, Olivier Dumoulin, and Françoise Thelamon, 91–102. Publications de l'Université de Rouen, 178. [Rouen]: Publications de l'Université de Rouen, 1992.

Vitz, Evelyn Birge. "The Liturgy and Vernacular Literature." In *The Liturgy of the Medieval Church*. Edited by Thomas J. Heffernan and E. Ann Matter, 551–618. Kalamazoo, MI: Medieval Institute Publications, 2001.

von Moos, Peter. "Literatur- und bildungsgeschichtliche Aspekte der Dialogform im lateinischen Mittelalter: Der *Dialogus Ratii* des Eberhard von Ypern zwischen theologischer *disputatio* und Scholaren-Komödie." In *Tradition und Wertung: Festschrift für Franz Brunhölzl zum 65. Geburtstag*, 165–210. Sigmarigen: Jan Thorbecke, 1989.

Wallach, Luitpold. *Alcuin and Charlemagne: Studies in Carolingian History and Literature*. Ithaca, NY: Cornell Univ. Press, 1959.

Walsh, Katherine. *A Fourteenth-Century Scholar and Primate: Richard Fitzralph in Oxford, Avignon, and Armagh*. Oxford, Clarendon, 1981.

Wardropper, Bruce W. *Introducción al teatro religioso del Siglo de Oro (Evolución del auto sacramental: 1500–1648)*. Madrid: Revista de Occidente, 1953.

Waters, Claire. *Angels and Earthly Creatures; Preaching, Performance and Gender in the Later Middle Ages*. Philadelphia: Univ. of Pennsylvania Press, 2004.

Wenzel, Siegfried. "The Continuing Life of William Peraldus's 'Summa vitiorum.'" In *Ad litteram: Authoritative Texts and Their Medieval Readers*. Edited by Mark D. Jordan and Kent Emery, Jr., 135–63. Notre Dame, IN and London: Notre Dame Univ. Press, 1992.

———. "The Dominican Presence in Middle English Literature." In *Christ Among the Dominicans: Representations of Christ in the Texts and Images of the Order of Preachers*. Edited by Kent Emery Jr. and Joseph Wawrykow, 315–31. Notre Dame: Univ. of Notre Dame Press, 1998.

———. *Macaronic Sermons: Bilingualism and Preaching in Late-Medieval England*. Ann Arbor, MI: The Univ. of Michigan Press, 1994.

———. *Preachers, Poets and the Early English Lyric*. Princeton, NJ: Princeton Univ. Press, 1986.

——. "The Seven Deadly Sins: Some Problems of Research." *Speculum* 43 (1968): 1–22.

——. *The Sin of Sloth: Acedia in Medieval Thought and Literature*. Chapel Hill, NC: Univ. of North Carolina Press, 1967.

West, Rebecca. "Purgatorio X." In *Dante's Purgatorio: Introductiory Readings*, II, 169–82.

Wetherbee, Winthrop. *Platonism and Poetry in the Twelfth Century: The Literary Influence of the School of Chartres*. Princeton: Princeton Univ. Press, 1972.

Wibbing, Siegfried. *Die Tugend- und Lasterkataloge im Neuen Testament*. Beihefte zur *Zeitschrift für die neutestamentliche Wissenschaft und die Kunde der älteren Kirche*, 25. Berlin: Töpelmann, 1959.

Wieland, Georg. "The Reception and Interpretation of Aristotle's *Ethics*." In *The Cambridge History of Later Medieval Philosophy from the Rediscovery of Aristotle to the Disintegration of Scholasticism: 1100–1600*. Edited by Norman Kretzmann, Anthony Kenny, and Jan Pinborg, 657–72. Cambridge, Eng.: Cambridge Univ. Press, 1982.

Wieland, Gernot. "Aldhelm's *De Octo Principalibus* and Prudentius' *Psychomachia*." *Medium Aevum* 55,1 (1986): 85–92.

Willemsen, Annemarieke. "Playing with Reality. Games and Toys in the Oeuvre of Hieronymus Bosch." In *Hieronymus Bosch. New Insights*, ed. Koldwewij and Vermet, 193–200.

Williams, Rowan. "Politics and the Soul: A Rereading of the *City of God*." *Milltown Studies* 19,20 (1987): 55–71.

Wilson, E. O. *On Human Nature*. Cambridge, MA: Harvard Univ. Press, 1978.

Zagorin, Pedro. *Ways of Lying: Dissimulation, Persecution and Conformity in Early Modern Europe*. Cambridge, MA: Harvard Univ. Press, 1990.

Zöckler, Otto. *Das Lehrstück von den sieben Hauptsünden: Beiträge zur Dogmen- und zur Sittengeschichte, in besonders der vorreformatorischen Zeit*. In O. Zöckler. *Biblische und kirchenhistorische Studien*, 3. Munich: Beck, 1893.

INDEX OF NAMES

(The index generally includes only names mentioned in the text of the essays.)

INDEX OF SUBJECTS

(The index generally includes only subjects mentioned in the text of the essays.)

STUDIES IN MEDIEVAL AND REFORMATION TRADITIONS

(Formerly Studies in Medieval and Reformation Thought)

Founded by Heiko A. Oberman†
Edited by Andrew Colin Gow

1. DOUGLASS, E.J.D. *Justification in Late Medieval Preaching.* 2nd ed. 1989
2. WILLIS, E.D. *Calvin's Catholic Christology.* 1966 *out of print*
3. POST, R.R. *The Modern Devotion.* 1968 *out of print*
4. STEINMETZ, D.C. *Misericordia Dei.* The Theology of Johannes von Staupitz. 1968 *out of print*
5. O'MALLEY, J.W. *Giles of Viterbo on Church and Reform.* 1968 *out of print*
6. OZMENT, S.E. *Homo Spiritualis.* The Anthropology of Tauler, Gerson and Luther. 1969
7. PASCOE, L.B. *Jean Gerson: Principles of Church Reform.* 1973 *out of print*
8. HENDRIX, S.H. *Ecclesia in Via.* Medieval Psalms Exegesis and the *Dictata super Psalterium* (1513-1515) of Martin Luther. 1974
9. TREXLER, R.C. *The Spiritual Power.* Republican Florence under Interdict. 1974
10. TRINKAUS, Ch. with OBERMAN, H.A. (eds.). *The Pursuit of Holiness.* 1974 *out of print*
11. SIDER, R.J. *Andreas Bodenstein von Karlstadt.* 1974
12. HAGEN, K. *A Theology of Testament in the Young Luther.* 1974
13. MOORE, Jr., W.L. *Annotatiunculae D. Iohanne Eckio Praelectore.* 1976
14. OBERMAN, H.A. with BRADY, Jr., Th.A. (eds.). *Itinerarium Italicum.* Dedicated to Paul Oskar Kristeller. 1975
15. KEMPFF, D. *A Bibliography of Calviniana.* 1959-1974. 1975 *out of print*
16. WINDHORST, C. *Täuferisches Taufverständnis.* 1976
17. KITTELSON, J.M. *Wolfgang Capito.* 1975
18. DONNELLY, J.P. *Calvinism and Scholasticism in Vermigli's Doctrine of Man and Grace.* 1976
19. LAMPING, A.J. *Ulrichus Velenus (Oldřich Velenský) and his Treatise against the Papacy.* 1976
20. BAYLOR, M.G. *Action and Person.* Conscience in Late Scholasticism and the Young Luther. 1977
21. COURTENAY, W.J. *Adam Wodeham.* 1978
22. BRADY, Jr., Th.A. *Ruling Class, Regime and Reformation at Strasbourg, 1520-1555.* 1978
23. KLAASSEN, W. *Michael Gaismair.* 1978
24. BERNSTEIN, A.E. *Pierre d'Ailly and the Blanchard Affair.* 1978
25. BUCER, M. *Correspondance.* Tome I (Jusqu'en 1524). Publié par J. Rott. 1979
26. POSTHUMUS MEYJES, G.H.M. *Jean Gerson et l'Assemblée de Vincennes (1329).* 1978
27. VIVES, J.L. *In Pseudodialecticos.* Ed. by Ch. Fantazzi. 1979
28. BORNERT, R. *La Réforme Protestante du Culte à Strasbourg au XVIe siècle (1523-1598).* 1981
29. CASTELLIO, S. *De Arte Dubitandi.* Ed. by E. Feist Hirsch. 1981
30. BUCER, M. *Opera Latina.* Vol I. Publié par C. Augustijn, P. Fraenkel, M. Lienhard. 1982
31. BÜSSER, F. *Wurzeln der Reformation in Zürich.* 1985 *out of print*
32. FARGE, J.K. *Orthodoxy and Reform in Early Reformation France.* 1985
33. 34. BUCER, M. *Etudes sur les relations de Bucer avec les Pays-Bas.* I. Etudes; II. Documents. Par J.V. Pollet. 1985
35. HELLER, H. *The Conquest of Poverty.* The Calvinist Revolt in Sixteenth Century France. 1986

36. MEERHOFF, K. *Rhétorique et poétique au XVIᵉ siècle en France.* 1986
37. GERRITS, G. H. *Inter timorem et spem.* Gerard Zerbolt of Zutphen. 1986
38. POLIZIANO, A. *Lamia.* Ed. by A. Wesseling. 1986
39. BRAW, C. *Bücher im Staube.* Die Theologie Johann Arndts in ihrem Verhältnis zur Mystik. 1986
40. BUCER, M. *Opera Latina.* Vol. II. Enarratio in Evangelion Iohannis (1528, 1530, 1536). Publié par I. Backus. 1988
41. BUCER, M. *Opera Latina.* Vol. III. Martin Bucer and Matthew Parker: Flori-legium Patristicum. Edition critique. Publié par P. Fraenkel. 1988
42. BUCER, M. *Opera Latina.* Vol. IV. Consilium Theologicum Privatim Conscriptum. Publié par P. Fraenkel. 1988
43. BUCER, M. *Correspondance.* Tome II (1524-1526). Publié par J. Rott. 1989
44. RASMUSSEN, T. *Inimici Ecclesiae.* Das ekklesiologische Feindbild in Luthers "Dictata super Psalterium" (1513-1515) im Horizont der theologischen Tradition. 1989
45. POLLET, J. *Julius Pflug et la crise religieuse dans l'Allemagne du XVIᵉ siècle.* Essai de synthèse biographique et théologique. 1990
46. BUBENHEIMER, U. *Thomas Müntzer.* Herkunft und Bildung. 1989
47. BAUMAN, C. *The Spiritual Legacy of Hans Denck.* Interpretation and Translation of Key Texts. 1991
48. OBERMAN, H.A. and JAMES, F.A., III (eds.). in cooperation with SAAK, E.L. *Via Augustini.* Augustine in the Later Middle Ages, Renaissance and Reformation: Essays in Honor of Damasus Trapp. 1991 *out of print*
49. SEIDEL MENCHI, S. *Erasmus als Ketzer.* Reformation und Inquisition im Italien des 16. Jahrhunderts. 1993
50. SCHILLING, H. *Religion, Political Culture, and the Emergence of Early Modern Society.* Essays in German and Dutch History. 1992
51. DYKEMA, P.A. and OBERMAN, H.A. (eds.). *Anticlericalism in Late Medieval and Early Modern Europe.* 2nd ed. 1994
52. 53. KRIEGER, Chr. and LIENHARD, M. (eds.). *Martin Bucer and Sixteenth Century Europe.* Actes du colloque de Strasbourg (28-31 août 1991). 1993
54. SCREECH, M.A. *Clément Marot: A Renaissance Poet discovers the World.* Lutheranism, Fabrism and Calvinism in the Royal Courts of France and of Navarre and in the Ducal Court of Ferrara. 1994
55. GOW, A.C. *The Red Jews: Antisemitism in an Apocalyptic Age, 1200-1600.* 1995
56. BUCER, M. *Correspondance.* Tome III (1527-1529). Publié par Chr. Krieger et J. Rott. 1989
57. SPIJKER, W. VAN 'T. *The Ecclesiastical Offices in the Thought of Martin Bucer.* Translated by J. Vriend (text) and L.D. Bierma (notes). 1996
58. GRAHAM, M.F. *The Uses of Reform.* 'Godly Discipline' and Popular Behavior in Scotland and Beyond, 1560-1610. 1996
59. AUGUSTIJN, C. *Erasmus. Der Humanist als Theologe und Kirchenreformer.* 1996
60. McCOOG S J, T.M. *The Society of Jesus in Ireland, Scotland, and England 1541-1588.* 'Our Way of Proceeding?' 1996
61. FISCHER, N. und KOBELT-GROCH, M. (Hrsg.). *Außenseiter zwischen Mittelalter und Neuzeit.* Festschrift für Hans-Jürgen Goertz zum 60. Geburtstag. 1997
62. NIEDEN, M. *Organum Deitatis.* Die Christologie des Thomas de Vio Cajetan. 1997
63. BAST, R.J. *Honor Your Fathers.* Catechisms and the Emergence of a Patriarchal Ideology in Germany, 1400-1600. 1997
64. ROBBINS, K.C. *City on the Ocean Sea: La Rochelle, 1530-1650.* Urban Society, Religion, and Politics on the French Atlantic Frontier. 1997
65. BLICKLE, P. *From the Communal Reformation to the Revolution of the Common Man.* 1998
66. FELMBERG, B.A.R. *Die Ablaßtheorie Kardinal Cajetans (1469-1534).* 1998

67. CUNEO, P.F. *Art and Politics in Early Modern Germany*. Jörg Breu the Elder and the Fashioning of Political Identity, ca. 1475-1536. 1998
68. BRADY, Jr., Th.A. *Communities, Politics, and Reformation in Early Modern Europe*. 1998
69. McKEE, E.A. *The Writings of Katharina Schütz Zell*. 1. The Life and Thought of a Sixteenth-Century Reformer. 2. A Critical Edition. 1998
70. BOSTICK, C.V. *The Antichrist and the Lollards*. Apocalyticism in Late Medieval and Reformation England. 1998
71. BOYLE, M. O'ROURKE. *Senses of Touch*. Human Dignity and Deformity from Michelangelo to Calvin. 1998
72. TYLER, J.J. *Lord of the Sacred City*. The *Episcopus Exclusus* in Late Medieval and Early Modern Germany. 1999
74. WITT, R.G. *'In the Footsteps of the Ancients'*. The Origins of Humanism from Lovato to Bruni. 2000
77. TAYLOR, L.J. *Heresy and Orthodoxy in Sixteenth-Century Paris*. François le Picart and the Beginnings of the Catholic Reformation. 1999
78. BUCER, M. *Briefwechsel/Correspondance*. Band IV (Januar-September 1530). Herausgegeben und bearbeitet von R. Friedrich, B. Hamm und A. Puchta. 2000
79. MANETSCH, S.M. *Theodore Beza and the Quest for Peace in France, 1572-1598*. 2000
80. GODMAN, P. *The Saint as Censor*. Robert Bellarmine between Inquisition and Index. 2000
81. SCRIBNER, R.W. *Religion and Culture in Germany (1400-1800)*. Ed. L. Roper. 2001
82. KOOI, C. *Liberty and Religion*. Church and State in Leiden's Reformation, 1572-1620. 2000
83. BUCER, M. *Opera Latina*. Vol. V. Defensio adversus axioma catholicum id est criminationem R.P. Roberti Episcopi Abrincensis (1534). Ed. W.I.P. Hazlett. 2000
84. BOER, W. DE. *The Conquest of the Soul*. Confession, Discipline, and Public Order in Counter-Reformation Milan. 2001
85. EHRSTINE, G. *Theater, culture, and community in Reformation Bern, 1523-1555*. 2001
86. CATTERALL, D. *Community Without Borders*. Scot Migrants and the Changing Face of Power in the Dutch Republic, c. 1600-1700. 2002
87. BOWD, S.D. *Reform Before the Reformation*. Vincenzo Querini and the Religious Renaissance in Italy. 2002
88. PELC, M. *Illustrium Imagines*. Das Porträtbuch der Renaissance. 2002
89. SAAK, E.L. *High Way to Heaven*. The Augustinian Platform between Reform and Reformation, 1292-1524. 2002
90. WITTNEBEN, E.L. *Bonagratia von Bergamo*, Franziskanerjurist und Wortführer seines Ordens im Streit mit Papst Johannes XXII. 2003
91. ZIKA, C. *Exorcising our Demons*, Magic, Witchcraft and Visual Culture in Early Modern Europe. 2002
92. MATTOX, M.L. *"Defender of the Most Holy Matriarchs"*, Martin Luther's Interpretation of the Women of Genesis in the *Enarrationes in Genesin*, 1535-45. 2003
93. LANGHOLM, O. *The Merchant in the Confessional*, Trade and Price in the Pre-Reformation Penitential Handbooks. 2003
94. BACKUS, I. *Historical Method and Confessional Identity in the Era of the Reformation (1378-1615)*. 2003
95. FOGGIE, J.P. *Renaissance Religion in Urban Scotland*. The Dominican Order, 1450-1560. 2003
96. LÖWE, J.A. *Richard Smyth and the Language of Orthodoxy*. Re-imagining Tudor Catholic Polemicism. 2003
97. HERWAARDEN, J. VAN. *Between Saint James and Erasmus*. Studies in Late-Medieval Religious Life: Devotion and Pilgrimage in The Netherlands. 2003
98. PETRY, Y. *Gender, Kabbalah and the Reformation*. The Mystical Theology of Guillaume Postel (1510–1581). 2004

99. EISERMANN, F., SCHLOTHEUBER, E. und HONEMANN, V. *Studien und Texte zur literarischen und materiellen Kultur der Frauenklöster im späten Mittelalter.* Ergebnisse eines Arbeitsgesprächs in der Herzog August Bibliothek Wolfenbüttel, 24.-26. Febr. 1999. 2004

100. WITCOMBE, C.L.C.E. *Copyright in the Renaissance.* Prints and the *Privilegio* in Sixteenth-Century Venice and Rome. 2004

101. BUCER, M. *Briefwechsel/Correspondance.* Band V (September 1530-Mai 1531). Herausgegeben und bearbeitet von R. Friedrich, B. Hamm, A. Puchta und R. Liebenberg. 2004

102. MALONE, C.M. *Façade as Spectacle: Ritual and Ideology at Wells Cathedral.* 2004

103. KAUFHOLD, M. (ed.) *Politische Reflexion in der Welt des späten Mittelalters / Political Thought in the Age of Scholasticism.* Essays in Honour of Jürgen Miethke. 2004

104. BLICK, S. and TEKIPPE, R. (eds.). *Art and Architecture of Late Medieval Pilgrimage in Northern Europe and the British Isles.* 2004

105. PASCOE, L.B., S.J. *Church and Reform.* Bishops, Theologians, and Canon Lawyers in the Thought of Pierre d'Ailly (1351-1420). 2005

106. SCOTT, T. *Town, Country, and Regions in Reformation Germany.* 2005

107. GROSJEAN, A.N.L. and MURDOCH, S. (eds.). *Scottish Communities Abroad in the Early Modern Period.* 2005

108. POSSET, F. *Renaissance Monks.* Monastic Humanism in Six Biographical Sketches. 2005

109. IHALAINEN, P. *Protestant Nations Redefined.* Changing Perceptions of National Identity in the Rhetoric of the English, Dutch and Swedish Public Churches, 1685-1772. 2005

110. FURDELL, E. (ed.) *Textual Healing: Essays on Medieval and Early Modern Medicine.* 2005

111. ESTES, J.M. *Peace, Order and the Glory of God.* Secular Authority and the Church in the Thought of Luther and Melanchthon, 1518-1559. 2005

112. MÄKINEN, V. (ed.) *Lutheran Reformation and the Law.* 2006

113. STILLMAN, R.E. (ed.) *Spectacle and Public Performance in the Late Middle Ages and the Renaissance.* 2006

114. OCKER, C. *Church Robbers and Reformers in Germany, 1525-1547.* Confiscation and Religious Purpose in the Holy Roman Empire. 2006

115. ROECK, B. *Civic Culture and Everyday Life in Early Modern Germany.* 2006

116. BLACK, C. *Pico's* Heptaplus *and Biblical Hermeneutics.* 2006

117. BLAŽEK, P. *Die mittelalterliche Rezeption der aristotelischen Philosophie der Ehe.* Von Robert Grosseteste bis Bartholomäus von Brügge (1246/1247-1309). 2007

118. AUDISIO, G. *Preachers by Night.* The Waldensian Barbes (15th-16th Centuries). 2007

119. SPRUYT, B.J. *Cornelius Henrici Hoen (Honius) and his Epistle on the Eucharist (1525).* 2006

120. BUCER, M. *Briefwechsel/Correspondance.* Band VI (Mai-Oktober 1531). Herausgegeben und bearbeitet von R. Friedrich, B. Hamm, W. Simon und M. Arnold. 2006

121. POLLMANN, J. and SPICER, A. (eds.). *Public Opinion and Changing Identities in the Early Modern Netherlands.* Essays in Honour of Alastair Duke. 2007

122. BECKER, J. *Gemeindeordnung und Kirchenzucht.* Johannes a Lascos Kirchenordnung für London (1555) und die reformierte Konfessionsbildung. 2007

123. NEWHAUSER, R. (ed.) *The Seven Deadly Sins.* From Communities to Individuals. 2007